MW00806187

MULTIPLE INJUSTICES

CRITICAL ISSUES IN
INDIGENOUS STUDIES

Jeffrey P. Shepherd and Myla Vicenti Carpio
SERIES EDITORS

ADVISORY BOARD
Hōkūlani Aikau
Jennifer Nez Denetdale
Eva Marie Garroutte
John Maynard
Alejandra Navarro-Smith
Gladys Tzul
Keith Camacho
Margaret Elizabeth Kovach
Vicente Diaz

R. AÍDA HERNÁNDEZ CASTILLO

MULTIPLE INJUSTICES

Indigenous Women, Law, and Political Struggle in Latin America

THE UNIVERSITY OF
ARIZONA PRESS
TUCSON

The University of Arizona Press
www.uapress.arizona.edu

© 2016 The Arizona Board of Regents
All rights reserved. Published 2016
First paperback edition 2018

ISBN-13: 978-0-8165-3249-0 (cloth)
ISBN-13: 978-0-8165-3868-3 (paper)

Cover design by Leigh McDonald
Cover illustration produced in Pilar Hinojosa's Sumi-e workshop in the Feminine Prison of
Atlacholoaya, Morelos.

Publication of this book is made possible in part by the proceeds of a permanent endowment created
with the assistance of a Challenge Grant from the National Endowment for the Humanities, a federal
agency.

Library of Congress Cataloging-in-Publication Data
Names: Hernández Castillo, Rosalva Aída, author.
Title: Multiple injustices : indigenous women, law, and political struggle in Latin America / R. Aída
    Hernández Castillo.
Other titles: Critical issues in indigenous studies.
Description: Tucson : The University of Arizona Press, 2016. | Series: Critical issues in indigenous studies |
    Includes bibliographical references and index.
Identifiers: LCCN 2016008678 | ISBN 9780816532490 (cloth : alk. paper)
Subjects: LCSH: Indian women—Latin America—Social conditions. | Indian women—Legal status,
    laws, etc.—Latin America. | Indian women—Political activity—Latin America. | Indian women
    activists—Latin America.
Classification: LCC E59.W8 H46 2016 | DDC 305.48/898—dc23 LC record available at
    https://lccn.loc.gov/2016008678

Printed in the United States of America
♾ This paper meets the requirements of ANSI/NISO Z39.48-1992 (Permanence of Paper).

CONTENTS

ILLUSTRATIONS

ACKNOWLEDGMENTS

T HIS BOOK CLOSES A CYCLE OF TWENTY-FIVE YEARS of activist research with indigenous women throughout which I have had the privilege of establishing academic and political dialogues with distinct "wise women" collectives (*colectivos de mujeres sabias*). To thank all who have accompanied me on this journey during these years is not an easy task; please forgive me for omissions. I want to use this space to acknowledge the generosity of those who, from their academic work, political struggles, or friendship, have made this book possible.

At an institutional level, I received the support of the Center of Research and Advanced Studies in Social Anthropology (CIESAS), my work center for twenty-five years. I also received specific financial support for different projects from the National Council of Science and Technology in Mexico (CONACYT) and the NORGLOBAL Program of the Norwegian Research Council.

My gratitude to Jeffrey P. Shepherd and Myla Vicenti Carpio, editors of the Critical Issues in Indigenous Studies book series, and to Allyson K. Carter, editor in chief of University of Arizona Press, for inviting me to participate in this most interesting editorial project. My thanks also to the anonymous readers for their valuable commentaries that helped me to substantially improve my book.

In the academic world, increasingly influenced by neoliberal, competitive, and individualistic values, it is a true privilege to have a working space characterized by solidarity and social commitment. With my research and teaching team in CIESAS Mexico, I have enjoyed the stimulating presence of a new generation of researchers and the pleasure of our collective work. María Teresa Sierra, Rachel Sieder, Mariana Mora, María Bertely, and more recently, Lola Figueroa, Carolina Robledo, and Genner Llanes have been not only colleagues but indelible friends.

The members of Decolonial Feminisms Network (Red de Feminismos Descoloniales)—Sylvia Marcos, Margara Millán, Guiomar Rovira, Raquel Gutiérrez, Meztli Yoalli Rodríguez, Mariana Favela, Mariana Mora, Verónica Gutiérrez Nájera, Oscar González, and, for a time, Aura Cumes—have been fundamental interlocutors in my political and academic life.

Thank you to all the members of the Continental Network of Indigenous Women (Enlace Continental de Mujeres Indígenas—ECMIA) whose struggles and theorizations I have learned from during these last twenty years. To the Zapatista women who have been an inspiration for a generation of Latin American feminists who believe in the possibility of the construction of a "more just world in which many worlds fit."

The Sisters in the Shadows Editorial Collective of Women in Prison (Colectiva Editorial de Mujeres en Prisión Hermanas en la Sombra) have been, during the last seven years, a space of collective reflection and sorority that has not only helped me reflect critically on the Mexican penal justice system but has also helped me to rethink my conceptions of captivity and liberty. To Marisol Hernández del Aguila, Rosa Salazar, Susuki Lee Camacho, Leo Zavaleta, Martha Elena Hernández Bermúdez, Maria Elena Basave, Rocío Solache, Alejandra Reynosa Alarcón, Galia Tonella, Honoraria Morelos (R.I.P.), Máxima Pacheco, Carolina Corral, and, to my feminist poets, Elena de Hoyos and Marina Ruíz, my deepest gratitude. My acknowledgment to Pilar Hinojosa, also a member of our collective, for giving me permission to use a painting of her Sumi-e artistic workshop at the female prison of Atlacholoaya as a cover of this book. To Inés Fernández Ortega and Valentina Rosendo Cantú, to all the women of the Indigenous Organization of the Me'phaa People (*Organización del Pueblo Indígena Me'phaa*—OPIM), to Abel Barrera and all the members of the Center of Human Rights of the Mountains of Guerrero Tlachinollan, to my colleague and dear friend Héctor Ortíz Elizondo, my gratitude for all the lessons received during the litigation before the Inter-American Court of Human Rights. Their courage and commitment with the people of Guerrero have been an inspiration for me.

To Ixkic Duarte Bastian, Lina Rosa Berrío Palomo, Morna Macleod, Susana Mejía, Shannon Speed, Lynn Stephen, Maylei Blackwell, Irma Alicia Velásquez Nimatuj, Margo Tamez, Juan Herrera, Odilia Romero, Violeta Zylberberg, Patricia Artía Rodríguez, Beatriz Canabal, Adriana Terven, Claudia Chávez, Alejandro Cerda, Juan Carlos Martínez, Manuel Buenrostro, Elisa Cruz, Liliana Vianey Vargas, Emma Cervone, Cristina Cucuri, Leonor Lozano Suárez, Ana Cecilia Arteaga, and Natalia de Marinis, students and researchers who have participated in distinct collective projects in which this book is based: my acknowledgement of sharing their knowledge with me. Their way of living and understanding of academia fills me with optimism and allows me to think about the emancipatory possibilities of committed social sciences.

To Chandra Mohanty, Mercedes Olivera, Emma Chirix, Veronica Schild, and Jane Collier: critical feminists whose academic work have inspired some of my theoretical and methodological searches. To my *brujitas* (little witches), Liliana Suárez-Navaz and Francisca-James Hernández, who taught me the meaning of a "lifelong friendship."

To my professors, dear friends, and male allies who have supported my projects in the different stages of my academic career: Andrés Fábregas, George Collier, Renato Rosaldo, Rodolfo Stavenhagen, and Boaventura de Sousa Santos. To a whole team of translators, professional or amateurs, who have supported me translating or reviewing different chapters of this book, among them are my dear nephews and nieces Mark Quintero, Adriana Pou, Ana Christina Gaeta, and Efrén Hernández, and the professionals Jana Schroeder and Alejandro Reyes. To Mercedes Pisoni, my assistant and dear friend, who patiently helped me to review and correct the final manuscript.

My gratitude to the Center of Latin American Studies (CLAS) at the University of Cambridge and to its directors Charles Jones (2011–2014) and Joanna Page (2014–present); to the master of Christ College, Frank Kelly, who, during my sabbatical year within the framework of the Simón Bolívar Chair, gave me the hospitality and the space to finish this book. A special and grateful acknowledgement to my colleague and friend Sarah Radcliffe with whom I had the possibility of discussing several of the chapters of this text, enriching it with her observations. To the *gran anfitriona* (main host) of CLAS, Julie Coimbra, whose heartfelt support toward my family and me was key to making our time at Cambridge an unforgettable experience.

To the memory of my dear friends who died when I was writing this book: my *compadre* Otto Maduro; my political "adviser" and friend, the Judge Cesar

Barrientos Pellecer; and my colleague Marianella Miano. All of them brilliant scholars who worked for social justice.

To my sisters and brothers Alma, Mario, Evelia, Efrén, Angélica, and Alina, who have been my primordial community where I learned from childhood the importance of collective work and solidarity. Without their support and affection, since I decided to leave Ensenada at seventeen years old to study in Mexico City, I would not have been able to pursue my academic career. To the memory of my beloved parents Don Efrén and Doña Chava, examples of generosity and strength.

Finally, to my son Rodrigo Álvarez Hernández and to my life partner Richard Cisneros López, two supportive, patient, optimistic, and affectionate men who have been by my side, helping me with the writing and surrounding me with joy during the hard British winter in which this book was finished. *Gracias por ser una parte fundamental de mi vida.*

Ocotepec, Morelos, September 2015

MULTIPLE INJUSTICES

INTRODUCTION

T HE LAST TWO DECADES have been witness to two political and discursive transformations that have deeply affected the lives of the original
peoples of Latin America. On the one hand, there is the emergence of
a discourse in relation to indigeneity that has linked local struggles across the
continent with a transnational movement that places racism and political and
cultural rights at the center of its demands. At the same time, a series of constitutional reforms recognize the multicultural character of Latin American
countries that has led to a de jure recognition of legal pluralism.

Now, it is common to write and talk about the struggles and rights of the
indigenous peoples without exploring the historical roots of the concept of *indigenous*.[1] What we see in the last decades is the transformation of a legal and
analytical term into a concept of self-ascription. The creation of new collective
imaginary and transnational spaces has allowed a sharing of experiences, thinking of common strategies, and establishing of links between groups so diverse
as the Maori of New Zealand, Adivasi in India, and Mayans from Guatemala.
Discourse about "the indigenous" has traveled on the rural roads of five continents, arriving at the most isolated villages through workshops, marches, and
meetings. In these collective spaces, community leaders, members of NGOs, and
the followers of liberation theology have made popular the concept of "indigenous" as referring to "original peoples" and of denouncing the effects of

colonialism in their lives and territories. The local terms of self-ascription, such as Zapotecs, Mixes, Aymaras, Navajos, and Evankies, create a new identity: to be indigenous, which came into being through construction of an imaginary community with the other oppressed peoples around the world. Several analysts mention that the movement for indigenous rights was transnational at its birth (Brysk 2000; Tilley 2002), in that its origins went far beyond local struggles and self-ascriptions.

In the first moment of legislative reforms on the recognition of indigenous rights, denominated by some scholars as the new "multicultural constitutionalism" (see Van Cott 2000), the new legislations were considered as the Latin American states' response to the demands of the continental indigenous movements and, thus, as a political achievement of their struggles; later analysis problematized these perspectives. In Latin America, the Ecuadorian lawyer and anthropologist Diego Iturralde was one of the first to mention that the logics of collective and autonomous rights of indigenous peoples were compatible with the neoliberal reformist logics of the Latin American states (Iturralde 2000). Sometime later, this critical line was popularized with the concept of "neoliberal multiculturalism" offered by Charles Hale to indicate that the neoliberal agenda required a more participatory civil society and decentralization process compatible with the demands of the indigenous peoples for greater participation and autonomy (Hale 2002). At the judicial level, the limited recognition of indigenous law and the spaces of community justice in the majority of Latin American states have not included political rights or territorial autonomy, resulting in an additive justice that contributes to decentralization as demanded by international financial organizations (Sieder 2002).

Other critical voices have gone beyond questioning the limitations of multicultural reforms by problematizing the construction of indigenous identity itself as a political space, revealing the effects of the power of legal activism (Engle 2010). One important critique claims that legal activism around indigenous rights derives from an identitary definition with historical links to "millenary cultures," "original peoples," and an alterity clearly defined from differentiated cultural logics. Thus, these critical perspectives question the conception of indigeneity that emphasizes "alternative epistemologies" and "holistic cosmovisions" because it excludes human collectives that, although they share the experience of racism and colonialism, have been marked by territorial mobility and cultural hybridity.

Analysts of Afro-descendant (see Hooker 2005; N'gweno 2007; Wade 2006) and mestizo identities formulated and reclaimed from "below" (de la Cadena 2000, 2005; French 2004) have shown that the struggles for indigenous rights have reified essentialist definitions of culture that replace the struggle against racism with that of cultural recognition. Karen Engle speaks of "the dark sides of virtue" in order to refer to the reification of indigenous cultures (Engle 2010). Critiquing the multicultural framework, she writes: "As the right to culture has developed over the years, I contend that it has largely displaced or deferred the very issues that initially motivated much of the advocacy: issues of economic rights, dependency, structural discrimination, and lack of indigenous autonomy" (Engle 2010, 2).

These criticisms seem to echo a broader debate that has developed, especially in the United States, around what has been termed "identity politics." Questions about the ways in which cultural and ethnic identities politicized spaces of mobilization against various types of oppression come from different positions along the political spectrum. From a feminist perspective, Micaela di Leonardo has questioned the new forms of exclusion created by identity politics and the difficulties it engenders when building political alliances (di Leonardo 1997). She comments that "identity politics is always doomed to failure both because it denies the need to organize nonmembers for particular political goals and because of its essentialism, its falsification, oversimplification of the workings of identity even in the present" (di Leonardo 1997, 67).

From a Marxist perspective, several Anglophone scholars have warned of the dangers that identity politics entail in terms of the fragmentation of anti-capitalist struggles (see Aronowitz 1994; Hobsbawm 1996; Gitlin 1993; Smith 1994). Some of these authors have painted oversimplified portraits of the political agendas of anti-racist, feminist, or sexual diversity social movements, stating that "identity politics is a rejection of the notion that the working class can be the agent for social change . . . Rather than representing an advance, [it] represents a major step backward in the fight against oppression" (Smith 1994, 4).

While this book does not intend to respond to these criticisms, which would first entail clarifying how these authors understand identity politics, what I will do is confront the homogenizing portrayals of social movements whose political demands are not limited to an anti-capitalist struggle (although they do not exclude it). The indigenous women's struggles analyzed in this book evidence how colonialism, racism, and patriarchal violence have been fundamental elements for the reproduction of capitalism. To represent indigenous movements in the Americas as identity movements that focus their struggles on cultural rights is to simplify the many dimensions of their strategies of struggle. Recognizing the historical and political heterogeneity underlying indigenous women's movements that demand rights and the use of laws as tools for struggle is a first step toward the construction of political alliances.

I consider that these critiques of identity politics point to challenges that could arise when claiming cultural rights and mobilizing politically from an identitary space. However, there are other forms of constructing a more inclusive indigenous identity. Through case studies in Mexico, Guatemala, and Colombia, I illustrate the ways in which indigenous communities and organizations question essentialist discourses.

In this book, I deliver an account of the tensions between the productive capacity of law and discourses of rights as forms of governmentality (which construct a certain type of indigenous identity that responds to the requirements of neoliberal citizenship) and the counterhegemonic answers to these discourses from organized indigenous women. In dialogue with critical perspectives on legal activism, I recognize the political uses of cultural differences by the nation-states. However, I am interested in analyzing the answers that social actors, defined as "indigenous," are giving to these politics of representation.

The construction of indigeneity is not a process that occurs only in one direction; the hegemony of governmental definitions is fragmented by discourses and representations constructed from daily life and the political practices of social movements that these politics claim to regulate.

I conducted fieldwork mainly in indigenous regions of the Mexican states of Chiapas, Guerrero, and Morelos, but I have also included an analysis of organizational experiences of indigenous women and their appropriation of rights discourses in Guatemala and Colombia. I participated in two collective research projects that included these two countries. They represent two national contexts in which multicultural reforms have been very different and their impact in the spheres of justice dissimilar. Creating a dialogue between the experiences of indigenous women of various regions of Mexico and those of Guatemala and Colombia enables observation of how various national contexts and political genealogies influence the appropriation or rejection of discourses on women's rights.

Regarding multicultural reforms, Colombia was the first country in the continent to promote a constitutional reform that, since 1991, recognizes the collective rights of indigenous peoples and indigenous jurisdictions in semiautonomous regions known as *resguardos*.[2] Although only 3.4 percent of the population defines itself as indigenous (1,378,884 people in 2014, according to the National Institute for Statistics and Censuses), the strength of the national indigenous movement is evident in the consolidation of political and cultural projects. The establishment of the Intercultural Autonomous Indigenous University (Universidad Autónoma Indígena Intercultural—UAIIN) and the fortification of their spaces of justice thanks to the Indigenous Law School (Escuela de Derecho Propio), promoted by the Regional Indigenous Council of Cauca (Consejo Regional Indígena del Cauca—CRIC), are closely linked to these constitutional and multicultural reforms. As we shall see in chapters 2 and 3, these organizational experiences have led Colombian indigenous women to prioritize discourses on indigenous rights over gender discourses.

Paradoxically, although 41 percent of Guatemala's population defines itself as indigenous (4,710,440 people in 2015, according to the National Statistical Institute), there has been no constitutional reform in that country that recognizes indigenous rights or spaces of indigenous justice. In this context, indigenous organizations have resorted to international legislation, such as the International Labor Organization's "Convention 169," as a legal recourse to claim their rights. As a result, indigenous women have established multiple dialogues with international cooperation, the continental indigenous women's movement, and the Mayan movement, which vindicates the right to Mayan *cosmovision* and law.[3] These various dialogues have given rise to very heterogeneous indigenous women's organizations, which appropriate discourses on indigenous and human rights or lay claim to a communal feminism from the perspective of their own cosmovisions.

The productive capacity of law and the appropriation of discourses on rights have been very different in each of these contexts. While it is possible to speak of "neoliberal multiculturalisms" in Mexico, Guatemala, and Colombia, the effectiveness of their forms of *governmentality*[4] has been highly dependent on the political and organizational genealogies of each region.

If we consider the hegemony of the state as an unfinished process, we can understand that the neoliberal multiculturalist agenda is not completely successful. Its need to strengthen civil society and promote decentralization opens new opportunities for indigenous peoples to increase spaces of autonomy and self-determination. It is a contradictory process, and I will analyze the counterhegemonic answers to the multicultural reform by indigenous women.

The productive capacity of the law, which creates the identities it purports to represent, as theorized by Michel Foucault (1977) and documented by feminist legal anthropologists (see Alonso 1996; Collier, Maurer, and Suárez-Navaz 1995; Engle Merry 1995), produces more than sub-alternized identities, as many of these critics have emphasized. There are also new indigenous identities that emerge in the framework of the new multicultural reforms that are confronting the hegemonic definitions of culture and indigeneity. This book demonstrates that legal pluralism in Latin America has been the result of contradictory processes of hegemony and counterhegemony in which the social actors have appropriated and vernacularized discourses on rights, confronting (and often transforming) hegemonic perspectives of liberal justice.

Several authors have documented "the use of the law from below," demonstrating how, through litigation in national or international spaces of justice or through the political use of discourses on rights, social movements are diversifying their strategies of struggle and challenging the limited meanings of liberal law (Rajagopal 2003; de Sousa Santos and Rodríguez-Garavito 2005). Indigenous women, whose political struggles I analyze in this book, have taken action at different levels of justice, challenging the narrow meanings of culture, identity, and rights, which are often shared by administrators of justice in their communities, in public prosecutors' offices (*ministerios públicos*), and in international tribunals.

In this introductory chapter, I will present theoretical reflections that emerged from the research projects that provide the empirical basis of this book. Some reflections relate to the impact of the indigenous women's movements on hegemonic practices and discourses, as well as their appropriation of the discourses on rights. Others refer to legal pluralism and the cultural construction of discourses on law and custom in the framework of postcolonial relationships. I finish with a reflection on state violence as a patriarchal semantic answered by the new discourses on indigenous women's rights.

Organized indigenous women are developing diverse forms of cultural politics from within organizations where women's rights are central to their political agenda, and also from those where local demands are the priority. The political agenda of organized indigenous women decenters not only the discourses of power about law and custom but also hegemonic discourses on indigeneity, gender, modernity, and tradition. In a wider sense, they are redefining what they understand to be justice and rights from their collective struggle and daily practice. This introduction is focused on these destabilizing elements.

CONFRONTING ETHNOCENTRIC PERSPECTIVES ON SOCIAL MOVEMENTS

One of the first challenges of working with indigenous women's movements is the construction of a conceptual framework that permits us to understand their organizational processes and does not reproduce the analytic ethnocentrism that has been dominant in the study of social movements. There is a tendency in the literature on social movements to establish typologies that implicitly create hierarchies, ordering movements, for instance, according to the level of emancipatory potential, or reifying the dichotomy between material and cultural demands as mutually exclusive. Many of these dichotomies underlie the critiques of identity politics made from the perspective of some Marxists. First, they construct a limited representation of the political agendas of the social movements in question (in this case, rural and indigenous women's movements), and then they disqualify their emancipatory potential.

The organizational experiences that I analyze in this book reveal the limitations of the perspectives on social movements in which the analysts project their values and utopian horizons as universal parameters in order to measure the transformative capacities of social actors. From these perspectives, as the political agenda of the organization comes closer to that of the analyst, the emancipatory potential is seen as greater, and the analysis takes on very ethnocentric representations of social movements in Latin America. During the turmoil of peasant movements in the continent in the 1980s, Alain Touraine claimed that Latin American social movements did not exist since their collective mobilizations (related to economic needs) lacked a sense of the "historicity" that would allow them to be a part of a wider political project (Touraine 1987).

Feminist analysis has also been marked by "political evolutionism" in the typification of women's movements in Latin America. The clearest example is the work of Sheila Rowbotham who differentiates between "women in movement" (to refer to those women who act together to achieve common objectives) and the concept of "women's movement" (to describe those who create gender demands of a feminist character) (see Rowbotham 1992).

These dichotomist typifications have been widely questioned by feminists of the Global South (see Álvarez 1990; Hernández Castillo 2008; Kabeer 1998; Wieringa 1992). They argue that these perspectives underestimate the central contributions of poor organized women to the destabilization of the current social order when they ignore how these women negotiate with power and re-construct their collective identities within their strategies of survival.

What this type of analysis ignores is the cultural dimension of the mobiliza-tions for material needs. In the case of the women of marginal neighborhoods in Ecuador, Amy Conger Lind has shown how poor women not only struggle for their basic necessities but they also modify the preexisting conceptions of gen-der and development when resisting collectively the forms of power present in patriarchal institutions (see Conger Lind 1992, 11).

From within their productive and economic organizations, indigenous women have responded to hegemonic definitions of tradition and culture on the part of official *indigenism*[5] and national indigenous organizations, proposing the need to change those elements of "custom" that exclude and marginalize women. They have confronted the hegemonic definitions of development by rejecting mega-projects such as the Puebla Panama Plan[6] and monocultural visions of citizen-ship, while participating actively in political struggles for constitutional reforms that recognize the collective rights of their peoples.

In many of these mobilizations, organized indigenous women have appro-priated discourses on rights to promote their material demands for land or ser-vices, their cultural rights for an intercultural education, and their own justice in terms of indigenous rights. In other cases, they have confronted state vio-lence against them and their peoples, or violence by their spouses, appropriating women's rights or human rights discourses. As I will show in the various chap-ters of this book, these processes have implied not only an imposition of the discourses of NGOs and the international bodies that finance them but also a re-appropriation (what some authors call a "vernacularization") of rights dis-courses (Levitt and Engle Merry 2009) or an alternative human rights ontol-ogy (Speed 2007, 2008).

Several women's organizations analyzed in this book have, as a central piece of their political agenda, demands on cultural rights that are based on a wider concept of culture that includes the agrarian and territorial demands of their peoples. Again, the dichotomy between the material and cultural demands does not recognize the existence of social movements for which the politics of recog-nition is linked to the politics of redistribution.

In this context, the concept of cultural politics (see Álvarez, Dagnino, and Escobar 1998) can be useful in describing the destabilizing potential of mobili-zations by indigenous women, be they in relation to agrarian demands, the col-lective rights of their peoples, or their own gender rights. While using alternative conceptions of social peace, nature, economy, development, and/or citizenship in their mobilizations for the demilitarization of their regions, or for the recognition of indigenous autonomy, organized indigenous women destabilize culturally dominant meanings. Through these cultural politics, we are reminded of the cultural dimension of their material struggles and the material dimension of their cultural struggles.

Within political science, sociology, and cultural studies there exists a tendency to group indigenous organizations and women organizations together with ecological and other organizations born of "new" postindustrial movements due to an emphasis on identity as a mobilization space and the cultural character of their demands. However, many women's organizations with whom we work combine longstanding demands for land, agrarian credit, and the financing of productive projects with new demands of autonomy and the recognition of the collective rights of their peoples or specific gender rights. Although they are organizing around the central theme of culture, historical demands for land and sustainable development are integral parts of their autonomic demands.

This consideration allows us to question the abrupt division between classist movements of the past and the identity movements of the present. These are divisions that some analysts of the "new" social movements take for granted. For many organized indigenous women, their political genealogies reveal previous experiences of militancy within peasant organizations centered on agrarian and labor demands. Their survival as a community required the consideration of land and labor as critical to indigenous peoples; in this sense, their "class politics" were also politics of identity. The cultural politics developed by indigenous women through local, national, and international organizations have implied a decentering of hegemonic discourses and a confrontation with relationships of domination occurring at diverse levels of power. Some have had to pay a high cost for their actions by suffering political violence on the part of army and paramilitary groups (see chapter 5), and even by suffering the domestic violence of their own partners (see Hernández Castillo 2001a). Many others have had to confront subtler forms of symbolic violence; for instance, some have experienced communitarian rejection that manifests through the isolation and gossip on the part of those that consider them a "bad example" for other women to follow (see Artía Rodríguez 2001; Hernández Castillo and Zylberberg 2004; Zylberberg 2008).

A closer inspection of the ways in which the cultural politics of these organized women destabilize the dominant cultural meanings about tradition, justice, and rights could help us to understand the violent response on the part of powerful sectors inside and outside of their communities.

DECENTERING FEMINISM AND RECONCEPTUALIZING GENDER FROM INDIGENOUS PERSPECTIVES

Some feminist discourses in Latin America have reproduced ethnocentric perspectives on popular women's movements when analyzing the emergence of indigenous women's organizations. This has resulted in the exclusion of indigenous women's organizations by feminist movements for what they see as the limitations of a political agenda that does not place gender rights at its center.

In the best of cases there is a condescending recognition of the importance of getting closer to these new spaces in order to "raise consciousness" that will bring organized indigenous women closer to "true feminist awareness." While self-appointing the right to define "true feminism," they have disqualified those indigenous women who have opted to work together with men in mixed organizations that combine demands of recognition with demands of redistribution.

In chapter 2, I reconstruct the distinct genealogies and experiences of the indigenous women's movement in Mexico, Guatemala, and Colombia in order to understand the manner in which they have or have not appropriated the discourses of rights as well as the tools and critiques of Latin American feminisms.

Some sectors of the indigenous women's movement have developed a discourse and practice on "indigenous feminisms," such as some members of the Kaqla group in Guatemala and the Coordinating Committee of Indigenous Women in Mexico (Coordinadora Nacional de Mujeres Indígenas en México—CONAMI). The centrality of women's rights in their struggle has brought them closer and more attuned to the agenda of feminist organizations. This opens the possibilities of diverse political alliances.

Some members of the indigenous women's movement, especially in Mexico and Guatemala, have begun to speak of the existence of an indigenous feminism and a communitarian feminism, prioritizing thought and practices that transform gender, class, and racial inequalities. This emerging indigenous feminism has questioned both patriarchal violence in their communities and the racism and ethnocentrism of mestizo urban feminisms (see Álvarez 2005; Cabnal 2010). These critiques point to the intersection of multiple forms of oppression; some authors, such as Lorena Cabnal (2011), a Maya-Xinca indigenous woman from Guatemala, have termed this a "patriarchal crossroads." She says in this respect:

> As a communal feminist I want to contribute with my thoughts to the paths of shrewdness where women are contributing from various places. I do it from this ethnic identity as an indigenous woman, because from this essentialist place I can be critical based on what I know and live. However, I also do it from my political identity as a communal feminist. This allows me not only to be critical of the ethnic essentialism that is in me, but also to approach the analysis of my reality as an indigenous woman with a communal, anti-patriarchal focus that continuously weaves its own concepts and categories. It names with authority my oppressions, but also my acts of rebellion, as well as my transgressions and creations. (Cabnal 2010, 11)[7]

This search for a language of their own to articulate the multiple forms of oppression suffered and to analyze the exclusions exercised by urban feminisms is reminiscent of similar positions developed by Chicano and black feminists in the United States in recent decades. The similarity of the experiences of internal colonialism, racism, and patriarchal violence has perhaps prompted some organized indigenous women in Latin America to resort to some of the theorizations made by "women of color." This is the case with the concept of "intersectionality," popularized by the work of African American feminist Kimberlé Crenshaw, which refers to how different systems of domination, such as racism, sexism, and homophobia, mutually constitute each other, creating systems of oppression that reflect the "intersection" of multiple exclusions (Crenshaw 1989).[8] The intersectional perspective points to how, in specific historic contexts, different social categories such as gender, race, and class intersect to produce social hierarchies. This perspective was revisited by the International Indigenous Women's Forum when it proposed that violence against indigenous women should be understood not only as a product of gender inequality but also as the intersection of colonialism, racism, poverty, and social exclusion (FIMI 2006). Recognizing these intersections entails seeking more complex strategies of struggle that go beyond liberal feminism's claim to "women's rights."

Importantly, the organizational experiences analyzed in this book are not limited to those that claim an indigenous and/or communal feminism but also those that reject the term feminism altogether (and even discourses on women's rights) and instead seek ethical referents in their own epistemologies to confront violence and to build a life with dignity.

These sectors have rejected the concept of feminism and opted to claim indigenous cosmovision as a space from which to rethink the power relations between men and women. This explicit disassociation with feminism, based on a stereotype of feminists as separatists who are not concerned with political alliances, informs many of the perspectives shared by popular women's movements, which, unfortunately, many feminists reinforce. The reluctance to understand the genesis of these political proposals and non-Western epistemologies, as well as the imposition of a feminist agenda that is insensitive to cultural diversity in Latin America, justifies many indigenous women's rejection of the concept of feminism.[9]

Similar processes have arisen in other parts of Latin America. Patricia Richards documented how Mapuche women in Chile rejected not only feminism but also the concept of gender. They relate it to separatist standpoints that are in conflict with their own worldviews: "Whereas feminist movements in some nations have advanced women's rights by challenging gender norms and relations, many Mapuche women find the concept of *gender* objectionable; this term implies for them an adherence to the Western ideas imposed on them. The language of rights better represents their multiple concerns, particularly when they contextualize it within the Mapuche worldview" (Richards 2005, 210). In spite of hegemonic feminisms'[10] resistance to and rejection of these culturally situated perspectives, their proposals begin to occupy an important place within the continental indigenous women's movement.

Indigenous women are developing their own theorizations through their organic intellectuals who have participated in continental events in the past decade. These theorizations inform the resolutions of the First Summit of Indigenous Women, where the declarations of the concepts of complementarity and duality were the central focus of the debates in the panel on education, spirituality, and culture. In contrast to the stark individualism promoted by globalized capitalism, indigenous women reclaim the value of "*community*: understanding this term as a life where people are intimately linked with their surroundings, under conditions of respect and equality, where nobody is superior to anybody." In contrast to a predatory neoliberal model of development, they declare "*equilibrium*: which means to watch over the life and permanence of all beings in space and nature. The destruction of some species affects the rest of the beings. The rational use of material resources leads us toward balance and rectitude in our lives." In contrast to violence and domination of the strong over the weak, upon which is premised the liberal conception of survival of the fittest, they propose "*respect*: which is based on the indigenous concept of the elders being those who are most respected, an attitude that extends to all other beings in nature. The Earth is a woman, mother and teacher who is the sustenance of all beings. It is equal treatment amongst beings, under the same conditions." In contrast to the superiority of the masculine over the feminine, which is claimed by patriarchal ideologies, they propose "*duality or dualism*: in which the feminine and the masculine in the same deity are two energy forces found in one, which permit the balance of vision and action. They represent the integration of everything that guides us toward complementarity. By considering the Supreme as dual, father and mother, one can act with gender equity. This attitude is fundamental for the eradication of machismo." In contrast to the fragmentation of the productive process—promoted by maquiladora development, the segregation of the labor force, the fragmentation of collective imaginaries, and the rejection of a systemic analysis that allow us to locate the links between different forms of struggle—they propose "*la cuatriedad*: this concept signifies the totality, a cosmic balance, that which is complete as represented by the four cardinal points, unity and the totality of the universe. By seeing ahead and behind as well as to the sides, it is possible to struggle for unity. It is a force capable of transforming the inequalities that our people suffer due to neoliberal and globalized politics" (Cumbre de Mujeres Indígenas de las Américas 2003, 132).

Taking as a point of departure the conception of cosmovision and spirituality, some Mayan women proposed a gender concept that implies:

> A respectful, sincere, equal, and balanced relationship, that in the West would be considered equity of respect and harmony, in which both the man and woman have opportunities, without it presupposing additional responsibilities for the woman. Only then can one be spiritually healthy with humankind, the earth, the sky and those elements of nature that provide us with oxygen . . . For that reason, when we talk of a gendered perspective, we are talking about the concept of duality based on an indigenous cosmovision in which all of the universe is ruled in terms of duality. This sky and earth, happiness and sadness, night and day, they complement each other, one cannot exist without the other. If we had ten days with only sun, we would die; we would not be able to stand it. Everything is ruled in terms of duality as, undoubtedly, are men and women. (Estela, an indigenous woman from the Asociación Política de Mujeres Mayas, Moloj, Mayib' Ixoquib' [Political Association of Mayan Moloj, and Mayib' Ixoquib' Women, Guatemala]; Gabriel Xiquín 2004, 45)

From these perspectives, it is evident that the concept of complementarity does not serve as an excuse to avoid speaking about power and violence as part of gendered relations, but rather, on the contrary, it becomes a tool to analyze the colonizing attitudes of indigenous men, and it proposes the need to rethink culture from the perspective of gender equity.

This claim in favor of an indigenous cosmovision and spirituality being capable of laying the foundation for a greater equilibrium between men and women seems to resonate with the writings and political proposals of some Native American feminists in the United States. Just as Paula Gunn Allen analyzes with respect to English colonialism, a sector of Mayan women argues that it was the Christianity brought by the Spanish colonizers that imposed the patriarchal structures currently existing in indigenous societies and that, by contrast, Mayan spirituality and cosmovision are based on a balance between the male and the female (Gunn Allen 2002 [1986]). Although in both cases the historic accuracy of these representations has been questioned, what interests me in the analysis of the processes of vernacularization is to what extent these discourses regarding cosmovision and spirituality have allowed indigenous women to confront contemporary practices of exclusion and violence that attempt to find legitimacy in "tradition and culture."

Morna Macleod has analyzed the link between gender and cosmovision in the practices and political discourses of the Mayan movement and has shown us the emancipatory significance that cosmovision is having for an important part of the Guatemalan indigenous women sector (Macleod 2011). Recognizing indigenous women's theorizations, and learning from their emancipatory potential, does not imply an idealization of contemporary indigenous cultures. The proposals of these indigenous women engender an indigenous epistemology based on important values that they want to recuperate as well as activate, and that in no way suggest that they represent the cultural expression already shaping their daily lives. To disqualify these proposals because they do not share urban feminist perspectives of equality, or because they are not based on concerns for sexual and reproductive rights (at least not in the same way in which urban feminists understand these rights in urban and *mestizo* regions), means reproducing the patriarchal mechanisms that silence and exclude those political movements.

There are those indigenous women who claim, from their cosmovision, the need to construct an indigenous feminism that derives from their own culture. Alma López, a Maya K'iche' activist and ex-council from the Department of Quetzaltenango, comments:

The feminist movement that comes from the academy has little to do with us. That is why we do not appreciate something that has nothing to do neither with our reality nor with our culture. I think it is necessary to reconstruct the feminism of indigenous women. All of us have to construct this without separating ourselves from the historical and theoretical arguments. The philosophic principles that I would recuperate from my culture are equity, the complementarity between men and women, between women and women, and between men and men. Today this famous complementarity of the Mayan culture does not exist, and to affirm the contrary is an aggression. It only remains in history; now there is only total inequality. However, the complementarity and equity can be constructed. I would recover the double approach, the idea of *cabawil*, the person that can at the same time look ahead and look back, can look to one side and another, see black and white. Recuperate with all the sadness that can be my reality as a woman and reconstruct myself with all the good that I have. Recognize that there are women different from myself, that there are mestizas and indigenous, that there are blacks, that there are urban and peasants.[11]

Alma and other indigenous women in different parts of Latin America are constructing their own epistemological and political projects about which we have much more to learn. A questioning of our own ethnocentrisms and racisms is a necessary first step in establishing intercultural dialogues on conceptualizations of women's rights, and for constructing political alliances based on what we have in common, while at the same time recognizing our different visions of the world. The chapters of this book are part of an effort to establish constructive dialogues and political alliances derived from what we share while recognizing our internal differences and distinct visions of the world.

DECENTERING THE DICHOTOMY BETWEEN LAW AND CUSTOM

The analysis of the experiences of indigenous women in different contexts of justice in Latin America has been inserted into a broader political debate between the defenders of legal monism and those who advocate for judicial recognition of the legal pluralism that exists de facto in all Latin American societies. In this political context, different discursive constructions have arisen regarding law and custom that seem to give continuity to the old anthropological discussions about the normative systems of colonized peoples. In other works, I have analyzed the legal anthropological debates in relation to law and custom and the manner in which this academic production contributes to the construction of this dichotomy (see Hernández Castillo 2002a). Some discourses used by colonial governments to control the colonized population claimed that indigenous peoples have their own normative systems (Malinowski 1982 [1926]) and that, confronted with similar problems, they find the same solutions as a European judge (Gluckman 1955). Other discourses argued that law is characteristic of societies with centralized governments and so the existence of law was a sign of a superior level of development (Radcliffe-Brown 1952). If the "aboriginal" peoples had laws, these were part of the "indirect rule" that was used by the local colonial administrative authorities and their institutions to control the colonized population. If, on the other hand, colonial governments accepted that indigenous customs could not be considered laws, then it was necessary to impose upon them the normative systems of the colonizing countries. Neither the recognition nor the rejection of their indigenous law implied real access to justice because of the context of colonial domination in which it occurred.

In the case of Latin America, the context of the continuity of internal colonialism and the coloniality of power and knowledge have been powerful influences (see Quijano 2000). Both the representations of the indigenous "uses and customs" (*usos y costumbres*) as a colonial legacy and the claim to "indigenous law" as an ancestral product of their own epistemologies are being used as discourses of power that limit and control indigenous autonomy.

The analysis of the colonial and neocolonial contexts in Latin American shows us that discourses in relation to equality, as well as to cultural difference, have been used as forms of domination and control of indigenous peoples. An emphasis on equality can lead to an ethnocentrism that imposes the vision of the world emerging from the West as an optic through which to see the social processes, institutions, and judicial practices of other societies. At the same time, to emphasize cultural difference can be an instrument to "Orientalize"[12] non-Western societies and construct them as "Other" to the discursive construction of a "Western subject" characterized by discourses of rationality and progress.

With respect to the defenders or the detractors of legal pluralism in Latin America, there are, on one hand, the defenders of legal monism derived from the liberal perspective on law who tend to represent the so-called uses and customs as pre-political residuals that are to be discarded. In many cases, the critiques of the recognition of indigenous legal systems have shown the racism that continues to exist in Latin American societies (see Escalante Betancourt

2015). In the Mexican context, the renowned jurist Ignacio Burgoa Orihuela, an important opponent of indigenous autonomy in the late 1990s, warned of the danger of indigenous peoples returning to "human sacrifice" if the right to their normative systems was recognized (Avilés 1997). Even anthropologists such as Roger Bartra have participated in this debate, pointing out the colonial origin of present-day indigenous cultures and warning about the "seeds of violence and anti-democracy" that would bring forth the recognition of these "uses and customs" (Bartra 1996).

Within these political debates, women's rights have been utilized as arguments against the recognition of indigenous normative systems and local autonomy. Analysts and academics who have never written a line in favor of gender justice began to write on the manner in which recognition of indigenous legal systems could affect women's rights.

At the same time, there has been limited recognition of indigenous jurisdictions that do not respond to the indigenous peoples' autonomic demands for political and territorial redistribution. On one hand, institutionalizing the spaces of indigenous justice has created the mechanisms of vigilance to limit its jurisdiction and, in many cases, has created new spaces under state control, as is the case of the denominated Indigenous Courts (see Buenrostro 2013; Martínez 2013). In this context of legal pluralism, indigenous law has come to play a role similar to alternative dispute resolution or restorative justice in the United States, approaches that offer civic spaces for the resolution of conflicts and contribute to the decentralization of the legal state apparatus. In many countries of Latin America, state recognition of indigenous legal systems and spaces has occurred primarily because of the inability of some states to impose their law in all of the national territory (and not because of a formal recognition of indigenous autonomy). Often, indigenous legal systems are tolerated only until the power of the state is affected. This type of decentralization, although it is a positive characteristic of democratic federalism, has little to do with the autonomic demands of the indigenous peoples for whom the recognition of their legal systems should accompany the recognition of their political and territorial rights.

In a parallel manner, in response to the racism that has prevailed in the representations of the mistakenly called "uses and customs," (*usos y costumbres*) some sectors of the indigenous movement have idealized their legal systems, representing them as an ancestral law that reflects harmonic and conciliatory cosmovisions (see Ticona Colque 2009; Zapeta 2009). With respect to Mayan

Law (Derecho Maya), the Maya-Cakchiquel anthropologist Aura Cumes has questioned idealized representations that do not allow seeing its historical development and its internal dynamic (Cumes 2009). These ahistorical and essentialist visions of Mayan Law do not recognize or confront those exclusions that occur in spaces of community justice. In relation to the justification of the exclusion of women Cumes states: "The political discourse about Mayan Law proposes that women are the counselors of men in private space. In other cases, it is mentioned that women are not being excluded from the legal spaces because they accompany their husbands in cases that require their presence. . . . The political claims of Mayan Law usually do not problematize women's exclusion. To have fostered a purist idea of Mayan Law also has had its costs" (Cumes 2009, 47).

As we will see in chapter 3 of this book, several legal anthropologists reproduce representations of indigenous law as ancestral laws founded on their cosmovision, and as completely isolated from the state's positive law. These reproductions have contributed to the construction of an essentialist political imaginary in relation to indigenous peoples that once again colonize them by erasing the dynamism of their own cultures. Some advocates of inter-legality and legal pluralism in Latin America have emphasized the essentialist and functionalist viewpoints on indigenous law that represent it as an autonomous legal space. They have pointed out the existence of a multiplicity of legal practices in the same sociopolitical space that often constitute each other and that interact by means of conflicts or consensuses (see Collier 1998, de Sousa Santos 1998b; Sierra 2004a; Sieder and MacNeish 2013; Wolkmer 2001).

Both racist and idealized views of indigenous law are ahistorical perspectives that negate the complexity of indigenous legal spaces of justice. In this formulation, it seems that there are only two possible representations: the nineteenth century one that views indigenous cultures and their "uses and customs" as primitive and backward (thus, to be dispensed with), and the essentialist ones that represent indigenous law as millenary, conciliatory, and democratic. However, the voices and practices of organized indigenous women in different parts of Latin America have come to challenge both representations by questioning those "uses and customs" that exclude them, and by pointing out the dynamic and changing nature of their indigenous law. In different regions of Latin America, indigenous women are struggling, from within their customary law, to include their demands for a dignified life without violence.

As we shall see in different chapters of this book, these are polyphonic voices, from different political genealogies, that are demanding from the state their collective and territorial rights. They are doing so before their communities and indigenous organizations as they emphasize their right to change cultural forms that cause violence and exclusion toward them. The voices of indigenous women challenged the liberal representations of their traditions that have been used to dismiss indigenous "practices and customs," saying instead that indigenous communities' normative systems are being reconstituted and that indigenous women are playing a fundamental role in that process. In the framework of struggle for indigenous autonomy and a legislative reform that recognizes the collective rights of the indigenous peoples, Zapatista Commander Esther focused on enumerating the inequalities and exclusions permitted by the current legislation. She argued that the constitutional reform demanded by Zapatista women would serve to "allow us to be recognized and respected, as women and as indigenous persons—our rights as women are included in that law, since now no one can impede our participation or our dignity and integrity in any endeavor, the same as men." In this historic intervention before the Mexican legislative congress, the Zapatista leader proposed: "What I can say is that indigenous people recognize now that there are customs that we must combat and others that we must promote and this is noted in the more active participation of women in the decisions of our community. Now women participate more in the decisions of the assembly, now we are elected to positions of authority and in general we participate more in communal life." (Commander Esther 2001, 9).

In chapters 2 and 3, I describe the manner in which the indigenous women of Mexico, Guatemala, and Colombia are determining the reconstruction of their own legal systems and confronting the liberal perspectives of indigenous law that negate indigenous autonomy. At the same time, they are rejecting the use of "tradition and custom" as arguments to justify their exclusion from community life.

CONFRONTING STATE VIOLENCE AND PATRIARCHAL SEMANTICS[13]

Although my analysis of the organizational experiences in Mexico, Guatemala, and Colombia emphasizes the political creativity of indigenous women and their capacity to resist and confront the discourses of power that tend to define them as subordinated victims of their own cultures, I cannot omit the context of structural violence in which these political processes occur. The testimonies of indigenous women who are victims of military violence that will be analyzed in this book reveal the use of sexual torture by governmental agents as part of a patriarchal semantics of violence and impunity developing in distinct regions of Latin America within a process of accumulation by dispossession (see Harvey 2003).

From a feminist perspective it is important to analyze the links between occupation through violating the bodies of indigenous women and the occupation of their territories and expropriation of their natural resources. These simultaneous processes correspond to the logics of neoliberal capitalism embedded as it is with gender and racial inequalities.

Taking into consideration the political economic analysis of late capitalism as developed by David Harvey, I recognize that the stage of capitalist development in which we now live is very similar in its violence and expansion to the stage of original accumulation in which the colonial forces were strengthened by dispossession, privatization of land, forced expulsion of subjugated peasant farmers, dispossession of their natural resources, and mercantilization of the alternative forms of production and consumption of colonial populations (Harvey 2003). These processes appear to repeat themselves in the current stage of globalization.

The liberation of markets did not bring the "harmony" predicted by liberals and neoliberals; rather, it deepened inequalities within capitalist countries and brought forth a crisis of over-accumulation when they produce more than can be consumed. The exploited workers receive less of what they produce, for which there is a sub-consumption that obliges capitalists to increase their territories of reinvestment and consumption. The logic of capital requires always an "external assets fund" to overcome the over-accumulation; therefore, there was immense pressure to sign the North American Free Trade Agreement, opening the borders to products and capital and allowing the process of accumulation to continue through the dispossession and privatization of natural resources (such as water, land, and forests). This dispossession has never been a peaceful process (not now, or in the process of original accumulation). The resistance of those peoples whose territories and resources are mercantilized has been confronted with colonial violence in the past, and now they are confronted with the violence of the neoliberal states (violence that is legitimized through the law).

We are before a new onslaught of capital that appropriates the territories and resources of native peoples through neocolonial strategies that criminalize social movements and use sexual violence as a repressive strategy in the processes of dispossession. As repression in Latin America has a long history that begins before the current moment of dispossession, the phenomenon to which we are witnesses in the last decade is the legitimization of the criminalization of dissidents through judicial reforms that pretend to combat delinquency while creating a legal framework to incarcerate and attack social movements. Examples of this are the penal reforms of 2008 in Mexico that criminalize social protest, and the recent anti-terrorist law in Chile that has incarcerated thousands of Mapuche activists who struggle for control of their territories. The strategy utilized by these governments involves lodging federal charges such as "the obstruction of means of communication," "destruction of federal property," or "kidnapping" so that, in the judicial files, they do not appear as charges of political dissidence. Thus, filing these other criminal charges instead enables the state to label and treat them as criminals, and then to subject them to violence under this framework (see Hernández Castillo 2010a).

These processes of dispossession and violence have been configured by the racial and gender hierarchies that continue to prevail in our societies. Indigenous peoples and peasants have resisted the privatization and mercantilization of their resources, drawing from epistemologies and visions of the world that actively challenge the utilitarian and individualistic perspective of capital; it is for this resistance that they have been constructed in hegemonic discourses as "retrograde and anti-progress" or, in the worst case, as "violent terrorists." At the same time, indigenous territories are being violated by transnational mining, energy megaprojects, and the War on Drugs—all often producing displacements of populations that leave their lands "free" for capital to acquire.

In this assault of violence and dispossession, the bodies of women have been converted into territories to be invaded and violated. The rapes of women participants in resistance movements are not only punishment for transgressing gender roles, but they are also a message in the semantics of patriarchal violence. Paraphrasing Rita Laura Segato, the language of sexual violence toward women employs the signifier of the female body to indicate the possession of what can be sacrificed for the sake of territorial control (Segato 2008). Controlling women's bodies through sexual violence is a way to demonstrate control over the territory of the colonized. Native American authors, such as Andrea Smith, show us how the construction of indigenous women's bodies has been a part of the linguistic etymology of colonization since its inception (Smith 2005a, 2005b). This is a message that repeats itself in this new stage of accumulation by dispossession.

In the Mexican case, women's participation in social movements of resistance (most evident in the Zapatista movement and in peasant and teachers' movements like those of Atenco, Guerrero, and Oaxaca) has disrupted gender roles in indigenous communities. It is not a coincidence that, in the face of the "destabilizing danger" that these women represent for the local and national powers, they become targets of male violence. Zapatista women and the members of the Indigenous Organization of the Me'phaa People (Organización Indígena del Pueblo Me'phaa—OPIM) have raised their voices to denounce the impacts of neoliberal economic policies and so-called security policies on their peoples (and specifically on the lives of women). Their voices have reached international tribunals, constructing new self-representations that destabilize patriarchal semantics. Chapter 4 analyzes the experience of Inés Fernández Ortega and Valentina Rosendo Cantú who were raped by members of the Mexican army in 2002 and were members of OPIM. After eight years of impunity, they opted to take their case before the international justice system because of the lack of answers to their demands on the part of the Mexican judicial apparatus. Both women placed representatives of the Mexican state on the bench of the accused before the Inter-American Court of Human Rights, achieving a guilty sentence for "military institutional violence."

The testimonies before international justice, as well as the memoirs, resolutions, and internal documents that emerge from national and international congresses of indigenous women, are a source of theorization that speaks of other ways of understanding women's rights and their links with the collective rights of indigenous peoples. Theorizations emerging from these voices give an account of the utopian horizons that organized indigenous women are constructing on the recuperation of the historical memory of their peoples.

The existence of organized women in some communities or regions has become a synonym of political radicalism. Organized women have transformed themselves into a symbol of resistance and subversion, placing them at the center of political violence in the three countries addressed in this book. The army, police forces, and paramilitary groups have turned women's bodies into their battlefield. Counterinsurgency strategies against political-military movements or, in the case of the War on Drugs, the combat against narcotics trafficking, are used as an excuse to militarize or paramilitarize the indigenous regions of Mexico, Guatemala, and Colombia. Sexual violence, more than a simple repressive act, is a message in the patriarchal semantics in order to promote demobilization and eventually displacement and dispossession.

In the Mexican state of Guerrero, where Inés Fernández Ortega and Valentina Rosendo Cantú were raped, there have been important mobilizations against mining concessions in indigenous territories. According to government reports, there are forty-two mining areas ready for exploitation in that state. However, these mining sites coincide with 200,000 hectares of territories inhabited by members of the Nahua, Me'phaa, and Na Savi indigenous communities. These peoples of the mountain and Costa Chica regions of the state experienced the granting of mining concessions located in their territories without previous consultation. The same events are happening in the Guatemalan departments of Huehuetenango and San Marcos, where Mam women have led the resistance movements against mining companies (see Macleod and Pérez Bámaca 2013).

We observe a territorial coincidence when locating on a single map the regions with granted mining concessions and mobilizations of resistance against these dispossessions, and the regions where the War on Drugs has left thousands of victims, missing people, and displaced communities. This overlap should oblige us to establish analytical links between both phenomena. In this onslaught of violence and dispossession, women's bodies have also become territories to be invaded, destroyed, disappeared, and violated.

Simultaneously, in collusion with drug trafficking, these security forces that discard racialized bodies also use sexual violence as a tool for political repression. Amnesty International's reports document sixty sexual aggressions against indigenous and peasant women by members of the armed forces within the last five years, especially concentrated in the states of Guerrero, Chiapas, and Oaxaca (precisely the states where there is great organizational activity and significant movements in resistance against dispossession and militarization).

From a patriarchal ideology that continues to consider women as sexual objects and as depositories of the family's honor, actions like rape, sexual torture, and bodily mutilations of indigenous women are seen as an assault on men of the enemy group; they are a form of colonizing their territories and resources. However, it is important to remember that this semantic of violence pervades not only the dominant groups but also society as a whole.

Organized indigenous and peasant women have responded to this counterinsurgency strategy by denouncing it in national and international forums. Their voices have come to destabilize the patriarchal semantics that attempt to utilize sexual violence on their bodies as a form of colonization. The leaders of OPIM, Inés Fernández Ortega and Valentina Rosendo Cantú, have opted to take their cases before international justice because of the lack of response to their demands on the part of the Mexican judicial apparatus. The Inter-American Court of Human Rights has not only been a space for pursuing justice, but also, through the process of lawsuits, new political alliances have been formed and new women's leaderships have been consolidated.

In the cases of Inés Fernández Ortega and Valentina Rosendo Cantú, their cultural identities and their peoples' history have marked the specific manner in which these women lived through their rapes and their consequent search for justice. Both women have begun to organize around their rights and those of their people. Their rapes interpreted and lived by them and their families from the standpoint of historical memory relate the presence of the army and security forces to the violence and impunity experienced in their regions. The rapes and torture experienced in the framework of recent history form part of a "continuum of violence" that has marked the relationship of the indigenous peoples of the region with the Mexican army. As I analyze in chapter 4, this culturally situated interpretation of their rapes as part of a series of community grievances has resulted in demands for collective compensations that include the demilitarization of the mountain region of Guerrero, where the Me'phaa communities are located.

Contrary to the demobilization effect often caused by repressive violence, these women's response has been a greater organization and strengthening of leadership. They have appropriated human rights discourses whereby their specific rights as women directly relate to the collective rights of their peoples.

While Inés and Valentina have utilized human and women's rights discourses in spaces of international justice, they have destabilized the liberal rights discourses that view rape only as an individual's problem. In this sense, their legal performances have contributed to the construction of subjectivities that reject the liberal conceptions of personhood. Their experiences contrast with the construction of subjectivities described by Sally Engle Merry in the cases of women who decide to denounce domestic violence in Hawaii, where the state's law constructs them as "free and autonomous subjects" who elect the rational option of using legality instead of maintaining family ties and preserving the "honor" of the family (Engle Merry 1995).

Among the compensation claims before the Mexican state is the construction of the Me'phaa Women and Men's Rights Center. It will have as its principal objective the creation of spaces for collective reflection in order to analyze the different levels of violence that exist in the region and promote indigenous and gender rights.

The lesson these experiences have taught us is that, in order to undo the neocolonial strategies of violence toward indigenous and peasant women, it is not enough to denounce the complicity between transnational capital and the processes of accumulation by dispossession. It is also necessary to change the set of shared meanings that conceive of women's bodies as a disputed and controllable territory, the epicenter of masculine power. The patriarchal complicities between neoliberal power and social movements must be deconstructed in order to break the chain of signifiers that allows the rape of women to be messages in patriarchal semantics. In many of the organized spaces analyzed in this book, indigenous women are reflecting on the use of sexual violence as a tool for counterinsurgency. New gender discourses are destabilizing the patriarchal meanings of the female body in indigenous movements. To name sexual torture, and to link it to distinct forms of state violence (as well as other strategies of dispossession and accumulation), is one way of breaking with the patriarchal meanings that have been constructed on the violation and occupation of organized women's bodies.

THE CONTENT OF THE BOOK

The chapters that form this book systematize my experiences of twenty-five years of research and activism with indigenous women's organizations. During these years, I have learned to widen my concept of gender justice and to question many of my liberal premises on rights and emancipation. These intercultural dialogues have taught me important lessons about how to decolonize my own feminism and have led me to question the manner in which I understand resistance to patriarchal powers in contexts of neoliberal globalization.

This book is a product of a long academic trajectory during which I have participated in various individual and collective projects whose common denominator was a concern with access to justice for indigenous women and their appropriation of rights discourses. The various chapters reflect my own theoretical, political, and methodological search, from my perspective of "awareness raising" through feminist activism in the late 1980s to my recent work in dialogic, collaborative research with incarcerated indigenous women. Despite the differences in time and space among the various chapters, three theoretical axes traverse the book: the vernacularization of rights discourses, the hegemonic and counterhegemonic uses of legality by the state and indigenous women in contexts of legal pluralism, and the limits of resistance in the context of neoliberal governance strategies and state violence.

Since the late 1980s, I have participated in different legal activist processes from a dual position as a feminist and as a critical anthropologist who recognizes the limitations of liberal discourses on rights. In the 1980s and 1990s, as member of a feminist organization that runs a center for women and children who are victims of violence, I participated in the legal and educational services delivered by this organization. Through this experience, I learned from our practice the possibilities and limitations of the justice system in relation to violence against women.[14] At the same time, my dialogues with indigenous women's organizations in different regions of Latin America have led me to question the ethnocentric perspectives of urban Latin American feminisms and to search within decolonial theories for some epistemological guidance to rethink my own feminism.

The collaborative research projects "Indigenous Women Between Positivist Law and Community Justice in the Highlands of Chiapas" (1998–2000) and "Old and New Spaces of Power: Indigenous Women, Collective Organization and Resistance in Guatemala, Mexico and Colombia" (2002–2005)[15] were formulated in these periods of my feminist activism and contribute to chapters 1, 2, and 3. The objective is to analyze indigenous women's appropriation of discourses on rights, the development of their own conceptualizations in relation to a dignified life, and how spaces are used within state and community justice in their struggle against violence.

Thus, I began to develop the theme of collaborative or activist research from a project on state law and communitarian justice in the highlands of Chiapas, and it has been my methodological approach in later projects, documented in chapter 1 of this book. Similar concerns led me to work with María Teresa Sierra on the project "Globalization, Indigenous Rights and Justice from a Gender and Power Perspective: A Comparative Proposal" (2006–2010). In this project, we addressed "the transformation of the relationship the state has with the rights of indigenous peoples from the privileged view on the dispute over rights and justice in times of intense changes marked by neoliberal globalization, multicultural politics and the processes of political transition which affect the nature of the state and society in Mexico and Guatemala" (Sierra, Hernández Castillo, and Sieder 2013, 13). At the beginning of this project, our concern centered on the impact of multicultural reforms in the area of indigenous justice.

However, in the course of our research, fundamental changes came about in the relationship between the Mexican state and the indigenous peoples, displacing the multicultural discourse for discourses on development, national security, and the war against drug trafficking (changes that impact indigenous women and men in a differentiated manner). The 2008 penal reforms in Mexico criminalized social protest and specifically impacted the organized indigenous population; these new state reforms forced me to return to an analytical focus on the state's justice. This analytic focus, in turn, led me to propose that we were witnessing a transition from a "multicultural state" to a "penal state" (Hernández Castillo 2013, 299–335), necessitating a case study that explores the relationship of indigenous women to the penal justice system.

In this context, I found a new space of feminist activism by participating in a literary workshop for incarcerated women and by contributing to the formation of their Sisters in the Shadows Editorial Collective of Women in Prison (Colectiva Editorial de Mujeres en Prisión Hermanas en la Sombra). In chapter 1, I give an account of the methodological strategies developed in this new collaborative project. The life histories of indigenous women written by the incarcerated women themselves (see appendixes 2, 3, and 4), and the creation of spaces for collective reflection focused on the experiences of exclusion, were the basis of the intercultural dialogues that inform chapter 5.

My path of legal activism led me to participate in the elaboration of an expert witness report at the petition of the Inter-American Commission on Human Rights (IACHR) and the Center of Human Rights of the Mountains of Guerrero Tlachinollan. The case was *Inés Fernández Ortega v. México*, presented in April 2010 before the Inter-American Court of Human Rights. The experience of this lawsuit gave me the opportunity to analyze a third space of justice, which until now was outside of my study of penal and community justice in indigenous regions: the space of international justice.

The project "Women and Rights in Latin America: Justice, Security, and Legal Pluralism," coordinated by my colleague Rachel Sieder, allowed me to document and analyze this experience in the framework of a collective project that included case studies from Bolivia, Guatemala, Ecuador, Colombia, and Mexico. Chapter 4 is the product of this project and enriched by the theoretical debates we had in the permanent seminar, "Gender and Legal Pluralism," that we organized at the Center for Research and Advanced Studies in Social Anthropology (CIESAS) from 2010 to 2013. The analyses of indigenous justice done by Sieder in Guatemala and Leonor Lozano Suárez in Colombia contributed in a fundamental manner to chapter 3 on indigenous justices (Lozano Suárez forthcoming; Sieder forthcoming).

The context of legal pluralism in which the indigenous women of Mexico, Guatemala, and Colombia develop their struggles for justice, and appropriate or negotiate the discourses of rights, reveals the political creativity with which women are responding to the discourses of power of the state and to hegemonic discourses within their own communities and organizations. These polyphonic discourses come from distinct political genealogies and reveal contradictory consciousness that in many ways reproduce hegemonic perspectives on the "socially appropriate feminine activities," while at the same time allowing for the construction of new meanings on culture, justice, and rights. In this sense, to recognize the construction of new subjectivities by discourses of power does not imply rejecting the possibility of constructing, from this contradictory consciousness, political projects that point toward social justice.

In chapter 1, titled "Activist Research on Justice and Indigenous Women's Rights," I discuss the importance of activist research not only as a methodological tool but as a new epistemological path for the collective construction of knowledge in alliance with indigenous and women's movements. I also refer to the challenges of legal activism in the framework of neoliberal multicultural states in Latin America. This chapter discusses my process of learning and the challenges I have encountered in almost thirty years of collaborative research and legal activism in the area of gender justice, as well as describing the methodological bases that orient this book's chapters.

In chapter 2, "Multiple Dialogues and Struggles for Justice: Political Genealogies of Indigenous Women in Mexico, Guatemala, and Colombia," I reconstruct the history of the processes of organization that have created new political identities and new discourses and practices in relation to indigenous and women's rights in Mexico, Guatemala, and Colombia. From bibliographic and hemerographic research that has included internal documents elaborated by the indigenous women's movements, the use of oral history,[16] and the ethnographic register of several organizational spaces, I reconstruct the dialogues of power that have constituted these new forms of being indigenous and the struggle for social justice through the appropriation of the discourses on rights.

In chapter 3, "Indigenous Justices: New Spaces of Struggle for Women," I analyze the possibilities and limitations of communitarian justice spaces for indigenous women. The acknowledgement of the so-called indigenous com-

munity law (what is known as Tribal Law in the United States) by the majority of the Latin American constitutions has meant changes in the spaces of
communitarian justice in indigenous regions. Based on ethnographic research,
I will examine the appropriation of community justice spheres by organized
indigenous women in Mexico, Guatemala, and Colombia and their reinvention
of indigenous law from a gendered perspective in the context of the new multicultural reforms.

In chapter 4, "From Victims to Human Rights Defenders: International
Litigation and the Struggle for Justice of Indigenous Women," I reflect on the
possibilities and limitations that come with international lawsuits to understand how indigenous women appropriate discourses of rights in international
spheres of legal activism. After having approached the challenges faced by
women in spaces of communal indigenous justice, I am interested in including
another level of inter-legality that arises in the scope of international justice.
Based on the analysis of the cases of Inés Fernández Ortega and Valentina
Rosenda Cantú before the Inter-American Court of Human Rights, my aim
is to approach the way in which violence, racism, and gender inequalities affect
the lives of indigenous women and determine their lack of access to justice.

In chapter 5, "From the Multicultural State to the Penal State: Incarcerated
Indigenous Women and the Criminalization of Poverty," I analyze the other
side of the multicultural reforms: the effects of the penal reforms on access to
justice for indigenous women. Centering my analysis on the Mexican context, I
examine the experience of indigenous women in the sphere of criminal justice.
I explain the recent changes in the relationship between indigenous peoples
and the Mexican state in what I call a transition from a "multicultural state" to
a "penal state." I analyze the way in which the official discourse has abandoned
multicultural rhetoric and adopted one of development and national security,
with matching legislative reform that criminalizes poverty and social protest. I
then offer a national perspective on indigenous women and federal penal justice to focus on the experiences of imprisoned women at two correctional institutions—called Female Social Correctional Centers (Centro de Readaptación
Social—CERESO) in Mexico: one in San Miguel, in the state of Puebla, and
another one in Atlacholoaya, in the state of Morelos.

The book ends with a "Final Thoughts" chapter, which I intentionally chose
not to call "Conclusions" because, rather than the conclusions of a positivist
research study, what I put forth are some reflections on the contributions that
indigenous women's struggles are making to Latin American feminisms and

gender justice in the Americas. Their theoretical and political lessons have been fundamental to rethinking Latin American feminist anthropology from new, decolonizing perspectives.

Getting closer to the discourses and practices of indigenous women in their struggles for justice has not been for me only an academic curiosity or a compliance with a research objective. Rather, I consider that the intercultural dialogues in which I participated through the frameworks of these different projects are a fundamental step to constructing political alliances based on the recognition of difference. To speak of feminisms and women in plural, and to recognize the differences among us, should not imply an impossibility of seeing our similarities. Our diverse struggles develop in the same global context of economic domination that influences local powers and resistances.

1

ACTIVIST RESEARCH ON JUSTICE
AND INDIGENOUS WOMEN'S RIGHTS

I N THIS CHAPTER, I would like to reflect on the methodological routes that
are the basis for this book, with emphasis on the epistemological possibilities of activist research.

In my experience as an academic and an activist, working for almost three
decades advocating for women's rights in contexts of cultural diversity, I have had
to confront both disparaging remarks from the positivist academy and skepticism from anti-academic activisms. The reflections I am presenting here are in
response to these two positions. Specifically, I defend the epistemological wealth
resulting from conducting research in alliance or collaboration with social movements, and I propose that social research can contribute to developing critical
thought and destabilize the discourses of power in struggles waged by movements working for social justice.

As a legal anthropologist, I have confronted the epistemological and political tension resulting from consistently maintaining a critical perspective of
positive law, as a practice and as discourse, and in relation to human rights as
universalized, globalized discourses, while at the same time being involved in
initiatives supporting political struggles for recognition of the rights of indigenous peoples at both national and international levels.

Some authors have proposed that these are two conflicting approaches: either
you engage in critical analysis of law and the *juridization*[1] of political struggles,
or you elect to reify the hegemonic perspectives of law and rights and support

legal activism. From these perspectives, struggles for recognition of cultural rights tend to reify hegemonic definitions of culture and indigenous peoples and end up limiting political imaginaries around justice (Brown and Halley 2002).

In opposition to these perspectives, I have attempted throughout my academic career to always maintain a posture of critical reflection in relation to law and rights, while at the same time participating in initiatives that support the struggles to achieve justice for indigenous peoples and organizations, appropriating and re-signifying national and international legislation.

The perspectives that discredit legal activism end up silencing subaltern groups, once again, by disregarding the legal counterhegemonic discourses and practices developed in the Global South. Many of the indigenous women with whom I have walked side by side during the last decades share my critical perspective on law and my skepticism about state justice. However, in various political contexts, I have opted to make use of legal discourses, defending the constitutional rights of these women, and have elected to take their struggles to arenas of state and international justice. The scope and the limitations of these decisions have depended greatly on the organizational and political contexts in which these legal struggles have taken place. Law and rights are not ends in and of themselves for these indigenous women but rather another language into which their demands for justice and a dignified life are translated. The chapters in this book are focused on these translations and these polyphonic appropriations.

FROM COLLABORATIVE RESEARCH TO EPISTEMIC DIALOGUES IN LATIN AMERICA

In the last decade, "activist anthropology" in North America (see Naples 2003; Hale 2008; Speed 2006, 2008) and the "modernity-coloniality group" (Castro-Gómez 1998, 2000; Castro-Gómez and Mendieta 1998) have issued a new call to decolonize the social sciences. They question "extractive methodologies" and confront positivist perspectives that, in the name of "scientific neutrality," end up reifying the status quo.

The questioning by these authors is vital at a time in which structural reforms are imposing new neoliberal logics on the spaces where research is taking place, discrediting anything produced in academic settings that does not respond to the needs of capital and the state by labeling it as "ideological." As such, it is important to historicize these theoretical perspectives and to remember that criticism of "extractive research" and the call to recover local knowledge through more collaborative methodologies have been key to the development of Latin American social sciences for decades. Critical anthropologists, dependence theorists, promoters of co-participative research and participatory action research, and rural feminists dedicated much of their writing during the 1960s and 1970s to reflecting on the need to decolonize the social sciences and understand how knowledge might be used to achieve social justice.

In 1971, some of these intellectuals signed what was referred to as the Declaration of Barbados in which they made a public commitment both to the liberation struggles waged by the continent's indigenous peoples and to the decolonization of the social sciences.[2] Over four decades later, we continue to battle against the phantoms of positivist and apolitical social science that simultaneously discredit any attempt to connect academic reflection with activism as "social work" and conceal their own political commitments to the status quo (see Gross and Plattner 2002).

In response to these efforts to discredit—that, unsurprisingly, frequently occur in places where assistance and financing for research are determined—it is necessary, once again, to demonstrate that critical thinking is not contrary to academic rigor. Building a research agenda in dialogue with the social actors with whom we work actually strengthens anthropological knowledge, as opposed to deviating from it, and makes it possible to transcend the limited academic world.

Although these debates seem to repeat themselves in the social sciences in a cyclical manner, the theoretical and political arguments made are not the same, even though they may appear to be. Changes in conceptualizations of power and the existence of the historic truth define significant differences between Marxist anthropologists who promoted action research in the 1960s and those of us who continue to declare the need for collaborative research today. The latter research based on "dialogues of knowledges" (*diálogos de saberes*) recognizes the partial nature of our perspective, the multiplicity of the subject positions characterizing the identities of social actors (including their relations of subordination), and the limitations of our situated knowledges.

Following Donna Haraway, I believe it is necessary to lend a new meaning to the concept of objectivity, acknowledging the historic and political context from which we construct our knowledge (Haraway 1991). In her feminist analysis of patriarchal science, she speaks to us about "situated knowledge," a concept that acknowledges the historic and social context from which reality is being perceived. At the same time, she does not give up the possibility of knowing, nor does she relativize the ethical and explanatory value of any knowledge. From Haraway's perspective, the alternative to relativism

> is partial, locatable, critical knowledges, sustaining the possibility of webs of connections, called solidarity in politics and shared conversation in epistemology . . . Relativism is the perfect twin mirror of totalization in the ideologies of objectivity: both deny the stakes in location, embodiment and partial perspective; both make it impossible to see well. Relativism and totalization are both "God tricks" promising vision from everywhere and nowhere, equally and fully, common myths in rhetoric surrounding Science. But it is precisely in the politics and epistemology of partial perspectives that the possibility of sustained, rational, objective inquiry rests. (Haraway 1991, 329)

Based on a concept of "positioned objectivity," some authors have more recently vindicated epistemological contributions from activist anthropology (see Naples 2003; Hale 2008; Speed 2008; Leyva et al. 2013). They define the latter as that which is carried out in alignment or in connection with a group of people organized in their struggle, and in collaborative relations with this group in producing knowledge. They argue that this provides a privileged perspective from within and a certain theoretical innovation that cannot be achieved if one is positioned as an external, distant observer.

The main rupture I find between our positioning in relation to socially committed or activist anthropology based on epistemic dialogues, and the positioning of our professors in the 1960s and 1970s, is that we no longer assume that we have a "historic truth" to share or that it is our responsibility to "increase the awareness" of popular sectors. Acknowledging these differences does not imply denying the path taken up to now. It is important to learn about and recover the experiences from past decades and not to pretend that we have reinvented the wheel when we once again speak about participatory research and the decolonization of theory.

Since the 1960s, the pedagogical and political proposals made by Brazilian Paulo Freire inspired an entire generation of social scientists who developed a series of methodological strategies for recovering the knowledge of popular sectors, promoting processes of political awareness-raising, and, through these processes, achieving social transformation. In the case of Mexico, these ideas led to a series of research projects linked to indigenous and peasant organizations in an attempt to build a bridge between the academic interests of researchers and the concrete needs of these sectors. What evolved as action or co-participatory research became popular during the 1970s and is considered by many to be one of Latin America's main contributions to the world's social sciences.[3] The Participatory Research Network, created by Orlando Fals Borda, Francisco Vio Grossi, and Carlos Rodríguez Brandão, proposed "the integration of people with researchers, to learn about and transform their reality, and in this way achieve their liberation" (Hall 1983, 19).

The political effervescence generated by these new methodologies coincided with the emergence of an indigenous and peasant continental movement questioning Latin American national projects that not only excluded these sectors economically and politically but also denied them the right to their cultural identities. These new voices created new challenges in the relationship between anthropologists and the "objects" of their study. At a number of continental indigenous conferences, the use of anthropology for the domination and control of indigenous peoples was denounced (see Bonfil 1981).

The voices of these new social actors played a part in the politicization of many Latin American social scientists who were in contact with this changing reality. Some decided to renounce academic work and become involved as participants or advisors to indigenous, peasant, and popular organizations. Others opted to create independent spaces for research in order to engage in a different type of social science practice, with a greater commitment to dialogue with social actors. Some examples in Mexico were the Mayan Institute of Anthropological Advice in the Mayan Region (Instituto de Asesoría Antropológica para la Región Maya), directed by Andrés Aubry; Circo Maya, coordinated by Armando Bartra; and the Center of Activist Research for Women (*Centro de Investigación-Acción para la Mujer*—CIAM), founded by Mercedes Olivera.

In Chiapas, where I lived and worked for fifteen years, co-participatory research was popularized by some independent researchers linked to nongovernmental organizations and the Catholic Church, whose pastoral work in this region was guided by liberation theology. Action research consisted of "recovering" the knowledge of popular sectors with regard to their social reality, assisting in its systematization and promoting "conscientization." Although this research model proposed the transformation of hierarchical relations between the researcher and the researched, the theoretical premise (inherited from Marxism, that intellectuals can awaken the conscience of the "oppressed") was based on a paternalist perspective of popular sectors and popular knowledge considered to be "distorted" by a "false consciousness."

This was part of the inheritance reproduced and eventually confronted by those of us who, from our feminist perspective, have opted for more collaborative research in recent years. Many feminist anthropologists, including myself, working in academic institutions or independent organizations, decided to take up the idea of supporting processes of the empowerment and conscientization of women from popular sectors through our research. Nevertheless, critical reflection has led some of us to acknowledge that we were reproducing some of the ethnocentric perspectives of Marxism. Now, the "infallible method" is not historical materialism, but rather gender analysis that has emerged from a Western intellectual tradition and that is generally quite insensitive to cultural differences.

The epistemic dialogues presented in this book arose from a self-critique of my own trajectory as a feminist working in an indigenous region characterized by racism and racial hierarchies. The voices of organized indigenous women, together with critical reflections on the colonialism in the discourse of academic feminisms, led me to question the methodologies used by the feminist organization to which I belonged during the late 1980s. The organization was located in San Cristóbal de las Casas, a city of ladinos surrounded by marginalized neighborhoods of indigenous Tsotsil and the administrative hub of a mostly indigenous region.

However, it was not only academic feminist readings that made me question the colonizing practices of some hegemonic urban feminisms. Living for long periods of time in Mayan communities in the highlands and border regions of Chiapas brought me closer to other forms of knowledge and to the political and organizational experiences of indigenous peoples. I reformulated many of my Marxist and feminist perspectives on resistance and social struggle, incorporating a critique of racism and internal colonialism as a fundamental focus in political struggle.

During those years, I found myself experiencing state repression and the criminalization of social movements at a personal level, as a number of my friends suffered repression and sexual violence carried out by government forces. These experiences led me to participate in forming a broad movement of women against state violence, and against sexual and domestic violence in particular. This movement became the Collective Spaces for Women (Colectivo de Espacios para Mujeres—COLEM) feminist organization, to which I belonged for ten years. My experience in COLEM, questioning and fighting patriarchal violence, and my work as an anthropologist in the Center for Research and Advanced Studies in Social Anthropology (Centro de Investigaciones y Estudios Superiores en Antropología Social—CIESAS), reflecting on the racism and internal colonialism affecting indigenous peoples, led me to think about political alliances and the need to construct a policy of solidarity among diverse social actors.

In 1994, the Zapatista movement connected struggles against neoliberalism, racism, and patriarchy, becoming the first political-military movement in Latin America that vindicated women's rights as a fundamental part of its political agenda. Its influence has been highly important (both theoretically and politically) for an entire generation of feminists, myself included, who have taken on the task of decolonization as a basic condition for reformulating our feminist agenda.

My double identity as an academic and a member, for ten years, of a feminist organization that worked against sexual and domestic violence through a center for assisting women and youth—especially indigenous women—led me to confront discourses that idealized indigenous cultures. This idealization occurred, from a significant sector of Mexican anthropology, alongside the ethnocentrism of a significant sector of liberal feminism. In a polarized context where women's rights have been presented as contrary to the collective rights of peoples, it has been difficult to vindicate more nuanced perspectives on indigenous cultures. In particular, it is hard to find perspectives that acknowledge the dialogues of power of which they are constituted and, at the same time, demand the rights of indigenous peoples to their own culture and to self-determination.

At this political crossroads, indigenous women have been the ones who have given me clues about how to rethink indigenous demands from a nonessentialist perspective. Their theorizations in relation to culture, tradition, and gender equity (as expressed in political documents, final reports from events, and public discourses, but also systematized in the writings of their intellectuals) are fundamental perspectives for the epistemic dialogue needed for the decolonization of feminism.

The proposal that we have been working on, together with other academic colleagues and activists participating in the Decolonial Feminisms Network (Red de Feminismos Descoloniales), arises from questioning the homogenizing, generalizing perspectives of patriarchy and "women's interests" that have characterized a significant sector of Anglo-Saxon and European feminism (see

Millán et al. 2014). When the idea of a pre-existing collective subject, in this case "women," is rejected, and when any collectivity is considered to be a product of alliances among diverse actors, we are presented with the challenge of constructing a political agenda on the basis of dialogue and negotiation. In this task, research has a great deal to offer in learning about and recognizing other knowledges and other ways of being in the world.

The epistemic dialogues that we propose from the perspective of activist research—unlike co-participatory research—do not intend to transform reality because of a method or theory considered to be infallible. Rather, the intention is that, together with the social actors with whom we are working, we reflect upon and deconstruct the issues in a shared social reality. Then, based on these dialogues, we jointly develop a research agenda that will make our knowledge relevant for the movements or social actors with whom we are collaborating. In co-participatory research, the commitment of social scientists with the objects-subjects of their study was an easy decision: it was a matter of simply taking sides with those who were marginalized, as opposed to those who were responsible for exploitation. However, to the extent that our analyses of power become increasingly complex, we find ourselves obliged to reject the homogenizing, harmonic representations of subalterns by acknowledging the different levels of inequality experienced by social collectives. Some committed social scientists are confronting new ethical and methodological dilemmas. If we recognize that our representations and analyses—of indigenous peoples, migrants, women, and religious minorities, to mention a few—may have political implications for these groups, it is important to acknowledge the shades of gray that exist between the blacks and whites emphasized in past analyses.

When we renounce the certainties offered by Marxism in the co-participatory research of the 1970s and 1980s, we face new challenges in conducting socially committed research. The social actors with whom we work (in our case, women) often seek, through the collaborative relationship, "infallible answers" to the problems they are facing, more than a critical questioning of shared reality. In addition, we have lost the apparent clarity derived from conceiving of the differences between "the dominant" and "the dominated" as emerging from a single axis of subordination: class. When we consider the plurality of relations based on subordination, any perspective of homogenous collectives is destroyed, and the task of recognizing a collective interest that should be supported by the researcher becomes more complicated. Nevertheless, recognizing these challenges should lead us to something more than political demobilization. Instead, we must search for creative ways to generate dialogues of knowledges that will allow us to propose strategies for struggle that are more congruent with the complex realities we are facing.

From the perspective of feminist anthropology, the link between the production of knowledge and political commitments to social transformation has been, since its origins, an axis around which its theoretical and methodological proposals revolve (see Moore 1996). For this very reason, feminists have made important contributions to a critique of the networks of power that legitimize and reproduce scientific positivism—contributions that have not always been recognized by contemporary critical anthropologists or postmodern theorists.[4]

In the case of Latin American feminist anthropology, these critical perspectives have not arisen exclusively in the theoretical, academic setting. These critiques accompanied political and methodological practices that have taken these debates to the spaces where political struggles are taking place, to popular education workshops, and to spaces of collective organizing in which many feminist academics, myself included, are participating.

This has been my experience as a feminist academic linked to a public center for research and graduate studies (CIESAS), while at the same time collaborating and/or being part of various collective efforts focused on building a more just life for women. The topics of my critical analysis of Mexico's national project, spaces of justice, and development policies—to mention some that I have addressed in my work—have not only been problems for academic research but also concerns that I have been able to share with other women with whom I have participated in organizations and/or established epistemic and political dialogues.

In the sections that follow, I will introduce four different experiences in collaborative research with indigenous women that serve as the bases for this book.

The four action research experiences that give sustenance to the chapters of this book are, first of all, my work as companion and ally, for over twenty-five years, to a continental indigenous women's movement that has experienced different local organizational processes in Mexico, Guatemala, and Colombia. These activist research experiences allowed me to systematize the various political genealogies of indigenous women in these regions through their oral histories and official documents (Hernández Castillo 2006a, 2006b, 2008), and to support the publication of their own theorizations and critical reflections (see Hernández Castillo 2006b; Martínez and Florentino 2012; Méndez et al. 2013; Painemal 2005; Rivera Zea 2005; Romay 2012; Sánchez Néstor 2005; Villa 2012;

Vargas Vásquez 2011). Second, I worked for ten years (1988–1998) as a member of the legal and educational areas of the Women and Children's Support Centre (CAMM) in San Cristóbal de las Casas, Chiapas, where my research on communal justice and legal pluralism contributed to rethinking our legal defense strategies for indigenous women (see Hernández Castillo 2002a, 2005; Hernández Castillo and Garza Caligaris 1995). Third, I participated in the elaboration of anthropological expert witness reports and their presentation at the Inter-American Court of Human Rights in cases of military violence against indigenous women (see appendix 1). Finally, I currently participate as a member of the Sisters in the Shadows Editorial Collective of Women in Prison (2008–2016), where I performed anthropological research on indigenous women's experiences with penal justice (see Hernández Castillo 2013).[5]

In these experiences, the dialogical construction of knowledge was one of the main objectives and challenges for those of us participating in these projects as women researchers/activists and activists/researchers.

CHRONICLER AND ALLY OF INDIGENOUS WOMEN'S ORGANIZATIONS

In the 1980s, when I participated as a member of a broad women's movement in Chiapas, one of the main challenges we faced, as a feminist organization with a project of struggle against domestic and state violence, was the construction of political alliances with indigenous women's organizations in the region. During those years, the issue of racism was taboo in feminist organizations, and the unwillingness to talk about racism reproduced the universalizing discourses of the feminisms of the Global North, speaking of women's rights as shared rights and excluding class, ethnicity, and sexual preference from the discussions.

In this context, there was little recognition of the ethnic and class hierarchies that marked the women's movement in Chiapas. The struggle against state violence and the militarization of indigenous regions, both of which increased after the Zapatista uprising in 1994, was the central axis of many of our struggles (see Hernández Castillo 2001a, 2002b).

In October 1995, in the context of the peace talks between the Zapatista Army of National Liberation (Ejército Zapatista de Liberación Nacional—EZLN) and the federal government, a round table called "Indigenous Rights and Culture" was established to discuss the EZLN's demands, with participation by the Zapatista general command, representatives of civil society allied with the

Zapatistas, and government representatives. The dialogue was organized in seven workgroups, one of which was "Situation, Rights, and Culture of Indigenous Women;" as a women's organization, we were invited by the Zapatista general command to be part of their group of advisers. My participation in this space allowed me to recognize, once again, how internalized racism expressed itself, even among female mestizo activists who claimed to be sympathizers with the Zapatistas. Both the Zapatistas and the government's representatives invited indigenous and mestizo women to participate in the adviser groups and, for five days (October 18–22, 1995), discussed the women's specific demands, many of them included in the Women's Revolutionary Law elaborated by Zapatista women.[6] To the surprise of many of us, the ideological and political differences between indigenous Zapatista women and the indigenous women invited by the government (many of whom were members of the official Institutional Revolutionary Party (Partido Revolucionario Institucional—PRI), took a secondary role when a mestizo feminist treated an indigenous woman of the government commission with arrogance and disrespect. The Zapatista women stopped the "feminist in solidarity" in her tracks for reproducing, in this political space, the racist and condescending ways in which many urban women often treat indigenous women.

After this experience, many of the indigenous women's organizations supporting the Zapatista struggle started to create their own spaces for organization and political discussion, spaces to which only a few non-indigenous feminists were invited as allies and observers (without the right to speak or vote).

It was in this context that, in 1997, the National Encounter of Indigenous Women's "Building our History" was held and attended by over 700 indigenous women from various regions of Mexico, with the participation of Commander Ramona, one of the main political figures of *Zapatismo*.[7] This meeting gave birth to the Coordinating Committee of Indigenous Women in Mexico (Coordinadora Nacional de Mujeres Indígenas—CONAMI), in which non-indigenous women could participate only as observers, and only by invitation. Many feminist activists who had worked from within their organizations against violence toward indigenous women felt offended by this decision, interpreting it as "treason," as expressed in this first encounter by the well-known feminist lawyer Martha Figueroa. Learning to listen and to put aside our tendency to take an excessively large role in the public encounters was an indispensable requirement in order to collaborate with them.

In this new political context, collaborative research is no longer just an ethical and political decision made by researchers, but also a demand of the indigenous

FIGURE 1. The author with participants in the Congress of the Continental
Network of Indigenous Women in Guatemala, 2015. Photograph
from R. Aída Hernández Archives.

organizations themselves. These organizations do not allow anyone to appropriate their knowledges, to "ethnograph" their spaces, or to assign themselves
the right to representation without first clarifying the purpose of the research.
Throughout the last twenty years I have had the privilege of being invited as an
ally to several of these women's organizational spaces, including CONAMI and
the Continental Network of Indigenous Women (Enlace Continental de Mujeres
Indígenas—ECMIA) created in Quito, Ecuador in 1995. I have oftentimes contributed behind the scenes with logistical tasks; with the elaboration of reports,
press documents, or popular education manuals; and, a few times, with facilitat-
ing or moderating in workshops on women's rights. This access to their program
documents, interviews with their leaders, and the knowledge of the internal dynamics of their organizational spaces allowed me to reconstruct the political genealogies presented in chapter 2.

I consider myself an unofficial chronicler of indigenous women's movements. Many times it was my task to elaborate audiovisual materials used in the
workshops on violence against women, such as the videos *Enough! Seven Stories
of Domestic Violence*; *Rights of Women in Our Customs and Traditions*, and *Under
the Shadow of the Guamúchil: Life Stories of Incarcerated Peasant and Indigenous*

Women (Ya basta! Siete historias de violencia doméstica, los derechos de las mu-jeres en nuestras costumbres y tradiciones, and *Bajo la sombra del Guamúchil: Historias de vida de mujeres indígenas y campesinas en reclusión).* Other times I have taken on the task of denouncing, through the written press, radio series, or other journalistic publications, the violence and repression suffered by their movements.[8]

Recognizing myself as an ally does not imply erasing or ignoring the structural inequalities that distance me from many of the indigenous women with whom I work. Class differences, my position as a tenured university professor in a society characterized by economic inequalities (where job insecurity in the academy is the norm rather than the exception), my place as a mestizo woman in a racialized society where mestizos are constructed by the national discourse as "the national norm," and my situation as a heterosexual woman in a profoundly homophobic society mean that I produce my knowledge from a highly privileged space of enunciation. Recognizing these sites of privilege is important, not in order to deny the possibilities of intercultural dialogues and alliances, but to construct them based on a critical reflection of their structural context of inequality.

This recognition is not always easy, nor are dialogues always supportive and constructive, but recognizing our internalized racisms and working on them from within academic and political spaces is a fundamental step toward building alliances. My collaborative research with indigenous women's organizations has also involved the task of building bridges with urban feminist organizations, taking the issues of racism and feminist exclusions to political and academic spaces. Publishing this book in English and translating their testimonies and reflections into that language is yet another attempt to contribute to build bridges with different women.

EXPERIENCES FROM WORKSHOPS ON GENDER VIOLENCE AND INDIGENOUS JUSTICE

One of my first experiences in building bridges between my legal anthropological research and political activism took place during the 1990s in the Mexican state of Chiapas, where I was a member of a feminist organization working to end all forms of violence against women (see Hernández Castillo 2002a). Drawing on my education in anthropology, I wanted to contribute to the outreach and organizational work promoted by COLEM, and so I proposed to my colleagues that we conduct collaborative research aimed at exploring the possibilities and limitations of national law and indigenous normative systems in addressing sexual and domestic violence.

A team of activists (including myself) who worked in CAMM, and who represented three different disciplines (law, pedagogy, and anthropology), held a series of workshops with a group of bilingual indigenous women. We shared basic knowledge regarding the way in which positive law confronts sexual and domestic violence, and they shared with us their experiences and knowledge regarding spaces of indigenous justice.

Using tools from popular education, we planned the workshops to serve not as traditional spaces for training "popular defenders" but as spaces for discussion in which both the indigenous participants and CAMM members shared knowledge for seeking together the best tools for legal defense work. Based on the methodological action research proposals developed under the influence of Paulo Freire's pedagogical work, we intended for the workshops to fulfill the double function of contributing to both the research and training of popular defenders who would be able to move fluidly between entities imparting justice in their communities and such entities at the state and national levels.

Participants in the workshops were all women from organizations or community leaders who had previous contact with CAMM and who had expressed an interest in reflecting on, and receiving training about, their rights. The group consisted of twelve women: six of them were bilingual teachers from the municipalities of Chilón, Jitotol, Simojovel, and Tila, and they spoke Tsotsil, Tseltal, and Chol; the other six were members of crafts cooperatives, two from the Zinacantán municipality, two from Amatenango del Valle, and two who had migrated to the city of San Cristóbal de las Casas from Tenejapa and Chamula. We never viewed the experiences of these women as representative of the feelings and thoughts of "indigenous women." These participants were all young women who had, in one way or another, confronted the prevailing gender roles in their communities. Through their work as teachers or craftswomen, they had contact with other organized women, both indigenous and mestizo women, and their perceptions and discourses were influenced by the ways in which they were constantly crossing cultural borders. All of them participated in broader indigenous organizations with cultural and political demands. These included the Teachers Union of New Education for Mexico (Unión de Maestros de la Nueva Educación para México) and the National Plural Indigenous Assembly for Autonomy (Asamblea Nacional Indígena Plural por la Autonomía—ANIPA), and two participants were originally from communities that were part of the new autonomous regions created because of the Zapatista uprising.[9] If their experiences were representative of something, it was that these women were from a minority sector of women who played very active roles in indigenous organizations and who were reformulating the way in which gender roles are understood.

The challenges we faced in conducting the workshops were greater than we had imagined when we initially proposed a space for exchanging knowledge. For those of us who were CAMM members, our professional training and work experiences had a profound impact on our perceptions of what would be involved in this type of exchange, and on our own perceptions of state law and customary law. The lawyers on our team, despite their critical perspective on law (resulting from their feminist activism), continued to view state legality as a fundamental tool for constructing a more just life for indigenous and mestizo women. Their perceptions of "customs and traditions" determined their understandings of a normative system, learned during their university studies. For the pedagogue on our team, the priority was to assist participants in reflecting on inequalities between men and women and, to whatever degree possible, to contribute to building a gender consciousness. Recognizing the cultural specificity of the indigenous women was only a first step toward finding the similarities that could unite all the women in a common front.

As an anthropologist, I debated between my cultural relativism and global feminist activism. I attempted to break with generalizing discourses on "women" and to understand the cultural logics that impacted their gender relations and normative systems. At the same time, I recognized the similarities and complicities between indigenous and non-indigenous patriarchal institutions. The main challenge was both reconciling the different levels of emphasis we placed on law, gender, and culture, and attempting to critically analyze our own conceptualizations. The second challenge was to do away with the idea of the existence of a "false consciousness" (which sometimes underlies the conception of popular education as a "conscienticizing" tool), and to learn to listen and understand the experiences and perceptions of the women participating in the workshop.

The indigenous women, for their part, had to face practical difficulties involved in attending the workshops, such as the insecurity on the roads to and from their communities, many of them militarized or under the control of paramilitary groups, as in the case of *Paz y Justicia* in the Chol municipality of Tila.[10] Those who came from zones of Zapatista influence had to suspend their participation in some of the workshops due to the various "red alerts" declared by the EZLN.[11] Still another challenge for the indigenous women participants was assuming the commitment involved in defending other women in their communities, where "getting involved in someone else's problems" was viewed negatively, almost as bad as "gossiping," and akin to creating conflict. Their parents questioned some of them when they attempted to explain their interest in learning more about the law, "due to the dangers they would be exposed to if they got involved in problems with the government."[12]

Despite all of these limitations, we were able to work together for a year's time, with monthly meetings lasting two or three days, until, for various reasons associated with political problems in the region, it was no longer possible for the women to travel to San Cristóbal. We decided to suspend the final workshops, replacing them with visits we made to the areas where they worked. This research presented us with the challenge of deconstructing and analyzing the premises underlying positive law and indigenous law as social practices and discourses that reflect the inequalities between genders. With their limitations and historical specificities acknowledged, we could explore the real possibilities they offered for constructing a better life for women.

Already at that time, a number of us on the team had begun to feel uncomfortable with the "didactic" style of feminist workshops. We pointed to the need for transforming such workshops into spaces for dialogues of knowledges (*diálogos de saberes*) in which both the indigenous women and CAMM members could critically reflect upon community justice and state justice, and in which we could dare to question our certainties. Resistance to bringing definitive solutions to the issues we discussed was at times discouraging for the women participating.

Our idea was not to present national law as simply a tool for state control and domination or to vindicate it as the panacea against ethnic and generic oppression. Nor was it our intention to demonize indigenous law or to idealize it as a space for cultural resistance. Instead, our proposal was to explore the possibilities and limitations of both, in relation to the specific problems of indigenous women, with the aim of seeking alternatives more congruent with the cultural and social context in which our organization carried out its work against sexual and domestic violence.

It was, of course, not easy to come to these collective spaces for constructing knowledge with doubts in our minds. It would be much more comfortable to assume that we had truths to "share," and to take on the role of "trainers" and/or those who "awaken consciousness." The latter would offer a certain legitimacy and power in collective spaces that was not easy to acquire from a position of uncertainty. Nevertheless, this experience, and others that followed, taught us that being open to decentering and destabilizing our visions of the world and strategies for struggle can be more productive for constructing a common project. Such lessons can allow us to find paths that we had not been able to imagine when we believed we had all the epistemological cartographies for an emancipatory agenda readily available.

For example, what indigenous women revealed about networks of power at various levels of justice, paired with their proposals for reinventing traditions under new terms, can provide clues for redefining the debate between cultural relativism and universalism. Through the testimonies shared at the workshops, and in the interviews conducted within the framework of this research (as well as in the documents from congresses, conferences, and forums), a concept of dynamic, changing culture becomes evident. Unlike the liberal critics of multiculturalism, the indigenous women from Chiapas do not reject their culture in the name of equality but rather demand the right to their own culture while fighting for the construction of equitable relations within their own families, communities, and organizations.

In later collaborative research projects with organizations of indigenous women from various regions of Latin America, we found similar perspectives in which, based on their political reflections, these new voices have come to question the dichotomous perspectives between feminist universalism and "Indianist" cultural relativism. Indigenous women from Mexico, Guatemala, and Colombia, whose experiences we will analyze in the next chapter, have simultaneously demanded from the state the right to cultural difference. and demanded from their communities the right to change the customs and traditions they consider to be unfair. In various documents generated in these new spaces for discussion, indigenous women have demanded their rights as national citizens and have taken up the demand made by the continental indigenous movement to maintain and recover their traditions. However, they have done so from a discourse that proposes the possibility of "always changing while staying the same, and always remaining the same while changing."

CULTURAL AFFIDAVITS AND ACCESS TO JUSTICE

Another way in which anthropologists are beginning to engage in legal activism is through expert witness reports or anthropological affidavits for litigation cases at national or international levels. The multicultural reforms of the last decade have brought changes in codes for criminal proceedings that permit the use of expert evidence of a cultural nature. These anthropological affidavits are reports prepared by specialists who acknowledge the cultural context of the accused or the plaintiff, whichever the case. The fundamental objective of the affidavits is to provide information to the court regarding the importance of cultural differences in understanding a specific case. For many anthropologists who promote the use of cultural affidavits, this means that indigenous peoples will have a better possibility for access to justice. Laura Valladares, a member of the board at Colegio de Etnólogos y Antropólogos Sociales (CEAS), one of the professional associations that certifies experts, states the following:

> Cultural affidavits have a relevant role in contributing to the construction of processes for procuring justice in conditions of greater equity for indigenous peoples and their members, and also contribute to creating scenarios of legal pluralism. It is a tool that makes it possible to initiate a dialogical relation between positive law and indigenous normative systems, as well as engage in the construction of a society that respects cultural diversity. (Valladares 2012, 11–13)

In the case of Mexico, the August 2001 revision of Article 2 of the Constitution, known as the "Law of Indigenous Rights and Culture," specified modifications in the Federal Codes for Criminal Proceedings, recognizing the right to a translator when the plaintiff or defendant does not speak Spanish fluently. This modification offers the possibility of expert opinions on cultural factors involved in the action being prosecuted.[13] Prior to these reforms, lawyers who represented indigenous defendants, some of them pro bono defense attorneys with the National Indigenist Institute (Instituto Nacional Indigenista—INI),[14] attempted to diminish a sentence or secure the release of an indigenous inmate by appealing to the already-repealed Article 49a of the Federal Code of Criminal Proceedings. The repealed article considered a reduced sentence for those who were in conditions of "extreme cultural backwardness." In other words, they appealed to an article that reproduced racism in Mexican society. Despite the multicultural reforms that have been implemented, this argument continues to be used by many lawyers and cultural expert witnesses. Thus, despite their "good intentions," they are reifying and reproducing racist perspectives on indigenous peoples (see Gitlitz 2015; Escalante Betancourt 2015; Verona 2015).

While the use of cultural affidavits may represent progress in achieving access to justice in comparison to racist perspectives that appealed to "cultural backwardness," these affidavits constitute a legal tool that raises new ethical and epistemological dilemmas for anthropologists (like myself) who defend legal activism.[15] On the one hand, this tool reproduces hierarchies in relation to knowledge, legitimizing the cultural knowledge of anthropologists over and above the knowledge of indigenous peoples themselves. As anthropologists, in this formulation, we are the ones who have legitimate cultural knowledge that can be acknowledged by the operators of justice. In this sense, then, we have the last word in terms of what is a "genuine indigenous cultural practice" or "genuine indigenous law." Yuri Escalante Betancourt, one of Mexico's most renowned cultural experts, describes this dilemma in self-critical terms:

> Who is the most competent expert for clarifying the cultural differences sought by judges, or in other words, who can be the best expert to present the truth before justice in matters of cultural analysis? An anthropologist trained under Western theories or someone from the community where the legal controversy arose? Does the anthropologist's authority not turn into authoritarianism by attempting to know what a native person already knew? (Escalante Betancourt 2012, 41)

The anthropologist's role as a "cultural translator" for the operators of state justice becomes even more complicated by the need to accept the rules of legal discourse where the complex, contextual perspectives of anthropological analysis often have no place (see Carrasco 2015). In Australia, where anthropologists have a long history of preparing cultural affidavits in support of the struggle for the recognition of the territorial rights of aboriginal peoples, David Trigger describes the contradictions faced when they accept the "rules of the game" in state justice (Trigger 2004). He writes that there is "a tension here between the necessity for a researcher to fit investigations into this legal context, yet maintain professional independence such that one's own disciplinary standards and practices are not swamped by the force of the legal process" (Trigger 2004, 31–32).

For example, the legal process requires "positive truths" with regard to the culture of indigenous peoples that often involve reproducing essentialist representations of their cultures. The diversity within communities and the different perspectives in relation to culture and traditions between genders and generations remain invisible in these homogenizing cultural descriptions. It is because of these power games in which anthropologists participate in spaces of justice that authors like Karen Engle warn about "the dark sides of virtue" in reference to the reification of indigenous cultures often involved in legal activism associated with their rights (Engle 2010).

What is the solution to these dilemmas? Shall we maintain ourselves at the margin of legal spaces and allow the "truth technologies" used in legal systems to continue to speak of "cultural backwardness"? Is it possible to critically analyze these knowledge-power systems and their productive capacity while at the same time attempting to use discourses on rights and legal spaces as emancipatory tools?

Because of my anti-essentialist perspectives on indigenous cultures and my criticism of the way in which anthropologists in countries like Colombia were becoming "purist guardians of indigenous culture" through cultural affidavits (see chapter 3), I previously rejected any invitation to participate as an expert witness in legal processes. However, my reticence to prepare anthropological affidavits or participate as an expert in litigation processes fell apart when two indigenous women leaders of the Me'phaa people who were raped by members of the Mexican army decided to take their case to an international court and asked me to accompany them in this process.

In March 2009, I was invited by the Center of Human Rights of the Mountains of Guerrero Tlachinollan (Centro de Derechos Humanos de la Montaña de Guerrero) and the Center for Justice and International Law (Centro por la Justicia y el Derecho Internacional—CEJIL) to prepare an anthropological affidavit to be presented to the Inter-American Court of Human Rights in the cases denounced by Valentina Rosendo Cantú and Inés Fernández Ortega. These two women, members of the OPIM, were raped by soldiers in February and March 2002, respectively. Since then, they have fought at the national and international levels both for justice to be served and in order to denounce the effect of the country's militarization on the lives of indigenous women and their peoples. This was a case that deserved an affidavit characterized by sensitivity to the intersections of gender, class, and ethnicity, and to the way in which these multiple exclusions had impacted the victims' vulnerability, their experience of violence, and the lack of punishment for the crimes. The request from their legal representatives was to prepare an affidavit that I would later present orally to the Inter-American Court and that would explain the impact on the communities of the sexual violence experienced by the two women.

This invitation was the beginning of an intercultural dialogue with both of these women and with other women in their organizations. Through this dialogue, I have learned from their courage in confronting and denouncing state violence and from their profound analysis in which they conceive their experiences of violence not as individual but as part of a collective history that has been characterized by a *continuum* of violence against indigenous peoples. This analytical perspective has been evident in their denouncements and their demands for compensations to their communities, including the region's demilitarization as a central element. The way in which they have formulated their denouncements, testimonies, and discourses throughout these ten years of struggle (as well as the demand for compensations before the Inter-American Court) reveals the cultural construction of a sense of personhood that is constituted mutually by the individual and the collective. An act as seemingly individualized as rape was experienced and analyzed as part of the historic violence against these women and their peoples.

Because of the political clarity with which both Inés and Valentina analyzed and denounced the sexual aggressions against them, I doubted for a moment, given my ethnocentric prejudices, if their testimonies had been faithfully translated from Me'phaa into Spanish in the documents I was reading. When I was invited, together with my colleague Héctor Ortíz Elizondo, to participate as experts in their denouncement before the Inter-American Court, I had not yet met them personally, and I was concerned that their organization and the human rights entities representing them were prioritizing their own political interests above those of the two women. Indeed, I worried that the denouncement might actually be a process of re-victimization.

While it is true that these paradigmatic cases tend to be evaluated in a positive manner by feminist organizations, judging by the impact they have had on gender jurisprudence and public policies, we know very little about the real-life consequences. The accusation process has brought new experiences upon the women who dared to confront the state's power by taking their complaints beyond national borders. It was this concern that led me to hesitate when I was invited to participate as an expert witness before the Inter-American Court in the cases of Inés Fernández Ortega and Valentina Rosendo Cantú. Were these two women truly those wanting to take this complaint before the international tribunal? Or were human rights organizations pressuring them to carry out this "strategic litigation?"

With these questions in mind, I made my first visit in March 2009 to Barranca Tecuani, a Me'phaa community of some 500 people in the municipality of Ayutla de los Libres in Guerrero. This is where I met Inés Fernández Ortega, a small woman with a penetrating gaze and inner strength. Any doubts I had dissipated when she told me: "It is I who wants to accuse, so that justice is done, so that the *guachos* (soldiers) know they cannot get away with it, so my daughters and other children in the community do not go through what I went through, so that all the women in the region can roam through the mountains without fear."[16] Her conviction that the complaint was necessary, not only for herself but for all Me'phaa women, made it clear to me that this was a community leadership very different from others I had known.

One of the key objectives of the expert witness report was to demonstrate that the sexual violence suffered by Inés had an impact not only on her and her family but also on the women of her community and organization (see the entire Expert Witness Report in appendix 1). This process brought me close to Inés and the women from the OPIM, and I learned not only of their courage but also of their sense of collective solidarity and communitarian cohesion.

Now I understand that the need for a report of this kind came not just from the legal representatives but from Inés herself, who since the beginning of this process insisted that her rape was part of a series of aggressions against her people and her organization. It is for this reason that it cannot be treated as an isolated event. Her conviction forced her lawyers to justify before the Inter-American Court the demand of communitarian compensation for a case of an individual sexual violation, a legal strategy that had not been used before at this entity of international justice. It was because of Inés Fernandez Ortega's firm decision to use the Inter-American Court as a forum for an accusation of a chain of violent events (in which her rape was only one link) that it was necessary to elaborate this anthropological report, giving me the privilege of meeting these women from whom I continue to learn every day.

While the details of this case will be analyzed in chapter 4, I would like to emphasize in terms of methodology that OPIM members and other members of the women's families carried out the entire process of collectively preparing the affidavit. At Inés's request, the discussion around collective compensation demands took place at a workshop coordinated by Héctor Ortíz Elizondo and a psychologist, Clemencia Correa, who also participated as an expert before the Inter-American Court. In this workshop, as in others held later, Inés insisted on expanding the discussions beyond her experience of violence in order to reflect on how militarization was affecting all the men and women in the region. She pointed out that her case was not unique and that many women were remaining silent out of fear of reprisals. This type of work allowed us to transcend the essentialist perspectives of culture by incorporating history and an analysis of political context into our affidavits.

It is important to acknowledge that our participation as experts in the Inter-American Court reproduced, to some degree, a hierarchization of knowledge

FIGURE 2. The author with the members of the legal team that represented
Inés Fernández Ortega in the Inter-American Court in Lima, Peru.
Photograph from R. Aída Hernández Archives.

by turning ourselves into the "voice of their culture" in the eyes of international
law. However, the collaborative nature of the research on which the affidavit
was based allowed us to incorporate their voices, analyses, and perspectives into
the expert report presented. This dynamic continued after the case was won,
in the subsequent stage of implementing the sentence. At that time, we were
invited, together with Héctor Ortíz, to facilitate a workshop to discuss the sentence and the mechanisms for implementing the collective compensations. The
Mexican state's conviction for "institutional military violence" became a tool
for collective reflection on the part of Inés and the women in her organization.

The "technologies of truth" implemented in the Inter-American Court
constructed a type of victimized identity that denied Inés's and Valentina's social agency. They became only victims of the repressive state (see Merry and
Bibler Coutin 2014). But both women destabilized these identitary constructions when they used the sentence of the Court as a tool for fighting against
the state's militarization and violence, assuming an identity as human rights
defenders.

I do not wish to overestimate the impact of these cases in the Inter-American
Court of Human Rights, but I would like to point out that they were paradigmatic sentences in which, for the first time, the Court demanded collective

compensations for a case of individual grievances. This speaks of the way in which liberal dichotomous conceptions around gender rights and collective rights are beginning to be destabilized in arenas of international justice.

Some critical perspectives on the Inter-American Court suggest that despite the importance this court has acquired in Latin America, it is a very limited space for international justice when it comes to gender justice:

> We are beginning to see the decisions of the Court invoked before domestic courts as supranational precedents, and this can also be found in the drafting history of legislative reform bills and the justification of public policy papers. Most importantly, unlike other international dispute resolution mechanisms in the field of human rights that are open to receiving complaints from the region, the Court offers victims of human rights abuses the possibility of a legally binding decision. For this reason, it tends to be favored among Latin American victims. Against this backdrop, it can be said that the Court's case law is a tremendously useful tool for human rights practitioners, NGOs and academics in the Americas. This being the case, it is certainly a matter of concern that in 18 years of decisions on individual petitions, there are only six cases that can be said to refer in a significant way to women's rights. Four of those decisions failed to adequately identify and manage the gender sensitive issues that arose from the facts. (Palacios Zuolaga 2008, 10)

Since Patricia Palacios Zuolaga wrote this text criticizing the Inter-American Human Rights Court's lack of gender policy, there have been some changes that speak to the potential impact of discourses and practices of resistance on these supranational spaces of justice. The cases of Inés and Valentina were preceded by the *María da Penha v. Brazil* case, involving domestic violence. The Brazilian state was found responsible for violating María da Penha's right to legal guarantees and protection, due to an unjustifiable delay and the negligent handling of domestic violence in Brazil. Because of the compensations demanded by the Court, Brazil issued one of the most advanced laws against domestic violence in all of Latin America, known as the "María da Penha Law." In 2009, the case of *Gonzalez & Co. v. Mexico*, also known as the "Campo Algodonero" case, was presented to the Inter-American Court. In this case, the mothers of eight women murdered in Ciudad Juárez, whose bodies were found in *un campo algodonero* (a cotton field), filed a complaint against the Mexican state for negligence and impunity in its handling of the denouncement. This case was paradigmatic because the compensations demanded by the Court included a recognition of structural conditions that facilitate femicide in the region.

Obviously, the sentences handed down by an international court cannot, on their own, change the structural conditions that make violence against women possible. They are only tools for a broader struggle. Their implementation brings new contradictions and, in some cases, new vulnerabilities for the women demanding justice, as we will see in chapter 4. Nevertheless, my experience accompanying the denouncements by Inés Fernández Ortega and Valentina Rosendo Cantú has led me to reconsider my critical position on cultural affidavits, and to think that perhaps, as anthropologists, we have something to offer to legal activism.

PENITENTIARY WORKSHOPS: ORAL HISTORIES AS A TOOL FOR DISARTICULATING MULTIPLE OPPRESSIONS

Another one of the important methodological experiences contributing to this book derives from my work in penitentiary writing workshops with indigenous and peasant women imprisoned at a social readaptation center (Centro de Readaptación Social—CERESO) in the Mexican state of Morelos. I arrived at the Women's Atlacholoaya CERESO in 2008 with the idea that my anthropological research on Mexico's justice system had something to offer in improving women's access to justice, without imagining the way in which the reflections and experiences of these women would change my life.

Through this experience, I have been able to verify the importance of oral history as a tool for feminist reflection and as a strategy for destabilizing racist and sexist colonial discourses. While feminist theorists have written a great deal on the importance of recovering the history of daily life and telling the stories of women's experiences through oral history (see Wolf 1996; Reinharz 1992; Fonow and Cook 1991), I had not imagined how the collective reconstruction of individual histories could serve to build sisterhood among diverse women and facilitate the writing of a counterhistory that would reveal the way in which the coloniality of power defines the lack of access to justice for indigenous and peasant women.

Oral history, in this context, has ceased to be a "methodological tool for researchers," instead becoming a means of collective reflection that exposes how

FIGURE 3. Participants in the penitentiary writing workshops at a "social readaptation center" (*Centro de Readaptación Social*—CERESO) in Atlacholoaya in the Mexican state of Morelos. Photograph from R. Aída Hernández Archives.

ethnic and class hierarchies impacted the trajectories of exclusion and lack of access to justice experienced by the incarcerated women. Contrasting the experiences of diverse women exposed the hierarchies that define the Mexican justice system. As indigenous and non-indigenous women, peasant factory workers and professionals, homosexual and heterosexual women shared their life histories and reflected on the multiple exclusions of the Mexican society.

Expecting to have an ethnographic approach to this penitentiary environment, I planned to undertake field research by recording the life stories of indigenous women in the women's CERESO in Morelos. This particular CERESO was established in 2000 to replace the old penal complex at Atlacomulco in the state of Morelos, as a response to criticism over the dreadful living conditions for its inmates. As a modern correctional facility, the new detention center includes a section designed exclusively for women, unlike most penal complexes that have been built with men in mind and later adapted to fit female inmates (Azaola and Yacamán 1996).

The women's section of the CERESO in Morelos has the highest number of female prisoners in the state: it houses 205 inmates, 34 percent of whom are under preventive detention and 65 percent are sentenced inmates; additionally, the prison houses fifteen minors.[17] The penitentiary's installed capacity is for only 120 interns in spite of the fact that it is considered to be a model penitentiary due to its modern infrastructure and the inclusion of sports and educational facilities (Velázquez Domínguez 2004).

In accordance with the methodological design of our collective project, I was interested in using collaborative methodologies inside the penitentiary environment. This entailed new challenges for me since it was not the same as working with organized women fighting for social justice. An alternative would have been to approach a human rights or women's organization that would like to sponsor our research team's project. At any rate, collaboration came through a different channel.

An obstacle to carrying out the research was the resistance of prison authorities to granting research permits for correctional centers anywhere in the country. Nevertheless, most of the inmate programs for "reentering society" (*readaptación social*) are of a cultural and educational nature. Many universities, like Mexico City's Autonomous University (Universidad Autónoma de la Ciudad de México) and the National Autonomous University of Mexico (Universidad Nacional Autónoma de México—UNAM), and special government institutions such as the Social Rehabilitation Patronage or the Morelos State Social Reentry, are involved in these endeavors. It was through one of these cultural programs that I enter to the female prison of Atlacholoaya, for first time.

Through a personal contact, I managed to enter as a guest in a workshop that was taking place at the Atlacholoaya Women's Center. Elena de Hoyos, a feminist poet, was conducting a workshop titled "Woman: Writing Can Change Your Life." It had been going on for a year, involving between ten and twelve inmates—none of them indigenous—with educational levels ranging from the completion of elementary school to technical education. When I introduced myself and explained my interest in writing life stories of incarcerated indigenous women, they offered to do the interviews themselves with their fellow inmates if I provided the proper methodological training.

This was the beginning of a space for dialogue and collective construction of knowledge that has brought new challenges for me as an academic and activist. What began as a writing workshop has become the Sisters in the Shadows Editorial Collective of Women in Prison, which has already published seven books, as well as various articles for cultural and penitentiary magazines. The

stories and denouncements in these publications have played a part in the review of prosecution files and the release of a number of women who were unfairly imprisoned.[18]

The formal goal of the "Life Histories" workshop, in which ten writers were
involved (all of them inmates at the Atlacholoaya CERESO), was to "train participants in the technical elements of elaborating life histories, as a literary and
reflective asset for gender inequality." The workshop has been taking place since
October 2008, and the women involved have undertaken their own projects,
each elaborating the life history of one of their fellow indigenous inmates. Once
a month, the indigenous women whose histories are being summarized take part
in the workshop to listen to progress made and to comment on and question the
ways in which their lives are being represented by the workshop members.

This collective process has allowed us to create new bonds between indigenous
and non-indigenous women and has opened up a reflective sphere on racism and
exclusions in Mexican society, reproduced within the penal environment.

Through these dialogues, we confront ethnocentric perspectives on defining
a dignified life while questioning perspectives on "backwardness and progress"
that tend to delineate the contrast between the lives of indigenous women and
urban mestizo women. When we compare their histories, we realize that, in
most cases, the "national system of justice" does not represent "progress" in relation to community forms of justice:

> Since detention, most of us have suffered beatings, mistreatment, insults from the
> servants of the law, and in some cases, certain extortions that aren't subject to pro-
> ceedings. Like magic, the medical reports and testimonies of these aggressions
> disappear in the trajectory from the prosecutor's office to the prison. And some
> little lines appear saying that the accused, now the alleged person responsible,
> appeared of her own free will to give her statement. The *costalazos*[19] don't leave
> any signs, but they have damaged my inner flesh. (Colectiva Editorial de Mujeres
> en Prisión Hermanas en la Sombra 2012, 32)

As participants shared their life histories, they came to realize that sexual and
domestic violence takes different forms, and while it is more private in urban
settings, it is still there. By contrasting their histories, reflecting on them, and
writing them down in a collective text, the women were able to both denounce
the racism, sexism, and classism in the penitentiary system, and to construct new
subjectivities by denaturalizing violence. In the spaces of collective reflection

created for the reading of their life histories, participants expressed the need to strengthen themselves from within to confront violence and, especially, to teach their daughters outside of the prison how to avoid reproducing the types of relationships they had experienced. In an exercise completed within the framework of the workshop, participants wrote letters to women who have been mistreated psychologically and physically:

> Break the chains of subjugation caused by the lack of high esteem. Find yourselves again and look around you. Life shouldn't be like it was for our mothers. We need to construct our own way of thinking and communicating with our spouses, instead of repeating the ways of life from our families. To have our own way of living, to know how to express our own feelings and to teach our children to express their own feelings both with the people around them and with their romantic partners. To know how to say "no" to violence.[20]
>
> Woman, if you dare to break the silence, you may be able to put an end to the pattern of violence that surrounds you and that you may actually be reproducing. It's understandable that if we live in a violent home, sooner or later we will reproduce the violence . . . but today, I encourage you to reveal yourself to fight against what humiliates you, what tramples on your dignity. Listen, you are invaluable. Don't remain silent. Shout, and fight for your rights, because after all, you're a woman.[21]

My experience has been by no means unique. Literary workshops have been a point of entry for many academics into the penitentiary realm, and a number of analysts have pointed out the complicities that occur between instructors and authorities in penal institutions since workshops act as means to feed the penal system's control and domestication needs (Bruchac 1987; Olguín 2009). The way in which the contents of the literary workshops respond to the cultural context of inmates and allow or hamper critical reflection shapes the hegemonic or counterhegemonic role these vehicles may have.[22]

With this in mind, my intention for the "Life Histories" workshop has been to encourage intercultural exchange between indigenous and non-indigenous women and to promote critical reflection on the chain of ethnic, gender, and class inequalities that gave rise to their reclusion. The participants have begun to elaborate their own theorizations and reflections that they incorporate into their biographical narratives, thus rendering hybrid and novel forms that go beyond mere life histories.

With the intention of socializing this knowledge, participants have begun to write a column in the monthly journal *¿Y ahora que sigue?* (Colectiva Editorial de Mujeres en Prisión Hermanas en la Sombra 2009a) published inside the penitentiary. In the article that introduced the workshop, one of the inmates described the importance of this effort to build connections between diverse women within the penal system:

> The *Life Histories Workshop* is important to me because it opens a door to an unknown world that must be considered in order to eliminate the inequalities we experience in our country. It is also a way to sensitize our hearts in order to create a sisterhood among women of different social classes. In my small space in the female prison area, where different minds, customs and certainties of women inhabit, it is interesting to join our voices and outline life histories, liberating them from this place and causing the outside world to know and think about the reality we live in here. This workshop will help achieve women's unity in a shared common goal. It is a way towards mutual support as spokespersons of real stories. Personally, it has allowed me to live a new experience in the world of writing, and feel proud for supporting those who have been silent for too long. My writing will serve those who wish to tell their story. For illiterate women, this workshop has been a means to liberate their story, to unburden themselves on a receptive ear, and to recover the courage to be a woman that society took away from them. (Colectiva Editorial de Mujeres en Prisión Hermanas en la Sombra 2009b, 3)

Thus, intercultural dialogue takes place not only between the researcher and the inmates, but among the inmates themselves, all of whom have had different life paths and contrasting ways of experiencing gender inequalities and state justice. Discussing similarities and differences has been a central part of the workshops:

> Personally, I feel this workshop helps me to get to know my companions better, learn about their ideas, and express ourselves better. I hope it also helps us become closer. I believe it is helping me to be a better person, to express my feelings and thoughts, and be more sensitive to my companions. For illiterate indigenous women, our work has been a way of making their lives known, and along with theirs, our own, as a form of mutual help. (Colectiva Editorial de Mujeres en Prisión Hermanas en la Sombra 2009b, 3)

In the seven years since this collective process began (spanning 2008 to 2016), four of the participating indigenous women have learned to read. They are now writing poems and short stories and are co-authors of the book titled *Mareas cautivas* (Colectiva Editorial de Mujeres en Prisión Hermanas en la Sombra 2012):

From different places	De diferentes lugares
with different languages	de diferentes idiomas
but the most beautiful	pero lo más hermoso
all of us spiritually free	todas libres espiritualmente
even though society calls us	aunque la sociedad nos diga
jailed women,	las presas,
forgotten women,	las olvidadas,
scum, despicable women	la escoria, las malas
we are creative women,	somos mujeres creativas,
warrior women,	mujeres guerreras,
roses in captivity	rosas en cautiverio
doused by our own tears	regadas con nuestras propias lágrimas
fertilized with our own pain	abonadas con nuestro propio dolor
prisoners with great hope	presas con mucha esperanza
captives loved by the Lord,	cautivas amadas por el Señor,
phantasm women,	mujeres fantasmas,
women victims of circumstances	mujeres víctimas de las circunstancias
warrior women	mujeres guerreras
women who struggle	mujeres que luchan

De diferentes lugares (From Different Places) by Leo Zavaleta, Me'phaa/Tlapanec woman who learned to write while imprisoned, in *Mareas cautivas*. (Colectiva Editorial de Mujeres en Prisión Hermanas en la Sombra 2012)

Seven women have been released from prison after their prosecution files were reviewed, and two of them continue to participate and write in a literary workshop coordinated by writer Elena de Hoyos outside the penitentiary. Those who continue to be imprisoned have been constructing a group identity as the Sisters in the Shadows Editorial Collective of Women in Prison, becoming a reference point for all female inmates by proposing new ways of interacting with each other, as a sisterhood, and by questioning racism and sexism in the penitentiary through their writings.

Inside the prison, within the limits of what Michel Foucault called a "total institution that constructs subordinated identities," the women of Atlacholoaya have been able to destabilize the discourses of power and denaturalize inequalities through their own writings and the public readings of these writings (Foucault 1977). These have taken place in both the classroom designated for the writing workshop and in the *tertulias literarias* (literary gatherings) organized in the prison's collective spaces.[23]

The creative ways used by these women to theorize gender violence, penitentiary racism, and solidarity among diverse women—through their poetry, essays, and short stories—have led me to rethink the forms that feminist theorization takes and to expand my teaching curriculum to include these dissident voices in the courses I teach on gender theory. Breaking through the limiting borders of academic settings and studying the theorizations emerging from experiences of (and resistance to) multiple oppressions are fundamental steps toward the decolonization of our feminisms.

As a researcher, I have been able to contribute to these dialogues by providing specific information on the technicalities of state justice mechanics. I share specific data on the rights violations I observe from their testimonies or judicial records (if I have access to the files). I direct them to proper pro bono legal counseling and try to follow the process. I also share with them the stories of indigenous women who are fighting for their rights in different parts of Latin America. Together with their theorizing, this has been fundamental to fostering our reflection circle.

I must point out the limitations of this type of activist research: this type of academic and cultural work does not destabilize the penal system, nor does it greatly modify the institutional control over the minds and bodies of incarcerated women. I recognize these limitations, and it is in the framework of these limitations that I try to contribute to denouncing a corrupt, sexist, and racist justice system that not only impacts the lives of incarcerated women but also threatens my own and other women's lives who are still on the outside.

Ruth Wilson Gilmore, one of the most thoughtful critics of the United States penal system, questions the brand of activism that struggles to ameliorate the living conditions inside penitentiaries or that tries to free men and women unfairly imprisoned, stating that this kind of activism does not address the root of the problem (Gilmore 2008). Similarly, Ben Olguín has stated the need for direct action against prisons through an abolitionist movement, based on his work with Latino prisoners in correctional facilities in California (Olguín 2009).

Thus, given prevailing prison conditions, the only feasible activism, according to Gilmore and Olguín, is to strive toward getting rid of prisons altogether.

In my view, this abolitionist initiative lacks historical perspective and is hardly realistic for modern-day Mexico. Their critical perspectives on "reformism" can have a demobilizing effect in circumstances where there is no cultural or political climate for promoting the abolition of prisons. There are some small-scale, yet significant, activities that can be achieved within prisons: specifically, accompanying the critical reflection and organization of inmate women and denouncing the correctional system's injustices, racism, and sexism. These activities can help to improve the living conditions of thousands of women whose minds and bodies are being subjected to neoliberal state control.

In addition to these micro-level efforts, we can conduct a critical analysis at a systemic level that may assist us in finding and denouncing the control and incarceration of indigenous men and women within the broader scope of neoliberal policies that impoverish broader sectors of Latin American peoples, and criminalize social dissidence and poverty. We analyze this in chapter 5 of this book.

FINAL REFLECTIONS

In this chapter, I have attempted to demonstrate that critical reflection on the discourses on rights and state justice does not exclude possibilities for appropriating and re-signifying these discourses on the basis of legal strategies that recognize legal pluralism. Establishing intercultural dialogues on rights and justice confronts the state's regulatory discourses, and it is an opportunity for destabilizing our certainties and expanding our emancipatory horizons.

As a feminist, collaborative research with indigenous women has contributed to a process of reformulating my own conceptions of gender rights and has led me to criticize my own complicities in the processes of "erasing" other perspectives and expectations in relation to justice for women.

The voices of organized indigenous women in the Continental Network of Indigenous Women, the experiences of Inés and Valentina, and the women who participated in the workshops on "Gender Violence and Indigenous Justices" ("Talleres sobre violencia de género y justicias indígenas") and the penitentiary workshops on "Life Histories" ("Talleres penitenciarios de historias de vida") are a source of theorizations that speak to us of other forms of understanding women's rights and their connections to the collective rights of peoples. The theorizations arising from these and other spaces being created in different regions of

Latin America point to new utopic horizons that organized indigenous women are constructing as they recover the historic memory of their peoples. My intention in this book is to reflect on the effects of resistance and the process of decentering hegemonic discourses in the rhetoric and practice of indigenous women who are defending other ways of understanding justice and rights.

In the research studies that are the basis for this book, we have attempted to establish epistemic dialogues on the basis of research and organizational work. In these dialogues we have discussed and analyzed different conceptions and experiences of subordination and resistance. These methodological and political searches reflect what Boaventura de Sousa Santos has called an "ecology of knowledges," which does not imply a rejection of Western scientific knowledge but rather an opening to other forms of knowledge for constructing better strategies for transformation and social coexistence in a collective manner (de Sousa Santos 2009).

In our case, an "ecology of feminist knowledges" does not discard the knowledges accumulated by Western feminism but instead attempts to change its hierarchical relationship to the emancipatory knowledges of indigenous and peasant women in different regions of the world in the construction "of another possible world, or in other words, of a more democratic society, and a more balanced society in its relation with nature" (de Sousa Santos 2009, 116). Vital to this ecology of feminist knowledges are the contributions of indigenous intellectuals who—from their academic settings or from their political activism—are developing their own theorizations in relation to the collective rights of their peoples and the rights of women. In many cases, these theorizations are presented in the form of final reports from conferences, political manifestos, and autobiographies, or, in other cases, they are systematized by appropriating or reformulating theoretical discourses. However, in both cases, these are perspectives that have opened up new spaces of reflection for the feminist academy. I hope this book will contribute, if even minimally, to the emergence of this ecology of feminist knowledges so urgently needed in the construction of a more just world.

2

MULTIPLE DIALOGUES AND STRUGGLES FOR JUSTICE

Political Genealogies of Indigenous Women in Mexico, Guatemala, and Colombia

T HE LAST TWO DECADES IN LATIN AMERICA have given rise to organized movements of indigenous women. These movements' collective
demands are combined with those that are gender specific. We could
say that there has been the birth of a new political identity, one that does not
dilute within the political identities of indigenous people, or within gender
identities of feminist movements.

In this chapter, I reconstruct the history of organizational processes that have
given way to the upsurge of these new identities and new discourses and practices in relation to the rights of indigenous women in Mexico, Guatemala, and
Colombia. Engle Merry's (2006) concept of the appropriation or vernacularization of the discourses of rights on the part of the indigenous women of these
three countries has had as an antecedent a history of political struggles in which
women's participation has been fundamental. Confronting the essentialist perspectives of the indigenous women, which represent them as a homogenous
group of "permanent victims" of diverse systems of oppression, I am interested
in emphasizing the multiple organizational genealogies that have marked the
internal heterogeneity of the continental movement of indigenous women.

I use the metaphor of the dialogue to refer to the different discourses that
interact in the context of social hierarchies and semantic tensions. Indigenous
women have been constructing their own political agenda and reconstructing
their collective identities in interaction with diverse social actors. These dialogues

have been in the contexts of inequality marked by power relationships but have had a productive capacity constructing new indigenous identities that confront, negotiate, or reject the hegemonic discourses in relation to the "indigenous" and to "womanhood."

It is important to acknowledge that political dialogues with feminist, religious, and political-military organizations (or with international cooperation) have been marked by class, gender, and ethnic inequalities that locate indigenous women in a sub-alternized space of enunciation. However, as I will demonstrate throughout this chapter, this does not deny their capacity to appropriate, re-signify, or reject discourses and practices regarding social justice, rights, and gender relations promoted from these spaces.

The reconstruction of indigenous justice spheres that I analyze in chapter 3 has had an organizational history in which the struggle for social justice and the recognition of their own cultures have been central. To understand how indigenous justice is constructed, it is necessary to recognize the history of struggles that have preceded the recognition of their cultural rights.

Some analysts locate the appearance of these new social actors in 1992, in the context of the commemoration of the "500 Years of Indigenous, Black, and Popular Resistance," when organizations from across Latin America mobilized against the celebration of the "5th Centennial of the Encounter between Two Worlds" and denounced the continuation of the colonial project in Latin American countries. In the context of these mobilizations, which included congresses, encounters, seminars, and workshops, indigenous women from across the continent had the opportunity to share their views and experiences. They brought forward the argument that it was not possible to fight against the exclusion of indigenous people in national societies without first recognizing the exclusion of women within those indigenous communities.

In the concrete case of Mexico, the armed uprising of the EZLN on January 1, 1994, made visible the presence of women inside the national indigenous movement. What set the Zapatista movement apart from other guerrilla movements in Latin America in which women have participated was the foundational inclusion of gender demands through the so-called Women's Revolutionary Law.

However, it is not possible to understand the participation of indigenous women in these historical moments, or the emergence of gender issues in the political agenda coming from indigenous organizations, if we do not recognize both the long history of struggle and resistance in which they have been participating since the colonial period (see Gall and Hernández Castillo 2004) and the multiple dialogues that have influenced the construction of their political identities. The peasant movements, political-military organizations, liberation theology, rural feminism, international agencies, and even state institutions have contributed to creating spaces of encounter for indigenous women and have contributed elements to the construction of culturally situated gender agendas that appropriate or reject elements of the different discourses regarding women's rights.

A dialogic perspective of these political identities will allow us to see these organizations of indigenous women not as pillars of millenary resistances, nor as conglomerates of passive subjects who mechanically replicate discourses and practices on rights that come from outside, but as subjects constructing social agency from their local cultures and struggles.

Recognizing the productive capacity of global discourses does not deny the ability of social actors to re-signify these discourses and, on many occasions, even produce alternative discourses that are globalized through the same communication networks.

New discourses on the rights of indigenous women (those women who define themselves as feminists, as well as those who emphasize their ethnic adscription through a discourse on cosmovision) are confronting globalization from above. They stand against the perspective that signals the homogenizing force of capital, underestimates the capacity for resistance by local cultures, and sets up the surge of a global "postmodern condition" that tends to erase cultural specificities (Jameson 1989, 1990). It is evident that all of the indigenous organizations in Latin America are in dialogue with global discourses. New communication technologies have enabled greater contact with, and the participation of, other social groups, such as Native American communities from Canada and the United States, human rights organizations, and feminist networks, which are part of global structures of communication and information in which contemporary indigenous females participate (Lash and Urry 1994, 64). The elements found in these structures of communication have been appropriated and integrated into a new political identity promoted through those same global communication networks. The "new customs" these women claim have appropriated elements of discourses on human rights, women's rights, and ecology from different organizations with which they had contact. More than an imposition of certain global perspectives, what we see are new spaces of intercultural dialogue in which indigenous and non-indigenous people have shared their visions of the world. It is important not to idealize these spaces, which are still marked with structural inequalities, but neither should we underestimate the capacity of appropriation and re-signification by social actors.

The different political ideologies and personal histories of organized women have changed the way in which they and their organizations prioritize (or not) the gender demands and/or collective demands of their people. The great internal diversity is the strength and weakness of the continental movement of indigenous women. To reach consensus or set up general demands has implied negotiating political perspectives on how they live their culture and conceptualize their rights and relationships between men and women. Given the diversity of voices that come out of indigenous women's organizations, it is tempting to legitimize some and silence others, representing as "authentic" those who claim the indigenous cosmovision as a space of resistance and disqualifying as "acculturated" those who appropriate the discourses on women's rights and propose the existence of an indigenous feminism. In the other extreme, there is also a tendency to label as "conservative and essentialist" those who reject feminism from ethno-political movements and to legitimize or open spaces in political and academic debates for only those who are closer to the agenda of urban and occidental feminism. Both perspectives can result in new strategies of "discursive colonialism," which deny the complexity and richness of these new political identities (see Mohanty 1991 [1986], 2002).

This chapter tries to take into account these multiple dialogues to comprehend the diverse paths taken by different indigenous women organizations and the possible coincidences and divergences in their struggles for justice and their appropriation or rejection of the discourses of women's rights.

My approximation of the organizational processes of indigenous women has given priority to the ethnographic perspective of their day-to-day lives. I have taken this approach because many specialists on social movements have limited themselves by speaking only of the movement's political agendas, analyzing their official documents or describing to us the "great political events" in which these movements have participated and reflecting on their allegiances, achievements, and limitations without offering us details to understand the day-to-day lives of these movements. It is precisely by coming closer to the everyday lives of such social movements that we can better understand how power relations are built within the organizations, how negotiations with different political conceptions take place, and how collective identities are built. In this chapter, I have decided to include some key ethnographic perspectives in order to give the reader a closer look at the human dimensions of the political and social processes that I analyze.

I introduce each political dialogue with an "ethnographic window" to reveal some of the tensions that occur in the construction of women's collective spaces and in the vernacularization of rights discourses. It is an attempt to approach the everyday reality of these women's movements through a description of their agreements and disagreements, revealing how they have appropriated anti-capitalist discourses of political-military movements, rights discourses of feminism, or discourses on cosmovision and their own epistemology of indigenous movements.

FIRST ETHNOGRAPHIC WINDOW: "RELIGION, THE OPIATE OF THE MASSES"

The "National Encounter of Indigenous Women" is a meeting of 350 women from sixteen states in Mexico (according to the organizers) who gather in the municipal auditorium of Chilpancingo to discuss their problems as women and as members of indigenous peoples.

The heat is terrible, and many women are sitting on the floor, fanning themselves with the folder that was given to them upon arrival, nursing their children, or watching them run and play on the stairs of the auditorium. They all await the inauguration. The meeting is scheduled for 9 a.m., which depending on the indigenous community could be 11 a.m., 12 p.m., or even 1 p.m. No one is in a hurry, and everyone knows that things will start when they have to start. They use this time to get to know new people, to look at the *huipiles*,[1] table cloths, or non-industrial soap that other women are selling. The members of the Network of Rural Promoters (Red de Promotoras Rurales) also have their stand; their flyers work as a fan for many of the indigenous women in attendance, while others look through the information with interest and put them in their backpacks to take back to their communities. The women feel a great responsibility to share everything that was learned with those at home who could not make the trip.

While we wait, we hear the rumor that the Zapatista delegation, whose participation had been announced by the organizing committee, had canceled their trip. Some say that there is a new "red alert" and they were not given permission to assist; others say that the money supplied by the government of the state of Guerrero to fund the event was the main reason why the Zapatistas declined the invitation. Some women stated, "For a few pesos the government will take all the credit of our event"; others argued, "It was a mistake to accept the economic help"; and still others pointed out, "They did not put any conditions to financially support the event, and we needed the money."

The event starts with a notorious discontent manifested by many and a huge distrust by some. A woman of "knowledge" is elected to direct a ritual of gratefulness to Mother Earth; she is a traditional midwife from Oaxaca who is acknowledged by many as a spiritual leader. The opening ceremony starts with the midwife burning copal while praying in Zapotec.[2] Her voice is low; her prayer is almost a whisper, a sweet chant that is accompanied by the circular motion of the incense. First, all the women follow the ceremony in silence; they form a half circle around an improvised altar. As time goes by, and the ceremony continues, some of the women begin to talk, and the volume of the chatter gradually increases until the Zapotec prayers become a musical background. Someone finally starts the assembly, and the women slowly begin to enter the hall, a place with very little airflow and no air-conditioning. I don't even notice when the ritual is over; by the time I look around, we are already inside the auditorium.

The topics of the event are selected in the plenary meeting: the two key topics are the participation of indigenous women in the autonomy processes of the Indian peoples of Mexico and indigenous women and their rights in the Mexican Constitution, local codes, and international legislation. Finally, the action and operation plan commences. It is evident that bilingual women or women who are monolingual in Spanish are the leading voices of the event. The counselors of a feminist organization, Kinal Anzetik, are present, but they manage a low profile, respectfully avoiding a dominant role and allowing the indigenous leaders to coordinate the workshops.

The absence of the Zapatista delegation creates a tension in the discussion groups; the debates digress from the agreed topics. At several tables the role of state funding in community projects is debated. There are different perspectives among the participants. Many argue that, in very poor regions, the money from programs like Progress and Solidarity (PROGRESA and *Solidaridad*)[3] is a resource that allows women to meet family expenses, and they cannot afford to say "no." Others say that is a way of losing autonomy, of "owing a favor to the government," and that through taking this money, little by little, one becomes "official" or co-opted. Some praise the way autonomous Zapatista regions do things, receiving no help from the government and surviving with dignity. There is tension in the round tables.

During one of the breaks, I approach some of the more participative women, the ones who have defended their ideas in the round table with more conviction. My aim is to do interviews to get to know their opinions on the event and the topics discussed and (if possible) to reconstruct their political genealogy. I approach a beautiful woman with silver hair going down to her waist; she wears a Mixtec huipil, and I imagine right away that she is one of the "spiritual leaders of the event," for her presence, her gray hair, and her elegance make her look like a priestess. She is a cheerful woman but convincing in her judgment and opinions. She is one of those who outright opposes receiving state funding. I ask her for an interview and she agrees. The following day, after having several informal talks during the breaks, we look for a quiet place to record the interview.

My first question has to do with the tension I sense at the discussion tables. Assuming her knowledge of indigenous cosmovision and her experience in ritual spaces, I ask her if there is any relation between the interruption of the ritual to Mother Earth and the problems flourishing at the worktables. In hallway conversations I had overheard that the ceremony had not been completed and, for that reason, things were not going according to plan. I was interested in knowing the opinion of my new Mixtec friend on this subject. Upon hearing my question, she opens her eyes in surprise and bursts out in laughter, "Please, the things that people make up to continue ignoring the fact that we need more grassroots work, more reflection prior to the event to come in here with clear ideas. This is where we lack, not in the ceremony or in the prayers. Have you not heard that religion is the opiate of the masses?" Her response leaves me petrified; with that one phrase she breaks every stereotype I had about "indigenous women of knowledge" and all my prejudices about the existence of "an indigenous perspective" on politics. Indeed, I am dealing with a woman of knowledge, but her knowledge comes from a long background in left-wing militancy. Her participation as a youth in the Communist Party, and later the guerrilla movement headed by Lucio Cabañas,[4] are the origins of her radicalism. For her, as for many more indigenous women of Guerrero of her generation, the Communist Party was a source of knowledge and experience that continues to mark their political militancy. This is where she gets the conviction that criticism of the state and capitalism must be central in any indigenous women movement; everything else is complementary.

The specific historic nature of the coast and highlands of Guerrero has greatly influenced the political agenda of many women in these regions, noticeably centering a class perspective (rather than a gender or ethnic one). Maybe it's one of the few indigenous areas in Mexico where the Communist Party achieved support in the indigenous and peasant sectors.[5]

This political genealogy explains why the final declaration of this "Second Encounter of Indigenous Women" will be called "Benita Galeana Declaration," after one of the most important communist leaders in Mexico (a Guerrero native and an active participant in support groups to the peasant, railroad, and teachers' movements).[6]

In the case of other countries, like Guatemala and Colombia, the guerrilla movements have influenced the formation of feminine leadership within the indigenous movement in many different ways, as we will see.

DIALOGUES WITH POLITICAL-MILITARY MOVEMENTS

It is evident that the EZLN has contributed to visualizing indigenous women as political actors in the Mexican context, and it has also aided the elaboration of gender demands coming from indigenous movements in other regions of the continent (see Kampwirth 2004; Klein 2015; Millán 2008, 2014; Rovira 1997). In my previous works, I have analyzed how the inclusion of gender demands in the "official" Zapatista discourse has contributed to legitimizing the demands of indigenous women in the national agenda of the indigenous movement. It has also disrupted existing gendered power structures and caused new tensions to arise within the indigenous community under Zapatista influence (see Speed, Hernández Castillo, and Stephen 2006).

However, Mexican Zapatismo has not been the only political-military movement that contributed to the formation of female leaders within Latin American indigenous movements. Despite the fact that guerrilla movements considered feminism a "bourgeois ideology" that divides people and weakens their struggle, many of these guerrilla groups integrated women into their troops and political consciousness. This unintentionally impacted the education of women who would later have relevant participation in female movements and feminist organizations.

While, for political-military movements of the 1960s and 1970s, rights discourses were unimportant (as was their impact decades later), a political imaginary was developed around "social justice." And this imaginary was later appropriated by women within those movements to denounce the exclusions and gender violence often reproduced among revolutionaries.

FIGURE 4. Armed insurgent woman of the National Liberation Zapatista
Army (EZLN) in Chiapas. Photograph by Mariana Mora.

Recent feminist analyses have centered their critique on the sexism and misogyny that characterized the revolutionary discourse and practice from the
1970s and 1980s. While acknowledging the importance of this criticism, it is
also necessary to reflect upon the reasons these mestizo and indigenous women
had to join these struggles, despite the costs to their personal lives and the cultural and political capital they acquired during years of activism.[7]

In the three countries analyzed in this chapter—Mexico, Guatemala, and
Colombia—political-military movements have had different impacts on the
lives of indigenous men and women. In all three regions, counterinsurgent violence produced massacres, displacements, and paramilitarization that upset the
lives of indigenous communities. Sexual violence was used as a counterinsurgency strategy against women from indigenous and peasant communities who
sympathized with revolutionary movements, and this violence is a part of the
historic memory of many of today's indigenous women's organizations.[8] Simultaneously, organizational processes in political-military and/or displaced

people's movements provided tools for indigenous women to begin questioning not only state violence but also the exclusions experienced in their own communities and organizations.

It is impossible to understand the actuality of an anti-capitalist agenda in many indigenous women's organizations in these three countries without acknowledging the importance of political-military movements in the development of their female leadership. The ethnographic window with which I began this section reveals the tension that continues to exist in Mexico between organized women who lay claim to traditional indigenous religion (as the result of a religious syncretism between Spanish Catholicism and local pre-Hispanic religions), and those who, from a Marxist standpoint inherited from their revolutionary past, reject those religious practices (which they consider alienating) without, however, putting aside their indigenous identity. A brief overview of the history of revolutionary movements in these three countries will allow us to understand the different impacts of those movements on the development of organizational and political spaces for indigenous women.

The triumph of the Cuban revolution helped create a state of revolutionary agitation in all of Latin America during the 1960s and 1970s. Political-military movements of Marxist influence started to appear throughout the whole continent.[9] In the case of Mexico, between 1965 and 1980, twenty-nine guerrilla groups were formed with approximately 2,000 militants among their ranks. Two of these movements had an important influence in regions where indigenous movements, with significant female participation, would later develop. One of these movements was the Party of the Poor (PDLP), led by Lucio Cabañas; the other was the National Revolutionary Civic Association, headed by Genaro Vázquez. Both guerrilla movements had an influence on the Sierra Atoyac in Guerrero. Lucio Cabañas and Genaro Vázquez were formed in the teachers' struggle; both had peasant roots and managed to incorporate indigenous peasants from the mountains of Guerrero into their organizations. Even though, at this time, none of these organizations considered that demands made specifically by women should be part of their political agenda, women had an active participation in the urban guerrilla movement and were fundamental supporters for the guerrillas in the mountains of Guerrero. Many rural teachers joined the PDLP and played an important role in the political formation of indigenous women in the region.

Their leadership within the movement made them a target of state repression when the so-called dirty war began. An event that started one of the worst eras of repression in the history of Mexico was the kidnapping of Senator Rubén Figueroa Figueroa by the PDLP in May of 1974. That year, 173 people disappeared, many of them by the military, mainly in the Sierra de Atoyac and mountainous regions. Many women were among those who disappeared and, years later, we would find out that sexual abuse was used as an important weapon against the insurgents during the "dirty war." Toward the end of 1974, Figueroa was rescued and Lucio Cabañas was killed. Figueroa was later elected governor of Guerrero. At the end of his administration he was responsible for over a hundred disappearances. By 1981, the official number released by the Political Prisoners' Refugee Defense League would be 330.

The state of Guerrero was the laboratory of the Mexican military against the insurgence. As in Colombia and Guatemala, paramilitary groups were used to violently raid mountain populations, creating the highest number of political disappearances in the history of the country. The historical memory of this violence has marked the present struggle of indigenous women in the state of Guerrero, as we will see in chapter 4 with the analysis of the experience of Inés Fernández Ortega and Valentina Rosendo Cantú.

As part of the so-called low intensity warfare, political measures were taken with the objective of dividing the movement and demobilizing their followers. "Health campaigns" were carried out; National Company of Popular Subsistence (Compañía Nacional de Subsistencias Populares) stores (state-sponsored) were everywhere, lowering their prices or giving away their merchandise; and branches of the Mexican Institute of Coffee were opened in order to have a direct relation with the combative coffee-growing industry. "Political orientation courses" were given to *ejido* and municipal commissioners in order to detect sympathizers or militants of the armed movements.

The guerrilla movements of Lucio Cabañas and Genaro Vázquez were finally dismantled, but the seed of resistance stayed in Guerrero, as it remains one of the most combative states for the teachers' movement, as well as for the struggle for land and (most recently) for the rights of indigenous people. Despite the fact that in the 1990s the peasant movement began to claim their indigenous cultural roots with the formation of the organization 500 Years of Resistance Peoples Council, the class perspective of the guerrilla movements in the 1970s still influences the political discourse of the indigenous leaders of this region, as we saw in our first ethnographic window. The class perspective inherited from this revolutionary history is reflected in the economic and social rights demanded by organized indigenous women in their rejection of neoliberal economic policies and in their active participation in mobilizations against the megaprojects that threaten to displace them from their lands.

In Guatemala, the guerrilla organizations that came together in the Guatemalan National Revolutionary Unit (Unión Revolucionaria Nacional Guatemalteca—URNG) had, in their majority, a strong indigenous social base and an outstanding participation of the women as combatants and bases of support. In particular, two of the political-military organizations that joined the URNG, the Guerrilla Army of the Poor (Ejército Guerrillero de los Pobres—EGP) and the Organization of the People in Arms (Organización del Pueblo en Armas—ORPA), following the important incorporation of indigenous men and women, were forced to confront the orthodox Marxist analysis of the time and they developed a more profound reflection about indigenous issues. These reflections were systemized into now-historical documents such as "The Indigenous Peoples and the Guatemala Revolution" ("Los Pueblos Indígenas y la Revolución Guatemalteca") by EGP and "Racism I and II" by ORPA, where they signaled the importance of recognizing structural racism as a fundamental element in the oppression of indigenous people. In her academic work, Morna Macleod refers to these documents as "precursors in Latin America of the reflection and incorporation of the indigenous people in the revolutionary processes" (see Macleod 2008, 134); however, Macleod also shows us the marginal relevance of these reflections in the political practices of Guatemalan guerrilla organizations, where indigenous militants had a subordinate role to the ladino leaders. Regarding the participation of women in the Guatemalan guerrilla organizations, other authors have shown that, despite the importance of female participation, the URNG never managed to incorporate specific gender demands in their political agenda. Like other guerrilla movements, it considered feminism as a petite bourgeoisie ideology that divided the struggle of the people (see Kampwirth 2002). The life-stories of ex-combatants tell us about the sexism and the machismo that marked the relationships between men and women within the guerrilla (Arriola 2000; Colom 1998; Stoltz-Chinchilla 1997). However, testimonies collected by MacLeod and Silvia Soriano recognize the spaces of political and organizational formation that these armed movements provided to a whole generation of indigenous and mestizo women formed in the heat of the battle (Macleod 2006, 2011; Soriano 2006).

As in Colombia and Guerrero, the counterinsurgence and the "low-intensity warfare" profoundly impacted the lives of many different women who were forced to abandon their communities and take refuge in Mexican territory or live in the Guatemalan mountains for years. The counterinsurgency campaigns included 626 massacres in the late 1970s and early 1980s, leaving a balance of more than 42,000 deaths and 400 ravaged villages. More than 1.5 million people were victims, 80 percent of whom were Mayan Indians. This genocide marked the lives of thousands of Mayan men and women from Guatemala, who were forced to abandon their country and to restructure their communitarian spaces in exile.

It was in this refugee stage that the paths of Mexican and Guatemalan indigenous women merged in Chiapas and together started to develop some specific thoughts about women's rights; these would later give place to organizations with gender-specific claims, like Mother Maquín, Mother Earth, and Ixmucamé (*Mamá Maquín, Madre Tierra* e *Ixmucamé*). These organizations were formed in the refugee camps of Mexico and played a fundamental role in the repatriation process. During this time, the dialogues with feminist NGOs were fundamental in formulating an agenda within refugee organizations. CIAM, founded in 1989 by Mercedes Olivera, played a fundamental role in the support of organizational processes of refugee women. The objective of CIAM was to work with women who became refugees or were displaced because of an armed conflict in Central America and Mexico; through collaborative research they would help these women develop a gender consciousness and identity, and appropriate the discourses of women's rights while simultaneously demanding their rights as indigenous peoples and as refugees.

Although many of the CIAM workshops were, at this time, targeted at refugee women, the interaction with Mexican peasant women with whom the land was shared made the gender-inequality issue a hot topic at the round tables of peasant and indigenous Mexican organizations. The learning experience of the refugee contributed to form a female leadership that played a relevant part in the rise of a movement of Mayan women in Guatemala (see Macleod 2011).

Years later, the Zapatista movement was created in the same region where the refugee camps were established in the 1980s. Since the first public appearance of EZLN on January 1, 1994, the large number of women within the ranks drew attention, as did their political influence within the organization. Many of them were at the front of the occupation of different municipalities, and the names of Commander Ramona, Commander Trini, Commander Andrea, and Lieutenant Ana María quickly became symbols of indigenous women's resistance. The participation of women in the guerrilla leadership is another important difference between the insurgent movements of Guatemala and Colombia and Zapatismo. However, the main difference between Zapatismo and the other guerrilla movements was the inclusion of gender demands in their agenda through the Revolutionary Women's Law. This law was the result of a query performed by many Zapatista women among its members and support bases. According to a statement released by Sub-Commander Marcos, this law is "the first Zapatista uprising":

> Susana, Tsotsil, is mad. A while ago they were mocking her because all the other people at the CCRI say she was the one to blame for the first EZLN insurgence in March of 1993. "I'm pissed-off" she tells me . . . "The comrades say that last year's *zapatista* uprising was my fault" . . . She would later find out what it was all about: in March of 1993 the comrades were discussing what would later become the Revolutionary Laws. Susana had to go to dozens of communities in order to speak with the female groups and formulate the Women's Law. (Sub-Commander Marcos 1994, 9)

The Revolutionary Women's Law contains ten points: among them, indigenous women's right to political participation and to leadership positions; the right to a life free of sexual and domestic violence; the right to choose how many children to have and take care of; the right to a fair salary; the right to choose who to marry; and the right to good health services and education (among others). Even though all indigenous women do not know this law in detail, its existence has become a symbol of the possibilities of a fair life for women. In a certain sense, it has contributed to creating what Karl-Werner Brand calls a "cultural climate" that denaturalizes inequality toward women; in other words, the Revolutionary Women's Law is the expression of a specific configuration of conceptions of the world in a certain time frame that "generates a certain sensibility for some problems; narrows or broadens the horizon of what seems socially or politically viable; determines the guidelines for political behavior and lifestyle; leads psychosocial energy outwards to the public sphere or inwards to the private sphere" (Brand 1990, 2).

It was within the context of this cultural climate that many indigenous organizations with whom I have been working in Mexico started to integrate the topic of inequality between men and women into their spaces of collective reflection. The argument was that it was not possible to fight for justice for indigenous people while women were being treated poorly on a day-to-day basis;

FIGURE 5. The Revolutionary Women's Law has been fundamental for the Zapatista women and their support bases in Chiapas. Photograph by Mariana Mora.

thus, this issue started to become relevant in regional and national meetings of the indigenous movement.

Parallel to this, the relations between men and women in Zapatista communities have been influenced by this law that in many ways opposes the "custom" (see Millán 2014). Indigenous law and justice systems are being reformulated in many communities of Chiapas in dialogue with the new Zapatista laws as well as national and international laws. We are talking about processes that are difficult and full of contradictions, which we have analyzed in other works (see Speed, Hernández Castillo and Stephen 2006). However, it is evident that the silence has been shattered and that the new Zapatista voices have come to denaturalize violence and female exclusion, placing their demands within the rights discourses.

Finally, to address the influence of revolutionary movements in the contemporary indigenous women's organizations, I would like to mention the case of Colombia, where indigenous women have not had significant participation in any guerrilla movements, but where they have nonetheless made an impact in the organizational spaces for the displaced, and in the mobilization against violence and paramilitarization. Although the armed conflict in Colombia is considered to be the longest in Latin America, the indigenous population has steered clear of these political-military organizations and, most of the time, the indigenous community has maintained a neutral position in regards to the armed conflict.

The first cells of the present-day Colombian guerrilla movement go as far back as the 1940s and 1950s when self-defense groups where assembled in response to the repression landowners unleashed on the Colombian peasantry. The period was known as "the era of violence" (1948–1953).[10] These peasant cells refused to abandon arms when an agreement was reached between liberals and conservatives, who took turns in power. Neither of those governments enacted any significant changes in the agrarian policies of the country toward the peasant population.

In the beginning of the 1960s, a broad popular movement called the People's United Front (Frente Unido del Pueblo) was born, led by the revolutionary priest Camilo Torres. Thus was established the first autonomous regions known as Independent Republics. The government's response was a wave of state repression that forced Camilo Torres to retreat into the countryside and join the National Liberation Army (Ejército de Liberación Nacional—ELN), a movement inspired by the Cuban Revolution and linked to the peasant resistance in the department of Santander. Around that same time, some peasant self-defense groups influenced by the Communist Party became the Revolutionary Armed Forces of Colombia (Fuerzas Armadas Revolucionarias de Colombia—FARC). Other organizations developed in the 1970s and 1980s. One of the most important of these was the April 19th Movement (M-19), very popular abroad for the spectacular actions they performed, such as the taking of the Dominican embassy, and their strong urban presence.[11]

Colombia's guerrilla movement has been recognized as an essentially peasant political-military movement. To date, it has not made any demands of an ethnic nature, with the one exception of a small organization known as Comando Quintín Lamé, who, in the 1980s, received considerable support from the indigenous population in its area of action in the Cauca department. This was also one of the few guerrilla movements that included indigenous women within its militants. This organization came together from the radicalization of one sector of the Regional Indigenous Council of Cauca (*Consejo Regional Indígena del Cauca*—CRIC) that, as a response to the state's pressure, decided to take arms to defend the indigenous population of the region.[12]

However, in contrast with Mexico and Guatemala, guerrilla organizations have not been an important organizational space for indigenous women in Colombia but rather the trigger of a series of population displacements that has forced women to organize and often become mediators between the parties involved in the conflict.[13] In the 1980s, the administration of conservative Belisario Betancur realized the danger of the guerrilla advance and developed a dual strategy: on one hand, he offered amnesty to guerrilla organizations (creating divisions between them); on the other hand, he promoted the formation of paramilitary groups that would confront those would not accept the amnesty. As a result, a negotiation period began, a process that culminated with the signing of peace treaties that demobilized the M-19, EPL, Comando Quintín Lamé, and the Workers' Revolutionary Party (PRT). The FARC was the only guerrilla movement that continued at war by 2016. This strategy of paramilitarization has deeply marked daily life in Colombian society and, in a specific manner, the realities of indigenous men and women. An alliance among the military, landowners, secret service, and drug-traffickers creates paramilitary groups that, unlike the death squadron of Guatemala or the paramilitary groups of Chiapas, do not limit themselves to political assassinations and massacres; they also exercise true territorial power. In dozens of Colombian municipalities, the paramilitary has started to control aspects of everyday life. In this context of violence, more than 10,000 indigenous peoples have been displaced from their communities and 15,000 affected by the incursion of armed groups in their territories (see Ramírez 2011). The political path chosen by the indigenous organizations of Colombia is one of peace and a denunciation of the violence that the army, the paramilitary, and the guerrillas have exerted upon their communities.

Lina Rosa Berrío Palomo describes how, in this context, indigenous women have suffered the direct consequences of armed conflict: "The female body has been used by the armed actors (regardless of their ideology or their geography) to control and humiliate the enemy. To the army, paramilitary or the insurgency; women, particularly indigenous women, are seen as a war-trophy and a means of debilitating an adversary or as workers in domestic and sexual labors" (Berrío Palomo 2005, 155).

But indigenous women have not only been victims of the conflict. They have also transformed into social actors who promote demilitarization and peace. For example, we have seen in the different initiatives they have promoted a commitment to the denunciation of human rights violations in indigenous regions, like the "1st Meeting of Indigenous Women for Autonomy, Resistance, and Peace" in July of 2002. The interaction in these spaces has allowed these women to share experiences and to build new female leaderships that began to have a pivotal role in the indigenous Colombian movement; even without having any gender-specific demands, these interactions are contributing to the image of indigenous women as political actors. These experiences contrast with the indigenous women in Mexico and Guatemala, where the guerrilla movements of the 1970s and 1980s did manage to incorporate into their ranks indigenous men and women. They were forced to question in one way or another their Marxist perspectives that prioritized the class struggle, developing critical reflections on racism and incorporating specific demands of the indigenous people into their agendas.

In all three countries, political-military movements intentionally or unintentionally promoted the creation of spaces of collective reflection where indigenous women started to question not only state violence and capitalist exploitation but also the racism and exclusions they experienced in their communities. In the case of Mexico and Guatemala, women's active participation in revolutionary struggles was one of the factors that prompted indigenous women's organizations to assume class and anti-capitalist perspectives as central to their demands, despite later criticisms made of the racial and gender hierarchies reproduced within the guerilla movements themselves.

In contrast, the exclusion and violence exercised by various guerilla movements in Colombia against indigenous communities contributed to that country's indigenous organizations' rejection of the Marxist left, its armed strategies, and its exclusively class-focused perspectives. For Colombia's indigenous women organized in the CRIC and the National Indigenous Organization of Colombia (Organización Nacional Indígena de Colombia—ONIC), discourses on indigenous rights and human rights have been their main tools for struggle. Indigenous rights have been the language with which they have demanded their right to land and territory, as well as to their own political and justice systems. Human rights discourses have been fundamental to denouncing the military and paramilitary violence that has affected their peoples.

In parallel to these dialogues with political-military movements in these three countries, spaces were created for collective reflection linked to Catholic priests promoting liberation theology. In these spaces, another kind of discourse was constructed regarding "women's dignity" and "peoples' rights," as we shall see in the next section.

DIALOGUES WITH LIBERATION THEOLOGY

As I pointed out in the beginning of this chapter, many of the dialogues that have contributed to the appropriation of discourses on rights, and to the formation of new political identities as indigenous women, have occurred simultaneously. This is why it is impossible to understand, for example, the participation of an important sector of the indigenous population in the political-military and peasant movements of the 1970s and 1980s if we do not take into account the important role played by the progressive Catholic Church in promoting a critical consciousness in this sector of the population. The spaces for reflection and organizational processes promoted first by liberation theology and then by Indian theology have been fundamental for the appearance of social and political movements in different countries of Latin America and for the promotion of human rights and indigenous rights discourses. Through these movements, indigenous and mestizo men and women have questioned the structures of inequality that oppress and exclude them.

When reconstructing the history of the different spaces in which indigenous women are appropriating the discourses of rights, and in exploring the organizational genealogies of women that are involved in such spaces, I discovered that many of them had some kind of link to the Catholic Church or were educated in a Catholic boarding school. In some cases, the first experiences happened through projects in which no significant change in the life of these women was intended but, instead, in scenarios where women were searching for an economical alternative for them and their families (see Duarte 2011). In other cases, women started to organize through biblical reflection groups, which gradually turned into spaces to share their experiences and day-to-day problems (see Ever and Kovic 2003; Hernández Castillo 2004a).

Many of these spaces of biblical reflection came to be when the Latin American Catholic Church gave an important twist to their pastoral work after the Second Vatican Council (1962–1965), where a new social commitment to marginalized sectors of society was ratified. These reflections emerged in the European context and were taken up again during the Second Conference of the Latin American Episcopate (CELAM) that took place in Medellin, Colombia, in 1968. It was only after this conference that a movement started to build all over Latin America that posed the need for the Catholic Church to take a "preferential option for the poor."

Even before this critical thought systemized itself in the form of the liberation theology, priests committed to the social reality and marked by their contact with marginalized groups—like Camilo Torres, Domingo Lain, and Manuel Pérez in Colombia—tried to make bridges between Catholicism and Marxism, and opted to participate in political-military organizations. Although the writings of Camilo Torres were more of a sociological than theological nature, his reflections were an inspiration for all those priests who, years later, would turn into the main ideologists of the liberation theory.[14] Peruvian theologian Gustavo Gutiérrez, a close friend of Camilo Torres and his schoolmate at the Catholic University of Lovaina, was one of the first to systemize these thoughts in his now-classic book, *Historia, política y salvación de una teología de liberación*, published in 1973.

Among the main changes that this critical tendency of Catholicism brought to the table was a rejection of the paternalist Catholic tradition. Taking up the methodological proposals of Paulo Freire, who spoke in favor of awareness processes, the critical Catholic tradition advocated the development of a critical consciousness in these marginalized groups toward the structural roots of their oppression. The commitment of the Church of the Poor promoted the formation of social actors that would transform the conditions of oppression through collective organization. This organization happened in different countries of Latin

America, and it went from agrarian cooperatives and peasant and indigenous organizations to the revolutionary sites of the guerrilla organizations.

In the case of the Colombian Church, its episcopate (considered, along with the Argentinean Church, to be the most conservative of Latin America) rejected the proposals of the CELAM; many priests, devotees, and members of the ministry took up the Medellin documents as a Magna Carta that justified a completely new pastoral approach. The geographic location of Colombia, and the fact that the country hosted the "2nd Episcopal Conference" (1968), made it a privileged location for the birth or constitution of national headquarters for many Latin American institutes. For example, the Institute of Catequesis (ICLA) constructed its headquarters in Manizales; the Institute of Pastoral Liturgy for Latin America (IPLI), with its headquarters in Medellin; and the Latin American Pastoral Institute for Youth (IPLAJ) with its headquarters in Bogota—all became centers of formation for new political leadership among the popular sectors of Colombia and other countries of Latin America (see Bidegain 1985).

Even though, in these first stages of development of liberation theology, there was not (among their pastoral agents) a reflection on women's rights, the spaces of reflection became spaces of critique of different types of oppression: class, gender, and ethnicity. Ahead of his time, Camilo Torres had reflected since the 1960s about the specifics of oppression of women when writing for *United Front* (*Frente Unido*) magazine his "Message to Women," in which he pointed out:

> Colombian women have the conscience of being exploited not only by society, as most of Colombians, but also by men. Colombian women have fighting discipline, have shown generosity towards others, and have more resistance to physical pain. The Colombian woman, like any other woman, has more feeling, more sensitivity, and more intuition. All these qualities, in a first stage, should be exalted and placed at the service, not of the oligarchies or men as such, but rather at the service of a revolutionary ideal turned into the ideal of women. (Torres 1965, 8)

Though this perspective still had an image of women as "sensitive, intuitive, resistant" and considered revolution as the primary means to end their subordination, it started to recognize male oppression as a reality that had to be transformed in order to achieve a fairer life for everyone. A decade later, a female sector of the Colombian Catholic Church took up the reflection regarding the specificity of women and formed the Organization of Religious Women for Latin America (*Organización de Religiosas para America Latina*—ORAL) (1975–1976), which clearly subscribed to the liberation theology perspective and advanced the breakthrough of women as protagonists within the Church in Colombia. Since 1970, many religious communities had a massive exodus from inner-city areas to outer-city slums and poor peasant communities. Even though this group did not last very long, it was a fundamental part of the construction of a women's pastoral sector within the Colombian Catholic Church.

The women from ORAL worked on the promotion of Base Ecclesial Communities (CEB) inside the urban zones and Christian Peasant Communities (CCC) in the rural areas, spaces in which theological and political reflection on social inequalities was supported. From the CCC comes the so-called peasantry reading of the Bible (*campesinización* of the Bible), a biblical re-interpretation by the same peasant people. In these spaces of reflection, and in Catholic schools marked by liberation theology, some of the political actors of the Colombian indigenous movement were formed. Avelina Pancho, a Nasa woman, member of the board in the ONIC, and active member of the indigenous movements for almost twenty years, when being interviewed by Berrío Palomo, describes the cultural climate of the time and the importance that religious boarding schools had for many indigenous women:

> For me it was really difficult, I wanted to study, wanted to experience more and the only opportunity that I had, the only one my family could offer me was to study in that school, a boarding-school directed by nuns. Once in there I was between wanting to study and accepting their rules. I didn't like to pray, it was too big a sacrifice but I did like mass and especially Salvadorian mass, at that time the revolution was reaching a boiling point over there and I like that. I loved to read, help the priest organize events, going out to the community and celebrating, reflecting, I like all that. (Pancho Aquite and Berrío Palomo 2006, 35)

It is important to recognize that, in this encounter between priests, nuns, and indigenous men and women, the influence has been reciprocal. The pastoral agents have promoted spaces of reflection and the appropriation of the Gospel from the everyday reality of indigenous people; at the same time, indigenous men and women have brought their experiences, worldviews, and spirituality to the table. These dialogues have not only influenced the formation of regional and national spaces of organization for indigenous women but have also unsettled hegemonic views of the Catholic Church regarding indigenous people and women. The elaboration of an Indian theology by a new generation of Indigenous priests and theologians tells us about the new voices within the Catholic Church that are getting feedback from the experiences of indigenous men and women (see CENAMI 1991, 1994; Siller 1991; Illicachi Guznay 2013).

The new kind of relationship that was established among Catholic pastoral agents and the peasants of different regions of Latin America led to a rethinking of not only the style of work but also the very foundation of Western theology. From the indigenous ministry the existence of an Indian theology was asserted, its purpose being to recover the existential experience of God that indigenous people had before the arrival of the Spanish. This perspective assumes that Indian theology has always been dormant in the way Indian people feel about and relate to God, and tries to recover this experience and knowledge.[15] This movement claims cultural traditions of the indigenous peoples and their ritual practices as alternative, less individualist forms of conceiving of divinity.

The concept of Indian theology began to be used in workshops and preparatory meetings for the "500 Years of the Evangelization of America." In different Latin American episcopates, critical reflection began on the acculturating sense of evangelization and developed a "new vision towards indigenous cultures, positive, dialogic, of exchange, of growth and above all, that rejects the old disqualifying attitude, apologetic and even demonizing towards the cultures and religions that had predisposed their hearts, to assume a perspective that didn't do much honor to the missionary work, or the Indians, or the proclaiming of the Gospel" (Aguirre Franco 1997, 3).

In the context of these activities, the "Encounter of Indian Theology" for the Andean region of Chucuito, Peru, took place in 1990; in 1991, the "First Latin American Encounter of Indian Theology" was held in Mexico City; in 1993, the "Second Latin American Encounter of Indian Theology" took place in Colón, Panama; and there have been multiple regional encounters in the Mayan zone. Agents of the indigenous ministry of the Diocese of San Cristóbal played an important role in the regional encounters and in the two Latin American encounters and were responsible to promote the new Indian theology in indigenous communities.

Regarding the relationships between men and women, Indian theology emphasizes the complementary roles between genders that exist within indigenous cultures. However, these perspectives on indigenous cultures and the relations between genders contrasted very much with the concrete experience of indigenous women in Latin America, where the reflections of the women have been advancing along different paths from Indian theology.

In the case of Guatemala, the Dominican Sisters were one of the first to start developing specific work for women. This order in particular, since its foundation in Peru in 1820, had prioritized education with women through the foundation of schools for "ladies" of the upper and middle classes. Under the influence of the Second Vatican Council, the order gave a new turn in its ministry to widen their range to include the evangelization and formation of marginal indigenous and mestizo women. It is along this line that they started to work with Mayan communities in Guatemala, promoting their education and supporting productive projects. This work continued years later in the Mexican state of Chiapas between refugee and Mexican peasant women. In this new stage, the nuns of this order started to rethink the "promotion of women" and discuss, in the spaces of reflection, the inequalities between men and women:

> The initial topic of any group of women was always equality and what makes a man and what makes a woman and if God wants us to be under the rule of a *macho*. With the refugee women we did work on how to generate conscience and other women organizations for women emerged, such as Mamá Maquín.[16]

The work of Dominican nuns comes together with that of other religious orders like the Jesuits and the Maryknolls who were also influenced in a profound manner by liberation theology, developing an intense pastoral focus during the bloodiest decades of the armed conflict in Guatemala. Many Mayan women who, over time, would become important leaders of the movement were educated in the schools for "ladies" located in urban zones like the Socorro Indigenous Institute founded by religious order Bethlemite Daughters of the Sacred Heart of Jesus and the Colegio Monte María of the religious order of Maryknolls.[17]

Paradoxically, many of these priests and nuns came to Guatemala from Spain and the United States with the task of counteracting the influence of leftist ideologies with a missionary, anti-communist, and pro-development view. However, when they had the experience of living in Mayan communities and getting to know up-close the conditions of extreme poverty in which these people live, some of the priests became radicalized and assumed the "preferential option for the poor."

The Guatemalan Episcopate, led by Cardinal Mario Casariego, who was close to the oligarchy and the higher ranks of the army, opposed the lines coming out of the Medellin Conference. It was not until the 1976 earthquake, when a big part of the capital city and hundreds of peasant villages were destroyed, severely punishing the poorest, that a new profile of the Guatemalan Episcopate started to emerge. Expressed in a document known as "United by Hope," the social and economic character of the "natural" disaster was denounced. Later, in 1978, after the massacre of Panzos in which 160 Q'eqchi' Indians died, the Guatemalan Episcopate proclaimed itself against the counterinsurgent campaigns and broke all historical alliances that the hierarchy held with military dictatorships (see Melville 1983).

At the indigenous ministry level, a group of itinerant Jesuits developed important work on the formation of catechists and cooperative leaders from a critical and anti-systemic perspective. During the colonization processes of the jungle regions of Ixcán and El Petén, the Jesuits and Maryknolls promoted self-management processes and agrarian cooperatives, whose organization was always accompanied by reflection of political dynamics that contributed to the formation of a critical conscience among the Indian settlers. These experiences of community re-constitution in the context of colonization were fundamental to the formation of female leadership that would later influence the formation of a Mayan women's movement in the refuge.

Insofar as military repression deepened with the "scorched earth campaign,"[18] priests, religious sisters, and catholic catechists working in indigenous regions became radicalized, and many of them were linked to the political-military organizations, particularly the Guerrilla Army of the Poor (Ejército Guerrillero de los Pobres—EGP) that had its areas of influence in the departments of El Quiché and Huehuetenango, and to a lesser extent in the Organization of the People in Arms (Organización del Pueblo en Armas—ORPA).

Those links of Catholic organizations with the revolutionary movements caused in the army a particular hatred toward the progressive sectors of the Church. From 1976 to 1979 (before the worst stage of violence), the Guatemalan Church in Exile claimed that more than 350 leaders were kidnapped in three Ixil municipalities (Iglesia Guatemalteca en el Exilio 1982). In 1980, the Bishop of Quiché sent his religious members to exile, and at least three priests and catechists of the dioceses joined the guerrilla movements. It was during this stage that the paths of Guatemalan and Mexican indigenous women cross each other once again in the refuge. The arrival of 200,000 Mayan peasants from

Guatemala profoundly impacted local organizational processes, creating a space for the exchange of experiences that would result in the formation of a wider movement of indigenous women in Chiapas.

In order to give social support to the refugees, the Diocese of San Cristóbal de las Casas formed the Christian Committee of Solidarity, in which pastoral agents linked to liberation theology participated. With the refugees also came the priests and the religious sisters of the Diocese of Quiché, Guatemala, who were affected in their ministry work by the "scorched earth" campaigns promoted by the Guatemalan army. The organizational and reflexive work that began during the colonization of Ixcán continued in Mexican territory. The Dominican sisters kept developing pastoral work with women that aimed at recovering feminine spirituality and reflecting on the subordination and exclusion of women. Toward the end of the 1980s, a growing number of nuns started to identify with this new line of thought and came up with a proposal to open an area for women within the Diocese of San Cristóbal. For this area to be recognized, it had to be demonstrated that presence of this work existed at every level of the ministry. By this time, nuns of different orders worked at different levels of reflection, with Tsotsil, Tseltal, Chol, Tojolabal, and mestizo women.

Unlike the thought promoted by feminist groups, in the meeting between religious sisters and indigenous women, gender inequalities were not the only topic of debate; they also shared experiences and different ways of living and conceiving of spirituality:

> All of us as women wanted to follow Jesus Christ, but we wanted to do it from our being women and sharing with illiterate women of different ethnicities, we discovered that women feel God in a very different way. That too was a threat to the structure of the Catholic Church. Indigenous women are sometimes even more religious than us and express their religion in a very intimate way with God, they feel it in different things, they feel it in their culture, in nature, in their traditions, they feel it as they say, "In an inner force."[19]

While the followers of Indian theology claimed complementarity and the importance of the ritual of women, indigenous peasants from the Diocese of San Cristóbal (including Tsotsil, Tseltal, Chol, and Tojolabal) began to form groups of reflection about the inequalities among men and women and how their communities were impacted. They also reflected on the particular way to live their spirituality. The sisters linked to the women's section played an important role at the organizational level. One of them described the process that would lead, in 1994, to the articulation of the Diocesan Coordinator of Women (Coordinadora Diocesana de Mujeres—CODIMUJ), which is, to this date, the largest women's organization in that state and one of the largest in Mexico with seven hundred local groups and the participation of about ten thousand women (see Santana 2001; Gil Tébar 1991; Meckesheimer 2015).

One of the nuns who was very active in the promotion of women's rights, which were discussed in terms of "women's dignity," described this process of regional organization of indigenous women: "In the different zones the pastoral agents of the ministry visited the communities and in every community there was a small group of women who wanted to reflect on the Word of God. In every community they got together one or two hours and read a biblical text and this text helps them see how they are children of God. It also helped them see how we are living in community, as children of God if we are respected, if there's equality, if they take into consideration our opinion, if our contributions as women in socio-political organizations is being recognized, if by being women they consider us less or if we can give our word and our word is acknowledged."[20] This was the beginning, and seven hundred groups of women were formed, groups that would later articulate in the Diocesan Coordinator of Women (CODIMUJ).

In February of 1994, a month after the Zapatista uprising, and in spite of the environment of insecurity in some zones of conflict, representatives of the almost 700 groups of reflection met at San Cristóbal to articulate their efforts and to give a new name to the coordination: CODIMUJ. In these first meetings, the coordination reflected on the challenges faced by women in this new context of war, but efforts also focused on articulating new ways to approach the Gospel from a feminine perspective:

Along with the women from the CODIMUJ, we have a set goal, to read the Word of God with eyes, mind and heart of a woman. So the Word of God helps us see ourselves as children of God, but also that it would allow us to recognize God from our being women; because we always see the Word of God preached and summarized from the position of men, the catechists, but we women also want to discover the Word of God. As the Tseltales say, we want to experiment the sweetness of the Word of God, we want to get to know it, read it by ourselves, and get that sweetness out, we don't want anyone telling us how it tastes, we want to experiment by ourselves.[21]

When reading the Gospel in light of everyday life, indigenous women started questioning not only the inequalities they live through as indigenous and as peasants, but also as women. The alleged roles of "complementarity" claimed by Indian theology are not a reality for many indigenous communities of Chiapas, where women have been excluded from ritual, political, and organizational spaces.

This questioning does not imply that a claim for cultural identity does not exist; toward the state the demand for cultural rights is being made, but toward the community they demand the right to change the traditions that oppress and exclude them. We could talk of the appearance of a new gender conscience that poses the need to "reinvent" the tradition under new terms and that uses the discourse on "women's dignity" as a tool to question gender discrimination and violence.

An important influence in this movement has been the feminist theology developed within the Catholic Church, reaching indigenous women through their religious and secular advisors. In the promotion of feminist theology, a collective of Catholic women has had special relevance. Since 1979, the group called Women for Dialogue (Mujeres para el Diálogo) has advised and supported the work of religious nuns in diverse indigenous regions across the country with the objective of transforming the patriarchal structures of the Catholic Church and promoting biblical reflection from a gender perspective.[22] These are dissenting voices within the Catholic Church that, despite their strong criticism, have decided to fight their struggle inside the institution. The feminist theologists have taken up the "option for the poor" in order to reconstruct it as an option for the poor women, and they are fighting against the hegemonic patriarchal perspectives of the institutional church through the voices and texts of Ivone Gebara (1990) and Elsa Tamez (1988). Parallel to this, its influence has been felt in the ant work of hundreds of Catholic women that are accompanying the reflection and the organization of indigenous women in Mexico (see Mujeres para el Diálogo 1992; Meckesheimer 2015).

It is not possible to understand the importance of the participation of indigenous women in the Zapatista movement, or the movement of indigenous women for justice and rights that has followed the uprising, if we do not recognize the silent and constant work of the religious feminists in different indigenous regions.

The feelings of indigenous women toward the inequalities they experience every day, as well as their demand to re-appropriate ritual and organizational spaces, have been captured in the memories of meetings and internal reports, but have not been systemized inside the materials of reflection of the Catholic Church. Unlike Indian theology, which has been systemizing and legitimizing itself as a theological proposition through the work of Clodomiro Siller, Eleazar López Hernández, Bartolomé Carrasco, Gerardo Flores, Angel Barreno, and Aiban Wagua (to mention only a few names), women's perspectives in Indian theology remain undeveloped. However, in different regions of Mexico and Guatemala, indigenous women have started to develop their proposals on how to read the Gospel with the "mind and heart of a woman," and from that reading, they contribute to the rethinking of male-female relationships in a more equitable way.

Although in many of these spaces women's rights were not vindicated as such, a discourse started to emerge regarding "women's dignity," which questioned the exclusions that took place not only in the Catholic Church and its social pastoral ministry but also in the indigenous communities themselves. Reading the Bible with "a woman's mind and heart" implied developing a critical reading that selectively revisited those biblical passages that spoke of the importance of respect toward women and described their powers and religious and spiritual skills.

However, the "emancipatory" principles that some indigenous women found in the Catholic religion did not always coincide with other perspectives developed in other spaces that were more critical of institutional religions in indigenous and peasant movements. The critique of colonialism and its effects on the lives and culture of indigenous peoples of the Mayan movement in Guatemala (as well as a number of sectors of the indigenous movement in Mexico and Colombia) included a rejection of the spaces of the Catholic Church, including those that were historically considered to be allies.

The critique of colonialism and racism, and the defense of a cosmovision and a spirituality of their own, implied, for some indigenous women, rejecting the Catholic discourse that many indigenous women who developed politically in institutions or organizations related to the Church continue to reproduce (see Chirix 2013).

In the next ethnographic window, I will address the tensions that exist among organized indigenous women with different political genealogies who claim different perspectives regarding culture and gender relations. We will also see how, despite profound political and generational differences that sometimes hinder dialogue, bridges and alliances continue to be built based on shared experiences of exclusion and critical reflections.

SECOND ETHNOGRAPHIC WINDOW

BETWEEN GENERATIONS AND WORLDVIEWS: CHRONICLE OF THE WORKSHOP "SHARING EXPERIENCES: CONTRIBUTIONS AND CHALLENGES OF INDIGENOUS WOMEN IN THE STRUGGLE OF THEIR PEOPLE"

It is November 2005, and the participants of a collective project under my co-ordination[23] decide to summon the representatives of the indigenous organizations with which we work to discuss the results of our investigation. It is the end of a four-year cycle in which we have grown together, nurtured ideas, and rethought our feminism based on the dialogues and exchanges that we had with the indigenous women. The workshop, called "Sharing Experiences: Contributions and Challenges of Indigenous Women in the Struggle of their People," is almost a rite of passage that makes us reflect on the possibilities and limitations of these intercultural dialogues that have changed our perspectives and, in a way, our identities.

The meeting provides us with an opportunity, as female social activists, leaders, spiritual guides, or communitarian dissenters, to exchange experiences, reflect, and imagine possible futures together. Finally, we meet the social actors whose feats and accomplishments are talked about by the rest of our colleagues and teammates; we even get to know, in detail, the lives of some of them, especially those who wrote their life histories for a collective book we developed as a part of the same project.[24] It is the first time that all of us (investigators and indigenous activists) have gotten together as a group and dialogued.

Once more, the Catholic Church is the backdrop of the meetings of indigenous women because the workshop takes place in a Jesuit retirement center that we rented for the event. Representatives of the organizations with whom we work arrive at the event: Defensa Popular de Oteapan from southern Veracruz, Frente Indígena Oaxaqueño Binacional, Maseualsiuamej Mosenyolchicauanij from the northern sierra of Puebla, Titekititoke Tajome Sihuame of the highlands of Guerrero, Axale of the low mountains of Guerrero, the National Coordination of Indigenous Women of Mexico, the Political Association of Mayan Women (MOLOJ) from Guatemala, the Mayan women's group Kaqla, Mother Earth (an organization of Mayan women formed in the refugee camps), and Pop No'j of Guatemala (as well as people from communities with Zapatista support bases). The lack of resources does not allow us to invite representatives from the Colombian organization ONIC with whom Lina Rosa Berrío Palomo has worked.

We have assembled a heterogeneous group of indigenous women of different age groups, political genealogies, geographical proceedings, and cultural conceptions. This diversity has an almost symbolic manifestation in the coloring of their suits: some are worn on special occasions; others are for everyday use. Just one of the women is wearing jeans; she is one of the Guatemalan leaders formed in exile. Her experience in non-indigenous circles is manifested in her clothing but also in her deep knowledge of both realities, which allows her to be a bridge between indigenous Mexican and Guatemalan women.

The group of researchers is also heterogeneous; we are ten women from different geographical regions: Mexicans from the north, center, and south of the country; an Afro-Colombian; and an Uruguayan. There are also several other colleagues with multiple nationalities: a Guatemalan-Brazilian-Mexican, with U.S. citizenship; a Mexican-Argentinean; and an American-British-Guatemalan, now holding Mexican nationality. It is evident that the quest for identity and its definition is also a relevant theme in our lives. Among ourselves, there are some generational differences: there are those who were marked by their militancy in the student movement of 1968; another generation of our group was formed in the heat of the Central American revolutionary struggles of the 1980s; and the youngest are the generation that got into politics through Zapatismo. We all concur in having arrived at feminism through the door of the left.

In the first exercise, we elaborate some identity maps locating ourselves in the geographical and cultural space, and the color and creativity of those maps reflect the diversity of our group. In workshops, we discussed topics such as the challenges faced by female leaders in the indigenous movement, the gender agenda imposed from the international financial foundations, the relation between gender and cosmovision, the relation between the indigenous movement and rural feminism, and the impact of war and militarization on indigenous regions.

The members of the research team had proposed to "share our knowledge," but we ended up learning a lot more from our indigenous colleagues than what we could share. Every one of those women had the experience of years of struggle and knowledge constructed collectively with their organization and community of origin.

The diversity of experiences that come together in the workshop only enriches the debate: female spiritual leaders, Mayan feminist Guatemalans and Mexicans, women with a wide organizational career (such as the Nahua women from

Maseualsiuamej Mosenyolchicauanij in the northern sierra of Puebla), and younger women fighting to open up organizational spaces in their regions. The different political and organizational genealogies mark the way each of the participants understands the political strategies and the specific ways in which they are working for the rights of women. There are many common points but also many differences that are discussed with the political energy of someone used to standing up for their ideas and fighting for them.

The differences in the debates among diverse participants not only are related to content but also reflect differences in form. The Nahua women of Cuetzalán have a particular manner of participation: they don't speak very much, but when they do, they do it in a convincing manner. That prudent style (silent, negotiator) had caught our eyes in other female meetings. Despite the fact that Maseualsiuamej is one of the pioneer organizations in the work on women's rights, their leaders have usually opted to keep a low profile in the national movement and instead concentrate on their regional struggles. Their styles contrast with the energetic and emotional voices of the women of Guerrero, who share personal testimonies, political reflections, and even poetry they have written. The Guatemalan participants express their long years of militancy in different political movements, carrying in many ways "the directing voice" of the event. It is they who bring to the debate the topic of an indigenous worldview or cosmovision as a holistic form of relating to nature and society, and as a fundamental element to building fairer relationships between human beings.

It is around this topic that some of the tensions of the event are developed. For a new generation of women who have appropriated the global discourse on women's rights and have begun to talk about indigenous feminisms, the discourse around the complementarity of Mayan culture is problematic because of the political uses to deny the problem of machismo.

Without questioning in a confrontational manner the Mayan leader who is talking about cosmovision, one of the women from the feminist organization Kaqla responds to the harmonic representation that is being made of their culture by talking about the violence and discrimination that are still experienced by indigenous women in their communities. It is evident that the priorities in the political agenda are different: in the first case, the racism, exclusion, and internal colonialism of ladino society were placed as the main problems indigenous women have to face; in the second case, the need for developing a gender agenda that parts from a contemporaneous Mayan reality is brought up, one that would not limit itself to the criticism of ladino society. In this clash, differences and agreements have a long history in the Mayan Guatemalan movement.

According to the work of Morna Macleod, in the last few years a larger number of coincidences have been found because a greater recognition and appropriation of elements of indigenous worldview have been developing by Mayan feminists (Macleod 2008). At the same time there is also a greater recognition, though not in a public way, of problems with sexism and machismo by the women who claim the cosmovision as a space of political resistance.

The existence of shared cultural logics that persist despite political differences is evidenced at the end of our workshop when, after a long day of heated debate, the son of one of the Mayan feminists gets sick and starts to cry inconsolably. The first explanation of the mother of the child is that the intense debate and the strong energy of all the women participating have made the kid sick with fright: *susto*. The first solution to this problem involves asking the Mayan spiritual leader to perform a "cleansing" on the child to cure him from the susto he suffers. Despite the differences that could exist between them, the knowledge and spiritual power of the women is recognized.

We end the event with the clear conviction that the diversity of the perspectives is where the richness of these different movements lies. Both the incipient indigenous feminism and the promoters of the Mayan cosmovision from a woman's perspective contribute to building fairer societies for indigenous men and women.

In the next section we shall see how these different perspectives regarding relations between men and women and how culture is understood and lived in different regions are influenced by political dialogues of organized women within peasant and indigenous movements.

DIALOGUES WITH THE PEASANT AND INDIGENOUS MOVEMENT

Two spaces that have been fundamental in the political formation of indigenous women are the peasant movements from the 1970s and 1980s and the indigenous movements (which acquired a greater visibility since the commemoration of "500 Years of Indigenous, Black, and Popular Resistance," at the beginning of the 1970s). In some regions, they are the same social actors that, in the first instance, mobilized under a peasant identity with agrarian demands; in a second moment, they claim their ethnic identities mobilizing around their territorial and cultural rights.

Some authors have located the transition from the peasant movements to the indigenous movements as a change from the old social movements to the new social movements. This characterization indicates that the prior would organize around claims of class, their objective being to change existing economic models, and they would tend to confront the state, while the latter would encompass different classes and articulate themselves around their identities looking for the transformation of society's cultural systems. In other writings, I have questioned these dichotomous perspectives with respect to peasant and indigenous movements in Latin America that do not consider the cultural dimension of the struggle for land: in other words, for the indigenous people, land is much more than a natural resource and is related to the reproduction of their way of life (see Rus, Hernández Castillo, and Mattiace 2003). The peasant movements of the 1970s and 1980s fought not only for a piece of land but for the right to reproduce their way of life and to defend Mother Earth from the predatory forces of an industrialization model with little respect for nature. Similarly, the indigenous movements of the 1990s and the present century fight not only for their cultural rights and autonomy but also for cultural recognition and economic and political redistribution of resources and power. In the context of these struggles, indigenous women have had an important role, several times being at the forefront of the mobilizations. In most cases, though, they do not hold leading roles and tend to reproduce gender roles when taking care of the logistics of the movement. In Mexico, Guatemala, and Colombia, the spaces of encounter of the peasant and indigenous organizations have been the political and organizational schools for hundreds of women, where they have been able to unite and share their struggles and strategies for resistance.

After World War II, peasant struggles began to develop all over Latin America, demanding agrarian redistribution, the right to form unions, and better salaries. Paradoxically, these demands echo the unfulfilled promises of the "Alliance for Progress," promoted since the end of the 1950s by the John F. Kennedy administration. An important aspect of this initiative was to persuade the Latin American governments to perform agrarian reforms. The reasoning behind this was that the redistribution of land and the proliferation of family-owned farms would turn the potentially insurrectionary peasantry into a conservative and stabilizing force of rural societies. In fact, many Latin American governments designed programs of agrarian reform under the influence of the "Alliance for Progress." These rural modernization initiatives were a double-edged sword, for they created the cultural climate that legitimized the right to land and the obligation of the government to dissolve *latifundios* and promote the agrarian redistribution. As expected, the groups of power that controlled the agrarian economy opposed these transformations, and in countries such as Guatemala and Mexico, the promotion of the colonization of the rainforest was the escape valve the governments found to respond to agrarian demands without impacting the interests of the large landholders.[25]

Facing the unfulfilled promises, large peasant confederations began to form in all three countries; these confederations led mobilizations and the taking of land, such as the National Association of Peasant Users (Asociación Nacional de Usuarios Campesino—ANUC) in Colombia, Committee of Peasant Unity (Comité de Unidad Campesina—CUC) in Guatemala, and the Independent Central of Agricultural Workers and Peasants (Central Independiente de Obreros Agrícolas y Campesino—CIOAC) in Mexico.

In the case of Colombia, the agrarian struggles of indigenous people take very different forms from the peasant movements of Mexico and Guatemala. This is due in part to the specific forms of indigenous communities since the colonial time, where the resguardos and the *cabildos* were fundamental as territorial spaces and political institutions.[26]

Even though ANUC has been an important space in the peasant struggles of Colombia, a large part of the indigenous population has abandoned its ranks because they feel it doesn't take into account the particular problems of indigenous peoples. The agrarian demands of indigenous peoples have been rather contained in their territorial demands because of their respect for the resguardos.[27]

This kind of indigenous territoriality has its origins in the colonial time when the Catholic Church opposed the dispossession of the native people and the appropriation of their work force; it also demanded from the Spanish Crown the recognition of land for the Indians. Thus, with a clear Christianizing purpose the first resguardos appear. Many of these indigenous territories were expropriated during the Republic, under the ideological justification of "progress," and their habitants became settlers of the haciendas. From this plunder, many of the indigenous mobilizations in Colombia have happened in a very specific manner for the recovery of the resguardos (including land and political control over territory) and not exclusively for the agrarian rights.

While in Mexico and Guatemala the indigenous peasants would mobilize for the distribution of land, the indigenous Colombians fought for the legal recognition of the existence of resguardos. In this context, the cabildo became the political instrument in the struggle of the indigenous population (see Sánchez Botero 1998). The peasant struggles, led by Quintín Lamé, proposed the cabildo constitution as the first stage in the struggle for the recovery of the reservation territories. Since then, and thanks to the political influence of the thought of Quintín Lamé, the organizational specificity of the indigenous peoples' struggles was clearly established (see Rojas 2006). These spaces of political organization have been preferred over the agrarian leagues, the armed groups, or the political parties.[28]

This specificity of the peasant struggle in Colombia turned the indigenous movement in this country into one of the pioneers in the claiming of the indigenous ethnic identities as political mobilization spaces. In 1971, the first regional indigenous association in Colombia was created as one of the first in Latin America: the Regional Indigenous Council of the Cauca (CRIC), followed by others in the Indigenous National Council of Tolima and the Regional Embera Waunana Organization. These local organizations were the organizational schools of hundreds of indigenous people who, ten years later, would form ONIC (see Berrío Palomo 2005). The centrality of indigenous rights sustained within the indigenous movements of Colombia can help us understand the emphasis on collective rights of organized indigenous women of that country over their gender specific demands. The fight for autonomy, territory, culture, natural resource control, health, bilingual education, and the impulse of economic communitarian organizations have been priorities to the women of the ONIC.

In the Guatemalan case, the emergence of the national peasant movement was directly linked to the dialogues with liberation theology. The pastoral and cooperative work of the priests and sisters at the start of the 1960s was the basis for the formation of the Committee of Peasant Unity (CUC). This organization was born on April 15, 1978, from the union of peasant, communitarian, Catholic, and indigenous work since the First National Assembly. It was on this same date that its name was chosen and organizational structure defined; it operates in three regions: the coast, highlands, and the central region of Chimaltenango. The political context in which CUC emerged was important, in that its demands and mobilizations go beyond the agrarian demands of a peasant movement. Their militants became the fiercest opposition of the military regime of Guatemala and, for that same reason, were victims of political repression and violence. The mobilization against obligatory military recruitment and the Civil Self-Defense Patrols (PAC), against the repression, against the cost of living, against the exploitation in the fincas, and for the respect of human rights, for a fair salary, and for the recovery of Mother Earth, put CUC at the center of state repression. The most significant example is the massacre of the Spanish embassy on the January 31, 1980, when they peacefully occupied this precinct to demand the ceasing of the massacres that the army was performing in the central and northwestern Guatemalan highlands. The government responded to this action by sending the police and the army to massacre everyone. Thirty-nine occupants, among them peasant members of the CUC, laborers, students, committed Catholics, and diplomatic personnel, were burned alive. From 1981 to 1985, the repression and dislocation of the CUC took place, ceasing to have a public expression. Many of the leading political actors were radicalized, joining the ranks of the Guerrilla Army for the Poor (EGP).

Despite the fact that CUC, like all the peasant organizations from that time, did not consider the demands of women in their agenda, from its ranks came many of the main leaders of the actual Mayan movement from that country. The figure of Maya K'iche' leader Rigoberta Menchú (Nobel Peace Prize winner in 1992), whose father was assassinated in the Spanish embassy, became a symbol of the resistance of the indigenous people of the continent and, in a more particular manner, the resistance of indigenous women and their capabilities for political leadership.

In 1992, the National Indigenous and Peasant Coordinator (CONIC) broke with CUC and started to develop some ethnic claims using the discourse of indigenous rights, making it the first peasant organization to assume cultural demands. Some years later, members of the CONIC managed to meet with Mayan intellectuals to talk about their differences and form what is now known as the Mayan movement of Guatemala. This movement put on its political agenda the indigenous rights of the Mayan people and the struggle against racism (see Macleod 2008). These two organizational and political schools nurtured many of the organized Mayan women who, from different political spaces, are claiming the need to consider inequalities between men and women as a serious problem to face within the indigenous and peasant movements.

In the Mexican case, the peasant movement has two main actors that mark in a specific way the agenda for women inside the movement: on one side, the state, and on the other, the rural feminists. Unlike the peasant movements of Guatemala and Colombia, the Mexican peasantry developed their struggles in permanent tension with the post-revolutionary government policies that appropriated the rhetoric and symbols of peasant struggle and, following a corporate policy, created an official peasant organization called the National Peasant Organization (CNC). The limited agrarian reform promoted by the post-revolutionary governments allowed a certain level of control over the peasantry, which between 1930 and 1970 tended to organize more around productive demands.

It was in the 1960s that the limitations of the agrarian reform became evident for an ample sector of the dispossessed peasantry forced to sell their labor at a low cost in the coffee fields or in agro-industrial businesses. During this time, the CIOAC is formed with the participation of members of the Mexican Communist Party (Partido Comunista Mexicano). The CIOAC has been led since its very beginning by agrarian leaders who have tried to provide an alternative to the corporative system of the Mexican rural programs. Since 1976, the political presence of the CIOAC increased, and it adopted a focused project, not having as a priority the struggle for land but mainly focusing on the formation of peasant unions for the credit and defense of the peasant as a worker.

These organizations allowed the indigenous peasants to converge with scholars and activists committed to the agrarian struggle to play the role of advisors or companions of the organizations. It was in this context that what has been denominated "civil feminism" in its peasant facet (see Hernández Castillo and Espinosa Damián 2011; Espinosa Damián 2009) or "rural feminism" (Mejía 2008) gets in touch with peasant and indigenous organized women. In some regions, such as the north sierra of Puebla, the students of the School of Postgraduates in Agricultural Sciences of the State of Mexico arrive with a clearly feminist agenda to promote the political reflection processes among the women of the organizations. In other areas, like the Chiapas highlands, advisors and indigenous peasants built together their gender agendas from teamwork, as we'll explore in the next section (see Garza Caligaris and Toledo 2004).

In the spaces of reflection that the advisors and feminist intellectuals could have promoted, inside of the peasant organizations, indigenous women experienced exclusion from the political decision-making processes, the administration of the economic resources, and leadership positions. These exclusions have led many women to demand and create their own spaces within the peasant organizations, as was the case of the Mexican Association of Women Organized in Network (Asociación Mexicana de Mujeres Organizadas en Red—AMMOR), or the spaces of women inside the National Plural Indigenous Assembly for the Autonomy (Asamblea Nacional Indígena Plural por la Autonomía—ANIPA). Many others decided to separate themselves from mixed-gender organizations to form exclusive female organizations such as the organization of artisans Maseualsiuamej Mosenyoltchicauanij in the Sierra Norte of Puebla that emerged from a division of the Regional Agricultural Cooperative Tosepan Titataniske (see Mejía 2010).

Many of these experiences converged in 1997 in the context of the National Encounter of Indigenous Women, "Building our History," that I described in chapter 1, and formed the National Coordinating Committee of Indigenous Women in Mexico (*Coordinadora Nacional de Mujeres Indígenas en México*— CONAMI). This experience has been unique in the history of the indigenous movements in Mexico because it is the first national organization that puts at the center of its agenda women's rights (see Blackwell 2009). In their presentation pamphlet, they state their objectives as:

> Strengthening the leadership of indigenous females from a gender perspective, starting this from our cultural identity; establishing a communication network at a national level for indigenous women; provide training and education to indigenous women at a national level; to manage economic resources to implement regional productive projects, for training and for service for the Indian people; sensitizing the indigenous people and national society on the respect of human rights of indigenous women, including a gender view; in regards to the training, you must take into account an appropriate methodology considering the identity and gender according to our world-view. (Coordinadora Nacional de Mujeres Indígenas en México 1997, 1)

All these experiences in peasant and indigenous organizations were the antecedent that allowed a minority group of indigenous women, proceeding from different regions of Latin America and with different organizational stories, to start articulating their struggles with a political agenda in which they combine their demands for women's rights with the autonomic demands of their people. Since 1995, these women have opted to build their own spaces independent from the national indigenous movement and feminist movements of their countries. The first Continental Encounter of Indigenous Women took place in the city of Quito, Ecuador (1995); the second in Mexico (1997); the third in Panama (2000); the fourth in Lima, Peru (2004); the fifth in Kahnawake, Canada (2007); and the sixth in Hueyapan, Mexico (2011). Additionally, the Summit of Indigenous Women of the Americas, conducted in 2002 in Oaxaca, Mexico, extended the participation of women from indigenous groups from other continents. From these encounters, a Continental Network of Indigenous Women (Enlace Continental de Mujeres Indígenas—ECMIA) has been formed in which indigenous women from Latin America, the United States, and Canada converged (see Rivera Zea 2005).

Inspired by these transnational spaces, different struggles are being launched on many fronts. On one hand, the organized indigenous women have united

FIGURE 6. Participants in the "Panel on Gender and Ancestral Justice" in the
Congress of the Continental Network of Indigenous Women in
Guatemala, 2015. Photograph by Raquel García.

their voices with the Latin American indigenous movement to denounce economic oppression and racism that marks the insertion of the indigenous people in national projects. These women are developing their own discourses and political practices from a culturally-located gender perspective that questions both sexism and essentialism of the indigenous organizations as the ethnocentrism of hegemonic feminism.

In some contexts, this struggle for social justice for indigenous peoples and women has come from an appropriation of transnational discourses on human rights; in other contexts, however, these discourses have combined with a rhetoric that claims indigenous cosmovision as a more holistic way of relating to nature and society (as we saw in our second ethnographic window).

There is, however, a minority sector of organized indigenous women in the three countries who define themselves as "feminists," although usually nuancing the term as "indigenous feminism" or "communal feminism" and asserting the importance of the struggle against racism as a fundamental axis of their political agendas. For these indigenous women, the dialogues with feminist organizations, and their agreements and disagreements, are an important component of their political genealogies.

DIALOGUES WITH FEMINISMS

In Latin America, the decade of the 1960s represented a turning point in the history of national feminisms because, after the Conference of Women that took place in Mexico City in 1975, the Decade of the United Nations for the Advancement of Women (1975–1985) was declared. This initiative legitimizes many of the feminist demands worldwide. It is true that, in Mexico, Guatemala, and Colombia, the emerging feminist movements contributed to creating the cultural climate that denatured oppression and violence toward women. However, case studies have shown that, only in the Mexican context, experiences from rural feminisms or civil feminisms developed that centered around rural work and came into dialogue with peasant and indigenous organizations (and which, in many ways, contributed to the formulation of a gender agenda from indigenous women).

As I mentioned in the previous section, it was in the context of peasant mobilizations of the 1960s that feminist militants started to develop their work in the rural areas of Mexico, combining their support with productive projects for indigenous women's education for the promotion of gender consciousness. Many of us came from a left-wing militancy, linked with solidarity to the struggles of national liberation in Central America, or with political organizations that developed their work with popular and peasant sectors of Mexico.

From the lessons learned from the rural women, we consider that the feminist agenda should be linked to a reflection on economic and social inequalities that mark the lives of poor women. The tensions between those who focus on the decriminalization of abortion and those who fight for a feminist agenda that centers its strategies on the inequalities of gender and class have marked the history of Mexican feminism and constitute some of the challenges to be overcome in building a national feminist movement.

Since the formation of the Coalition of Feminist Women in 1976, and later with the creation of the National Front for Women's Rights and Liberty (Frente Nacional por los Derechos y la Libertad de las Mujeres) in 1979, the decriminalization of abortion, and the fight against domestic violence were the demands of the hegemonic feminism in Mexico. This hegemonic feminism has been fundamentally urban in its theorization, primarily from the academy, and constructed from the center of the country. Its hegemony has been defined not in the sense of legitimizing their worldview in a broader society but in relation to other popular and rural feminisms whose voices have not been heard in the large international feminist events and whose political practices have developed outside of international financing agencies.[29]

To this day, the stories of Mexican feminism written from the academy (see Lamas 1992; Lamas et al. 1995; Lau Jaiven 2002; Bartra 2002) continue to use the term "popular feminisms" to refer to the nongovernmental agencies that, since the 1980s, supported the organizational processes of poor urban and rural women. These authors ignore the women from the popular sectors who developed their own critique toward gender inequalities. When mentioned, these women are represented as passive victims whose consciousness will be raised by the feminists and whose mobilizations responded exclusively to practical demands. Gisela Espinosa Damián, who has been a witness and participant in the construction of this feminism since the very beginning, signals that "the epithet *popular feminism* should not be applied to civil organizations, for it was the women from poor urban neighborhoods who coined the term and assumed that identity" (Espinosa Damián 2009, 82). Espinosa Damián proposes to differentiate between a "civil feminism" conformed by civil organizations, whose members are generally middle-class professionals working with popular sectors, and a "popular feminism," referring to "processes featuring women from popular sectors who build their own organizations but also participate in mixed organizations and combine the struggle to transform the gender inequalities and to favorably reposition women with other type of demands" (Espinosa Damián 2009, 87).

It was during the 1980s, a time of political effervescence inside the women's movement, that national events were held and indigenous and peasant women converged with these women from popular sectors in the First National Encounter of Women in 1980. This event is considered a turning point in the history of popular feminism and was convened by groups close to liberation theology and feminist civil associations such as Communication, Exchange, and Human Development in Latin America (Comunicación, Intercambio y Desarrollo Humano en América Latina).[30] Some five hundred women from urban and rural backgrounds assisted with the event, which had as one of its objectives the discussion of the role and problems of women in popular movements. According to the testimony of one of the organizers, indigenous peasant women attended the event from Veracruz, Chiapas, Michoacán, Morelos, and from the Emiliano Zapata Peasant Organization (Organización Campesina Emiliano Zapata) and the Emiliano Zapata Peasant Union (Unión de Comuneros Emiliana Zapata de Comuneros) (see Espinosa Damián 2009).

In the case of Chiapas, it was the context of the peasant movement of the 1980s that brought left-wing activists and indigenous women from different regions of the state together in meetings, workshops, and congresses. Outside the official agendas of these events (that were mainly focused on agrarian problems), women started to share experiences and reflect on their own lives. The inequalities within the family, community, and organization started to be a topic of conversation in the extra-official spaces of the peasant movement. In these dialogues, the organizations' advisors, nuns linked to liberation theology, and activist scholars not only were witnesses or companions but also built our own feminist agenda. We broadened our critiques to the inequalities of the "capitalist system" by reflecting on gender exclusion and racism.

An important event that marked this meeting between a civil feminism and an indigenous women's movement was the First Encounter of Indigenous and Peasant Women of Chiapas. It was held in San Cristóbal de Las Casas in 1986 and was summoned by scholars and activists of the Autonomous University of Chiapas (Universidad Autónoma de Chiapas) and by the Organization of Indigenous Healers of the State of Chiapas (Organización de Médicos Indígenas del Estado de Chiapas—OMIECH). Sonia Toledo and Anna María Garza Caligaris, promoters and chroniclers of this event, told us how the popular education methodology was used to explore, with indigenous women, conceptions about their own bodies, sexuality, and the suffering of women (Garza Caligaris and Toledo 2004). Working in this way, they

> sought to build different relations than those developed in organizations traditionally dominated by men. Despite the fact that we inherited and recreated the distinction between advisors and advised and that tensions and specific conflicts were generated, these types of encounters allowed us to create new dynamics of reflection and interaction. The work and the political participation of women were valued; the expression of affection and self-worth was emphasized. (Garza Caligaris and Toledo 2004, 213)

Despite the structural inequalities that separated professional women from indigenous women, these dialogues marked the organizational processes and political agendas of both groups.

Different feminist civil associations were the result of these dialogues, and they opted for prioritizing the work with indigenous and peasant women. I became a feminist in this context and I was part of one of these experiences through the Women's Group from San Cristóbal (Grupo de Mujeres de San Cristóbal), founded in 1989 and renamed as COLEM in 1994. This organization emerged from a series of rapes against women who were members of nongovernmental organizations that took place during 1988 and 1989. Initially organized as a broad front against sexual and domestic violence, over time, the movement was consolidated as a civil association, and our work extended through educational, legal, and health areas, including workshops to promote gender consciousness.[31] Similar experiences developed in other indigenous regions of the country, as was the case of feminist organization Comaletzin AC, founded in 1987, whose members promoted the development of gender perspectives with indigenous and peasants from Morelos, Puebla, Sonora, and Chiapas.[32] The Center of Investigation and Action for Women (Centro de Investigación y Acción para la Mujer—CIAM) was another group founded in 1989 to support the organizational processes of indigenous women of the Chiapas highlands and Guatemalan refugees.[33] Women for Dialogue worked in Veracruz and Oaxaca, and the advisors of the Team of Women in Solidarity Action have worked with Purépecha women from Michoacán.[34]

These pioneer organizations have been followed by many more that have established constructive dialogues with indigenous women. Important examples of these dialogues are the work of Kinal Antzetik with the women of the CONAMI and many other feminist organizations that are part of the National Network of Rural Advisors and Promoters (Red Nacional de Asesoras y Promotoras Rurales).

However, the processes of institutionalization of feminist organizations that characterized the 1990s in Latin America, and which some authors have called the "NGOization of feminism" (see Álvarez 1998) or the "neoliberalization of feminism" (see Schild 2015), have brought about new challenges for the construction of political alliances between organized indigenous women and urban feminisms.

These authors have warned of the confluence that is under way between the neoliberal system's need to dismantle the welfare state and build an "individualist ethos" oriented toward the rationality of the market, and the role that feminist NGOs are playing by taking on tasks that were formerly the responsibility of the state and by contributing to the development of new female subjectivities that respond to these needs (see Schild 2014, 2015). In these power games, the appropriation of discourses on gender rights by neoliberal states has allowed them to attenuate the political radicalism of feminist agendas:

The institutionalization of a gender rights-based agenda has taken a very specific form in the context of broad neoliberal economic restructuring. The new discourse of "modernization" championed by governing elites is permeated by an individualized ethos of neoliberal politics whose core elements are the terms and values of market rationality, individual choice, personal responsibility, control over one's own fate and self-development. Neoliberalism is the new hegemony, understood not as a done deal or fixed ideology, but in the sense eloquently articulated by the anthropologist William Roseberry, as "a common material and meaningful framework for living through, talking about and acting upon social orders characterized by domination." (Schild 2014, 27)

In the following ethnographic window, we shall see how this process of institutionalizing the gender agenda takes place in the neoliberal context and how gender, ethnic, and class hierarchies influence the way in which universalist discourses regarding women's rights try to be imposed through international funding mechanisms.

THIRD ETHNOGRAPHIC WINDOW

GENDER HIERARCHIES IN WOMEN RIGHTS: COMPLICITY AND DISAPPOINTMENT

In May 2004, I felt ashamed to be part of a "tribunal"—one of those that are recurrent in different parts of the world to enable international agencies or feminist NGOs to judge the pertinence of the gender agendas of poor women in the Global South and decide whether their work on behalf of women's rights is worthy of receiving financial support. These public "trials" are not recognized as such by the "experts" who evaluate the proposals of the applicants and who end up playing a role of power through decision making and the imposition of values similar to that of a jury. On this occasion, the international financing was channeled through a prestigious feminist NGO in Mexico, which provided scholarships to indigenous women so that they could work for sexual and reproductive rights in their regions of origin.

Thinking, naïvely, that maybe my participation in these spaces could influence the construction of broader and less ethnocentric definitions of women's rights, I accepted the invitation from the NGO that administered these scholarships to be part of the group of "experts" that would evaluate the projects of the applicants.

The interviews and presentations of the projects took place at a swanky hotel in a town of the Mexican state of Morelos. The indigenous women of different parts of the country had traveled to this place in order to make a public defense of their projects. The six members of the panel were feminist scholars and/or activists, all non-indigenous, and the majority were from Mexico City. Seated in a semi-circle next to the board members of the NGO and the regional director of the international agency that was giving the financial resources for the scholarships, we started the interviews of the applicants.

One by one, the indigenous women passed in front of the "jury," some completing their presentations in perfect Spanish, while others presented in Spanish mixed with their own indigenous language; some did their presentation with the aid of a previously prepared flipchart, while others were proficient in the use of PowerPoint and the computer. All of them answered the questions of all six evaluators. It was Amanda's turn, a Nahuatl women from southern Veracruz with fifteen years' experience working as a health promoter. Through the flipchart, she spoke to us about the importance of traditional medicine for the self-care of indigenous women, the holistic conceptions of health that were relevant to indigenous medicine, and the importance of recovering them in attention to women's problems. The director of the funding agency, a bit tired by the lack of mention of women's reproductive rights, interrupted Amanda and asked her directly:

"How do you define reproductive health? What does your proposal have to do with women's reproductive rights?" A bit surprised by the interruption, Amanda responded, repeating a standard definition that appeared in the promotion pamphlets for the scholarships. The NGO official countered by asking "What do you think about abortion?"

Amanda was stunned by the question, and kept silent.

"Do you think indigenous women have a right to decide over their body?" continued the interviewer.

Amanda responded with another question: "Decide what?"

The official started to get desperate by the lack of concrete answers on the part of the applicant. The rest of us observed in complicit silence the obvious harassment. "What do you know about feminism?" the interviewer asked.

Amanda responded in paused manner, "I think that is ok that women have rights, but I differ with those feminists who fight men and want to separate both worlds."

"Which feminists are these?" asked the NGO official, "can you name any?" Amanda was about to burst into tears, when, outraged by the "display" of power we were witnessing, I interrupted the spokeswoman of the financing agency by saying, "I think you are mistaking the place and the person to whom to ask these questions; if you want, I can give you a long list of exclusionary or intolerant feminists."

Amanda was awarded the scholarship and, to my good fortune, never again was I invited to participate in these "trials." This experience provides an account of the way international financing is making an impact on gender agendas of indigenous women, legitimizing some struggles and delegitimizing others. Some feminist organizations have been accomplices to these impositions, prioritizing a gender agenda that has reproductive health and, more specifically, the right to abortion and to contraception, in the middle of it.

These spaces of encounters and conflicts among feminists and indigenous women are not exclusive of the Mexican reality and account for the way in which the discourses and practices around women's rights are not always spaces of resistance. They also articulate how these discourses could even play a role as globalized localisms (that is, local knowledge that has become globalized and is presented as "universal") when attempting to impose views on a free and rational individual as the subject of legal rights. These conceptions have roots in a specific place in space and time: the "European Illustration" (see de Sousa Santos 1998a). With time, they have acquired the character of globalized localism (that is, they have become transnational practices that impact local conditions) when becoming imperative by international agencies that, with the mediation of national states and feminist NGOs, have imposed a homogenizing conception of universal gender rights. In our last section, we will talk about the contradictory role of these discourses and transnational practices.

DIALOGUES WITH STATES AND INTERNATIONAL AGENCIES

It is important to consider the economic and political context in which feminist NGOs and international agencies have increased their influence in the promotion of universalist perspectives on "women's rights" in indigenous and peasant regions of Latin America.

The neoliberal hegemony described by Verónica Schild has not only implied the reduction of the social functions of the state and a redesign of its intervention in the economy to allow the "free" operation of the markets, but it has also enabled the promotion of new forms of governance to ensure that citizens take care of their own well-being (Schild 2014). Commercial opening, deregulation, and the reduction of public services have been followed by the promotion of public policies toward a new model of "market citizenship." It is in this context that feminist NGOs, with their programs for women's "empowerment," have contributed to developing the new subjectivities required by the neoliberal system (see Schild 2015). In their advocacy of new targeted "anti-poverty" programs that reject general subsidies in order to apply them to specific populations, many NGOs have found a new source of financing as mediators in the programs directed toward indigenous women.

In this new role as intermediaries, many feminist NGOs have taken on the task of mobilizing the "social capital" of indigenous women for the purpose of development (Radcliff 2008). Paradoxically, many of the methodologies of popular education that formerly served to promote collective reflection on class and gender inequalities are now used as training tools to develop citizens who are "responsible for themselves."

Although it is important to consider that these neoliberal economic and social reforms have implied the reformulation of the state's forms of governance creating a new "market citizenship" (one in which indigenous people are increasingly responsible for their own welfare, self-regulation, and successful competition in the free play of social forces; see Harvey 2001), it is also important to recognize that, in many contexts, these reforms have created new opportunities for autonomous organization, generating new responses and strategies of resistance.

Like other dialogues described in this chapter, the dialogues with international agencies, NGOs, and government representatives have been contradictory processes in which spaces of encounters and reflection for indigenous women have been created and in which some of their initiatives have been supported economically. However, they have tended to impose a gender and development agenda that does not always correspond to indigenous women's needs (see Radcliff and Pequeño 2010). In some contexts, the state initiatives have helped to co-opt women's movements that are more radical in their political and economic demands.

The emancipatory or regulatory potential (de Sousa Santos 1998b) of women's rights promoted by state public policy in Latin America has depended, to a large extent, on the social tissue of the regions in which they are applied. It has also depended on the capacity of the social actors to give the state initiatives another sense more in tune with its cultural context. It is necessary to recognize, for example, that leadership scholarships for indigenous women (to which I make reference in our "Third Ethnographic Window") have allowed strengthening the ant-like work of many women within their organizations by locating their specific demands inside the political agendas of the indigenous movement.

Despite the economic and political power that lies behind the liberal and universalizing definitions of women's rights (see Schild 2015), these discourses and practices have been responded to and given new meanings by organized indigenous women struggling for fairer relations between men and women. Their discourses are based on definitions of personhood that transcend Western individualism, understandings of a dignified life that go beyond the right to property, and concepts of equity that include not only complementarity between genders but also between human beings and nature.

These contradictory dialogues, with a gender agenda formulated and imposed from the Global North, have existed since the 1970s. In that decade, the topic of women was incorporated by international development agencies and international cooperation. The inequalities between men and women, as a problem for the development of national projects, began to be acknowledged by the states and the international community, in part as a response to the pressures of feminist movements but also because of what the exclusion of women meant for capitalist development in certain circles of public life.

In the decade of the 1970s, a series of international conferences took place, and they marked a breakthrough in public policies for women and their inclusion in the priorities of international cooperation. In 1973, the Food and Agriculture Organization of the UN organized the World Food Summit, for the first time recognizing the contribution of women in the production of food and the nutrition of the family. A year later, in 1974, the UN conference on population in Bucharest placed, in the center of international debate, the problem of overpopulation. They identified the woman, in her reproductive role, as the main figure responsible for the reduction of the average number of children. International financing began to be promoted so that the governments of the so-called Third World would lower their birth-rates, assuming that poverty could be reduced simply by reducing fertility.

It was in 1975 that the topic of women acquired international relevance, with the Conference on Women in Mexico City, which established the declaration of the United Nations Decade for Women (1975–1985). A product of these initiatives was the Convention on the Elimination of All Forms of Discrimination Against Women, adopted by the general assembly on December 18, 1979, and entered into force on September 3, 1981.

These initiatives, and the commitments that states acquired from the signing of international conventions, contributed to a cultural climate that legitimizes the struggle of the feminist movements worldwide and, in a certain way, denaturalizes gender inequalities.[35] But parallel to this, a discourse and a hegemonic practice started to build around women's rights that imposed certain visions of the world and delimited the radicalism of the initial demands of the feminist movements.

More than structural transformations or initiatives to change discriminatory gender ideologies, what we initially see in all three regions is the emergence of governmental programs to support productive projects or training workshops that reproduce traditional gender roles or promote "individual empowerment" so marginalized women could be responsible for their own welfare. Since the 1960s, "Third World" women are becoming the main beneficiaries of the welfare programs operated by national and international aid agencies. These welfare programs were conceived of to alleviate the needs of poor women exclusively in regards to their roles as mothers and housewives. Thus, the dichotomy between well-being and productivity was created, impacting the perspectives on development of the principal international agencies. The most important resources should be directed at a productive activity that is market-oriented and the assistance directed at well-being. Secondary and residual aid was directed at vulnerable and dependent groups, such as women and children. To the extent that economic growth is considered, it was the dominant objective of development; these welfare programs had, in large part, a residual character and the programs were offered only when the principal planning requirements had been met and they were dispensed at times of economic austerity (see Kabeer 1998).

However, under the influence of a widespread feminist movement in Europe, the United States, and Latin America, these representations of women as dependent and outside the productive and market activities started to be rejected by many women (in the academy as well as in the same development agencies). This criticism was advanced and documented in the now-classic work of Esther Boserup, *Women and Economic Development*, in which the productive role of women was defended and directly challenged the orthodox equivalence between women and domesticity (Boserup 1983 [1970]). Boserup argued that many colonial and postcolonial governments have systemically overlooked women in the diffusion of new technologies, extension services, and other inputs (thanks in part to their view of the world). Their work was fundamental to diminishing the emphasis on the investment for well-being as a new perspective in equality for women in the development process. However, despite her critical feminist perspectives, Boserup reproduced an ethnocentric vision that is still relevant in the rhetoric of development (Boserup 1983 [1970]). Knowing that poverty and underdevelopment problems of women in the "Third World" is a problem of lack of access to technology and to the market economy, the modernization of the productive processes would imply a larger participation (in terms of equality with men) in the benefits of development.

This opens up a new paradigm that is known as Women in Development (WID), through which the emphasis on well-being is substituted with an emphasis on effectiveness and the promotion of support for productive projects aimed at women. The idea that women were productive agents whose true potential had been underutilized was the basis of this new phase in development policies. With the growing influence of a free-market philosophy in funding agencies, support for projects of social well-being have been reduced to a minimum.

The experiences of the women supposedly "benefited" by the WID focus show us that the participation in new productive projects, the appropriation of new agricultural technologies, and the integration into the market economy, when they are not accompanied by substantial changes in family and community structures of gender domination, result in a policy for female exploitation. Now women had to deal with housework, subsistence activities, and the new productive projects promoted by WID, while the men of the families appropriated the meager economic benefits of these programs. Although the WID focus was important to ending the old political equivalence of women/reproduction/well-being, the equivalence of women/production/effectiveness constituted the new hegemonic discourse on women's rights that has been exported by international funding agencies.

These "localized globalisms" on women's rights have been promoted by Latin American governments as part of the initiatives to incorporate women into a model of development and comply with international commitments to promoting public policies that strive for gender "equality." The underlying logic in many of the government programs aimed at rural and indigenous women is that the process of development would advance in a much smoother way if women were incorporated into it.

The United States Agency for International Development (USAID) has been an important vehicle for globalizing an agenda for women's rights that arises from the WID, and whose underlying logic is that women constitute an untapped resource capable of providing economic benefit to development. Under the influence of these global discourses, bestowing rights to women involves incorporating them into a model of development that seems like the civilizing horizon for all humanity; by contrast, local cultures are viewed as responsible for "stopping the development and excluding women." Pakistani feminist Naila Kabeer shows us the way in which this vision of the world is exported and imposed by the development agencies to the whole planet:

> There is a close relation between the world view that powerful development agencies have and the kind of knowledge they may promote, finance and act upon. Some explorations of the methodological foundation of this worldview have contributed in discovering the hierarchy of knowledge over which that worldview is built; a hierarchy that privileges certain types of information (scientists and positivists) over others (local and experimental); certain types of informers (neutral, impartial) over others (committed and involved). The origins of this hierarchy is in the epistemological liberal tradition that contemplates reality in an essentially atomized and typified manner. (Kabeer 1998, 85)

This discourse on women's rights and development presents itself as a "universal" perspective and is opposed to the cultural practices of indigenous people by defining these practices in a limited way. In this process of "culturization" of gender inequalities and "deculturization" of women's rights discourses, the Latin American states have played a fundamental role in the complicity of feminist NGOs. The modernizing and developmental discourse has tended to blame the "indigenous cultures" and the "customs and traditions" of female exclusion, presenting the panacea for development and women's rights as a "decultured" solution for that exclusion.[36]

Something similar has happened in the imposition of a universalizing conception of reproductive rights, wherein these priorities have been central in international cooperation. This view of reproductive rights has heavily influenced the public policy of the health-care sector, as in the political agenda of feminist organizations. Without denying the importance of the recognition of the existence of "reproductive rights," since the International Reunion on Women and Health in Amsterdam (1984), it is necessary to signal that the broader definitions of these rights (including the right to all economic and social conditions that enable the health of women) have been substituted by a regulatory discourse that reduces the concept of "reproductive rights" to birth control and the right to abortion.

Some important Global South feminists, such as Sylvia Marcos and Shu-mei Shih, refer to the network of power that underlies the discourse of reproductive health. They also talk about the silence and limitations of the discourse, declaring: "The global movement for women's health has focused much of its agenda on reproductive rights, as if several other important topics regarding women's health did not exist. Poor women are dying of starvation, from curable diseases and lack many other things that are indispensable for their wellbeing and survival" (Shih et al. 2005, 147). They continue: "The most extreme negative implication of population control through rhetoric of the reproductive rights is that it echoes the old imperialist paradigm of eugenics. While developed countries are promoting the reproduction due to the aging of their population and the low birth rates, in developing or underdeveloped countries there is a reproduction control in the name of 'right of choice of the women over their bodies'" (Shih et al. 2005, 148).

The globalization of liberal definitions of women's rights, that are presented as universal, has been used to justify military intervention by the United States in those countries whose "patriarchal and antidemocratic cultures" violate the rights of women. Charles Hirschkind and Saba Mahmood have analyzed the responsibility of the United States government in strengthening and establishing the Taliban regime in Afghanistan and the subsequent counterinsurgent use of human rights that the administration of George W. Bush used as an argument to justify military intervention in the region (Hirschkind and Mahmood 2002). In the Mexican case, the state and other groups of power have used similar arguments to deny political rights to the indigenous people.

In the next chapter we will see how organized indigenous women have confronted the representations of tradition that have been used to disqualify their cultures and legal systems by stating that the indigenous regulatory systems are in a revision process in which indigenous women are having a pivotal role.

FINAL REFLECTIONS

The new political identities that have been built in the context of these contradictory dialogues are a reflection of the heterogeneity of the Latin American indigenous movement and of the scope of their political demands. These new voices are being heard all along the continent, reflecting the concern for political and economic redistribution present in the peasant and political-military struggles of the 1970s and 1980s; these are demands for recognition not only of their ethnic identities but also of the gender identities of women.

What we see in this historical review is that the creation of spaces for collective reflection have been fundamental both for the emergence of discourses that denaturalize gender inequality and for the vernacularization of the discourses on women's rights. Many times these spaces have been created from the interaction with other social actors whose perspectives of justice and rights have been placed in dialogue with the local perspectives on a "dignified life" or a "just life." The majority of the collective spaces explored in this chapter did not have as their main objective the reflection on women's rights, but when women were included in the dialogue or debate on the exclusion of the poor or indigenous peoples, they acquired the analytical tools to reflect on other forms of exclusion, including their own exclusions as indigenous women. Thus, they develop new languages to name violence and exclusions that were previously naturalized. These moments are called "points of rupture" (Roseberry 1994), or "penetrations" (Willis 1981), in which the "common sense" (Comaroff and Comaroff 1991), or "doxa" (Bourdieu 1977), is questioned. In this way, what was previously assumed to be natural has ceased to be, and has been included within the limits of the debatable and questionable, causing a crisis in hegemonic discourses about indigenous and gender hierarchies. Some of those spaces for collective organization were promoted by the neoliberal states as forms of governmentality, manifested as "individual empowerment" and a "market citizenship," but indigenous women have developed counterhegemonic strategies to confront these discourses.

Through the different "ethnographic windows" in this chapter, the emergence of multiple discourses and diverse forms for naming women's exclusions were documented, as were as the multiple forms of imaging emancipation and justice. In the following chapters, we will look at how distinct forms of naming have influenced the types of political strategies that have been developed in each country in order to transform their own spaces of justice or appropriate the discourse of women's rights.

The political histories of distinct indigenous movements in Mexico, Guatemala, and Colombia have influenced the way in which indigenous women claim the rights discourse or develop their own concepts to analyze the exclusion and to name emancipation. In the case of Mexico, the Zapatista movement has been fundamental in order to legitimize the specific demands of indigenous women and in order to propose women's rights that do not contradict the demands for collective rights of their people. At the same time, the development of rural feminism that has been open to dialogues with indigenous women, and to reconsidering their strategies of struggle based on these critiques, have caused the rights-based discourse to be appropriated by the indigenous women's movement.

In the case of Guatemala, the themes of racism and internal colonialism have been central to the agenda of indigenous women and, in many cases, have been more important to their political agenda than the struggle against gender violence and exclusion. Also, the emergence and consolidation of the Mayan movement has created a cultural climate in which the discourse on indigenous cosmovision has converted into a language that negates the inequality between men and women based on the concept of complementarity. However, paradoxically, in other contexts, it has also been a way to claim their own language in the construction of more just relations between women and men. Before a masculine leadership that refuses to recognize its exclusions, utilizing the discourse of harmony and complementarity, the Mayan women have taken up the same discourse, giving it a new meaning as political inspiration in order to reconstruct a complementarity in equality that colonialism and patriarchal violence have destroyed. In reaction to these discourses, other critical perspectives between the Mayan women have denounced the dangers of essentialism, claiming a historical perspective of their cultures and their own rights, as we shall see in chapter 3.

In the case of Colombia, there have been experiences of war, displacement, and paramilitarization that have led indigenous women to organize for peace with justice and in defense of territorial rights. Their specific agendas as women have been much less central in their struggles than in the cases of indigenous women's organizations in Mexico and Guatemala. However, they began to develop strategies to confront the violence against women as part of the defense of the family and the community, as we shall see in the analysis of the School of Indigenous Law developed by ONIC in the region of Cauca.

The reconstruction of political genealogies of organized indigenous women shows us the diversity of experiences that mark their strategies of struggle. These multiple dialogues remind us that there exist other ways of imagining ourselves in the world and constructing emancipatory strategies. Although it seems commonplace to say that the cultural and social context determines the manner in which we construct our sense of personhood (and the manner in which we imagine justice), the monoculture of Western knowledge has universalized European local knowledge that is based on liberal and neoliberal individualism, proposing a linear conception of time in which "progress" is determined by specific forms of consumption marked by capital.

The voices of indigenous women that seem to emerge from the margins, from spaces erased by silencing strategies, come to destabilize our certainties. They question perspectives of progress and well-being that have been universalized together with the concepts of liberal rights that have given great support to contemporary democratic struggles. The certainties that, as "committed intellectuals" or as "feminist activists," we can "raise awareness" or teach the way and strategies to confront domination have fallen apart before the voices that question utopias of progress constructed from the political left or right. Behind these voices underlie other epistemologies that come from a concept that it is not possible to separate the individual and collective, where nature is not a resource at the service of human beings. These are voices full of contradictions that also reproduce discourses of power in relation to "womanhood" or the naturalization of racial hierarchies. It is not my proposal to idealize them; rather, I show that other spaces exist to think about the world and that other forms of theorizing about their transformation are available. The construction of political alliances between diverse social movements requires the construction of dialogues that denaturalize gender, class, and race hierarchies.

3

INDIGENOUS JUSTICES

New Spaces of Struggle for Women

N THIS CHAPTER, I analyze the possibilities and limitations of communitarian justice for indigenous women in Mexico, Guatemala, and Colombia.
I show how the vernacularization of women's rights discourses took place
based on the dialogues described in the previous chapter, and I document how
these new perspectives have influenced women's participation in the spaces of
communal justice and transformed what is understood by indigenous law.

I address different experiences of indigenous justice where women have
been able to influence the reconstitution of communal normativity in the
practices of justice, maintaining the tension between the analysis of neoliberal
forms of governance and counterhegemonic strategies with which indigenous
women in the three regions have responded to the constitutive power of state
legality.

The acknowledgement of "indigenous law" or "indigenous justice systems"
by most Latin American constitutions has meant changes in communitarian
justice in indigenous regions. The wave of constitutional reforms that has swept
the continent during the last three decades has had the common recognition
of the cultural diversity of the Latin American nations. In the vast majority of
the cases, it has resulted in the acknowledgement of indigenous law and local
justice spaces. These reforms, in some cases, have entailed a strengthening of the
political autonomy through the recognition of indigenous jurisdiction (Sánchez

Botero 2001). In other cases, we find processes of reconstruction or reinvention of communitarian justice (Sierra 2009, 2013, 2014; Terven 2009) and experiences of undermining the existent autonomy prior to constitutional reforms after the state creation of new indigenous tribunals that have overcome the local justice institutions (see Buenrostro 2013).

The coexistence of parallel spaces and indigenous justice has happened since the colonial era when Laws of the Indies (*Leyes de Indias*) recognized indigenous jurisdictions subordinate to the Spanish Crown.[1] The indigenous justice systems have gone through several reconstruction processes in permanent dialogue with the justice systems of the postcolonial nation-states. More than ancestral justices, they are historical products that incorporate the principles and epistemologies of the indigenous peoples, the moral and religious Catholic principles (a product of five hundred years of colonial occupation), and the legal proceedings taken from the law of the state. Despite the liberal reforms of the nineteenth century imposing a legal monism on most of the Latin American countries, these parallel systems kept functioning de facto and, in many contexts, were tolerated before the inability of the state to respond to the justice necessities of the indigenous regions.

The liberal and monocultural practices and discourses started to be openly questioned by a growing indigenous continental movement that denounced the continuity of internal colonialism and claimed not only their cultural recognition but their autonomic and territorial rights. The commemoration of the five hundredth anniversary of the wrongly termed "Encounter of Two Worlds," in 1992, created the conditions whereby indigenous representatives of the whole continent united their voices against racism and exclusion that characterized the national projects of the different Latin American countries.

The critical analysis of society worldwide, the indigenous movement, and the failure of indigenous policies of integration and acculturation have led a whole generation of Latin American anthropologists to sympathize and show solidarity with the indigenous struggles for rights. Since the 1970s, this link between the academic circles and the indigenous movements made possible the critical reflections of anthropologists (such as Guillermo Bonfil Batalla, Rodolfo Stavenhagen, Carlos Guzmán Bockler, Roberto Cardoso de Oliveira, and Héctor Díaz Polanco) that were appropriated and debated by indigenous leaders in confronting the *indigenista* projects that promoted acculturation in the name of development. Through different perspectives (all of them under the influence of theories of internal colonialism), this generation of critical anthropologists confronted the functionalist representations that U.S. cultural anthropology has created of the Latin American indigenous peoples as inhabitants of isolated communities that are harmonious and inheritors of an ancestral culture. In sharp contrast with these representations, the analysis of their insertion in systems of inequality, racism, and economic marginalization that were hidden under the discourse of national integration was denounced.[2]

In part, as a response to the demands of indigenous organizations during the 1980s, the process of legislative reforms began to recognize the multicultural character of various nations of Latin America. The discourse of legal monism was substituted by one of legal pluralism and cultural diversity, and by the need to develop multicultural public policies. These reforms differ greatly among countries, but the majority of them include the recognition of the multicultural character of the country, the collective rights of the indigenous people, the recognition of their normative systems, their autonomous governments, and the right to use and preserve their own indigenous languages.[3] It is from these reforms that government census recognized the existence of forty million men and women who recognize themselves as indigenous (approximately 10 percent of the inhabitants of Latin America).[4]

In this new political context, the defenders of the universal citizenship have raised their voices to reject or limit the reach of the multicultural reforms by trying to isolate the cultural dimension from the territorial or political aspects of the reforms. To separate the recognition policies from the policies of redistribution has been the strategy of the Latin American neoliberal states to mitigate the radicalism of indigenous demands. Many academics committed to helping the indigenous people have written and denounced the new obstacles these reforms create for indigenous autonomy (Hernández Castillo, Sierra, and Paz 2004). However, other voices have questioned the limitations of the struggles for indigenous rights from other political positions, pointing out the limitations of indigenous identity as a space of political mobilization, or denouncing the way in which it is used by neoliberal governments as a new strategy for control and regulation.

These perspectives analyze the multicultural constitutionalism as a new way of neoliberal governance that has brought the predominance of the discourses regarding rights as a path of "narrating or codifying" the indigenous identities that often give way to the construction of essentialist discourses on indigenous cultures (see Sieder and Witchell 2001, 201), displacing other discourses on social justice as those that referenced internal colonialism or economic exploitation.

These perspectives state that the multicultural reforms, by giving indigenous communities the responsibilities formerly belonging to the state, respond to a necessity of the neoliberal agenda to decentralize and promote a more participative civil society, leaving behind what was known as a regime of neoliberal citizenship (Yashar 2005). The social adjustment needed by the neoliberal model includes the construction of a plural state in which everyone participates, which can coincide with the political agenda of the indigenous people that demand greater autonomy and larger spaces of participation. Inside these perspectives, Charles Hale has popularized the concept of "neoliberal multiculturalism" to refer to the way neoliberal states have appropriated multicultural recognition policies as a strategy to silence or displace the more radical demands of the indigenous movement (Hale 2005).

Despite the efforts of later work that tried to demonstrate that countries with fewer structural reforms have adopted a multicultural agenda, and vice versa, the link between neoliberalism and multiculturalism is not as immediate (Van Cott 2005). These critical perspectives surrounding the multiculturalism of Latin American states have allowed us to nuance the achievements of indigenous movements and to reassess the centrality of legislative struggles within the political strategies of these movements.

It is in this political context that the issue of indigenous justice has come to occupy a central focus in the political claims of indigenous movements, as in the analytical concerns of Latin American legal anthropology. Was their recognition just a part of the neoliberal reform to cheapen the costs of the justice system? Was it only an "additive justice" that did not represent a real recognition of indigenous jurisdictions or political autonomy? Were the essentialists' perspectives of indigenous law, which were taking away its historical character, given a priority? Was this recognition a backward step for the rights of indigenous women?

Throughout the last decade, I have been able to participate in three collective research projects[5] that approached some of these questions in permanent dialogue with indigenous organizations. These organizations have appropriated rights discourses as part of their political struggle, and they claim the recognition of indigenous justice as a part of their autonomic rights. In our collective projects, we set out to explore the contradictions that exist between the new forms of neoliberal governance (through legal reforms) and the counterhegemonic uses of justice by indigenous men and women in their everyday practices (see Baitenmann et al. 2008, Hernández Castillo 2005, 2008; Sierra, Hernández Castillo, and Sieder 2013; Hernández Castillo and Terven forthcoming). These experiences revealed that the hegemony of the state is always an unfinished process. Thus, the multicultural neoliberal agenda is not entirely successful. In its need to strengthen civil society and promote decentralization, it has opened, once more, opportunities for indigenous people seeking to expand their spaces of autonomy and self-determination.

I have reservations about analyses of these experiences (and others that have taken place in other geographic and cultural contexts) that emphasize the productive capacity of state discourses on indigenous rights if those perspectives do not recognize the capacity of the social actors to reject or resist these constructions.

The impact of the multicultural reforms in spaces of justice is as diverse as the people who inhabit the continent; their "regulatory" or "emancipatory" character has depended on many factors. It is not the objective of this chapter to make an exhaustive analysis on the impact of those reforms, but rather to analyze some concrete experiences in which indigenous women have participated in processes of "reconstruction" of communitarian justice. I am especially concerned with taking into account their critical experiences of those "customs and traditions" that exclude them, and the transformation of those rules that discriminate against women.

Our studies have documented that systems of indigenous justice have certain practical advantages for indigenous men and women, being that the procedures take place in the language of the plaintiff, inside their communities, and under their frames of cultural reference. This does not guarantee that completely harmonious intercommunitarian relations take place, nor that conciliatory systems do not reconcile subordinated groups within a community by reaffirming their positions of subordination (Hernández Castillo 2002a). Often those who judge women are the men from the communities, according to patriarchal structures and gender-excluding ideologies (see Calla and Paulson 2008). However, in many regions of Latin America these discourses are being contested by women who claim a different way of being "indigenous" by reformulating communitarian justice under new terms.

In this chapter, I aim to approach the experiences of indigenous women in Mexico, Guatemala, and Colombia and their use of communitarian justice as spaces of cultural production of new indigenous and gender identities. Beyond the limitations of the multicultural reforms, they have created a cultural climate for negotiation about how the concepts of "culture" and "justice" are understood in indigenous communities. When practices that used to be seen as part of "life itself" are now labeled as "culture," and when ways of resolving the communitarian conflicts are named "indigenous law," new spaces of enunciation are created which are being occupied by counter-hegemonic discourses from indigenous women.

THE RIGHTS OF WOMEN REGARDING THEIR CUSTOMS AND TRADITIONS: ORIGINS OF A DEBATE

On the January 28, 1992, the Official Diary of the Federation (Diario Oficial de la Federación) announced a constitutional reform that recognized the pluricultural character of the Mexican nation, establishing in the second article that: "The Mexican nation has a pluricultural composition originally founded in their indigenous people." This reform, that according to the indigenous leaders of the time "arrived with 500 years of delay," marked the beginning of a new cultural climate in which the main political struggles of indigenous people occur through the demand of the recognition of rights.

Since the promulgation of this constitutional reform, the indigenous people of Mexico responded by demanding their participation in a public consultation to establish a regulatory law that defines in concrete terms how the reform is applied. The Zapatista uprising in January 1994 pressured government agents to respond to the indigenous organization's consultation demands. It was in this context that consultative forums were organized throughout the country, making use of the organizational networks of the official party (Institutional Revolutionary Party—PRI), and excluding the most critical voices within the indigenous movement. Ninety-nine percent of the participants in these forums were indigenous men, most of whom were close to the party in power. When questioning the organizers of these forums on the absence of indigenous women, they responded: "It's because women are not interested in politics." This provocative answer led me and other indigenous members of my organization[6] to contact midwives who are part of the Organization of Indigenous Healers of the State of Chiapas (Organización de Médicos Indígenas del Estado de Chiapas— OMIECH) and artisans of different crafts and agricultural cooperatives to propose the organization of a workshop to discuss the constitutional reform to the

second article. The workshop, "The Rights of Women with our Customs and Traditions," took place in San Cristóbal de las Casas, Chiapas, on May 19 and 20,
1994. More than fifty women attended: Tsotsiles, Tseltales, Tojolabales, and
Mames from very diverse communities (Grupo de Mujeres de San Cristóbal
1994). At the beginning, the objective was to discuss the second article, analyze
it, and reflect upon the possibilities that were opened for the access of justice for
indigenous women. However, given the arid nature of the legal language in the
constitutional text, the participants proposed including the Women's Revolutionary Law, made public by the EZLN in January 1994, which they felt much more
accurately articulated their everyday problems. The discussion groups were coordinated by two indigenous women of my organization: Juana María Ruíz and
Sebastiana Santiz (Tsotsil and Tseltal speakers, respectively) and by two members
of the OMIECH, Micaela Gómez and Pascuala López. The Mam women from
the sierra, who no longer speak their Mayan language, formed their own working
groups in Spanish, coordinated by Doña Cedema Morales, from the Nan Choch
cooperative. The bilingual teachers were the ones responsible for elaborating the
minutes and reading them aloud in the different languages to ensure that all participants' feelings were reflected in the summaries.

The discussions of article four were based on the definition of various terms
included in the first paragraph:

The Mexican nation has a pluricultural composition originally founded on its
indigenous peoples. The law shall protect and promote the development of their
languages, cultures, ways, customs, resources and specific forms of social organization, and shall guarantee its members effective access to state law. In the actions
and procedures regarding land in which they take part, their judicial practices and
traditions shall be taken into account in the terms established by law. (Mexican
Constitution, Article IV)

What does "pluricultural" mean? What is meant by "originally founded"?
What is the state law? What are the terms established by the law? The simple
act of translating these lines says something about the complexity inherent in
polling eight hundred pages with fifteen law initiatives in two days, as the state
government intended.

The support materials created by the Legal Anthropology Subdirection of the
National Indigenous Institute (INI) assisted with the task of analysis (Gómez
1992). Although the booklet pretended to make an apology for the advantages

that such an amendment would bring to the indigenous peoples, its own contents gave the participants some elements to question the benefits that they, as women, would derive from the amendment. An example from the booklet narrates the case of José, who was tried for killing cows for his son's funeral. His daughter-in-law said the cows were hers, and another witness commented, "he was accused of stealing the cows, but this is part of our tradition." The booklet explains: "in any trial, indigenous people may submit a cultural expert witness report as evidence; this means that the traditional authorities may explain that certain actions are part of the culture of their community, and are not considered as breaking the law. The court authorities will then take these elements into consideration" (Gómez 1992, 40). The questions came: But what if the cows belonged to the daughter-in-law? What if she was widowed and needed her cattle? When it says, "he was accused," who accused him? Was it the daughter-in-law? Then is the traditional authority going to take away the daughter-in-law's cows? These questions illustrate the complexity of making an "expert witness cultural report" when the traditional authorities do not equally represent all the community member's concerns.

The women, particularly those from the highlands, also debated the issues of forced marriage and selling girls into marriage. The women from Teopisca, and those expelled from San Juan Chamula, said, "We are forced into marriage in our communities. Boyfriends are not allowed. It is not a fair way to treat people; we are mistreated when we must marry by force. They should respect our decisions." Their counterparts from Chenalhó added, "It would be better to put down on paper that we women say some traditions do not respect us, and we want those traditions changed. Violence is not right. It's not fair that women be traded for money. Neither is it fair that women, because of 'tradition,' are not allowed to be representatives, or to own land. We don't want any bad traditions" (Grupo de Mujeres de San Cristóbal 1994, 22).

The positive aspects of tradition were discussed as well. The Tseltal women from Ocosingo spoke of the need to preserve their native language: "to show that we are indigenous and think differently than those who speak only Spanish." The women from the Sierra Madre spoke of the need to recover the respect for nature and for Mother Earth that their ancestors had before the arrival of pesticides and fertilizers. This knowledge has guided the agro-ecological co-ops where some women are members. Tsotsil women from the highlands spoke of the importance of traditional medicine, practices that midwives and other traditional healers of the OMIECH recover and promote.

A constant feature in all of the workshop groups was discussion on the right of women to own land and to have support for production projects. The women made an important point about the constitutional amendment that says, "In the actions and procedures regarding land in which they [indigenous peoples] take part, their judicial practices and traditions shall be taken into account." They pointed out that this could serve to reinforce the discrimination that many women are currently subjected to regarding their right to own land. Mam women from the sierra commented, "the problem here is that, if the traditional authorities say that we can't inherit land, Article Four is going to leave us women without land, and if we are widowed or have children, we are not going to get any land. Maybe this amendment goes together with the one that applies to Article 27, which doesn't benefit women either, or families" (Grupo de Mujeres de San Cristóbal 1994).

DIVERSE EXPERIENCES OF EXCLUSION

The encounter brought together women of very diverse experiences. Artisans, midwives, merchants, and peasants discussed the discrimination to which they are subjected in their work by their bosses, the government, and even by their indigenous male partners. Catholic, Traditionalist, and Protestant women shared their experiences of what being a woman in their communities is like in either urban settings or peasant organizations. Through socio-dramas and debates, women exposed the different forms that discrimination can take in the Chiapas sierra, rainforest, and highlands.

Regional, cultural, and organizational differences have marked different ways of "being a woman." Comparing experiences and finding common ground empowered the women to build social communities. Through a socio-drama analyzing the different ways in which indigenous peoples experience discrimination, they discovered different histories and experiences. For Tsotsil artisan women, discrimination came from the *cashlanes* (non-indigenous people), who showed no respect for them and refused to pay a fair price for their products. Discrimination also came from the government and its institutions, which not only did not support independent artisan organizations but actually hampered them. Discrimination came from the tourists, who treated them like animals in a zoo, disrespectfully aiming their cameras at them. Doña Margarita, a monolingual Tsotsil woman from San Pedro Chenalhó, amused us all with her impersonation of a tourist wearing sunglasses, taking pictures of the women while at the same time haggling over the price of their wares. When laughter subsided, there was something sad in the air, and someone spoke up: "This is not just a theatrical representation, this is how things really are. This is true" (Grupo de Mujeres de San Cristóbal 1994).

For the Tseltal in the Ocosingo rainforest, oppression came from the large cattle ranchers, from the middlemen to whom they had to sell their products cheaply in order to get them out of the jungle, from the ladino women who pay little for the vegetables they buy in the market, from the government that did not hear their voices, and from the officials in whose waiting rooms they languish. They spoke for the indigenous domestic workers who follow their mistresses, carrying the bags of groceries and haggling for them, because ladino women will not even attempt to speak to the Tseltal merchants.

Mam women from the Sierra Madre spoke of the experiences of their grandparents, who the government forced to give up their language so they could be told apart from their Guatemalan counterparts; they told of the time when their traditional clothes were burned in huge bonfires in the plazas as part of the effort "to civilize the Indians." They told us of the time when language was hidden, when the government forced them to forget. Their main problem is not the cashlanes or ladinos since ethnic barriers are not as unbridgeable in the sierra as they are in the highlands. Rather, it's the government and the public officials who create discrimination. In their socio-drama they told of how they are treated by public officials, of the disrespect with which they are addressed, and of the government's refusal to support their production projects just because they are women.

Tojolabal women from the municipality of La Independencia talked about discrimination in the health-care system. In their socio-drama they illustrated how they are treated by doctors who do perfunctory check-ups, and who don't bother to hide their disgust at the poverty of the women's clothes, giving them any pill just to get them out of the office.

The role-playing elicited amusement and laughter followed by intense debate in which Tsotsil, Tseltal, Tojolabal, and Spanish mixed and melted, translated back and forth with amazing skill and speed by the interpreters of the San Cristóbal de las Casas Women's Group and the OMIECH. Anger and outrage displaced laughter as women spoke about who mistreats them and why. Their responses were marked by their organizing experience and by the various levels at which they had considered the issues. For many Tsotsil artisans and midwives, discrimination came from cashlanes and *caciques* (political bosses). Racism has characterized inter-ethnic relationships, and the main issue is not being poor, but being indigenous.

A woman from the highlands remarked in Tsotsil: "We are looked down upon because we are Indians, we are not respected, we are deceived." The women from the sierra, members of agro-ecological co-ops and experienced participants in peasant organizations, warned, "This is what is apparent; but really we are all mistreated by the capitalist system." Tseltal women from the jungle added, "It's the rich people, the people who have power, who have exploited indigenous peoples for over 500 years." Someone objected, "But we are also mistreated by our own kind." Artisan women who had been thrown out of San Juan Chamula told of the indigenous caciques who had taken away their land and chased them out of their communities with impunity, while women from the sierra introduced the issue of domestic violence to the discussion.

Indigenous women are mistreated not only by the cashlanes, the wealthy, the government, the doctors, ranchers, and caciques, but also, at times, by their own male partners, husbands, fathers, or brothers. While commenting on a scene from the video *Ya no más: Siete historias de violencia doméstica* (No More: Seven Cases of Domestic Violence), produced by the Women's Group from San Cristóbal (Grupo de Mujeres de San Cristóbal de las Casas), someone said: "It is as if they have gone and looked at our own stories."

For the first time, the issue of "tradition" was discussed: "It's part of the tradition to force a woman to marry even if she dislikes the man." "Sometimes it's part of the tradition to trade women for cattle." "It's our tradition that the man who beats his wife has to pay one day's labor as penalty, only to go back and beat her again for telling on him." Someone points out, "This happens to us not because we don't speak Spanish, and not because we are poor, or uneducated, but because we are women. It's not understood that women are not things they can buy and then treat as they like." The insight with which these women generated class and race analyses has been a constant in the political debates about indigenous justice and the need to reform it.

As a final product of the workshop, the participants prepared the minutes that were sent to the state congress. This document was the basis of a video that circulated among the participating communities where Juana María Ruíz, a Tsotsil activist of the San Cristóbal de las Casas Women's Group, read the document in Spanish and Tsotsil so that those who do not know how to read or write could access it.[7] Despite the fact that this document was completely ignored by the congressmen (who never officially answered the representatives of the organizations), their elaboration implied a first effort to systemize the feelings of indigenous women before the legal reforms.

This workshop was also a turning point for me as an academic in my research concerns. The rejection of the idealizing perspectives of indigenous law and communitarian justice, as well as the liberal perspectives (many times marked by racism) that re-established legal monism, led me to explore less dichotomous visions in order to rethink the relation between collective rights and women's rights. The voices and experiences of indigenous women have contributed more complex visions of culture and indigenous justice and have made claims for more inclusive legal practices on indigenous law that consider diversity within diversity.

From this perspective, this book and my prior work on indigenous women rights are a part (be it only in a marginal way) of this field of power in which different definitions of culture and indigenous justice are confronted. My own positions regarding these topics have changed through time, from a skeptical criticism before the possibilities of indigenous justice (see Hernández Castillo 1994b; Hernández Castillo and Garza Caligaris 1995; Hernández Castillo 2002a), to positions that are much more open to the creative politics that have been used by indigenous women to claim their own spaces of justice as part of their demands for autonomic rights (see Sierra and Hernández Castillo 2005; Sierra, Hernández Castillo, and Sieder 2013).

In the following sections, I address some concrete experiences of the re-constitution of the indigenous justice systems through the participation of indigenous women, emphasizing the different ways women appropriate or reject global discourses on rights and justice.

NAMING CULTURE AND JUSTICE FROM A WOMAN'S STANDPOINT

In various regions of Mexico, Guatemala, and Colombia, indigenous women are appropriating global discourses regarding women's rights while also defending the right of their people to maintain their own spaces of communitarian justice and, in a broader sense, their rights for political and territorial autonomy.

We are talking about different experiences in which indigenous women have appropriated the new multicultural spaces to debate or redraw the ways in which culture and tradition are understood. The new context of recognition of the "multicultural" character of the nation has steadily influenced the indigenous people (especially the organic intellectuals of their movements) to reflect on their cultural practices, and to systemize, theorize, and philosophize on those same topics (see Sánchez Néstor 2005, 2012; Álvarez 2005; Cumes 2007a, 2007b; Chirix 2003; Grupo de Mujeres Mayas Kaqla 2000, 2004; López 2005; Velásquez Nimatuj 2003; Méndez 2013; Painemal 2005).

In the process of "naming" the culture, there are negotiations among genders that occur in order to establish a definition of it. These processes of "political creativeness" confront the critical views coming from feminism on the topic of cultural recognition. Ample literature from feminist theory suggests that both official and ethnic nationalisms have used women's bodies as the raw material in the construction of their political projects (see Yuval Davis 1997; Gutiérrez Chong 2004). These perspectives have signaled that recognition policies have led to a strengthening of cultural essentialisms that often serve the patriarchal interests inside of the group. Ahistorical representations of cultures as homogenous entities of shared customs and values give way to cultural fundamentalisms that see, in every attempt of women to transform practices that affect their lives, a threat to the collective identity of the group. Before these essentialist postures, there is a need to analyze cultural practices to demonstrate that many "traditional" practices that impact and distort the lives of women have changed through time. Many times these traditions have their origin in colonial contexts, and their modification or disappearing does not affect the identitarian continuity of the group.

When the transformations of certain traditions impact the interests of groups in power, arguments against the dangers of "cultural integrity" become stronger. These reflections prompt us to rethink the indigenous cultures from analytical perspectives that include the dialogues of power that constitute them. To deconstruct how some features are selected (and others are not) as representative of a culture or are seen as integral to an identity allows us to unveil the network of power behind the representation of "difference." Historical perspectives on indigenous identities enable us to see how some cultural elements change without anyone considering that this endangers the cultural integrity of the group (i.e., automobiles, cellular phones, or agricultural technology). At the same time, it is arbitrarily decided that other changes do constitute a cultural loss.

As we shall see in the following sections in the Latin American context, some academic defenders of indigenous rights have contributed to making idealized representations of these people without allowing the voices and questioning of women within the communities to be heard. Power groups have been using these representations in order to legitimize their privileges. At the same time, there have been liberal academic analyses that disqualify indigenous institutions and practices, arguing a lack of authenticity because of their colonial origin.

This is a discussion in which I have been politically involved. During the last decade, I included myself among the voices critical of the essentialism of the indigenous continental movement that would refuse to approach the topic of exclusions of gender and domestic violence in indigenous communities.

In the Mexican context, the polarization of the feminist and Indianist postures has deepened in the last two decades as a result of the Zapatista movement raising the need for constitutional reform that would recognize the autonomic rights of the indigenous people (see Hernández Castillo, Sierra, and Paz 2004). In this context, an important sector of Mexican liberal feminism made alliances with liberal anti-autonomic groups to pose the dangers faced by indigenous women of the recognition of the collective rights of their peoples. Suddenly, many academics, who had never before written in favor of indigenous women, started to become "concerned" for their rights, and even began to quote the work of some of the feminist academics writing about violence in indigenous regions. This juncture changed the context of enunciation for our academic work, raising the need for contextualizing our reflections about domestic violence beyond the cultural analysis. This change has included an analysis of state violence and signals the importance of the structural context in which this violence presented itself.

At this political crossroads, organized indigenous women have given us clues about how to rethink the indigenous demands from a non-essentialist perspective. Their theorizations regarding culture, tradition, and women's rights were formalized in political documents, memoirs of encounters, and public speeches. Indigenous women never asked for this "protection" from the liberal intellectuals or from the state, which limited the autonomy of their people. In contrast, they have claimed their cultural rights and their rights to self-determination. They fight from within the indigenous movement to redefine the terms in which tradition and custom are understood and to actively participate in the construction of autonomic projects.

INDIGENOUS WOMEN BEFORE COMMUNITARIAN JUSTICE IN MEXICO

In Mexico, in spaces of communitarian justice, a rethinking of the "traditions and customs" from a woman's perspective has occurred. In different parts of the country, the organizational processes of indigenous women have encouraged them to directly participate in the spaces of communitarian justice. These emerging experiences, whose analysis could not be generalized to all indigenous regions of Mexico, are having a symbolic importance in the new discourses and imaginaries surrounding indigenous law.

The three experiences that I would like to approach in this section are the spaces of Zapatista justice in the Juntas del Buen Gobierno in the Tseltal, Tsotsil, and Tojolabal areas of Chiapas; the case of the Estatuto Comunitario of Tlahuitoltepec, Oaxaca, in the Mixe zone; and, finally, the case of the Indigenous Court of Cuetzalán, Puebla, in the Nahuat area. These are three very different experiences regarding communitarian justice, for in the first case we have a completely autonomous space that is not recognized by the state, in which the Zapatista support bases are applying their own justice system with no intervention from state institutions. In the second case, it is an area of community justice that has been recognized by the constitutional reforms that have occurred in Oaxaca in the last decade. Finally, we have the case of an indigenous court that was created by the state itself in the frame of a series of legal reforms that aimed to decentralize justice, and which has subsequently been appropriated by indigenous organizations in the region.

Since the public appearance of the EZLN on January 1, 1994, the numerical and political importance of indigenous women at the inside of this military-political organization attracted attention. As I mentioned in chapter 1, what has set Zapatismo apart from other guerrilla movements in Latin America has been the inclusion of gender demands in their general platform of struggle through the Women's Revolutionary Law (see chapter 2). Although all indigenous women do not know this law in great detail, its existence has become a symbol of the possibilities of a just life for women.

The Women's Revolutionary Law has been fundamental in the reconstitution of Zapatista justice. The new structures and regulations of Zapatista justice have consolidated as an autonomous justice system since 1996, when the Mexican government did not acknowledge the agreements that had been made by their own representatives with the Zapatista command (see Fernández Christlieb 2015). The San Andrés Agreements laid the foundations of indigenous autonomy and were the basis for the creation of de facto autonomous regions that are not legally recognized by the Mexican state, but which have been tolerated, ignored, or repressed by the various administrations in the last two decades. In 2001, the Union Congress approved a new constitutional reform, known as the Law of Culture and Indigenous Rights (Ley de Derechos y Cultura Indígena), that

FIGURE 7. Zapatista woman from Chiapas: between tradition and women's rights. Photograph by Andrés Solorzano.

(in a very diluted fashion) incorporated some of the elements of the San Andrés Agreements. However, at its very core, this law violated the agreement made between the Zapatista Army and the federal government concerning rights to territorial autonomy and the management of natural resources (see Hernández Castillo, Sierra, and Paz 2004).

After an intense political battle for the recognition of indigenous rights that included protests, forums, and national meetings, the Zapatistas opted to build their own autonomous project apart from the state. This decision emerged from the dissatisfaction of the indigenous people at the consideration of the "indigenous law" amendment being framed as "treason" by the Mexican political class. The San Andrés Agreements enabled the development of this autonomous project. The autonomous Zapatista regions are political and administrative divisions located in the geographical territory of the rebel army, where they exercise ways of self-governance and where they implement different social and productive programs (i.e., education, health, or organic agriculture). These autonomous regions include many communities that established themselves in land recovered by the Zapatistas. This began in 1994 with the expropriation of the large cattle ranches that were the foundation of a large estate maintained with the exploitation of the indigenous labor force.

Zapatista autonomy has meant the rejection of the institutional government's presence and official social programs of education, health, and development. In parallel, autonomous systems have been created for health, education, justice, and sustainable development. These work in commissions where men and women of Zapatista communities participate in the organizations through a rotational position system.[8] As part of those commissions, the Commission of Honor and Justice was created for the enforcement of justice at a municipal level.

Since 2003, there has been a restructuring of Zapatista autonomy, with the aim of separating the military from civil authorities, and also with the aim of achieving greater coordination among the different regions. Five *Caracoles* have been created; these are administrative units that constitute the autonomous municipalities and have, as their maximum authority, the Juntas del Buen Gobierno. In her analysis on Zapatista justice, Mariana Mora Bayo gives an account of how the Zapatistas manage to compete for power with the state. They achieve this by enforcing justice not only for the Zapatista support bases but also for the non-Zapatista population that resorts to them (see Mora Bayo 2013).

This new autonomic system, through the Commission of Honor and Justice, complements the spaces of communitarian justice still current in the Zapatista communities, where the elders have a very important role as counselors in intracommunitarian conflicts but where the maximum authority is still the assembly. If the problems cannot be solved at a communitarian level they go up to Caracol's Commission of Honor and Justice, integrated by men and women of the Zapatista support bases.

The participation of women in the Commission of Honor and Justice itself implies a change from the previous dynamics of communitarian justice. This has proved a challenge to many women who are not used to speaking in public spaces, but it has been accepted as part of the new community commitments. Emiliana (member of the Commission of Honor and Justice, of Caracol IV, *Whirlwind of Our Words*) describes the challenges in learning about the repercussions of participating in these new spaces of government. She also gives an account of a new political consciousness that rejects racism and exclusion:

At first I did not want to accept this charge. I did not think I could do it, but little by little they convinced me. I said to them I cannot add or subtract, nor do

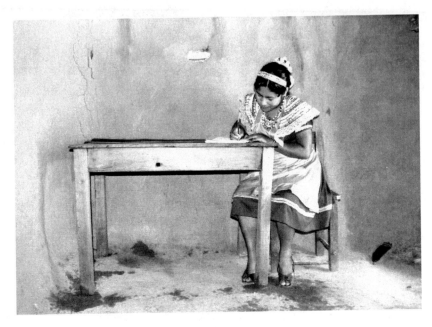

FIGURE 8. Tojolabal woman, member of the Commission of Honor and Justice, in a Zapatista autonomic region. Photograph by Mariana Mora.

I know how to read, neither do I speak Spanish very well. But my peers would tell me that I can very well do it, that I only need desire and enthusiasm to be able to learn anything . . . I realized that it was here where I could learn the most and where I would be able to help my people the most. I had been mistaken; I thought that the knowledge was in the city and that in my town I could not learn anything new. To be a good government we need to learn and teach, that's why I'm here to serve my people. I have my charge in the *Junta de Buen Gobierno* so that a *Caxlan* (white man) may never call *india patas rajadas* (dirty Indian) to a young woman like myself. (Mora Bayo 2014, 36)

These spaces of communitarian justice are still marked by gender ideologies that exclude women from many spaces of political decision. But despite this fact, the new generations of Zapatista women have appropriated the Women's Revolutionary Law in order to fight for a larger participation and for other types of conciliatory processes in which their voices may be heard. The work of the Commission of Honor and Justice means that there will be other young women in these justice forums that will struggle for their rights:

The work of *Honor y Justicia* is just like in the collectives. There we try to encourage your peers and you explain their rights to them. Even though we explain the women what their rights are, they don't always understand. In my town we talk about it. If your husband treats you badly is not because God wants it that way. They do not have the right to treat you like that. That is why we try to give talks to all women.[9]

The works produced by Margara Millán (2008, 2014) and Violeta Zylberberg Panebianco (2006, 2008) in the context of our first collective project (see Hernández Castillo 2008; Millán 2014), and also by Mariana Mora Bayo (2013, 2014) in the second project (See Sierra, Hernández Castillo, and Sieder 2013), show us the contradictions that this rethinking of communitarian justice produces for those authorities whose perspectives are still marked by patriarchal gender ideologies.

Zylberberg Panebianco describes the case of María Angélica, one of the members of the women's commission who wanted to divorce her husband because of the constant harassment she experienced from him and his family due to her political participation. Her continuous outings to regional meetings made her the target of community gossip, to which her husband responded with jealousy and abuse. Before the petition of divorce, communitarian authorities resorted to conciliation and asked both parties to reconsider their positions. María Angélica was convinced that she did not want to continue in that relationship, but peer pressure made her accept conciliation, which did nothing for her relationship (Zylberberg Panebianco 2006).

Mora Bayo discusses a case of rape that was sanctioned by the Commission of Honor and Justice with the sentence of "cleaning fifteen hectares of land" for the victim's family. The author points out in this regard:

This case raises a series of fundamental questions that link *Zapatista* justice to a gender focus. In what way does collective work in the public spaces of a community repair the damage of a violent aggression aimed at the body of a woman? In what way does this guarantee that the guilty party does not commit a similar crime? How does the crime victim participate in defining what would constitute reparation of the damage or an act of justice? (Mora Bayo 2013, 214)

These cases remind us of the persistence of moral/ethical perspectives marked by the Catholic tradition that oppose divorce and that continue to view the autonomy of indigenous women as a danger to "family integration." It is a deeply complex context in which various visions of the world overlap and generational confrontations occur regarding how women "ought to be feminine."

The relations between men and women in the Zapatista communities are being impacted by new regulations that, in many senses, are opposed to "tradition." Zapatismo represents, for many women, a rupture with a context of violence that was justified in the name of tradition:

> Before, sometimes women would get hit inside the house. The male peers would not know our rights. Now, we share with the men when we shower our children, before they would never do what was considered a woman's job. And now when we go to a meeting, for instance in CODIMUJ, and you have to stay all week, well the men stay home and help with the work. That is an important change.[10]

Communitarian justice is being re-formulated in many communities of Chiapas in dialogue with the new Zapatista laws, and in dialogue with national and international legislations. These are difficult processes, full of contradictions, but they emphasize the flexibility and historicity of communitarian justice and confront essentialist perspectives of indigenous law.

This phenomenon of rethinking community justice is not exclusive to the autonomous Zapatista regions. In the Mixe or Ayuujk municipalities of Santa María Tlahuitoltepec, where, since the 1970s, there has been an organizational movement for indigenous rights and communitarian autonomy, women have not been excluded from the political debates surrounding the "uses and customs."

The long history of struggle against PRI chiefdom, and for indigenous rights, has marked the political dynamics of this region, and the Mixe intellectuals have been pioneers in theorizing communitarian justice and indigenous autonomy. Mixe intellectual Floriberto Díaz has written, since the 1970s, about communitarian autonomy, anticipating the debates that would generate an indigenous movement for autonomy at a national level in the 1990s. Díaz is considered to be the foremost theorist of the political trend that claims "communality" as one of the main values for an indigenous democracy.[11]

Through this line of thought, the Mixe Defense Committee for Human and Cultural Resources (Comité de Defensa de los Recursos Humanos y Culturales Mixes—CODREMI) was formed around that time. This committee would later continue as the Assembly of Mixe Authorities (Asamblea de Autoridades Mixes—ASAM) and Services for the Mixe People (Servicios del Pueblo Mixe in 1988 to provide support, guidance, and management for communal and municipal authorities, as well as for organized groups of producers. These would later consolidate to form the Assembly of Mixe Producers (Asamblea de Productores Mixes).

All of these organizations have also been learning spaces for many Mixe women that have had an active participation in the political struggles of the municipality, and who have started to question the gender exclusions that take place in their community spaces. Thanks to this effort, Mixe women were incorporated into the musical orchestras of the municipality, and now they train alongside men in the most prestigious indigenous conservatory in the country: the Mixe Center for Music Training (Centro de Capacitación y Musica Mixe), with its headquarters in Tlahuitoltepec. This achievement was made possible by the indigenous movement in the region.

In this region, communitarian justice has always been in the hands of indigenous authorities, and they have worked with relative independence from state law. The community assembly has been the maximum advisory organ in the application of justice, and it has been the representative adopting the daily responsibility of the resolution of communitarian conflicts (Vargas Vásquez 2008, 2011). Paradoxically, this relative autonomy of community justice has been restricted considerably because of the constitutional reforms that recognize the so-called systems of uses and customs.[12]

The series of modifications in the local legislation that began to surface in Oaxaca in 1990 with the recognition of the "ethnic plural composition" of the state (article 16), and that in 1998 consolidated itself as the Law of Indigenous Rights of the State of Oaxaca, recognizes the right of the communities to have their own normative systems and methods of election for their local governments. This recognition has had contradictory effects. In one regard, it has reinforced the mechanisms of control of the state over community justice by increasing the presence of human rights state organisms. These state entities are the ones in charge of "overseeing" that community justice does not violate individual rights.[13] In parallel, the subject of indigenous justice has become a topic of political discussion inside the communities.

In this new political context, Mixe women have begun to reflect on those elements of communitarian justice that are consequential to their lives. A privileged space for these reflections opened in 2011 when the municipal government set out to elaborate a communal statute where the main norms and values of Mixe justice become systematized. Despite the contradictions that emerge from writing down procedural law (since these laws have been primarily oral), in the spaces of collective discussion of the communitarian laws (*estatuto comunitario*), different perspectives regarding Mixe culture and tradition were expressed and negotiated in public spaces.

Liliana Vargas Vásquez, a Mixe anthropologist member of our investigation team who has studied and participated in these reflection processes, describes this new cultural climate in Tlahuitoltepec, signaling that:

> The voices of indigenous women, whose protagonism has gone *in crescendo* since the *Zapatista* uprising, claimed that both communitarian justice and state justice have serious limitations to promote an equal development for indigenous women due to the social, cultural, and gender inequalities. Now, the importance of indigenous women's movements is that they come to question on one side the internal system, but at the same time they try to rethink the dynamics of their legal system with an aim towards collective development, dignifying and re-signifying human life. (Vargas Vásquez 2011, 5)

These proposals for "rethinking communitarian justice" have come through a group of organized Mixe women in the Network of Mixe Women (Red de Mujeres Mixes) and in the Group of Women in Action with Ayuujk Word and Thoughts (Grupo de Mujeres en Acción con Palabra y Pensamiento Ayuujk). The result has been the promotion of spaces of collective reflection with women from different communities in order to discuss their rights and experiences when dealing with Mixe justice. Other women from small communities in the municipality that are participating in the discussion workshops on communitarian laws have expressed, "If women do not begin to participate in a joint fashion in the communitarian assembly, there are going to be many empty spaces . . . as indigenous peoples we need to see real things, if years have gone by without the recognition of the importance of women, today we have to change" (Vargas Vásquez 2011, 45).

The re-formulation of communitarian justice with the participation of Ayuujk women is an incipient process that does not have an institutional structure as the Zapatista justice system does, nor does it have the legitimization of a Women's Revolutionary Law that supports the demands of organized women in the Mixe region. Rather, it is an experience that begins to mark the way in which Mixe communality is debated and conceived.

The third case I will reference for the Mexican context is the case of the Indigenous Court (Juzgado Indígena) and the House of the Indigenous Woman (Casa de la Mujer Indígena) from the Nahuat municipality of Cuetzalán in the sierra of Puebla. This experience has been analyzed by two members of our investigation team: Adriana Terven (2009) and Susana Mejía (2010) in permanent dialogue with María Teresa Sierra, who has performed studies in this region for several decades (Sierra 1992, 2004a, 2004b).

The Cuetzalán Women's Group is one of the oldest and most solid organizations of indigenous women in Mexico, organized specifically for women's rights but rooted in a political agenda that simultaneously demands the collective rights of their people. As in the case of Tlahuitoltepec, Cuetzalán has been characterized by a long history of peasant and indigenous organization in which women have played a fundamental role. Initially, the organizational processes were focused on better conditions for commercializing agricultural products (e.g., coffee, vanilla, fruits), playing a very important role in the agrarian cooperative, Tosepan Titataniske, founded in 1977. In the 1980s, and more clearly in the 1990s, the peasant agenda started to be complemented with a political agenda that claimed cultural and political rights for indigenous people.

During the mid-1980s, there was conflict between an important group of women from the cooperative Tosepan and the men managing the cooperative. The conflict was caused by critiques of the machismo and anti-democratic practices of the leaders of the organization who centralized the decision-making process as well as the profits generated by the artisan women. This pioneering group built a parallel space of productive organization that has centered the collective reflection on the participation of women and their specific rights. This is the origin of the crafts organization known as Maseualsiuamej Mosenyolchicauanij, founded in 1986, which, to this day, has been one of the main promoters of the rights of women in the Nahuat regions. The origins of this organization are described by one of its founders in these terms:

> At the beginning of our organization we came to realize the problems we had when we went out to our meetings, to the workshops, it was a battle inside the family where you had to convince your husband. Then we started to have our meetings, our workshops, where we reflected on our rights as women. It was important for us to know that we had our rights and that it wasn't normal that we suffered violence, beatings, or abuse, that was how we got to know about our rights . . . later, in 1995 we put together our first project, we requested the support of INI to have an ampler promotion among our communities.[14]

Unlike the processes in the Mixe region, in the Nahuat zone, the formulation of a women's rights agenda developed in close dialogue with rural feminist organizations working in this indigenous region for decades. Civil feminisms focused on the rural work and came into contact with indigenous and peasant organizations that, in different ways, contributed to the formulation of a women's rights agenda from indigenous women's perspectives. Many of these women came from a left-wing militancy, were linked to the national liberation struggles in Central America, or they were involved with political organizations that work with popular and peasant sectors of Mexico.

In the region of Cuetzalán, the feminist organization Comaletzin AC, founded in 1987, has been very important in the promotion of the discourses on rights. Its main line of actions and primary functions are "the training, organization, education and investigation with gender as an axis of analysis" (Comaletzin 1999, 2). This organization played an important role in the 1987 formation of the Network of Rural Promoters and Advisors (Red Nacional de Asesoras y Promotoras Rurales), formed by organizations concerned with gender and development in different rural regions of Mexico. Susana Mejía (a member of our research team) was one of the founders of this organization whose work has been fundamental in the advising and support of Nahuat women.

It is important to point out that the dialogues between rural feminists and indigenous women have been very important in the formulation of an indigenous political agenda with a gender perspective. Feminism has not been an "imposition" or "manipulation" from outside; rather, it has been a productive dialogue in which both the feminists from Comaletzin and the Nahuat women from Maseualsiuamej Mosenyolchicauanij have reformulated their visions and perspectives on culture and social justice. Indigenous leaders, such as Rufina Villa, have become intellectual and moral guides to rural feminists and have influenced Comaletzin to rethink its work strategies, looking to culturally locate their reflections on gender inequalities.

This organizational effervescence, and the long history of reflection and mobilization in regards to indigenous rights and women's rights, is what enables women and men from Cuetzalán to appropriate and influence the spaces created by the Mexican state as part of the neoliberal multicultural reforms. This is the case of the Indigenous Court, created in 2002 as part of the reforms to the judicial system (Ley Orgánica del Poder Judicial del Estado de Puebla) and as part of the reforms to the civil procedural code to include the practices, uses, customs, and traditions of the indigenous people as alternative means to contribute to ordinary justice.

These legal reforms can be read as a response to the demands of the political and cultural rights of the indigenous movement, or as a part of the decentralization measures that the neoliberal system needs in order to reduce the responsibilities of the state. Beyond the intentions behind the reforms, in some regions of the country, the spaces opened by multicultural policies have allowed the indigenous people to appropriate and give new meanings to these spaces of justice.

One of the main critiques of indigenous courts is that instead of the state recognizing the local spaces of justice in indigenous communities, as the Zapatistas demanded through the San Andrés Agreements, other parallel spaces of indigenous justice were created, promoted, and in many cases, controlled by the same state (see Maldonado and Terven 2008; Terven and Chávez 2013).

In the case of the Northern Sierra of Puebla, when representatives of the state judicial branch proposed the creation of the Indigenous Court of Cuetzalán, they encountered the organized response of Nahuat men and women who rejected the imposition of an indigenous attorney as the local judge. They countered with a proposal to create a council integrated with elders, men, and women of "knowledge" and experience in communitarian justice. This is the council responsible for electing the indigenous judge and his substitute. The local organizations (among them, Maseualsiuamej Mosenyolchicauanij) have given the Indigenous Court a new meaning that does not necessarily match with the original objectives of the legal reform. Terven and Buenrostro describe the objectives of the Indigenous Court of Cuetzalán in the following terms:

> The revitalization of the figure of the Council of Elders, a tradition practically in disuse throughout the region; to strengthen the figure of the indigenous Judge through the own values of the Nahuat culture and the mother tongue; and to define the normative practices. There has been a significant concern for the defense of gender equity in the legal practice. This process is largely driven by the indigenous women organizations, who supported by mestizo advisers, have done a great job in different areas privileging training over women's rights. This has promoted the transformation of gender relationships through the legal practice. (Terven and Buenrostro 2010, 45)

The impact of organized women in communitarian justice has been enabled by the participation of the members of the Maseualsiuamej in the council of the Indigenous Court, as they have prompted a "rethinking of the Nahuat law and the conciliatory processes" within the council. In 2003, they also created the *Maseuasiuatkali* (House of the Indigenous Woman), working in collaboration

FIGURE 9. Workshop on Women's Rights organized by the House of the Indigenous Woman (CAMI) in Cuetzalán, Puebla. Photograph by Susana Mejía.

with the Indigenous Court to treat victims of sexual and domestic violence. In the legal area of this house, two lawyers were invited to participate in what has been defined as a strategy of "intercultural defense with a gender perspective." This strategy of intercultural defense is described by Celestina Cruz Martín, Nahuat leader and coordinator of the "defense area" in the House of the Indigenous Woman, in the following terms:

> The decision was taken to have a hybrid method of legal defense, having both systems, the positive and indigenous, to reach a systemic method in the solution of conflicts related to domestic violence. This method takes up from the indigenous system the conciliation through dialogue and the making of agreements between aggressors and victims, looking for joint solutions to the problems of the relationship that generally end up in domestic violence. (Mejía, Cruz Martín, and Rodríguez 2006, 5)

This defense strategy combines the processes of conciliation and mediation inside of the House of the Indigenous Woman that are later legitimized through legal documents signed before the Indigenous Court. Simultaneously, self-help groups have been created for women victims of violence and for the aggressors that propose to reflect and confront the patriarchal ideologies that are behind domestic violence. Members of the House of the Indigenous Woman coordinate these groups, and their aim is to change the meaning of conciliation into a process that does not completely reinforce the subordination of women.

The three cases described in this section are experiences that claim indigenous communitarian justice and the rights of indigenous people to self-determination. Importantly, they do not claim a static "indigenous law" of millenary origin whose precepts cannot be modified; rather, they claim an indigenous justice system of procedural character that has been changing with time and that is capable of incorporating and enriching itself with experience and the reflections of organized indigenous women.

Paradoxically, while indigenous men and women critically reflect on their practices of justice and propose new strategies for the resolution of communitarian conflicts, many legal anthropologists are still reproducing essentialist perspectives of "indigenous" law and delegitimize those initiatives that do not respond to their own ahistorical visions of indigenous cultures and traditions.

BETWEEN MAYAN LAW AND HISTORICAL ANALYSIS OF COMMUNITY JUSTICE IN GUATEMALA: DIFFERENT PERSPECTIVES ON CUSTOMARY LAW

The Guatemalan Constitution has never been reformed to recognize the rights of indigenous peoples to their local spaces of justice. A package of constitutional reforms, including recognition of "customary law," was rejected by popular referendum in May 1999, following a major racist publicity campaign that warned that such reforms would jeopardize national unity. However, after the signing of the Peace Accords in 1996, multicultural winds began to impact public policies and spaces of justice. The Peace Accords, which put an end to thirty years of civil war, were signed by representatives of the Guatemalan National Revolutionary Unity (Unión Revolucionaria Nacional Guatemalteca—URNG) and the Guatemalan government on December 29, 1996. However, they did not include any commitments to modify the profound inequalities that characterize Guatemalan society and that, essentially, led to the civil war. A specific section, called "Identity and Rights of Indigenous Peoples," was included, however, and while it was not transformed into a constitutional reform, it did lay the groundwork for later multicultural public policies. At approximately the same time, Convention 169 of the International Labor Organization (ILO) was ratified in March 1996, serving to validate a set of terms and visions associated with the rights of indigenous peoples, including the right to their own systems of justice.

With respect to women's rights, the Peace Accords referred to the triple discrimination of indigenous women arising from their ethnicity, class, and gender, and established a commitment on the part of the government to develop policies inclusive of women in the areas of agriculture and development projects. The Peace Accords also ratified the government's responsibility: to criminalize sexual abuse; to consider the ethnicity of victims in cases of sexual violence; to establish the Office for the Defense of Indigenous Women's Rights (Defensoría de la Mujer Indígena—DEMI); and to fulfill its commitments acquired in international conventions with regard to women's rights.

In terms of access to justice, there are two parallel processes taking place in Guatemala, opening up new political debates around women's rights and justice. The first was the creation, in 2000, of DEMI in various regions of the country. DEMI has had strong support from international organizations dedicated to promoting women's rights and has focused on other new reforms to the justice system aimed at improving the coordination between state justice and community justice.

Many of the reforms in the legal arena responded to neoliberal tendencies to decentralize and diminish the justice apparatus, but they have also included some advantages for improving access to justice for the indigenous population through, for instance, the creation of more "lower courts" in all of the country's departments, the use of interpreters in legal entities, and the search for better coordination between state justice and community indigenous justice.

In Guatemala, the spaces for community justice had been profoundly affected by the army's counterinsurgency strategies, resulting in death or exile for many traditional authorities. However, these spaces continued to play a fundamental role in the resolution of local conflicts sparked by the wave of violence characterizing the post-war period. As in other regions of Latin America, new multicultural policies that referred to indigenous law opened up forums for political discussion regarding what was understood as Mayan law and whether or not its "recuperation" or "revitalization" was important (see Cumes 2009; Zapeta 2009). The emergence of indigenous organizations claiming their Mayan identity as a space for political mobilization (beginning at the end of the armed conflict) also brought the demand for Pan-Mayan law conceived of as "norms, authorities and practices of justice that are in some way shared by the country's twenty-one Mayan linguistic communities. Emphasized is the historic continuity of their legal norms and practices, which have changed over time but continue to represent a Mayan 'essence,' that is central to their own identity" (Sieder and Macleod 2009, 63).

The creation by Mayan intellectuals and activists of Indigenous Defenders' Offices in various regions of the country plays a fundamental role in promoting spaces of reflection on the collective rights of indigenous peoples, and on the ethical values to be recovered through Mayan law. These are civil NGOs composed of indigenous activists, some of them trained as lawyers specializing in state law who offer free mediation services in cultural matters, and who also accompany community authorities in processes for imparting justice, assisting in the strengthening of Mayan institutionality. In the framework of our collective project, Rachel Sieder analyzed the experience of the Indigenous Defenders' Office in San Cruz del Quiché (Sieder 2013). She pointed to the importance of these offices in reconstituting Mayan law as a strategy for reconstructing the social fabric following the armed conflict, especially given the lack of access to state justice in a context characterized by insecurity and organized crime violence. Based on an analysis of experiences in the coordination of Mayan law and official justice, she identified the challenges in these contexts of legal pluralism, stating:

> Such attempts at strengthening indigenous autonomy and respect for community authorities take place in a context of much violence, in which the functions of state security and justice are becoming increasingly more fragmented and privatized, and in which organized crime has colonized many parts of the state apparatus. Effectively, there is a kaleidoscope of legal, quasi-legal and illegal orders, or *contested or overlapping sovereignties*. (Sieder 2013, 235)

In the context of post-war violence, recovering Mayan ethical values in the resolution of community conflicts has become an alternative for constructing codes of coexistence that are based on Mayan culture and that permit the reconstitution of the social fabric. Those coming together to carry out this task have included traditional community authorities such as the *k'amal b'e* (guides), *ajq'ijab'* (Mayan priests), and *ajiyom* (midwives), as well as activists from the Mayan movement, with support from international development entities that have financed some of these initiatives.[15] José Angel Zapeta, a Mayan priest from the Nim Q'atab'al Tzij Kech Ajq'ijab organization of Mayan spiritual guides, describes the strengthening of Mayan law as one of his organization's priorities, stating "Mayan Law is profoundly formative, profoundly preventative, profoundly educational, from the moment we are in family life, in the life of the family nucleus and in the extended family, in which grandfathers and grandmothers play an important role, and in which elders play an important role" (Zapeta 2009, 198).

Nevertheless, these perspectives on Mayan law have been questioned, due to their lack of historical context, by a new generation of indigenous intellectuals who point to the importance of historicizing community justices and critically reflecting on them. Without denying that the tendency toward the "idealization of Mayan law" is a response to the historic discrimination by the Guatemalan state and society against forms of indigenous governance, these voices demand recognition of the colonial legacy prevailing in many of the normativities governing the life of indigenous communities (see Cumes 2009; Esquit and Garcia 1998). With regard to relations between men and women, the use of the discourse of complementarity between genders as a way to justify women's exclusion from various spaces of political power is questioned.

There is a debate between those who defend the Mayan cosmovision as a fundamental way to imagine a more just society based on the principles of complementarity, duality, and equilibrium (Ajxup 2000; Curruchich 2000; Jocón González 2005; Álvarez, 2005), and the Maya women who denounce the political uses of these discourses by those who intend to silence the violence against and exclusion of women that prevails in indigenous communities (Cumes 2009; López 2005). This debate continues to polarize the positions of Mayan men and women in relation to community justice.

From the most critical viewpoint, the reconstitution of Mayan law must include a broader and more inclusive process of deliberation, with participation by the various sectors of the community:

Women have great contributions for democratizing not only state law but also indigenous law. While racism makes it difficult to impact state law, it cannot be an obstacle for indigenous law. The democratization of indigenous law requires forms of deliberation or dialogue in which women's participation is important.

Criticizing the gender perspective is important if this leads us to the task of re-newing analytical and political categories, the use of which is pertinent in our realities. This will make it possible to continue to develop methodologies that will allow us to view reality and its relations of power with critical eyes. The funda-mentalist visions of indigenous cosmovisions can become a type of religion that, just like Christianity, makes us tolerate suffering. We don't want this version of indigenous cosmovisions, but rather one that is more revolutionary, that ques-tions and constructs new perspectives. This is where women's experiences should enter in, not only for becoming authorities in already-existing systems, but also for constructing new ways of thinking and understanding doctrinal principles of both state and indigenous law. (Cumes 2009, 47)

Efforts have begun to build bridges between those who defend Mayan law, and those who question its exclusions, through spaces for dialogue promoted by international development entities. One example was the event titled "In-digenous Women and Ancestral Justice," organized by the United Nations Development Fund for Women and held in Quito in October 2008, with par-ticipation by indigenous intellectuals and community authorities from Mexico, Guatemala, Nicaragua, Panama, Ecuador, Bolivia, Peru, and Colombia.

The event involved heated discussions between those who emphasized the importance of denouncing the violence taking place within indigenous commu-nities, and those who defended more harmonious visions of the spaces for their own justice and prioritized the defense of indigenous autonomy. At the end of the event, Mayan spiritual guide José Angel Zapeta, one of the staunchest critics of gender discourses in Guatemala acknowledged:

If there is *machismo*, we have to work on this because it can't be that a person who has a vision of equilibrium, who has an important vision of dignity as persons, women and men, girls and boys and the elderly, is suddenly beating, mistreating, this can't be. I will take many important lessons from here. Through the Indig-enous Women Defenders' Office, I have learned about the discrimination suf-fered by indigenous women in ordinary justice. And here, I have become aware, through your voices, that they are also treated unfairly in ancestral justice. We have to work on this with our Mayan authorities. Ancestral justice must be fair for women. I promise to take this matter to my organization. (Zapeta 2009, 200)

At the local level, the Indigenous Defenders' Offices have played a very im-portant role in creating spaces for reflection on violence against women and ways to confront this matter from the perspective of community justice. At the same time, in the case study conducted in the framework of our collective research, Morna Macleod has analyzed the work of various Mayan women's organizations at the regional and community levels that are defending the indigenous cosmovision, not as an excuse to silence conflict, but as an ethical principle that should be recovered in the search for more harmonious relations between men and women and also between human beings and nature (see Sieder and Macleod 2009; Macleod and Pérez Bámaca 2013).

Considering the contradictions denounced by Aura Estela Cumes in her valuable reflections on Mayan law, it is also important to acknowledge that the current political context has permitted the identification of problems that were previously naturalized as part of life, and it also has allowed for the negotiation of meanings about Mayan law and, with respect to the culture, for which legal recognition is sought.

NEW CHALLENGES IN INDIGENOUS JURISDICTIONS FOR COLOMBIAN WOMEN

Colombia has been a pioneering country in Latin America in the formation and consolidation of a national indigenous movement and in the implementation of legislative reforms that recognize indigenous jurisdictions in the procurement of justice. Despite the fact that only 3.4 percent of the population defines itself as indigenous (1,378,884 according to the National Population Census), the organizational processes of this population have made it possible to obtain political achievements, such as the recuperation of their territories— of approximately 250,000 hectares—as well as recognition of their forms of local authority and participation as a national social movement (CRIC 2004).

As we saw in the previous chapter, the Regional Indigenous Council of Cauca (Consejo Regional Indígena del Cauca—CRIC), created in 1971, is one of the continent's oldest indigenous organizations and one of the first to transcend struggles for land, demanding territorial control and political autonomy. CRIC's mobilizations were fundamental in assuring that the Colombian Constitution of 1991 would recognize the collective rights of indigenous peoples and indigenous resguardos (or reserves) as territorial jurisdictions. These reforms have been considered among the most advanced in Latin America in terms of recognition of indigenous rights. This is not only because they consolidated indigenous institutionality in the resguardos, but because they also specified other rights such as indigenous jurisdiction and indigenous law; the regulation of land distribution within the resguardos; recognition of territorial rights; and representation before the national government. The Constitutional Court also played a role in settling disputes between state and indigenous jurisdictions.

As part of the reforms to the judicial branch, a Special Indigenous Jurisdiction was also created with a high degree of autonomy. Although there has been criticism of the lack of a regulatory law for governing the coordination between state law and indigenous law, Colombia's Constitutional Court has developed jurisprudence for resolving the disputes that have arisen in the exercise of individual and collective rights throughout the last twenty years (Sánchez Botero 1998).

The Constitutional Court has also been responsible for developing a doctrine of "legal minimums," specifically stating that indigenous authorities— like all national authorities—may not kill, torture, or enslave any person and must provide some guarantees of due process. The important role played by the Constitutional Court in strengthening indigenous jurisdictions is unique in Latin America and has depended a great deal on progressive judges, like Carlos Gaviria Díaz (Constitutional Court Judge from 1993 to 2001), who have been committed to recognizing indigenous rights.

Nevertheless, the dissemination and analysis of some of these disputes by legal anthropologists, and by the Constitutional Court itself, has led to many debates on the vulnerability of women in the framework of indigenous jurisdictions where the possibilities for inter-legality are closed when no compensation is offered in indigenous justice.[16] It was precisely the analysis of one of these disputes, and the affidavit prepared by Colombian anthropologist Esther Sánchez Botero at a conference of the Latin American Network of Legal Anthropology (Red Latinoamericana de Antropología Jurídica) in the early 1990s, that led me to write for the first time against the idealization of community justice and acknowledge its limitations for indigenous women (see Hernández Castillo 1994b; Hernández Castillo and Garza Caligaris 1995).

In her presentation, later transformed into one of the chapters in *El caleidoscopio de las justicias en Colombia: Análisis socio-jurídico* (*The Kaleidoscope of Justices in Colombia: A Socio-legal Analysis*) (de Sousa Santos and García Villegas 2001), Sánchez Botero analyzes the case of an indigenous woman whose individual rights were framed in opposition to collective rights. This is a case in which the intervention by state justice weakened indigenous jurisdiction.

Tránsito, a Paez woman from the Cauca region, was murdered by her husband in an episode of domestic violence in which her husband, Alcides Cayapú Dagua, "knocked her down, put a burning log on her body, and when totally burned, dragged her body along a path until she died hours later. When he saw that she was dead, Alcides went to look for a pig 'for her final wake, because candles should be lit, and may many people come!'" (Sánchez Botero 2001, 168).

Legal anthropology provides the context for the case, explaining the norms and values that Tránsito violated "that led Alcides to *eradicate* her, considering her to be a social evil" (Sánchez Botero 2001, 169; emphasis added). Sánchez Botero provided a detailed analysis of the background for the case, specifically that Tránsito had a baby boy with a white man who raped her while her husband was in prison (paying for another murder). The son was adopted by Tránsito's sister-in-law only hours after he was born, causing his death, since the adoptive mother did not have breast milk to feed him and gave him cow's milk (considered taboo among the Paez people). In her analysis, Sánchez Botero addressed a number of violations committed by Tránsito that have nothing to do with a Judeo-Christian perspective on infidelity. Specifically, the mistakes Tránsito made included leaving her house only hours after giving birth, walking near a river, giving away her child without breastfeeding him, not having attended his burial, and approaching Protestant indigenous people. Each of these actions violated the community's cosmogonic and ethical conceptions, and consequently, the husband was acquitted in the community trial, considered to be a "protector and defender of the principles and ideals of the Paez culture" (Sánchez Botero 2001, 168).

The author does not justify or condemn the murder, but instead assumes the position of a cultural analyst who attempts to explain the internal logics that led to Tránsito's "eradication." What the author does question, however, is the intervention by state justice through the tribunal in Popayán, which weakens indigenous jurisdiction by judging the case and imposing a legal minimum that prohibits murder in national territory. As a result, Alcides was condemned to prison by state justice officials who disregarded the cultural reasons why he murdered his wife. The author concludes that "the case reveals the conflict between individual law—allowing a person to be respected in the framework of his decisions and religious convictions—and the possible consequences for the collective subject" (Sánchez Botero 2001, 173).

This case and other expert opinions by the same author led us to confront the harmonious visions of indigenous justice that do not recognize the internal power conflicts or the critical perspectives of minorities in relation to community norms (see Hernández Castillo 2002a). Homogenizing perspectives on indigenous cultures that fail to recognize the internal diversity that exists within indigenous communities end up silencing the voices of indigenous women whose practices of resistance are also part of the culture for which they seek recognition. Who speaks on behalf of culture? Whose voices are heard in anthropological expert's opinions, and whose voices are silenced? What are the ethical dilemmas for anthropologists when they become defenders of essentialist perspectives on culture that do not allow any space for the transformation of customary cultural logics? These are the questions that led us to search—in the voices and experiences of Colombian indigenous women—for some clues to understanding, from other perspectives, the tensions between collective rights and individual rights.

The context of legal pluralism we found was very different from that in Mexico and Guatemala. This was due to the persistence of the administrative forms imposed during colonial times that had allowed a certain regional legal autonomy, even prior to constitutional recognition of indigenous jurisdictions. This is evident in the indigenous resguardos and *cabildos* (local councils), which were both institutions imposed by the Spaniards and recognized by the Spanish Crown through royal titles. Paradoxically, these documents continue to be fundamental in the legal defense of territories (see Rappaport 2003).

The indigenous resguardos and their councils—despite various modifications made, and despite the plundering by landholders—have managed to survive to the present, with reconfigurations, in many cases, of their internal normativities and forms of imparting justice. With the recognition of the Special Indigenous Jurisdiction, CRIC included, as part of its political agenda, the strengthening of indigenous law and the restructuring of the councils to enable them to assume functions associated with imparting justice in the regions where this was no longer the case.

It was in this context that CRIC restructured itself internally and established itself as the Zonal Associations of Councils (Asociaciones Zonales de Cabildos), forming ten associations[17] that bring together a total of 115 councils. These councils are recognized by the communities and by the state as "traditional authorities." CRIC's Council of Chiefs (Consejería Mayor) is in charge of regional leadership and is composed of one delegate from each zone. Zonal Legal Committees are formed in some zones (especially the Northern Zone) and are in charge of coordinating local legal teams. The function of these teams is to assist the councils in resolving conflicts, collecting information and investigating cases, and defining the implementation of solutions (see Lozano Suárez forthcoming).

With the aim of strengthening indigenous normative systems and supporting the re-establishment of CRIC councils, a proposal was made to create a School of Indigenous Law within the Intercultural Autonomous Indigenous University (Universidad Autónoma Indígena Intercultural—UAIIN). This new project provides continuity to a history of more than forty years in which indigenous education has been one of CRIC's fundamental commitments. First, through informal educational programs, and then, with a more institutionalized university program, CRIC's commitment to education has been focused on not only building autonomy and strengthening cultural identities but also developing and disseminating strategies for defending its political project.

To contribute to this commitment, CRIC has a team of non-indigenous collaborators who have an organic connection to the organization's political project. Joanne Rappaport defines these researchers as:

> *colaboradores* [collaborators] who work full-time for ethnic organizations, whose everyday lives transpire in an indigenous milieu, and who submit to the risks and the discipline of ethnic organizations; *colaboradores* are, essentially, intellectuals from the dominant culture who are organic to the indigenous movement. Many of the most prominent members of this group function as interlocutors who stimulate discussion within the organization, but they rarely, if ever, publish their ideas in format other that internal documents and reports. This sector is almost totally ignored in the literature, perhaps because *colaboradores* do not fit neatly within the essentialist models that we have created for analyzing indigenous organizations. (Rappaport 2005, 129)

For the purposes of this collective research, we invited Leonor Lozano Suárez, an anthropologist who has collaborated with CRIC for the last twelve years and who serves on the teaching team at the UAIIN, to conduct a case study on the challenges experienced by the organization's women in relation to indigenous law. Due to her long history of collaboration with CRIC, Lozano Suárez was able to explore the women's feelings and, in response to their requests, conduct a participative diagnostic assessment of the main problems they are confronting in their family and community settings (see Lozano Suárez forthcoming).

In contrast to the essentialist perspectives of Colombian indigenous cultures that refuse to acknowledge that women can have critical perspectives on the practices that exclude them from community and organizational spaces, Lozano Suárez systematized the CRIC women's proposals based on the primary problems they face as women and as indigenous people. In her case study, she speaks of the internal negotiations taking place, aimed at influencing indigenous law and local spaces of power. In this regard, she comments that "education has been a field that has opened up spaces for women's participation and has been a privileged arena for building consciousness around gender identity and renegotiating gender relations" (Lozano Suárez forthcoming, 35).

In a previous project, Lina Rosa Berrío Palomo analyzed the experiences of Colombian indigenous women within the National Indigenous Organization of Colombia (Organización Nacional Indígena de Colombia—ONIC). These women questioned the visions of complementarity and equity between genders, pointing to the differentiated value placed in their communities on being a man or being a woman, and the symbolic prestige generated for a mother who has children of one sex or the other. In this regard, Yolanda Durán, the only woman on ONIC's Peace Team, stated the following:

> Well, in the generation of our cultures, boys are highly prized within our communities, for becoming authorities, becoming part of the structures, or in other words, for carrying out specific activities . . . So, women who have boys are highly regarded. They're like highly respected *compañeras*. But women who have girls have nearly no worth at all. They don't have the same possibilities as mothers who have boys.[18]

Despite this questioning, indigenous women in ONIC and CRIC have not opted to create their own organizational spaces, and instead they have worked to gain greater opportunities for participation within mixed organizations. Berrío Palomo contrasted this experience with that of the National Coordinating Committee of Indigenous Women in Mexico (Coordinadora Nacional de Mujeres Indígenas en México—CONAMI), in which indigenous women decided to create their own spaces for organizing. She pointed out that the long history of political participation at community and regional levels in Colombian grassroots organizations generated an imaginary of participation and identification with an ethnic discourse as having higher priority than specific gender demands.

Nevertheless, in the case of CRIC, analyzed by Lozano Suárez, there are some initial efforts to address women's specific problems in a framework of broader reflection on strengthening indigenous organizations. According to Lozano Suárez, there was discussion at CRIC's 12th Congress, held in March 2005, about the increasing problems of intra-family violence, fathers abandoning their children, early pregnancies, and rapes by paramilitary groups. As a result of the efforts of a group of women supported by both young people and the elderly, the assembly approved inclusion as the tenth point on the organization's program: "To work to strengthen the family as the nucleus of indigenous organization." Based on this "mandate" from the organization's 12th Congress, CRIC's Women's Program was created and allocated a budget for supporting its work in indigenous communities.

As part of these efforts to address the problems of violence and women's exclusion, members of CRIC's Women's Program, in coordination with UAIIN, promoted the organizing of a special *diplomado* (a diploma course), "Indigenous Families, Gender Participation, and Equity," designed for the delegates to indigenous councils, with participation of two hundred students from two class levels. There was, however, some resistance from male leaders to talking about women's problems separately from family or community problems. These leaders argued that indigenous thinking is based on integrality, and it is thus necessary to talk about families, not only women, since the latter would go against the organization's unity.

The indigenous women in CRIC do not reject or question these discourses, but instead, like Guatemalan indigenous women, they make use of the discourse of cosmovision to speak of the need for returning to the cultural values that will allow them to experience "integrality" with greater harmony. For example, attention has been given to the Nasa myth around the creating parents Uma and Tay, who have the same authority and whose knowledges and powers complement each other. According to Nasa cosmovision, all human beings are born in pairs. Women are born accompanied by a male Ksxa'w, and the Ksxa'w for men is female. In this regard, Lozano Suárez commented, "Women trust that these new languages, these indigenous epistemologies, will open the way for negotiating relations characterized by equilibrium and complementarity between men and women, and that they will be incorporated into the organization's narratives without dismissing them as 'feminisms from the outside'" (Lozano Suárez forthcoming, 30). Lozano Suárez highlighted the women's proposal for conceiving of the family in a broad sense, like the CRIC family in four dimensions, for placing debate and analysis of gender issues in a political organizational context in harmony with the culture's principles such as integrality and communality.

One of proposals emerging from the diplomado course is the creation of a permanent school on gender and family that will serve to create a space for reflection on ways to reconstitute integrality and communality from values of peaceful, equitable coexistence without exclusions and without violence.

The voices, and reflections on the voices, expressed in the work of Berrío Palomo and Lozano Suárez, speak to us of a dynamic, changing indigenous identity that, while founded on cultural community-based logics, rejects historical practices that exclude and violate women. The reconstitution of indigenous law, as promoted by CRIC, cannot remain on the sidelines of efforts made by the organization's women to construct new forms of coexistence.

FINAL REFLECTIONS

The "juridization of politics" has meant that the struggles for rights and for legality have come to occupy a central position in the struggles waged by indigenous peoples. We might say that these political initiatives established the language on the basis of which resistance would be expressed. Using the definition of hegemony from William Roseberry, we might assert that the reforms of multicultural constitutionalism can be analyzed as a new hegemony that has constructed "a common language or way of talking about social relationships that sets out the central terms around which and in terms of which contestation and struggle can occur" (Roseberry 1994, 360–61).

The language of rights is being appropriated and vernacularized by the indigenous men and women of Latin America in their struggle for new societal agreements with nation-states and within their own communities. The denouncement of violence and the exclusion of indigenous peoples by Latin American national projects and the exclusion of women by the ethno-nationalist projects of indigenous movements have taken place simultaneously, demonstrating to us the complexity of the current struggles for social justice in our continent.

Discourses of cultural rights, autonomous rights, and women's rights have involved a new language in political struggle that, in many cases, has replaced discourses of greater political radicalness, such as discourses on internal colonialism, sovereignty, and revolution. However, also in this process of the vernacularization of discourses on rights (see Engle Merry 2006), new meanings have been created around what is understood by culture, justice, and tradition, and in a broader sense, around what it means to be an indigenous woman or an indigenous man in our contemporary world. Legislative reforms in favor of cultural recognition and the creation or reconstitution of indigenous justice have been accompanied by processes of collective reflection and political creativity in which indigenous women have played a key role.

Over the last ten years, we have learned from the practices and discourses of these women who have led us to reformulate many of our theoretical paradigms and our own feminist practices. The voices speaking on behalf of culture have diversified, and this has confronted and destabilized purist and ahistorical perspectives of indigenous cultures. Also, we have witnessed the construction of new spaces for dialogue, negotiation, and confrontation in the reconstitution of indigenous justices. These are processes characterized by intra-community hierarchies and by relations of power, and in this sense, they have represented many challenges for women who have opted for transforming their spaces of justice while at the same time defending indigenous autonomy.

In the area of justice, we have learned that advocating, through our academic work, respect for indigenous jurisdictions does not mean denying or silencing the diversity of voices that, from within indigenous communities, are reformulating the way to understand justice and indigenous law.

A recognition of the productive capacity of academic knowledge leads me to position myself politically among the voices that demand a broad-based, non-exclusive definition of indigenous identity and that recognize the multiplicity of political experiences and genealogies characterizing a sense of belonging to this imaginary community. I thus reject the temptation to reify indigenous identities and their spaces for justice on the basis of authenticity-based criteria, whether involuntarily or strategically, since I believe this can contribute to creating new exclusions. Listening to and reflecting the diversity of voices spoken from the perspective of being indigenous, with the objective of strengthening indigenous justice, is a political responsibility for those of us who support, from our academic settings, the recognition of so-called indigenous rights.

In the next chapter we shall see how these processes of "juridization of politics" have also implied acting in transnational spaces of justice, where indigenous women have also had an influence in destabilizing hegemonic discourses on women's rights. These spaces of international justice, such as the Inter-American Court of Human Rights, have allowed some indigenous women to evidence the racism and patriarchal violence allowed and reproduced by Latin American states.

4

FROM VICTIMS TO HUMAN RIGHTS DEFENDERS

International Litigation and the Struggle for
Justice of Indigenous Women

I
N THIS CHAPTER I REFLECT ON THE POSSIBILITIES and limitations of
international litigation for indigenous women's access to justice. After examining the challenges faced by women when resorting to communal indigenous law, I include a second level of inter-legality that arises in the scope
of international justice. Based on an analysis of the cases of Inés Fernández
Ortega and Valentina Rosendo Cantú before the Inter-American Court of
Human Rights, I examine how the appropriation of discourses on indigenous
peoples' rights and human rights allowed these two women (and the women
in their organizations) to reflect on the historic grievances suffered by their
peoples and on the specific ways they have been experienced by women. The
experience of international litigation, its preparation, and the subsequent application of the Inter-American Court's sentence gave rise to collective spaces
where Me'phaa indigenous women shared their critical reflections on state
violence, justice, and impunity. Simultaneously, Inés's and Valentina's testimonies, and those of other women who supported them in their struggle,
demonstrate the tight link they establish between individual experiences of
sexual violence and the historic violence suffered by their communities and organizations. In these cases, the vernacularization of rights discourses implied
theorizing about and vindicating the connection between individual and collective rights by reconstructing the memories of grievances and demanding
collective reparations.

These case studies also reveal the way in which violence, racism, and gender inequalities affect the lives of indigenous Mexican women and determine their lack of access to justice. These two indigenous leaders, raped by members of the Mexican Army in 2002, opted to take their cases before international justice after the lack of response by the Mexican justice system. The Inter-American Court not only became a space through which to seek justice, but many collective efforts and new leaderships were developed throughout the denunciation process.

Through the ethnographic reconstruction of their workshops, political encounters, and the trial before the Inter-American Court, I will analyze the appropriation of the discourses on rights that Inés Fernández Ortega and Valentina Rosendo Cantú, as well as other women from their organization, have undertaken in order to denounce the violence, racism, and economic segregation they suffer in their communities.

Facing the concern that human rights discourses are becoming new forms of control that cause social protests to fall under the control of the state and contribute to the construction of neoliberal conceptions of the individual, my research aims to analyze the complexities of the vernacularization process of human rights discourse in the context of militarized violence and lack of access to justice.

This chapter is a product of a collaborative investigation that involved the carrying out of collective reflection workshops, the development of an anthropological expert report that was presented before the Inter-American Court, and the ethnography of national and international spaces of justice. My intention is to contribute to the debate surrounding the construction of a "subordinate cosmopolitan legality" by the popular movements of the continent (de Sousa Santos 2002; de Sousa Santos and Rodríguez-Garavito 2005; Engle Merry 2011).

Valentina Rosendo Cantú and Inés Fernández Ortega, both members of the Organization of the Me'phaa People (Organización del Pueblo Indígena Me'phaa—OPIM), were raped by soldiers of the Mexican Army in February and March of 2002. After eight years of the soldiers' impunity, Valentina and Inés opted to take their cases to international justice after the lack of response to their demands by the Mexican justice system. The Inter-American Court not only became a space in which to seek justice, but also, during the time it took to process their accusations, many collective efforts had been organized. Contrary to the demobilizing effect that repressive violence usually exerts, the response has been a greater organization and strengthening of female leaderships that have appropriated the human rights discourses as tools for their struggle. It is upon this dual process of female victimization and personal reconstruction in the struggle for justice that I want to center my analysis.

THE APPROPRIATION OF INTERNATIONAL LITIGATION IN THE STRUGGLE OF WOMEN

As a legal anthropologist and feminist, I confront the dilemma of conceiving positive law as a cultural product of liberalism critically, but at the same time, as an activist, I cannot cease to recognize the potential it has as a tool for the construction of a better life for women. Feminists, anthropologists, and jurists have widely analyzed the power mechanisms derived from positive law and the way in which state legal institutions reproduce ethnocentric and patriarchal perspectives that have ruled the cultural imaginaries of the Western world (see Engle Merry 1995; Facio 1992; Fineman and Thomadsen 1991; Hernández Castillo 2002a, 2004b). However, in certain contexts, positive law and state justice can be used by those same women to build spaces of resistance (Chenaut 2014; Hirsh 1994; Smart 1989; Sierra and Hernández Castillo 2005). In this case, international justice has had a repairing effect on the lives of the women who have been victims of sexual violence. It has also had a political effect in the denunciation of gender violence perpetrated by the Mexican Army and in the promotion of reforms that limit military legal jurisdiction.

International justice increasingly becomes the last resource of Latin American women who see their human rights violated by representatives of their governments, be it in a direct way or by negligence, and whose demands for justice go unanswered by the national system. In many of these cases, strategic litigation has helped refute gender discrimination and achieved legislative changes in favor of women's rights. Regarding domestic violence, we have the case of *María da Penha v. Brazil*, presented before the Inter-American Court of Human Rights in 2006, resulting in one of the most advanced laws on domestic violence (known as the "María da Penha Law"). In the matter of sexual violence, the following cases are to be noted: *MM v. Perú* was presented in 1998 before the Inter-American Commission on Human Rights (IACHR); the case of *MZ v. Bolivia* was also presented before IACHR in 2008. Both cases concern poor peasant women who were raped and could not find justice in their respective countries and decided to resort to international justice to achieve, as part of their compensation, public policies that favor women's rights.

Finally, there is the case of *Gonzalez & Co. v. México*, known as the case "of the Cotton Field," because the mothers of eight young women, whose corpses were found in a cotton field in the city of Ciudad Juárez, Chihuahua, filed the grievance. This is considered a paradigmatic case in strategic litigation favoring women's rights because of the international awareness that was achieved regarding the structural causes of gender violence. In 2009, the Inter-American Court ruled that the murders of women "of the Cotton Field" were part of a pattern of systemic violence based on gender, age, and social class, and the Court urged the Mexican government to provide compensation measures oriented to identify and eliminate what was defined as structural factors of discrimination. The ultimate aim was to transform implicit gender inequalities that generated the violence.

These experiences have led the Latin American and Caribbean Committee for the Defense of Women's Rights (Comité de América Latina y el Caribe para la Defensa de los Derechos de la Mujer—CLADEM), one of the foremost feminist networks that deals with gender justice, to deem international justice as an important tool in the progress of women's rights. It has achieved, through strategic litigation cases 1. the extraction of legal precedents for fighting gender-based violence in the international system of human rights protection, 2. the socialization of processes and results obtained with the women's movement and other social movements in a collective exercise of civic construction, and 3. Normative and public policies modifications, as well as friendly settlement agreements and compensatory actions obtained a) according to the resolutions obtained at the international level, or b) with the direct assumption of responsibility in a public act.[1]

As I explain in chapter 1, these paradigmatic cases tend to be evaluated in a positive manner by feminist organizations, judging by the impacts that they have had in gender jurisprudence and public policies, but I was concerned about the impact that the legal process could have in Inés's and Valentina's lives. It was not until I met Inés, and I heard from her the reasons why she wanted to denounce, that I decided to participate as an expert witness in the case.

The legal representatives of the Center of Human Rights of the Mountains of Guerrero Tlachinollan (Centro de Derechos Humanos de la Montaña de Guerrero Tlachinollán) placed at the forefront in their strategies the needs and decisions of

Inés and Valentina. For them, the complaint before the Inter-American Court was not an end in itself but a part of what they called "integral defense of the individual" that places not the lawsuit, but the victims, at the center of the process. Santiago Aguirre, member of the legal team of Tlachinollan, describes his differences with those who prioritize strategic litigation:

> These long justice processes have a component—almost structural and unavoidable—of ambiguity in the relationships that remain. You said it yourself just now: the victims can easily become flags, political symbols, and we can cease to see the person behind everything. What we can do as organizations to reduce that risk is to focus on the people we are accompanying through this process. But the idea that through the defense of a case, we are going to change "X," inevitably has this manipulation factor that is messed up. That is a component of strategic litigation. For that reason, we say that we do not recognize ourselves in strategic litigation, we like to think that we do an integral defense of the individual, we integrate psychologists, we have an anthropologist on the team. It is almost like those of us who wished to be tall, but we come from a very short family, it is the genetics of litigation. For that reason, we have a hard time making alliances with a new generation of lawyers that do strategic litigation.[2]

It was this political perspective of Tlachinollan, before the issue of international litigation and the conviction of Inés to take her grievance beyond the borders of her country, that led me to embark on a long journey that took me to Lima, Peru. In April 2010 I took part in the public audience summoned by the Inter-American Court of Human Rights with the aim to illustrate for the judges the content of the report I elaborated jointly with ethnologist Héctor Ortíz Elizondo as part of the supporting documents presented by the legal representatives of Inés Fernández Ortega (see appendix 1). This document served as the basis for the further development of the anthropological report in the case of Valentina Rosendo Cantú, in whose litigation I did not participate in a direct manner.

VALENTINA AND INÉS AGAINST MILITARY VIOLENCE

Although my research has focused on the case of Inés Fernández Ortega (for the obvious reason that I developed the cultural report surrounding her case and for having participated as a specialist in her hearing before the Inter-American Court), her grievance has been closely related to that of Valentina Rosendo Cantú, a member of the same organization who was also raped by the military one month prior.

On February 16, 2002, Valentina Rosendo Cantú, then a young woman of only seventeen years of age and the mother of a three-month-old baby, went out of her house (located in the community of Barranca Bejuco in the municipality of Acatepec, Guerrero). She headed toward the river in order to clean her clothes. As all the women in her community, Valentina walked nearly an hour to get to her destination since the communities in the region lack running water. That day, her sister-in-law offered to take care of Valentina's daughter since Fidel (her husband) was busy working on the construction of a communitarian school. Valentina never imagined that on that fateful afternoon her life would take a radical turn when she faced the violence and impunity of the military. While she washed her clothes, eight military men approached her with a list of names of presumed *encapuchados* (a name given to members of political-military organizations because they cover their faces with *capuchas/* hoods). Two of these soldiers, apparently the leaders of the group, proceeded to beat her and rape her when they did not get the answers they expected.

In subsequent interviews, Valentina reported that the list of presumed encapuchados had been supplied to the military by one of the local overlords with whom her family had problems for opposing the cultivation of narcotics.[3] Valentina, just like several women from Barranca Bejuco, was a member of OPIM, an organization formed in 2002 as a collective response to the continuous human rights violations of the indigenous peoples.

A month later, March 22, Inés Fernández Ortega, a twenty-two-year-old Me'phaa woman and a fellow member with Valentina in the women's section of the OPIM, was raped by a member of the 41st Battalion of the Mexican Army. The soldier assaulted Inés inside her home (and in front of her three children), with the complicity of two other military men. After the sexual attack, as the soldiers left, they took the meat that was drying on the patio. Along with this trifling loot, the soldiers also took the peace of mind of Inés and her family, who have not been able to sleep well out of fear of the military violence that continues to stalk the communities in the region.

Both women resorted to the community assembly to ask for their support in filing a complaint; they received conditioned support that was later removed out of fear of retaliation by the army. They later approached state justice through the prosecution department, where the racism that permeates the justice system was made evident since they were both denied the right to an interpreter, and a negligent medical staff treated them with contempt. In the case of Inés, the medical department "lost" the gynecological tests that were performed.

The testimonies of Inés and Valentina allow us to access a privileged point of view of those who have experienced the multiple oppressions that characterize the whole of Mexican society. The exclusion they both suffered on account of their ethnic, gender, and class background was revealed when both women tried to gain access to state justice. The ignorance of indigenous languages by government officials and the high level of monolingualism and illiteracy among the female indigenous population hinders their access to justice. The experiences of Inés Fernández Ortega and Valentina Rosendo Cantú with the authorities of the Public Prosecution Office (Ministerio Público), and subsequently before military justice, come to confirm these exclusions. As in the majority of the indigenous regions in Mexico, the Public Prosecution Office of Ayutla de los Libres and of Acatepec have mestizo employees who do not speak the indigenous languages spoken in the region (the Me'phaa or Tlapaneco and the Tu'un sávi or Mixteco) and do not have access to an interpreter or translator. For that reason, Inés Fernández Ortega asked for the support of Obtilia Eugenio Manuel, leader of OPIM, in order to file her grievance. In the interviews of Inés and Valentina, they both told us about how badly they were treated and with what lack of interest judicial authorities took on their case. These officials determined that the case was out of their jurisdiction since the presumably guilty party belonged to the Mexican Army, so they decided to turn it over to the military prosecution department.

The aforementioned research on indigenous women's access to justice states that the experiences of Inés and Valentina are almost the norm when it comes to judicial processes of indigenous men and women facing state justice. This is true despite the fact that in the reform to the 2nd Constitutional Article of 2001, the right to have an interpreter and anthropological reports is established. What we found in both cases is that these laws were unheeded since the departments do not have the adequate personnel to attend the demands of indigenous people since they know neither the culture nor the language of the complainants.

This violation of cultural and linguistic rights is not only a product of the lack of training and personnel, it is also accompanied by degrading and racist treatment by public officials. In many ways this behavior reproduces the racial hierarchies that mark Mexican society as a whole. In the case of indigenous women, this structural racism that state institutions replicate goes even deeper because of gender discrimination, and many times, they become victims of symbolic violence when government representatives treat their cases of sexual violence with a total lack of respect and sensibility. Such is the case of the medical examiner first in charge of certifying the rape suffered by Inés Fernández Ortega, who, when Inés solicited a female doctor to examine her, answered: "Who cares if a man examines you, was it women who raped you?"[4]

For ten years, Inés and Valentina traveled the roads of the Costa Chica in their native state of Guerrero looking for justice, facing the racism and misogyny of the state representatives. During the legal process before the Inter-American Court, both women endured death threats, criticism by community members, and family tensions. In the case of Valentina, this tension climaxed when her husband left her; in the case of Inés, this resulted in the torture and murder of her brother Lorenzo by "strangers." He had been her main support in her search for justice.

Going out and demanding justice had a heavy cost for both women. Inés had to leave her older daughter, Nohemí, who was barely a pre-teen, in charge of the younger children and the household. This allowed for Inés and her husband to head to the municipality in Ayutla de los Libres, to Tlapa, to Chilpancingo, or to Washington, DC. On the other hand, Valentina was forced to abandon her house, her family, and her cornfield when she left Barranca Bejuco after receiving several death threats by paramilitary groups linked to the army.

In their journey toward justice, both women encountered allies and built solidarity networks that have accompanied them for the last nine years. These include the members of Center of Human Rights of the Mountains of Guerrero Tlachinollan, the Peace Brigades, and the team of Amnesty International in México, among others. In the company of some of these close friends and allies, they crossed the border and went to Washington, DC, to present their case before the Inter-American Human Rights Commission, to finally take them to the Inter-American Court of Human Rights in 2010.

The cultural identities and regional history affected the way in which both women lived through their rapes and subsequent searches for justice. Both Inés and Valentina have begun to organize around their rights and those of their people. Their rapes are interpreted and lived by themselves and their families with a historical memory that links the presence of the army with the violence and impunity that has permeated the region since the 1970s as a result of the "dirty

FIGURE 10. Inés Fernández and her family with the author and the members
of Center of Human Rights of the Mountains of Guerrero Tlachinollan.
Photograph from R. Aída Hernández Archives.

war." In 1998, the massacre of "El Charco" occurred precisely in the municipality
of Ayutla de los Libres where OPIM has its main headquarters.[5] All of these
rapes and instances of torture constitute a part of the "continuum of violence"
that has marked the relationship between the indigenous people of the region
and the Mexican armed forces.

In February 2008, a series of events occurred that fed the fear and sense of
vulnerability of the members of the OPIM and the inhabitants of the region,
and stirred memories of a recent past of violence and impunity. These included
the murder of Lorenzo Fernández Ortega (Inés's brother and a member of OPIM);
the anonymous death threats to the organization's president, Obtilia Eugenio
Manuel; and the arrest warrants and detentions in April of that same year for
five of their main leaders.

The expert witness report that elaborated on behalf of Inés's accusation showed
us that sexual violation was an experience that impacted the whole community

because the Me'phaa people understand that the individual and the collective are closely linked, thus the experiences suffered by one individual are lived by the whole community. A reflection of this communal sense is the fact that most of the compensations for damage demanded by Inés to the Court are not for her personal benefit, but rather they include children and women of her organization and community. The testimonies and the actions of these women speak to us of experiences that were not perceived as personal affronts but as part of a continuum of violence that has affected their villages and organizations for some time now. The justice they demand is not limited to the incarceration of their aggressors but also includes the demilitarization of their region and the end of impunity and legislative reforms that would allow women and indigenous women access to justice (see Section 4, "Reparation Measures," in the Official Expertise Anthropological Report, in appendix 1). These were the compensations I had to justify before the Inter-American Court of Human Rights in my first experience in international litigation.

THE HEARING BEFORE THE INTER-AMERICAN COURT: AN ETHNOGRAPHIC APPROACH TO INTERNATIONAL LITIGATION

Although it is true that legal anthropology has had a special interest in ethnographically documenting dispute processes in spaces of communitarian justice (see Collier [1973] 1995; Garza Caligaris 2002; Moore 1996; Nader 1978, 1990; Sierra 1992, 2004a, 2004b), and to a lesser degree in spaces of state justice (see Barrera 2012; Chenaut 2014; Engle Merry 2000; Latour 2002), we have very few ethnographic descriptions that give account of the "cultural rituals" that develop in spaces of international justice.

Some authors have shared with us insight and theoretical reflections regarding their experiences as cultural expert witnesses when giving testimony in spaces of international justice (see Anaya and Grossman 2002; Hale 2005) or in UN meetings where women's rights are discussed (Engle Merry 2006), pointing toward the cultural dimension and practices that are produced in these spaces. However, it would seem the prevailing premise is that so-called indigenous law and communitarian justice are plagued by "culture" while the international right and its spaces of justice are only a "transparent" manifestation of the use of law.

In this section, I approach international litigation as a space of dispute in which cultural references and power relations among all actors that take part in this legal "performance" are revealed. Taking up the methodological proposal of Leticia Barrera, I assume that "The hearings are not discreet, but rather choreographed events, calculated to achieve an effect. They involve discursive repertoires that appeal to a segment of the population to which they are aimed" (Barrera 2012, 141).

Taking part in this legal performance were not only the involved parties but also a broad audience that included law students, members of human rights organizations, Peruvian indigenous women organizing against military violence, and feminist groups. By becoming itinerant, the Inter-American Court of Human Rights is sending a message of legality to all countries with membership in the Organization of American States, and this message is reaffirmed in these hearings.

The Inter-American Court was founded in 1979 as an autonomous judicial institution. It was formed out of the organization of American governments with the purpose of applying the American Convention on Human Rights and other international treaties.[6] It is a space of international justice to watch over and sanction any member that violates human rights. The Inter-American Court has its headquarters in San José, Costa Rica. The Costa Rican government donated a house so that a tribunal could be established and trials could be held there. However, since May 2005, the Inter-American Court decided to conduct itinerant sessions at various member countries. The trial of *Inés Fernández Ortega v. México* took place in the Palace of Justice in Lima, Peru. The Palace of Justice is a neoclassical building of gray granite and shiny multicolored marble floors that was built in 1939 and has become a symbol of judicial power in Peru. Two lions, sculpted in white marble, flank the sides of the entrance to the palace. The grandeur of the venue contrasts with the poverty of some of the streets in downtown Lima.

We arrived at the Palace of Justice on April 15, 2010: Colombian psychologist Clemencia Correa, Peruvian lawyer Marcela Huaita, and I (a cultural anthropologist) would testify as experts in the legal representation of Inés. The legal team consisted of the lawyers Vidulfo Rosales, Alejandro Ramos, and Jorge Santiago Aguirre, as well as the anthropologist Abel Barrera Hernández from the Center of Human Rights of the Mountains of Guerrero Tlachinollan. On behalf of the Center for Justice and International Law (CEJIL), the lawyers

Gisela de León and Agustín Martín. The advanced stage of Inés's pregnancy had prevented her from traveling to Lima; the Inter-American Court had denied the petition of the legal team for Inés to be substituted by the president of OPIM, Obtilia Eugenio Manuel. We all knew the power that Inés has when she speaks, and her absence added to the nervousness of her legal representatives. Her testimony, and that of her husband and daughter, as witnesses, were presented before a notary public in Guerrero and delivered in written format to the Inter-American Court (known legally as an affidavit). The strength of Inés's voice took over the room through a video that was played at the beginning of the hearing.

When entering the Palace of Justice, the first thing that caught my attention was the presence of a significant number of Peruvian indigenous women dressed in their traditional dresses, patiently waiting for the start of the hearing. We later found out that they were members of the National Coordinator of Women Affected by Internal Armed Conflict (Coordinadora Nacional de Mujeres Afectadas por el Conflicto Armado Interno) and the National Federation of Peasant Artisans, Indigenous, Native, and Salaried Women of Peru (Federación Nacional de Mujeres Campesinas, Artesanas, Indígenas, Nativas, y Asalariadas del Perú). Women in these organizations have been supporting other women victims of sexual violence during the internal armed conflict that, for more than twenty years, has altered the life of Peruvian society (1980–2000). Many of them came up to me after the hearing and told me how moved they were and how important it was to them that an indigenous woman like themselves would dare to confront the army and take her government to an international trial. The example of Inés Fernández Ortega encouraged them to think of the Inter-American Court as a space where justice could be achieved. Two of these women gave me brief written messages for Inés where they expressed their admiration.

The presence of these peasant women, most of them Quechua speakers, gave the tribunal a popular appearance that contrasted with the formality of the witness stand and the entire environment of the Palace of Justice. Being a public hearing, many law schools took their students to witness the first international litigation that the Inter-American Court held in Peruvian territory. All the excitement of the crowd turned into silence when the five male judges came into the room: Leonardo A. Franco, Manuel E. Ventura Robles, Alberto Pérez, Eduardo Vio Grossi, and Alejandro Carlos Espinosa, along with two female judges: Margarette May Macaulay, and Rhadys Abreu Blondet. Their black and red togas gave the ritual a sense of solemnity that made me think of public dissertations in European universities.

The paraphernalia of the ritual distanced the judges from the popular audience witnessing the trial. The Quechua women, to whom Inés's case echoed their own memories of military violence, silently witnessed a justice ritual that had little to do with the community justice with which many of them had been involved.

As the expert in charge of presenting the oral report before the court, I was not able to witness the whole hearing, as I was taken into a small room in the back area of the palace where I nervously waited my turn to talk before the tribunal. Before leaving I could see the ostentatious entrance of the party that represented the Mexican state. Besides the legal team, more than twenty government representatives appeared, including members of the Mexican embassy in Peru, the government of the state of Guerrero, and the national defense secretary, among others.[7] The government representatives were accompanied by a group of assistants who carried many boxes of documents. The numerous entourage and the "mysterious" documents contrasted with the five lawyers who carried their folders in their hands. Later, I learned that the documents submitted were reports of the diverse "mainstreaming of gender perspective" programs that the Mexican government promotes in their public policies; these were submitted as "evidence" that the Mexican state is concerned with women's rights.

The distribution of the two teams within the tribunal's space, the way both teams communicated internally, and the manner in which they approached the judges evidenced the power inequality that existed between the representatives of the Mexican government and the representatives of Inés.

The government's legal team opted for a strategy that partially recognized the responsibility of the Mexican state for misdemeanors of omission and delay in the delivery of justice. Without any witnesses or experts to support their defense, they started their participation in the hearing by saying they recognized:

First, the lack of specialized medical attention, which should have included the psychological part and not only the physical, to Mrs. Fernández Ortega. That it should have been delivered without delay, for it constitutes a flagrant violation to article 8.1 of the American Convention. Second, that the disappearance of the expert evidence taken from the victim also constitutes a flagrant violation of article 8.1 of the American Convention. Third, that despite the efforts of the authorities, both delay and absence of due diligence occurred in the investigations. Therefore, several violations to articles 8.1 and 25 on the American Convention, and as a consequence a violation to article 5.1 of the same legislation, for the damages caused to the psychological integrity of Mrs. Fernández Ortega. This is . . . the state's recognition of international responsibility for violations to the American Convention . . . that is presented today . . . with the finality that the Court dictates the demanded compensations by international law and its jurisprudence.[8]

This recognition excluded direct responsibility on the part of the Mexican Army for the use of sexual torture against Inés and the family, and the community impacts of "institutional military violence" throughout the last ten years. It also excluded the violation of the Inter-American Convention to Prevent and Eradicate Violence Against Women; the Convention Belem do Pará; and the Convention Against Torture and Other Cruel, Inhuman, or Degrading Treatment (all of which were violated by these actions). Despite the fact that the state began the trial recognizing its responsibilities, the team from Tlachinollan and CEJIL still had much to prove in order to achieve the expected sentence as a result of Inés's accusation.

When it was my turn to speak, two other specialists had already testified, and I had no knowledge of the course the hearing was taking. I started my declaration with a twenty-minute introduction in which I summarized the main arguments of my report based on a field investigation and interviews with Inés, her family, and members of her community. These points were 1) the impact that the sexual assault suffered by Mrs. Fernández Ortega had on the indigenous community, especially women; 2) the alleged affectation of the community tissue and the impunity; and 3) the possible compensation measures.[9]

The judges posed questions to me with the intention of clarifying parts of the presented document and the oral testimony that I had just presented. It was Judge Margarette May Macaulay, an Afro-Caribbean magistrate from Jamaica, who seemed to be the most knowledgeable about the report, and who subsequently confronted the Mexican government representatives more openly. Although it is true that all judges followed a pre-established protocol and constructed their questions based on the evidence provided beforehand, Judge Macaulay could not hide the special concern she had for Inés's case. Her career as a women's rights defender and promoter of legislative reforms against domestic violence and sexual harassment in her country allowed her to approach the case with political and cultural capital that the other judges did not appear to have. After the hearing, I found out that she was a member of the coordinating committee of the Caribbean Association of Feminist Research and Action.

Having judges like her in the Inter-American Court of Human Rights is likely an achievement of the Latin American feminist movement in the inter-American human rights system.

Although it is true that the gender sensibility of some judges may have helped obtain the sentence that was achieved in the end, the cultural arguments did not have the impact I expected, not even in the speech presented by Inés's legal representatives or in the summaries made by the members of the tribunal. To my surprise, both the lawyers of CEJIL and the ones from Tlachinollan did not include in their final statements the arguments we presented in our cultural report about the impact of Inés's rape on the community. In the workshops that we had with Inés and the members of OPIM, a lot of emphasis had been placed on the demand for demilitarization of the region as a guarantee of no repetition. Based on this collective reflection we had included in the demanded compensations of our report a section that read:

> The retreat of military forces from the region is seen by many inhabitants as an indispensable measure to guarantee no repetition. The presence of military forces without the proper application of international legislation on military conflicts, generates a situation of vagueness in which neither the members of the army nor the habitants of the zone are clear on whether or not the settlers are recognized as civilians or non-belligerent forces. It is from this situation that a mutual distrust was created that contributed to the conflicts and the violations to human rights. This vagueness could be solved if the Mexican government recognized the capacity of indigenous communities to decide on issues within their competence according to their culture as stipulated in Article 2 of the Mexican Constitution in regards to autonomy and Article 6 of Convention 169 concerning the right to consultation. (see appendix 1)

This argument was not taken up again in the oral statements of Inés's legal representatives. We later found out that they were included in the written statements, but it was decided that they would be left out because of the "few possibilities that the court would retake this demand" (see "Protection and Prevention Measures" in the Official Expertise Anthropological Report in appendix 1). This omission made me question the importance that human rights activists give to cultural reports.

We parted Lima with the conviction that each one of us had made our best effort, accomplishing the task that had been assigned to us. But it was almost impossible to make up for the impact that Inés's presence would have had on the Inter-American Court. There were many uncertainties regarding the contents of the sentence.

Five months later, on August 30, 2010, the Inter-American Court announced its sentence, declaring that Inés Fernández Ortega had been sexually assaulted and tortured by members of the Mexican Army in a context marked by poverty, discrimination, and what the tribunal called "institutional military violence."

The verdict of the Inter-American Court was, in itself, reinvigorating; after so many years of waiting, the complaints of Inés and Valentina were finally legitimized. The sentence was composed of sixteen points in which the judges demand that compensations are carried out in the area of justice by punishing the guilty parties; publicly recognizing the responsibilities of the state; modifying and implementing public policies that promote and facilitate the access to justice for indigenous women; establishing compensations of a communitarian nature, such as the construction of a Center for Women's Rights and a shelter; promoting legislative reforms that would limit the military jurisdiction; and establishing that civil regional tribunals must process cases of violations to human rights committed by the military. Other compensations considered in the sentencing included providing support for the education of Inés's daughters, as well as medical and psychological attention for the whole family. Finally, a monetary compensation was granted to Inés and her close relatives affected by the military violence.[10]

In the sentence, there was a mention of our report in several inserts (infra paragraph 243, 244 and 267–70) and it recognized the importance of the cultural context to determine the compensations, signaling: "The Court does not lose sight that Mrs. Fernández Ortega is an indigenous woman, in a special situation of vulnerability, which will be taken into account when the compensations for this sentence are awarded. Additionally, the tribunal considers the obligation of noticing a case that involves victims of an indigenous community, may require measures of communitarian reach."[11] Despite my skepticism about the little importance given to the cultural report in the oral statements by the legal representatives of Inés during the trial, the sentence showed us that step-by-step international justice starts to integrate the cultural context when interpreting the human rights of indigenous people. While it is true that in several previous cases the Inter-American Court had demanded community compensations, it had always been collective damages to peoples or communities;[12] this was the first time that a case in which a violation to the human rights of one individual resulted in communitarian compensations. Inés's concern that her case would be judged within the framework of a history of violence suffered by her people, and that measures would be taken to end that continuum of violence, appeared to find a response in this sentence.

THE RITUAL OF FORGIVENESS: PUBLIC ACKNOWLEDGEMENT OF RESPONSIBILITIES

Both the verdict and the "Act of Acknowledgment of Responsibilities of the Mexican State" for the cases of Valentina on December 15, 2011, and Inés on March 6, 2012, symbolize a political and moral triumph for both indigenous leaders, giving them the historic reason and probing the veracity of their claims so many times distorted by the operators of civil and military justice.

Valentina, the adolescent, premature mother, monolingual in Me'phaa, whose life was forever altered by two soldiers on February 16, 2002, made one of the most powerful politicians of the Mexican government apologize and recognize before her family, friends, thousands of TV viewers, and radio audiences the responsibility of the Mexican state in the violation of her rights. In front of Valentina and her daughter Jenny (now a pre-adolescent, and heir to her mother's strength and courage), Alejandro Poiré Romero, Mexico's Secretary of the Interior, apologized saying:

> The lack of timely and specialized medical attention to Mrs. Rosendo Cantú, the delay in the proper investigations, the damage of her psychological well-being . . . In addition to these, other actions against human rights were also committed and because of that the Mexican state recognizes in this public act its international responsibility for the violation to the rights of personal integrity, the dignity, the private life, judicial guarantees, judicial protection, the guarantee of access to justice without discrimination and the right of the children, convened in the American Convention on Human Rights, in the Inter-American Convention to Prevent and Punish Torture, in the Inter-American Convention on the Prevention, Punishment, and Eradication of Violence Against Women, "Convention of Belem do Para," in detriment of Mrs. Valentina Rosendo Cantú . . . Having recognized the responsibility of the government and invested as the representative of the state in this event: Mrs. Valentina Rosendo Cantú, to you, to your daughter, I put forth my most sincere apology for the incidents that

took place almost a decade ago and in which your rights were gravely infringed upon.[13]

This speech was translated simultaneously into Me'phaa to the mother of Valentina, seated next to her, and to the family members who accompanied her in the auditorium. Many of us in the audience were moved to tears, not only because of the strength and dignity this woman transmitted but because we knew the high price that she had paid for this symbolic gesture.

Three months later, on March 6, 2012, Inés Fernández Ortega received a similar apology on behalf of the secretary of state, this time in a completely different context and political climate. Unlike Valentina, Inés did not accept traveling to Mexico City to receive an apology but demanded that the "Act of Acknowledgment of Responsibilities" by the Mexican government be performed in the municipality of Ayutla de los Libres, with the partners and members of different organizations as the special guests.

Alejandro Poiré Romero (secretary of the interior), Marisela Morales Ibáñez (attorney general), Ángel Aguirre Rivero (governor of Guerrero), and General Rafael Cázares Anaya (director of human rights of the secretary of defense) all arrived in the central square of Ayutla de los Libres, surrounded by a large security team and a dozen other lesser public functionaries who fought over the chairs in the first rows and for a place in the group picture. Supporting Inés, on her side of the stand, were her husband Fortunato Prisciliano Sierra, Oblitilia Eugenio Manuel (the president of OPIM), and the director of Tlachinollan and anthropologist Abel Barrera Hernández. Both faces of contemporary Mexico were present in this trial, almost giving each other their back, without making eye contact and making clear the class and racial barriers that set apart both worlds. On one side, the face of power: excessively embellished, emotionless. On the other side: the face of Inés, the face of resistance with a stare of reproach and incredulity, strengthened by the cheers of the peasants who had come from different regions to witness this event. Among the audience accompanying her were the authorities of the Community Police of Guerrero (CRAC), peasants of Atoyac de Álvarez from Xochistlahuaca, students of the Raúl Isidro Burgos Rural Teachers' College of Ayotzinapa, and opponents of the La Parota Dam. Inés addressed all of them in Me'phaa, warning them:

> Listen to me, all of you, men, women and children: the people of the government, even though they say they are by your side, they will not keep their word, do not

listen to them. They committed this crime against me because I am poor. And not only against me but against other people . . . The Governor, though he is here, he will not keep his word. That is why I had to look for justice elsewhere, because here they would not listen to me. Today they tell us what we can do and what we cannot do. The government does not let us organize. The soldiers do not let us move freely throughout our communities. They are always close, as civilians, not necessarily in uniform. In this moment they are among us. (Transcription of the Spanish translation of Inés Fernández Ortega's speech during the public act of acknowledgement, March 6, 2012, Ayutla de los Libres)

From the large speakers located around the park came forth the deep voice of the interpreter who transmitted Inés's warnings to us. I got goosebumps when I heard the phrase "in this moment they are among us," as I noticed the presence of armed men wearing civilian clothes mingling with the crowd. Those men were identified by other members of the OPIM as members of paramilitary groups linked to the mayor of Ayutla, Armando García Rendón. One more time, Inés raised her voice to denounce the mockery that was taking place, for they publicly apologized without apprehending the people responsible for the assault she suffered. Nor did they acknowledge their accomplices who were moving about freely in the central park of Ayutla.

FROM VICTIMS TO HUMAN RIGHTS DEFENDERS

Throughout the ten years that have passed since the rapes suffered by Inés and Valentina, their paths have diverged. Valentina opted to leave her community after her husband abandoned her when he succumbed to the peer pressure that criticized Valentina for being a *"mujer de los guachos"* ("woman of the soldiers") and punished her for being brave enough to "shout her disgrace for everyone to hear." Without a man to support her, she felt vulnerable before a community that turned its back on her, when the mayor of Acatepec threatened to withdraw public works financing if they continued to support Valentina's claims. In a new urban context, she has learned Spanish and dared to cross the Atlantic to denounce, on European soil, not only her rape but also military violence as a counterinsurgent strategy against organized indigenous peoples. Her activism has brought her close to different networks of women who fight against violence, and her voice has become the voice of dozens of indigenous women who do not dare to denounce the impact that the militarization of their regions is having on their lives.[14]

Inés has opted to remain in Barranca Tecuani despite the fact that a part of her community has criticized and turned its back on her. In her testimonies, she told us how, at first, her community organized to kick the military out of the communal lands where they have camped out. However, this social cohesion began to fragment over time due to disagreements regarding what strategy to use in order to confront the threat that the army represents. In one of the interviews, Inés stated, "Before the attack, the community was together, but it was the government and fear that divided us. Alfonso Morales, one of the people who worked for the army told the women they should not accuse the *guachos* (military) for they would get in trouble. They are afraid that what happened to me will happen to them, this is why they do not want to support me, nor do they want to organize."[15]

However, the communitarian links of solidarity of those who were in agreement with Inés's claim for justice have flourished once again under the collective space of OPIM. Here, she has found the support that some of her colleagues from Barranca Tecuani denied her. She says, "the OPIM is now my family and my community, they have suffered with me the lack of justice, they are like my father and my mother."[16] It is in the company of other OPIM women that Inés has regained her leadership and has begun to discuss the terms of how the sentence will be implemented.

Inés and Valentina have decided to tell their stories to everyone who wants to listen. It is why her testimonies travel the web through a documentary titled *Looking Inside: Militarization in Guerrero* (*Mirando hacia adentro: La militarazación en Guerrero*), where they narrate not only the history of violence they have suffered but also their experiences in the search for justice.

The voices of Inés Fernández Ortega and Valentina Rosendo Cantú have joined those of their peers: Cuauhtémoc Ramírez, Andrea and Obtilia Eugenio Manuel, Fortina Fernández, and Orlando Manzanares, who have not let the violence toward women and the impunity that characterizes the present administration go undenounced. The Mexican government has not only failed to prevent feminicide, understood in a broad sense as "a category that includes all premature death of women caused by a gender inequality characterized by historical violence and systematic violations of their human and civil rights," as the investigation promoted by the 59th legislature on feminicidal violence in Mexico has shown us (Lagarde 2006, 156). But the Mexican government has

FIGURE 11. The author with Inés Fernández in Barranca Tecuani during the expert witness report research process. Photograph from R. Aída Hernández Archives.

also been directly responsible for the use of physical and sexual violence on the part of security forces as a repressive strategy against social movements.

The gender violence that the testimonies of Inés and Valentina highlight coincides with the Mexican government's signing of various international treaties supporting women's rights. Also, this coincides with the approval of legislative reforms that supposedly promote the elimination of all forms of violence against women.

It is in this context of impunity that the voices of Valentina and Inés claim justice for all those women who live in fear and have opted for silence. Before the eyes of Inés, to do justice does not mean throwing the soldier who raped her in jail. Rather, it means stopping the counterinsurgent violence in the Me'phaa region; demilitarizing the communities; providing security to children so they can walk through the mountain trails unharmed; having a women's shelter in the municipality of Ayutla de los Libres so that their daughters do not have to work as maids in the houses of mestizo families; knowing their rights and having a center so they can educate themselves as human rights defenders; changing the spaces of justices marked by racism and misogyny. These were some of the demands that were articulated during the collective workshops in which the community compensations that would be demanded in court were discussed.[17]

In the act of responsibility and acknowledgement, Inés added a new demand to her list of communitarian compensations and handed the secretary of state a document developed previously by OPIM that demands the implementation of a development plan for the region. Referring to the problems of extreme poverty and marginalization in which the lack of access to justice and the lack of health services are framed, Inés seized on the arrival of a high-level government representative to denounce not only military violence but also structural violence.

However, this supposed "development plan" has turned out to be a double-edged sword, for it has enabled government representatives to legitimize themselves before the local population with the delivery of limited resources for small projects. Some leaders of the region talk about the "danger of the goats," for there are funds being distributed among the people for the purchase of farm animals as a way of building loyalty to state power.

The perils involved in this new context are described by the director of the Tlachinollan Center in the following terms: "We are concerned because now the central topic for OPIM is the development plan, well that is something they feel and think is important: *if we do not make the most out of this juncture, now that the government is negotiating with us, we won't take advantage of it at all.* Then their priority was to focus on which projects and programs are necessary, rather than going forward with the demilitarization issue. And basically it was all about sitting, doing, and evaluating: *Well, we have the program Guerrero Without Hunger, where do we apply it? Here, here, and here.* It was only like taking existing social programs and broadening their coverage and redistribution."[18]

The old co-opting strategy that characterized the PRI administrations for more than seventy-five years is back with the presidency of Enrique Peña Nieto, and (at a state level) with the ex-PRI governor, Ángel Aguirre Rivero (who was governor for the Democratic Revolution Party until October 2014, when he was forced to resign after the mass kidnapping of forty-three students in Iguala, Guerrero).[19] The organizations confront new challenges with the presence (each time more violent) of organized crime that justifies the militarization of the region and the intensification of a policy of co-optation that jeopardizes its autonomy.

It is a political moment full of contradictions: on one side, the sentence has made possible the strengthening of the OPIM and, more specifically, the leadership of Inés at a local level; at the same time, it has justified the biggest intervention of local functionaries in the organizational dynamics of the region. However, we can acknowledge that the process following the trial has allowed Inés and the women members of OPIM to come together and reflect collectively on the origins of the violence that has affected their lives, and to devise strategies to end this violence. The voice of Inés has been multiplied in the voices of her organization's women, who have taken their experiences to Washington, DC, to Spain, to Cuetzalán, Puebla, to the Community Police of Guerrero (CRAC), to Tlaxcala, to different forums in Mexico City, all places where they have denounced sexual violence as a form of torture and denounced the impact of the militarization in the mountains and coast of Guerrero.

Thanks to the efforts and courage of Inés Fernández Ortega and Valentina Rosenda Cantú to demand justice, alongside Tita Radilla (daughter of the peasant leader assassinated during the "dirty war"[20]), they have convinced the Inter-American Court of Human Rights to rule in their favor against the Mexican state, forcing them to modify the Military Justice Code by limiting military legal jurisdiction. Since these historical cases of human rights violations by the military, these types of cases will not be judged in military justice systems, but they will have to go through the civilian justice system. In the current context of militarization, in the name of the War on Drugs, it is a fundamental policy shift that the military is not allowed to hide, within its complicity networks, the human rights violations it has committed.[21]

It is also important to recognize that the reform regarding human rights that was approved by the legislative power in June 2011 has a direct link with these three cases. Thanks to the struggle of these women, the agreements regarding human rights signed by the Mexican state have been recognized and integrated into the Mexican Constitution, strengthening the legal framework of access to justice for all Mexicans.

Finally, I want to mention that Inés's commitment to including all women of her organization as beneficiaries of the verdict set a precedent in international litigation since, for the first time, it was recognized that damage to an individual (in this case, the rape suffered by Inés) can affect a whole community when the cultural context of this individual is taken into account through an understanding of how sexual violence is lived and justice is imagined.

Despite delay tactics by government representatives in executing the sentence, Inés and the women of OPIM have continued with their organizational and reflection processes, collectively discussing the objectives and structure of the Community Center of Rights for Me'phaa Women that they seek to establish as one of the compensations owed by the state. In this process, other indigenous women fighting for a culturally situated women's rights agenda have come close, like the women of CRAC and the Nahuatl women of the Indigenous Women's Center in Cuetzalán, Puebla.

If the use of sexual violence as a form of torture was intended to terrorize and demobilize women, it is evident that the obscure powers that are behind counterinsurgent strategies did not take into account the courage and solidarity of the women from OPIM. Instead of the end of indigenous leadership, what we have seen is the rise of new human rights defenders who (just as Inés did) raise their voices not to denounce a personal experience of violence but to demand justice for all women, children, men, and elderly who are being affected by the violence and militarization of security forces.

FINAL REFLECTIONS

It is not up to me to evaluate the positive or negative impacts that the decision to sue the Mexican state have had on the lives of Inés and Valentina; only they know if all the risks, the abandonments, the fears, the threats, and the losses they have faced have been compensated with the sentence of the Inter-American Court. Only they know the impacts of the words "I extend my deepest apologies," uttered by the secretary of the interior. Their voices are now the voices of many silenced women, but only they know what is in their hearts. And yet, in the small amount of time I have known them, I know their responses would not be easy.

The context of militarization and paramilitarization, which Inés denounced, has now deepened; in February 2013, two hundred soldiers of the Mexican Army entered Barranca Tecuani again, without asking permission of the community authorities, and spread fear and insecurity among the inhabitants of the region.[22]

With the emergence of self-defense groups in the beginning of 2013 in Ayutla de los Libres, coordinated by the Union of Peoples and Organizations of the State of Guerrero (Unión de Pueblos y Organizaciones del Estado de Guerrero), the political landscape has acquired a higher level of complexity. The leaders of OPIM have denounced these self-defense groups, arguing that they have been infiltrated by the paramilitary members responsible of the murder of Inés's brother. To no avail, they highlight the inefficiency of the state security forces and, in many cases, the complicity of these security forces in organized crime. Their position regarding the self-defense groups has been that of deep distrust and, in many cases, a rejection of this strategy of self-defense. Cuauhtémoc Ramírez, president of OPIM, stated the following: "OPIM recognizes and supports the self-defense groups of the towns of Ayutla and Teconoapa in their armed fight against organized crime, but now the problem is the return of militarization to the region, which has been disastrous to the Mixteco and Tlapaneco peoples."[23]

In this military and paramilitary context, beginning the construction of a Community Center of Rights for Me'phaa Women has been quite a challenge. Even though some land has been purchased and a ceremony performed where they laid the first stone, the collective planning for the program has been constantly interrupted by the lack of security.

The success or failure of the co-optation policy that state functionaries promote will depend greatly on the ability of these communities to grow stronger at the organizational level. The total lack of trust of Inés toward any government initiative is, in this context, a fundamental element that confronts the "two-faced policy" that the state promotes.

On a personal level, as a member of a women's movement, I have seen myself grow through the teachings of Inés and Valentina, their examples of courage, their sense of collective solidarity, and their ways of knowing and being in the world. It is fundamental that these "different ways in which to be a woman" are considered when thinking about our political agendas and the strategic planning of our struggles. Their experiences with exclusion have to make us think of the need for a feminist anti-racist agenda. We cannot remain quiet before the violence that indigenous men and women suffer, or the criminalization of their social movements, or the incarceration of their leaders. As feminists and promoters of women's rights we take greater risks when we denounce state violence than when we denounce domestic violence. However, if we do not follow Inés's example and break our silence, our demands for gender equality may be appropriated and trivialized by the institutions.

What we have seen in the last decade is that the "mainstreaming of gender perspective in public policies" has had little impact in improving access to justice. The feminist agenda is partially taken up or, in a worst-case scenario, tolerated when the battle is constricted to the confines of the family space. As women organize and denounce the patriarchal nature of the state, they demand structural transformations, and it is at this threshold that the international treaties against violence are forgotten and state violence becomes a strategy to "retreat" women into the domestic space.

In the case of indigenous women, the ways that state violence manifests itself are also influenced by the racism that disqualifies violation complaints not filed in Spanish language. This makes them vulnerable before a justice system that does not recognize their language or their cultural context. It is also the structural racism that makes their lives and their testimonies of violence less relevant than those of students or intellectuals. The erasures of their experiences by ethnocentric perspectives of some feminisms allow us to address new forms of colonialism that continue to shape the realities of indigenous women. Further, the appropriation and institutionalization of the discourses of gender equality on behalf of the Mexican government deprives them of their critical radicalism. This institutionalization leads us to consider the need for including the critique of colonialism as a central theme in feminist agendas.

It is urgent to build alliances between feminist and indigenous movements, to make an echo out of women's voices, like those of Inés and Valentina, in order to denounce and disarticulate neocolonial strategies that use sexual violence as a counterinsurgent weapon.

So that the struggles of Inés and Valentina are not in vain, we need to appropriate their achievements. Legislative modifications and the sentence itself can have an impact in the access to justice for Mexican women if we turn them into tools of awareness and struggle, and if we use them in the painstaking task of constructing a democratic society. Inés and the women of OPIM have already begun this task by reflecting collectively on the sentence and the effects that the community center for women's rights may have once they build it.

5

FROM THE MULTICULTURAL STATE TO THE PENAL STATE

Incarcerated Indigenous Women and the
Criminalization of Poverty[1]

ALONGSIDE THE STATE'S POLICY OF APPROPRIATING RIGHTS discourses as forms of governance, in Mexico, we are witnessing the criminalization of dissidence and the stiffening of penitentiary measures that mostly affect impoverished indigenous men and women. The experiences of incarcerated indigenous women pose a productive site for analyzing the persistent contradictions between the rhetoric of acknowledging rights and the factual realms of state justice.

While in other chapters I have emphasized indigenous women's capacities for social agency before hegemonic discourses on justice and rights, this does not imply failing to recognize the structural limitations within which organized indigenous women have been appropriating and re-signifying discourses on indigenous and gender rights. Structural reforms have not only implied the state's retreat in regards to its functions for social well-being, as we have described in the previous chapters, but in many regions of Latin America, it has also meant its reinforcement in the area of security.

In the specific case of Mexico, in the course of the most recent administrations of Felipe Calderón (2006–2012) and Enrique Peña Nieto (2012–2018), we have witnessed a transition from a discourse that represented indigenous peoples as part of the "national cultural heritage" and that promoted multiculturalism, to a new discourse that represents indigenous peoples as "poor" or as "destabilizers of the social peace," criminalizing their social movements and their institutions of justice. It is in the context of what I have characterized as a transition from the "multicultural state" to the "penal state" that I examine indigenous women's experiences with penal justice.

Even in these spaces, where state violence against indigenous women's bodies is both symbolic and physical, these women have been able to engage in collective reflection and destabilize, with their writings, the dominant representations of them and their peoples. Based on an experience of activist research in a female penal space, I accompanied and publicized the creation of new counterhegemonic discourses by incarcerated indigenous women regarding Mexican justice, structural racism, and gender violence.

An initial moment of neoliberal multiculturalism, marked by the constitutional reforms of 2001, was followed by a process of criminalization of indigenous institutions of justice. In many cases, this has led to the imprisonment of indigenous authorities who oppose or obstruct the interests of local governments colluded with organized crime. Such is the case with the detentions of, and arrest warrants against, members of the Community Police of Guerrero (Regional Coordination of Community Authorities—CRAC) (see Hernández Castillo 2015). Simultaneously, the War on Drugs has justified the militarization of indigenous regions and the criminalization of poverty, incarcerating indigenous men and women who participate in planting natural drugs or who are involved in small-scale drug-dealing.

The criminalization of poverty is permeated by gender and ethnic differences. For those of us who are interested in women's experiences related to justice and equality, it is important to ask, how much does structural racism influence the way in which crime is constructed for racialized women? In this chapter, I explore the ways in which the penal system has become a means for domestication, for strengthening structural racism, and for frequently legitimizing slave labor for the globalized neoliberal economy.

I will first analyze the way in which the official discourse has abandoned multicultural rhetoric and adopted one of development and national security, with a matching legislative agenda. Then I analyze the growth of the penitentiary industries in Mexico and the new legislative reforms that create the settings for the economic exploitation of male and female prisoners. I will review debates about the new forms of neoliberal slave labor based on private penitentiaries and manufacturing. I will also offer a national perspective on indigenous women and federal penal justice in order to focus on the experiences of imprisoned women at two correctional institutions—named in Mexico as Female Social Correctional Centers (CERESO)—one in San Miguel in the state of Puebla and another in Atlacholoaya in the state of Morelos.[2]

Drawing on the experiences of indigenous and mestizo women members of the Sisters in the Shadows Editorial Collective of Women in Prison, I will also reflect on how these women have been able to destabilize the discourses of power, using writing as a tool to reconstruct their female identities and denounce penal violence. I close the chapter with some ideas on the impact of globalization in the realm of justice based on new forms of regulation and control according to transnational tendencies of constructing neoliberal penal states.

FROM THE MULTICULTURALIZATION OF JUSTICE TO THE CRIMINALIZATION OF POVERTY AND SOCIAL DISSIDENCE

Neoliberal multiculturalism in Mexico had its most salient moments during President Vicente Fox's administration (2000–2006), when he developed structural adjustment policies that worked to deregulate the state and encourage state withdrawal from critical social domains. Simultaneously, an official discourse was built on the multicultural character of the nation and the recognition of indigenous rights, structured around the so-called Law of Indigenous Rights and Culture, approved by the permanent commission of Congress on July 18, 2001, and published in the Federal Official Diary on August 14, 2001.

In spite of the recognition of Mexican cultural diversity, the law installed a view of multiculturalism that separates the concept of culture from its political and territorial dimensions and establishes a number of padlocks against indigenous autonomy. These conditions have led to national indigenous organizations rejecting the law.[3] Amendments were implemented in response to demands from international organizations such as the World Bank and the International Monetary Fund, aimed at promoting greater decentralization and local political participation, as well as transferring functions to civil society in order to break bureaucratic red tape and circumvent regional powers.

At the justice level, the recognition of local justice systems and the creation of Indigenous Courts, such as the ones described in chapter 3, were both responses to indigenous demands and a means to transfer state responsibilities to local communities. As several critics of Latin American states' multicultural reforms have observed (Hale 2005; Yashar 2005), recognizing indigenous rights in many contexts has implied leaving responsibilities that once belonged to the state on the lap of indigenous peoples and communities.

However, the national political context changed radically during the administration of President Felipe Calderón. Since 2006, the multicultural discourse has been replaced with a framing of indigenous people as poor, in need of integration into development processes, and as threats to national security. Regarding public policies, these changes entailed a substantial budget cut for the government agency that serves indigenous peoples, the National Commission for the Development of Indigenous Peoples (Comisión Nacional para el Desarrollo de los Pueblos Indígenas—CDI). These changes also involved a general omission of indigenous topics from the national agenda. During Vicente Fox's presidency, CDI's director, Xóchitl Gálvez, enjoyed the spotlight of the media, whereas her successors at CDI, Luis H. Álvarez (2006–2013) and Nuvia Mayorga Delgado (2014–2018), have kept low profiles, almost disappearing from media attention.

Because of these policy shifts, a number of programs that served indigenous peoples have disappeared, among them, the CDI's "Release of Indigenous Prisoners" program. Overall, this has meant the displacement of neoliberal multiculturalism and the establishment of a pro-development and national security policy that recants any recognition of indigenous peoples' cultural identities, seeing them now as poor or delinquent.

A later legal amendment, the constitutional reform on penal justice and public security of June 2008, became a landmark of the adoption of an authoritarian conservatism that upholds the War on Drugs banner. This conservatism has increased the vulnerability of indigenous peoples within the legal system while militarizing their communities and criminalizing social movements.[4]

This does not mean that public multicultural policies are not promoted; rather, they overlap and often contradict national security politics that turn indigenous citizens into poor and delinquents. As de Sousa Santos has pointed out (1998b), the state's heterogeneity allows for parallel existence of two different processes: on the one hand, the state is decentralizing social life through the promotion of multicultural reforms; on the other, it is recentralizing processes of state action in areas such as public security. He writes: "The death of social welfare provided by the state and of the safety nets that favored the citizen can coexist with the expansion of state social welfare and safety nets that favor companies and transnational capital" (de Sousa Santos 1998b, 30).

The penal law amendment, considered by some specialists to be the most far-reaching since 1917 (Zepeda Lecuona 2008), introduces oral trials as a way of cutting costs and providing swifter trials. However, it simultaneously installs lowers standards required to sustain an indictment and limits fundamental rights of people allegedly participating in organized crime. Some penal justice analysts, such as Sergio García Ramírez, have denounced that such reform infringes on human rights, arguing, "It includes some disturbing novelties of an authoritarian character, which impinge upon the penal system of a democratic society and leaves individual rights and guarantees at odds. These novelties could entail a treacherous shift on what has been gained so far and somber the road and destiny of the Mexican penal order, leading us in a trail to a 'guantanamization' of the Mexican penal justice" (García Ramírez 2007, 36).

The changes established by the amendment include widening prosecutorial discretion so that the prosecutor does not need to substantiate evidence before a judge in order to detain a suspect (Mexican Penal Code Amendment XVI, Sec. 1). Prosecutors only need to have data that "establish that a breach of law has been committed and that it is probable that the suspect was involved in it or actually committed it" (Mexican Penal Code Amendent XIX, Sec. 1).[5]

The power endowed on police officers is also widened since they can now perform research duties, a faculty formerly under the scope of public prosecutors alone (Article 21, par. 1). This power is also extended in the right to search and seizure without a legal warrant.

The scope of wrongful acts for which preventive detention is warranted has also been broadened, including those "against national security, the uninhibited development of personality and health" (Article 19, par. 2). The notions of "national security" and the "uninhibited development of personality," defined in such an ambiguous way, leads us to believe that the amendment is aimed at criminalizing social movements in the name of national security. In this sense, Barbara Zamora, a lawyer and human rights advocate, has pointed out that "Current reforms to the Constitution and the criminal law, approved under the pretence of fighting organized crime, terrorism and lack of public safety, are actually aimed at limiting constitutional guarantees and criminalizing and penalizing social protest actions, thus punishing with endless penal procedures and abhorrent sentences social leaders and anyone who dares to protest" (Zamora 2008, 2).

The potential of such reforms to help criminalize social movements is illustrated by the case against the leaders of the Peoples' Front in Defense of the Land (Frente de Pueblos en Defensa de la Tierra). This social movement, formed in 2006 in the town of Atenco, Mexico, has resulted in its leaders being sentenced to 60 and 120 years in jail, based on a penal law amendment that makes withholding of a public official tantamount to kidnapping.[6] The withholding of public officials in order to force them to perform their appointed duties has been a common practice in indigenous and peasant communities as a form of negotiation with authorities. When such practices were criminalized, they were typified as "illegal suspension of freedom," a felony punishable with one to four years of imprisonment. The new penal law reforms make this social movements' resistance strategy akin to the act of kidnapping performed by organized crime, and they apply a punishment so high that it amounts to life without parole.

The same thing is happening in regard to communal justice. Since the beginning of Enrique Peña Nieto's administration (2012), indigenous community police forces (which perform not only security functions but also administration of justice) began to be criminalized. In the last two years, several members of community police organizations in Guerrero and Michoacán have been imprisoned for *usurpación de funciones* (seizing and usurping authority) and *secuestro equiparado* (kidnapping). The latter has applied to the detention of offenders who are subjected to processes of reeducation by community authorities. The detentions in August 2012 of Nestora Salgado (the commander of the community police of Olinalá, Guerrero) and eleven members of the CRAC of the municipality of San Luis Acatlán, and their continued imprisonment without a sentence until February 2016, violate Convention 169 of the ILO (signed by Mexico and recognized in article 2 of the Mexican Constitution, and Law 701 of Guerrero, which recognizes the CRAC's jurisdiction as a system of indigenous justice).

Additionally, the penal law amendment creates a special regime for organized crime that strips those accused of many fundamental rights, while at the same time defining organized crime in a rather vague way. Alleged members of organized crime can be subject to preventive detention even before the investigation initiates, away from their relatives and lawyers, while formal accusations can remain pending for up to eighty days, and the identity of their accusers and witnesses can be kept secret (Article 73, fraction XXI, par. 1 and 11th transitory article of the amendment).

One could understand this toughening of penal procedures as an answer to the extreme violence displayed by organized crime, and it is possible to imagine, as a result, the risks taken by anyone who dares to denounce any of their members. Unfortunately, studies conducted on incarceration for "crimes against health" (*crímenes contra la salud*, the name given in Mexico to crimes resulting from the illicit drug trade) have shown that "only 10% of the cases involve amounts higher than $3,900 pesos (approximately $400 dollars) which indicates that most people currently sentenced for 'crimes against health' were involved in small scale drug trafficking. Thus, people found in prisons are not the major distributors but rather small time drug peddlers or even consumers who were found with amounts not much higher than those tolerated for personal use" (Azaola and Bergman 2008, 762). As a result, the stiffer sentences and the violation of due process will not be suffered by the higher ranking organized crime lords but rather by the impoverished classes and the marginal players in the criminal pyramid, among them, indigenous women who are frequently tricked into working as "mules" for drug transportation.

According to a congressional report, the number of women imprisoned during the last five years has increased 19.89 percent in sharp contrast with a mere 5 percent in the male population, mainly due to their involvement in drug peddling. According to the "Reform Proposal for the Cases of Female Prisoners for Drug Related Crimes" ("Propuesta de reforma en casos de mujeres encarceladas por delitos de drogas"), elaborated by NGOs that work with women's rights issues, drug-related crimes are the most common cause of the imprisonment of women at the federal level and the third at the local level (see Giacomello and Blas Guillen 2016).

In the last official census of the National Commission for the Development of Indigenous Peoples (Comisión Nacional para el Desarrollo de los Pueblos Indígenas—CDI) in 2006, 52 percent of detainees were processed for drug-related crimes (CDI 2006). Indigenous women are now hostages of the War on Drugs, while the Mexican government promotes the success of its security policy by incarcerating the most vulnerable social echelons: peasant, poor, and indigenous women.[7]

In this regard, Concepción Núñez, an advocate for indigenous women incarcerated in the state of Oaxaca, has declared that:

Certification policies, strongly linked to [drug] combat, are designed and imposed by the US, based on certifying or excluding countries that undertake the assignment of keeping drug trafficking at bay, basically a form of imperialist intervention . . . Certification and combat are logically related: in order to be certified it is necessary to demonstrate that the illicit drug trade is being combated. The higher the statistics of people detained, the more points earned in the approval and good behavior card of producer countries. Likewise, when acting in accordance with US defined recommendations and strategies. (Núñez 2007, 25–26)

However, the Mexican reform is not isolated from the global context, where there seems to be a trend to buttressing the infrastructure of the penal industry.

There is a legal build up as well that legitimizes the criminalization of poverty and political dissidence, as was the case with the USA PATRIOT Act against terrorism in the United States (Gilmore 2007; Wacquant 2009).

In light of the War on Drugs and the rhetoric regarding organized crime underlying the penal reform, the discourses on cultural diversity and the multicultural reforms that prevailed during the Fox administration have retreated into the shadows. At the same time, most laws related to indigenous rights remain without secondary legislation or the necessary administrative adjustments to enforce them. Even in those states that have passed secondary laws, such as Guerrero, indigenous justice continues to be criminalized when it interferes with the interests of local powers, as exemplified by the case of Nestora Salgado.[8]

The constitutional amendment in penal justice and public security seems to be having a greater impact on the relationship between indigenous peoples and national justice than the recognition of legal pluralism based on the approval of the Law on Indigenous Culture and Rights of 2001. The penal reform has allowed the Mexican government to demonstrate concern over combating organized crime in the face of U.S. and international public opinion, while simultaneously unfolding a repressive policy against social movements, now with a legal coating that legitimizes the incarceration of political dissidents by criminalizing them.

Both indigenous men and women taking part in resistance movements, and those who have been recruited by drug cartels (due to the extreme poverty produced by neoliberal reforms), are now confronting a penal justice system that recognizes neither their indigenous identity nor guarantees them access to rights recognized in article 2 of the Constitution.

During the current administration, indigenous peoples are seen either as poor peasants who must be integrated into national development through megaprojects, or as criminals who must be incarcerated by imposing on them a legal regime created for organized crime.

PENAL INDUSTRY OR NEOSLAVERY?

Within the complex web of oppression that has impacted the lives of incarcerated women, a new form of exploitation and colonization of their bodies has taken the "benign" form of yet another strategy of social reintegration, euphemistically called "labor therapy" (industrial penitentiary labor under the guise of occupational therapy and job training).

The global tendency to create "penal states," as Joy James (2005) has called them, has required the growth of penitentiary complexes at a global scale in order to criminalize, confine, and control the bodies of the most destitute echelons of society. The growth of the so-called prison industrial complex has required private investment to build and provide maintenance to infrastructure. The global tendency to subcontract the management of prisons is part of neoliberal structural reforms meant to reduce the state's social responsibilities.

The tendency to privatize prisons began in the United States during the 1980s, in the state of Kentucky, under Ronald Reagan's administration. Companies such as Kentucky Fried Chicken invested in the creation of a corporation named Corrections Corporation of America (CCA). CCA is currently the largest private corporation in the prison industry, handling contracts in different parts of the world.[9]

Clearly the case of the United States is unique in that it is the country with the highest number of incarcerated citizens. Studies on the subject reveal that approximately two million people are currently detained and five million people are on parole. This amounts to the United States having 5 percent of the world's population and 25 percent of prisoners on the planet (Gilmore 2007).

The increase in detentions has gone hand in hand with the growing privatization of prison facilities. In 2003, there were only five private prisons in the United States, holding 2,000 prisoners. By 2013, there were 100 private prisons, holding 62,000 inmates. It is expected that, in the coming decade, this number will increase to 360 facilities. Within these prisons, clothes, airplane parts, and even military equipment are being assembled, at costs far below minimum wage. This situation has led some scholars to maintain that the American prison industry's private contracting system encourages imprisonment: "prisons depend largely on that income. Corporation stockholders that use prisoners wish for longer sentencing. 'The system reproduces itself,' according to a Progressive Labor Party, who also contends that the penal industry resembles Nazi Germany in its use of forced labor and concentration camps" (Pelaez 2008, 7).

The same source also stated that the prison industrial complex is one of the most successful industries in the United States and is trading stocks on Wall Street. We should recognize that this model is being globalized because it caters to the needs of evermore polarized societies, strengthening social control while attracting low-investment industries due to its access to an extremely cheap labor force with no benefits or even labor rights.

Atlacholoaya and San Miguel, as well as all other Mexican penitentiary facilities, are part of what some scholars have called the "Global Prison," a local expression of a global trend to control people, products, and capital. This implies that "the building of prisons in itself, as well as the people held in them, are being structured by global factors: from free trade agreements and neoliberal economic restructurings, to the expansion of multinational corporations. Prisons are then both a local and a global occurrence or as is now said, glocal: a local product of global political, economic and cultural phenomena" (Sudbury 2005, xii).

The growth and privatization of the Mexican prison industrial complex is still in its onset, but there are already a few changes reflecting the reproduction of these glocal trends. In September 2009, the public security secretariat (SSP) revealed that Mexican builders with a capital of 200 to 400 million pesos were welcome to compete to design and associate with the government to build twelve new penal facilities to lodge 30,000 federal inmates.

The goal is to develop a new social reintegration model that includes employment and the cooperation of private investors such as Meyer Zaga, a textile industrialist who is already investing in penal facilities around the country. The SSP announced it was looking for experienced investors to build and provide maintenance for penal facilities, and it offered twenty-year contracts amounting to three million pesos for each yearly lease.[10]

The new penal manufacturing model has been in operation for a few years now in several prison complexes throughout the country. The innovation introduced in 2009 was the legal reforms to promote and reinforce the model, thus legitimizing the economic exploitation of male and female inmates. In April 2009, reforms to the law that establishes minimum norms for social readjustment of convicts were approved by 341 votes in favor (with four abstentions). Inmates must now contribute to their maintenance by participating in the penal industries. Legal reforms establish that 30 percent of wages earned by inmates will be used for their expenses in prison, an extra 30 percent for reparations, and the remaining 40 percent for their personal needs and the support of their families.

The reforms also allow investors to contribute to the "readjustment" of inmates through "labor therapy." The proposal for the amendment to the Minimum Norms Law argues that "according to the Public Security Secretariat there is a total penitentiary population of 219,754 inmates, of which 204,711 are mentally and physically fit for work. That is to say that there is enough human capital available and a large number of centers that could be equipped to build a solid penal industry in the country and could contribute to the continuity of the facilities, to the national economy, and to the reinsertion of inmates to society.[11] On these grounds, congressmen propose to amend the law with the goal of establishing spaces and facilities for the expansion of the prison industry.

Establishing industries within prisons would not imply economic exploitation nor would it deserve the label of "neoslavery" if inmates received fair wages and were granted their rights as workers as determined by the Federal Labor Law. Unfortunately, the advantages federal and state authorities offer investors in order to promote their participation in the penal industries, as well as the experiences of interns at Atlacholoaya and San Miguel, show that this is not the case.

For example, the section for the Social Readjustment and Prevention Secretariat on the website of the state of Mexico[12] invites businessmen to invest in the penal industry, enumerating the advantages this would have for them: they won't have to pay rent for services and facilities; they are exempt of taxes and social security fees; the labor is cheap, flexible, and abundant; punctuality is guaranteed; there is no need to pay benefits, yearly premiums, or vacation bonuses; there is no absenteeism and work hours are flexible; the payroll is handled by the Penal Industries Department; available machinery requires only maintenance fees; there is no need to provide food or uniforms; and investors are allowed to train and directly supervise the production and quality of the product. Therefore, business entrepreneurs contribute to inmates' readjustment and benefit society. In other words, inmates are at the complete disposal of the entrepreneur at any time when there is a need for labor. Wages vary from one-and-a-half to two dollars for twelve-hour workdays.

Among the businesses that already benefit from these privileges are, Chemicals and Manufacturing of Mexico SA of CV (fiber manufacturing), Design and Footwear SA of CV (shoe manufacturing), Fábrica de Brochas Perfect SA of CV (natural fiber manufacturing), Sport and Industrial Manufacturer (soccer ball manufacturing), Dr. Simi Enterprises (pharmaceutical), Maquila Tokai of Mexico SA of CV, Venetian Tiles SA of CV, Barece & Fucho (soccer ball manufacturing), Calva Mar (plastic suppliers), Serafín Plata (children's denim), Vicky Form (lingerie), Ovalle Plastic SA of CV (plastic suppliers), Pelotas Máxima SA of CV (baseball supplies), D Hadas & Deseos SA of CV (doll manufacturing), and Mayer Zaga (textiles), among others.

Although working in the penal industries is not mandatory, it is a means to reduce one's sentence and one of the few options available to acquire money while in prison. If the advantages for businesses of participating in the penal industry were not enough, these businesses are also exempt from partaking in public contract biddings in order to sell their products to the state. In a recent interview, an executive stated, "We are exonerated of participating in biddings, regardless of the sum, as long as we can demonstrate the high quality of our product and that we will be solving a problem for them."[13]

These labor conditions stand in stark contrast to those of other Latin American countries where governments have negotiated the entry of private capital in the prisons under decidedly fairer terms. In Argentina, for example, businesses cover the costs of local and national taxes, workers' retirement fees, insurance quotas, and labor insurance. Labor and tax expenses can constitute a 40 percent surcharge over the salary costs.[14]

A bed and bath linen manufacturer is currently operating at the San Miguel Puebla CERESO, and produces socks, towels, bed sheets, and seat cushions. Workdays are Monday through Saturday from 6 a.m. to 10 p.m., and the weekly salary is around 18 dollars per day.

Dr. Simi Enterprises produces mouth masks, paying five pesos for every two hundred masks by piecework (around 30 U.S. cents per 200 masks). The women we interviewed stated that the daily average that one inmate could make was between four and six hundred pieces, which amounts to a daily salary of one to one and a half dollars on a sixteen-hour workday.[15]

A Venetian tiles manufacturer that operates at the Atlacholoaya Morelos CERESO also pays by piecework to produce tiles, bath borders, and glass pebbles. The same facility also hosts a mouth mask sweatshop that manufactures boots, bathrobes, caps, and sheets, among other items. Wages here are also by piecework and do not differ much from those paid by Dr. Simi at San Miguel Puebla.

In the male section, there is a company called Maquila de Tokai and a textile company producing jeans, t-shirts, and vests. All these industries pay by piecework, which means that wages depend on the ability of interns to work and the hours they are willing to put in. The new penal sweatshop system, currently promoted and vouched for by national legislation, offers no minimum wages, benefits, or labor rights.

Some scholars refer to this labor system as "neoslavery" (Sudbury 2005; Herivel and Wright 2003). Others call it "neocolonialism," referring to its disproportionate impact on indigenous and racialized peoples in the continent (Segato 2007). Whatever the name, what is self-evident is that we are facing a global model that does not tend to the "readjustment" needs of male or female interns but rather caters to the social-control interests of penal states and to the need for accumulation of wealth of neoliberal economies.

In the case of indigenous prisoners in Mexico, this system is in line with colonial labor conditions that persist in export-oriented agricultural plantations heavily dependent on seasonal migration of indigenous labor. Economic exploitation and the absence of labor rights has been an unwavering feature in the history of indigenous peoples, and this is now taking new forms under a penal justice system that criminalizes poverty and strengthens exclusion.

INDIGENOUS MEN AND WOMEN IN THE MEXICAN CRIMINAL JUSTICE SYSTEM

But who are the indigenous men and women laboring under this new neoslavery economic model, and how many are they? It is difficult to provide exact and current data on the imprisoned indigenous population since the censuses have not been updated in the current administration.[16] Even the data available through other sources is not entirely reliable since it is the linguistic criteria that is usually applied in institutional records, and many people imprisoned do not state their ethnicity for fear of the racism that continues to prevail in various spaces of Mexican society, including prisons. As mentioned before, the CDI abandoned its Indigenous Prisoners Release Program due to budget cuts, thus keeping the indigenous census outdated. The last count was in 2006, meaning that available data for later years does not disaggregate the ethnic or linguistic variables.

The suspension, during the administration of President Felipe Calderón, of the penitentiary census formerly undertaken by the CDI is yet further evidence of the lack of concern of this government for indigenous populations. It also conceals the effects that the War on Drugs and the national security policies have on this sector.

The fact that available data is disaggregated by gender but not by ethnicity makes it hard to prove with "hard data" the amount that indigenous women are "contributing" to the Mexican government's War on Drugs. In this regard, Julia Sudbury has stated that:

From Mexico to South Africa, the rise in the incarceration rate has entailed a mega prison construction boom following on the USA model. But statistics that see gender but not race or class, do not account for the impact that prisons are having on indigenous and colored women. In said countries, oppressed and racialized groups have been disproportionately affected by the criminal justice system. The imprisoned women crisis can be seen as a poor working, indigenous and colored women crisis throughout the world. (Sudbury 2005, xiv)

Notwithstanding, the 2006 census and the review of the judicial proceedings files in two Female Social Correctional Centers (CERESOs) from the states of Morelos and Puebla allow us to determine trends in indigenous women's profiles (see appendix 3). According to the 2006 CDI census, out of a total number of 214,275 prisoners, 8,767 were indigenous (4 percent of the imprisoned population), of which 8,334 were men and 383 were women. Though the number of detained indigenous women seems low compared to non-indigenous women, one should consider the fact that many women do not declare their ethnic identity for fear of racism and the discrimination that still prevails in the sphere of justice. Even based on such limited data, we can observe a 122 percent increase in the number of imprisoned indigenous women, up from the 172 registered in the 1994 census (Azaola and Bergman 2008) to the 383 registered in the last disaggregated census of 2006.

The states of Oaxaca, Puebla, and Chiapas occupy the highest in number of incarcerated indigenous people. Out of these, 25 percent speak Nahuatl (the largest represented linguistic group), followed by Mayas (8 percent) and Zapotec (7 percent). If we keep in mind that language is still the main criteria used to determine inmates' ethnic identity, then it is safe to assume that most likely the numbers of incarcerated indigenous peoples is higher than the ones reported by the CDI.

In 2015, the National Commission on Human Rights (CNDH) published a special report on the prison conditions of women.[17] This report allows us to update some information on the prison population, even though its census is not broken down by ethnic self-identification. Prior to this report, there was a similar one published in 2013, whose recommendations are yet to be implemented. As part of the activities undertaken, information was gathered and visits were made to seventy-seven centers, among them the fifteen centers exclusively for women. At the time of the visits (February 2014), the latter housed 87.52 percent of the female prison population.

According to the 2014 report, there were 389 correctional centers in Mexico, nineteen of which depended on the federal government, including three military prisons administered by the Secretariat of National Defense; 282 were administered by state governments, eleven by the Government of the Federal District, and seventy-seven by municipal authorities. There are only fifteen centers exclusively for women (thirteen under state and two under federal administration). As a consequence, most women are incarcerated in mixed prisons, where there are problems of prostitution, inequality in the access to school and medical services, and a shortage of female personnel, issues that Elena Azaola (1996) has denounced for almost two decades. According to this most recent census, in 2014, women accounted for 5.08 percent (12,690) of the total prison population (249,912).

Women who commit a crime are more stigmatized than men; they are seen and treated in a harsher way, mostly suffering abandonment from their partners and families. Out of the 206 women held at the Female Correctional Center at Atlacholoaya, where I have been working for the last seven years, fifteen have children living with them, and only 40 percent receive visits, in strong contrast to the male population, where 70 percent receive visits (Ríos 2009).

According to studies conducted on how gender inequality taints women's relationships with penal justice, there is a similar tendency at the national level (Azaola 1996; Azaola and Yacamán 1996). Examining the inmates' judicial records from the Morelos CERESO and the San Miguel CERESO, we could confirm this trend among indigenous women.

Out of the thirty indigenous women incarcerated in both states, twenty-four speak Nahuatl, the most common language in those states.[18] Sixteen of them, the majority, are held for crimes against health, all of them for small-scale drug distribution, sentenced to terms from ten to fifteen years. Only three of them had criminal records, and none had been armed or arrested for a violent act. The state of Morelos registers the highest imprisonment terms, where the average is fifteen years. The women's ages range from twenty-two years to seventy-four years. Seventeen of them are illiterate, ten have some primary studies, and only three have some secondary education. None among the thirty women had a translator during their trials (see appendix 2).

During the personal, in-depth interviews we conducted, half the accused women denied having participated in drug sales, while the other half did admit being involved in drug distribution but argued economic duress and a lack of job alternatives. Several of the women declared that they did not speak Spanish before their arrest and learned it in prison. Monolingualism and illiteracy had some bearing on many of them signing written statements in which they acknowledged their involvement, without a clear understanding of the document's content.

H. M., a seventy-year-old Nahuatl-speaking woman, imprisoned in the Atlacholoaya CERESO for seven years, describes the experience of helplessness while arrested at a military roadblock when traveling to Mexico City in search for her son:

I still remember the day I arrived here. I was 63 years old. It seems like only yesterday. Just a few days earlier, I had been preparing the land for sowing. Later I took a bus to Mexico City. It never crossed my mind that it would be the last time I saw my hut! During the trip, I was thinking of going back to finish sowing in order to provide for myself. Then sometime around eleven or just before midnight, I cannot recall, the bus driver woke us up and asked us to step out of the bus. I was frightened; there were many soldiers in front of me. They surrounded us. In one corner of the bus there lied some suitcases, and since I was on that side they said "this is yours isn't it?" I told them they weren't, that I only had a bag with some seeds, plums and beans I was taking to a relative. That's what I said. However, they answered "sure granny, you are very funny. But you are traveling with this package at your side." No matter how much I argued, it was their word against mine. Later they took me to the lock-up. My things and the alleged package did not appear, but they insisted it was mine. Three days later I was transferred to the penitentiary, were someone read what I was told was my statement, though I had said nothing. I hardly spoke Spanish! No matter how I tried to explain that I had done none of the things written there they did not believe me, so I was sentenced to eleven years and eight or nine months.[19]

In other cases, the women's husbands were involved in small-scale drug distribution, and those activities backfired on them due to a number of circumstances. This happened to M. P. E., a forty-seven-year-old Nahuatl-speaking woman accused of crimes against health:

One afternoon my sister came over asking me if my husband had any marihuana. I told her I didn't know. "He'll be back soon," I said, "I will ask him; come back later." When my husband arrived, he didn't want to give her any. She said, "It's for my son. You know he's an addict." I felt sorry for her so I gave her some I took from my husband. Then the police arrived and said I was under arrest for selling drugs. I didn't speak Spanish then so I hardly understood what they were saying. They told me to say I had sold the marihuana to my sister so I answered: "but I didn't sell her anything, I gave it to her." I have no idea of what they wrote down because they wrote my statement. So when I was called to receive sentence I was told that I would spend ten years here. I have already been here six years. During that time, some fellow inmates took pity on me and corrected my Spanish. They taught me new words. With whatever I learned from them I started communicating, but I still don't know what actually happened.[20]

As we were able to confirm by reviewing the records of the proceedings for the thirty women imprisoned in Morelos and Puebla, the experience illustrated here by these two testimonies is the norm regarding trials of indigenous women and men in the federal justice system. The same type of testimony has been collected among female prisoners in the state of Oaxaca by Concepción Núñez, who has documented the institutional racism that has criminalized indigenous women in that Mexican state (see Núñez 2007, forthcoming).

These experiences are common despite the fact that the 2001 constitutional reforms established the right to assistance of an interpreter during proceedings and to anthropological expert witness report that could shed some light on the cultural context of the accused so that some extenuating circumstances could be argued in their favor.

The Federal Penal Code (CPF) and the Federal Penal Proceedings Code (CFPP) determine regulations for interpreters. These statutes state that the public prosecutor decides competence in Spanish language, which boils down to his common sense understanding of competence.

In December 2002, the CFPP was amended so that now articles 15, 18, 124, 128, 154, and 159 regulate the mandatory knowledge of interpreters and defense lawyers on indigenous languages, culture, and customary law. Nevertheless, as we learned from the judicial proceedings files, these regulations are unenforceable since tribunals do not have state-appointed defense lawyers of indigenous background or with at least some understanding indigenous culture.

However, this breach of linguistic and cultural rights is explained not only by the lack of qualified personnel that can promote access to justice for indigenous peoples. It is also a result of a larger framework of derogatory and racist behavior from public officers, a characteristic of the whole justice system that, in many ways, furthers racial hierarchies ingrained in society (see Escalante Betancourt 2015).

Regarding indigenous women, sexual violence bolsters this form of structural racism reproduced by public institutions, a tool frequently used during detention or as a latent threat during suspect examination. Feminist analysis has shown how prisons work as fields for control and domestication of female bodies, in which racism and sexism determine how poverty and dissidence are criminalized (Davis 1981; Díaz-Cotto 1996; Sudbury 2005).

Just as analysts of the United States prison system have shown how prisons are marked by the racialization that characterizes American culture, so have these racialization processes determined the experience of indigenous women in Mexico. As critical race theorists have pointed out, wherever societies are characterized by the existence of racial hierarchies, those situated in the lowest echelons tend to be overrepresented in the correctional system. The most studied case is that of the United States, evidenced by the findings of Loïc Wocquant, who contends that justice selectivity has a racial character:

> On a lifelong accumulated probability, a black man has a one on four possibility to serve at least one year in prison; a Latino has one in ten while a white man has one on 23 . . . Actually, the gap between whites and blacks is not the result of a sudden divergence in the propensity to commit crimes and felonies. It speaks rather of the fundamentally discriminatory police and judicial practices furthered on the "law and order" policy followed during the last two decades. (Wacquant 2000, 100)

Considering the Mexican context, both social scientists and public policymakers have refused to accept the existence of racial hierarchies and, therefore, have declined to analyze the institutionalized racism that characterizes the entire Mexican society. Despite the fact that a few authors have started to study racism in Mexico (Castellanos et al. 2008; Escalante Betancourt 2015; Gall 2003; Paris Pombo 1999), the myth of the "mixed race nation," promoted by post-revolution governments, is still being used to deny the existence of racial hierarchies and discriminatory practices against indigenous peoples in Mexico.

What is blatantly clear is that both graphic and televised mass media continue to promote a white, Eurocentric beauty standard that is foreign to the prevailing Mexican phenotype. In the same way, the wealthiest and politically

powerful social echelons are still predominantly white. In the midst of a hegemonic nationalist discourse held by the middle classes who embrace mestizo
identity, the truth is that not all mestizo identities are as valuable: the darker
the skin color, the lower you will be in the social pyramid. There are, of course,
exceptions; but a look at private school enrollment, populated by upper-class
children, is enough to prove that racial hierarchies build on class difference.

The penitentiary field reproduces these same hierarchies since either poor,
dark-skinned mestizos or indigenous peoples are the ones who suffer under
the power displayed by the penal state. In both women's correctional facilities
in which field work for this project was conducted (the Atlacholoaya and San
Miguel CERESO at Morelos and Puebla, respectively), the few blonde women
inmates had a higher level of education than the average prisoner. They enjoyed
special privileges, such as having separate cells and being given the lead charac-
ters in plays staged in prison. Rita Laura Segato ponders the hardships of naming this racialization of justice process in Latin America by pointing out that:

> We should wonder why it is so difficult to talk about race, pin it down with a name
> and realize what should be self-evident by observing the incarcerated population
> throughout the continent. . . . Trying to enunciate what is seen when entering a
> prison, declare the race of the imprisoned people, is hard because it touches the
> sensibilities of enshrined actors: the traditional academic left because it entails
> giving flesh and bones to the mathematics of class by rendering it with color, cul-
> ture, ethnicity and ultimately, difference. It touches a sociological chord because
> data for these topics is scarce and hard to pin down objectively due to the com-
> plexities of racial classification. It also strokes the sensibilities of the law operators
> and enforcement agencies because it hints at state racism. (Segato 2007, 145)

Even though the racialization of penitentiaries is hard to quantify, it is self-
evident once you experience any CERESO. There is a sharp contrast between
the skin color of people in power who benefit from drug networks and the
people in detention for their role in drug distribution. To illustrate such claims,
I will offer as an example the complicities between the drug cartels and public
officers in Morelos.

During the period when this investigation began, the state's public security
secretary was Luis Ángel Cabeza de Vaca, a tall, sturdy blonde man who had
held several public posts in the state before his appointment in public security. His close collaborator was Undersecretary Sara Olivia Parra Téllez, a tall,

blonde, and green-eyed professional who was assumed to be on good terms with the gangs that handle prisoner relations through the euphemistically called prison "co-government."

The detention of fourteen members of the Beltrán Leyva drug cartel in April 2009 uncovered a link between the cartel and the state's public security secretariat, as well as to the municipal public security secretary, Francisco Sánchez González. In May 2009, both were taken into custody, accused of taking bribes and protecting the Beltrán Leyva cartel. As a result, Parra Téllez and other minor officers had to step down. Now Cabeza de Vaca and Sánchez González face an indictment and have formed a sturdy defense team, while Parra Téllez has taken a different official post in the state government. Meanwhile indigenous women held at Atlacholoaya for "crimes against health" are doing up to fifteen years of prison time without clearly understanding the charges made against them.

The example shows how trafficking with controlled substances is just part of a social totality characterized by multiple social, racial, and gender inequalities. Accordingly, Santiago Castro-Gómez ponders how racialization determines the ways drug trafficking is criminalized: "Peasants and indigenous people in Latin America produce natural drugs (marihuana, coca leaves and poppy flowers); the racialized groups distribute them on the streets, while the white elites who reap the profits control its distribution and export. So when things go wrong or someone needs to pick up the bill, who will end locked up in jail? Peasant and indigenous" (Castro-Gómez cited in Núñez 2007, 24).

I am not implying that there are no racialized groups working for organized crime groups. They are part of those brown faces we see every time the TV transmits one of the "victories" on the War on Drugs. What I mean to say is that politically powerful groups that favor the survival and growth of drug trafficking networks are part of a white oligarchy that is usually spared the consequences of penal reforms allegedly aimed at combating organized crime.

ANALYZING INDIGENOUS WOMEN'S JOURNEYS OF EXCLUSIONS: AN INTERSECTIONAL APPROACH

Our own efforts elaborating twelve life histories of incarcerated indigenous women in the framework of the "Life Histories" workshop at Atlacholoaya CERESO in Morelos (2006–2015), paired with Meztli Yoalli Rodríguez's

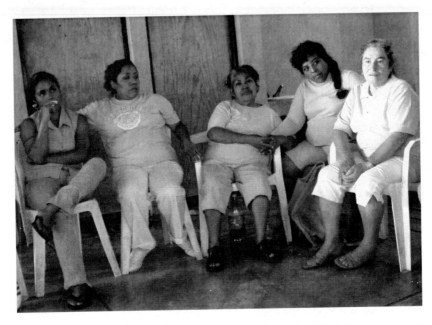

FIGURE 12. Participants in the "Life Histories" workshop in Atlacholoaya Correctional
Facility in Morelos. Photograph of R. Aída Hernández Archives.

additional ten histories by in-depth interviews at San Miguel CERESO in
Puebla, allow us to understand the journeys of exclusion that have distinguished
the lives of these women since birth.

Analyzing these life histories, we can find several common elements that
mark the oppressive experiences suffered by these incarcerated women: extreme
poverty and gender discrimination frequently manifested as sexual and domestic
violence and racism.

There is a trend in criminological studies, as well as among some social scientists, to use biographical narratives to do criminal profiling in order to link
dysfunctional family contexts to "criminal personalities." This practice weighs
on psychological factors to explain the causes of crime instead of contextualizing them within the larger framework of social processes (Garrido and Sobral
2008; Cavazos Ortiz 2005; Cuevas Sosa, Mendieta Dimas, and Salazar Cruz
1992). On the contrary, life histories in our project are tools to understand the
way in which systems of class, gender, and racial oppression are mutually constructed and are fundamental in the criminalization of poor women in Mexico.

In this sense, I would like to follow on the theoretical intersectional approach suggested by African American feminists as a means to analyze how the socially constructed discriminating categories such as class, gender, race, and generation interact, simultaneously configuring unequal social contexts (Crenshaw 1991; Hill Collins 1990; Hill Collins and Andersen 2007).

Rather than analyzing capitalism, patriarchy, and racism as three separate systems of oppression, I am interested in observing how they mutually construct each other and determine the social hierarchies in which imprisoned women are situated. In other words, capitalism, in its current neoliberal existence in Mexico, cannot be understood without recognizing its racialized and sexist character, features that situate indigenous peoples in general, and indigenous women in particular, in the lowest echelons of the social pyramid.

Likewise, imprisoned indigenous women's narratives allow us to access a privileged standpoint of those who have experienced, and are thus aware of, the multiple oppressions that characterize Mexican society. Considering the insightful collective sphere in which these narratives take place, we can say, following the feminist standpoint theory perspective (Hartsock 1983, 1997), that incarcerated indigenous women benefit from a certain epistemic privilege because their experiences of exclusion and exploitation allow them a more inclusive and critical perspective than those who live their social vantage points in a more naturalized and invisibilized way.

The experience of extreme poverty, frequently symbolized by the physical suffering of hunger, appeared in all their life histories as one of their most important childhood memories. Morelitos, a Nahuatl-speaking woman incarcerated at Atlacholoaya for drug-related crimes, expresses it in her own words:

> We slept on a *petate* (palm leaf mat); we ate on it. We cooked outside on a *fogón* (wood-burning stove) and when it rained, we cooked inside. Our village was far away from any big town; we were surrounded by hills. When we needed to buy groceries we walked to town. There was no doctor there, no sewage nor light or tapped water. To find water we had to carry it with beasts but those who had none simply did it by foot. We walked 30 minutes from the house to the water spring. We worked growing corn, squash and beans. What we grew is what we ate. Sometimes it wasn't enough so we only had a *tortilla* with *chile*.[21]

Hunger and violence also taint the childhood memories of Lila, a Nahuatl-speaking woman imprisoned for the same crimes at San Miguel, Puebla: "We lived near where the *milpa* (corn field) grew. My house was made of wood and there were only two big rooms. We all slept in the same room, my fifteen brothers, my mom and dad. Since we were plenty we did not eat too well . . . My dad was a driver. He carried sorghum, wheat or fruit. My mom stayed at home and washed clothes to earn some money."[22]

The negative effects of neoliberal farming policies on the peasant economy have been seen through the testimonies that articulate the necessity of abandoning the fields to migrate to the cities in search for a better life (as happened to several women from Guerrero who migrated to the city of Cuernavaca) or else accept growing and commercializing illegal crops such as marijuana and poppy flowers.

Altagracia, a Tlapanec woman arrested for drug-related crimes, described to us how poverty and the lack of resources to sustain her kids led her first to migrate and abandon her land, and then to drug trafficking:

> After giving birth we traveled from Guerrero to Cuernavaca and began living at the train terminal at Colonia El Vergel station. My husband started working as a construction worker, but we had eight kids so we were ten family members, including my husband and myself, so we weren't earning enough. Things were getting tough because I had to send my kids to school, dress them and give them shoes, so I started cooking *tamales*, *atole*, and bread and sold them. I also sent the kids to sell them, so they would help raise some money. I would wake up at 5 am and by 10 the bread was ready. After making the bread I would start with the *tamales* and *atole*. Life was tough for all the family. Kids would start working very young. But my husband began to be lazy, seen that I was pulling through. There were times in which he would stop working for a year and all expenses would be mine. I paid the water, the light, and school tuitions. During those times of duress for the family when we could hardly survive by selling bread and tamales, a woman called Alondra approached me and said she pitied me so she would help me earn some extra money by selling drugs.[23]

Hunger and poverty, intertwined with racialized economic exploitation, affect each family member in a different way. The rural communities from where many of the indigenous immigrants come were characterized by rural labor that had semi-feudal structures. The persistence of landlords who kept the workers in debt through the *tienda de raya* (credit system of the company store) is denounced in many of the testimonies by rural inmates. These landlords also took advantage of the inadequate comprehension of Spanish that indigenous people usually have.

Flor de Nochebuena, a Nahuatl-speaking woman imprisoned at Atlacholoaya for drug-related crimes, offers a life history that speaks about the structural and domestic violence chains that marked her childhood:

> Nights were short because we had to get up early at four o'clock to make breakfast: a few tortillas and an herbal tea with a pinch of sugar. My mother used to say: "on Saturday, when your dad gets paid, we will eat chicken." A promise hardly ever kept because every pay day the boss would tell my dad that he owed him money so the paycheck was never complete. My dad didn't wish to lose his job so he would bear whatever. Besides it was hard for him to confront the boss since he couldn't read or write and hardly spoke Spanish except for saying hello and "till tomorrow." So with the little that was left from a whole week's work we had to endure and be happy to share it among the siblings. Perhaps out of frustration facing such unfairness, he used to pick on us and used to hit us about anything. Like when we would be late taking his lunch to work, we would be punished.[24]

Flor de Nochebuena's experience with the kind of domestic violence generated by her father against the rest of the family members is not an isolated experience. All twenty life histories registered during the research account instances of sexual and domestic violence by fathers, uncles, husbands, bosses, or police authorities.

In spite of the fact that violence was not the central topic of the "Life Histories" workshops, the recurring discussion of the topic by indigenous and non-indigenous women alike forced us to dedicate several sessions to reviewing collectively the assorted experiences of violence suffered prior to incarceration and the probable similarities among such experiences.

The question arose: was there any relationship between the violence exercised by their fathers and the violence employed by their bosses or the sexual torture brought to bear by police? Answers led us to discuss the subordinated role of women in indigenous communities based on colonial and postcolonial relations and the subordinated role of women in society as a whole.

Correspondingly Native American feminists, such as Andrea Smith (2005a, 2005b), have pointed out the connection between domestic violence and neocolonial violence by stating that domestic and sexual violence in indigenous communities cannot be effectively eradicated unless the higher structures of violence, such as police brutality, indigenous rights violations, institutionalized racism, and economic neocolonialism, are confronted.

Critically articulating our discussions on these different types of violence allowed us to locate personal experiences of sexual and domestic violence within a wider frame in which the violence they have endured from the Mexican state is intertwined with the violence they suffered during childhood.

Many of the stories that emerged in the dialogues between indigenous and non-indigenous women began with memories of hunger and violence, as if there had been a predetermined script that all of them followed. But the interviews in which the stories were based had been conducted outside of the workshop, in different times and spaces, in accordance with the pace established by the women involved. It turns out that this was the first time that many of these women had had a chance to verbalize their experiences of childhood suffering and be listened to with respect and interest. One of the stories reads as follows:

Violence has been a part of my life since birth. My early memories do not include embraces and motherly tenderness. When I was five years old I began facing mistreatment and beatings. I saw how my mom's husband beat her and threw her out of the house. We come into contact with violence in different ways. Our stepfather not only disregarded feeding us, but he also kept us terrified with sudden outbursts of rage. He drank everyday so when he arrived we ran to hide under the mattress because if he saw us he would hit us. When he arrived late at night he would wake us up with strikes and yelling. This tragedy lasted for two years. My dear mother worked washing and ironing and we would lock ourselves without food until she came home from work.[25]

The further we advanced on the life histories, the clearer it became to me that our interview guides had been written from an ethnocentric perspective of lifecycles. We had imagined these women's lives split up in segments, which contradicted their actual experiences as indigenous women. For example, more than half the women interviewed had not attended school and, therefore, had no childhood recollection of the institution. Their memories where tied to the land as a work place and to the agricultural chores they completed from the age of five or six years old:

We were only my mom, my dad a brother and me in the family. We never learned Spanish. My brother was born sick; he laughed for no reason. I had to look after him since I was a child. I cooked for him, carried him while mom did the household choirs. I could not go to school because it was too expensive, so I went to the coffee plantation with my mom, from six in the morning till five in the evening. We ate tortillas with salsa and if we found any, also an avocado.[26]

Likewise, most interviewed women began their sexual life sometime between five and eleven years old, most of them in non-consensual relations. Therefore, the so-called adolescent stage had totally different characteristics than those among children during this stage in mestizo society. A persistent topic in their life histories was the experience of being snatched and raped during childhood, as a "tolerated" cultural practice in many indigenous and peasant regions, from which marriage or cohabitation ensued.

In spite of the pain with which these experiences were built, several women admitted that there was no consciousness or denunciation of those practices as tantamount to rape:

One Nahuatl women told me that when she was barely twelve a man snatched her by force and had her four days hiding on the hills. As was customary in her village, after abducting her, he asked to marry him. She was just a child who wanted to go back home to her brothers and goats. But her fate was now beyond her reach: "when I tried to go back home, my dad wouldn't have me no more." "Why would I want you like that?" I had left already; I had slept with that man.[27]

We heard a similar story from Carlota Cadena, who shared her story with Victoria, a Tlapanec woman from the Guerrero Mountain:

I was still a child, barely eleven years old, when this man snatched me. After having me for four days in a place called "Dead Bull," where he abused me, my mom and my uncle found me. When they arrived I told my mom I wanted to go back home with her, because this man had taken me by force and I didn't like him. But my mom didn't want me back, and said I had to put up with the situation and become my rapist's wife, otherwise I'd be any man's toy. In her view, I had no future if I refused to marry the man who abused me, since according to her any woman who had already been with a man and was no longer a *señorita* was worthless. Since my mom repudiated me and I refused to live with this man, I decided to live with my uncle, who was my mom's brother-in-law. But after a few days, the man called on my uncle's house. He asked for my hand to marry me, but I didn't like him and had no intention of marrying him, because I was just a child.[28]

So-called *robo de la novia* (bride kidnapping) is a common cultural practice in many Mesoamerican indigenous communities that, according to several kinship scholars, is usually a consensual decision taken by the couple to avoid the burden of petitioning the bride and incurring marriage expenses (D'Aubeterre 2003; Robichaux 2003). Nevertheless, during the last few decades, indigenous organized women have challenged this practice as another form of sexual violence and have rejected what they have called "bad customs," demanding their right to choose who to marry and how many children to have. Perhaps the "normalization" of the practice is due to versions collected among men, fathers, and older women, but for the new generations, this is an evident form of violence by which they are repulsed and which they wish to confront.

During the "Life Histories" workshop, indigenous women referred to those "snatchings" as kidnappings and denounced the sexual violence they had experienced, questioning the complicity of their parents in these experiences. In that sense, two of them commented:

Forcing us to marry our rapists was yet another form of violence. It was the ignorance and *machismo* of older days because, in my mind, if one of my kids happened to live that, I would ask "do you want to come with me?" So if she stays with the man then that's her free will. That's why it is important to speak to our children, right? I had no confidence with my parents; they had no time to pamper us. All day long they had to work, my father I mean, always on the field . . . he came back tired . . . all he wanted was food. And since he was *macho* he wanted to have many kids, so there was mom, having more and more babies.[29]

Old customs assumed that if a man *used* a woman, then she had no more honor, she was valueless, so it was best to stay with her rapist lest other men abuse her as well. In my home town people used to say "you'll get *pueblo*," meaning you would get gang raped when word got out that you had lost value. But those ideas must change; I tell my girls that they have worth as persons, not for their virginity, and we must put a stop to men, even if we must end up in jail for that.[30]

Seven of the women whose stories were written down during the workshop had started their sex lives in a non-consensual relationship, with a rape, also experienced domestic violence throughout their relationship. The onset had announced what would be a sequence of violence that would become the "normal" way of living as a couple:

> Having no alternative than living with her rapist, Lupita endured abuse during seven years. Physical and psychological violence was exacerbated by the fact that she wouldn't get pregnant. "We had been together for two years when he started beating me because he said I was a mule, because I couldn't have kids." "You are a mule, and for a mule I already have me. I want a woman that can give me children." There is no resentment in her voice, she simply describes the reality she had to endure, the same one her mother lived and one she envisions for her daughter. I have told her that her husband will beat her once or twice a year . . . that's how marriage is like; a chain of violence that is inherited from one generation to the next.[31]

Reading life stories out loud in the presence of indigenous women helped build an introspective setting in which women began to denaturalize violence and consider the need to gain inner strength to confront it in order to help their daughters to avoid reproducing the kind of relationships they had experienced. One activity undertaken during the workshop was to write a letter to physically and psychologically abused women:

> Break the chains of subjugation caused by the lack of high esteem. Find yourselves again and look around you. Life should not be as it was for our mothers. We need to construct our own way of thinking and communicating with our spouses, instead of repeating the ways of life from our families. To have our own way of living, to know how to express our own feelings and to teach our children to express their own feelings both with the people around them and with their romantic partners. To know how to say "no" to violence.[32]

The use of physical and sexual violence in police procedures throughout arrest and detention was also denounced during the workshops. These instances of violence usually took place as threats during questioning or more directly by police officers. This is what happened to Águila de Mar, who presented herself voluntarily at the public prosecutor's office to denounce a kidnapping and rape she had suffered at the hands of thugs who worked with her husband (a private security officer working for the state government, and whom she had also accused of domestic violence). Then she was charged with self-kidnapping and attempting to hire them to kill her husband. She recalls her experience of police violence:

> I arrived at the public prosecutor's office and was shown to a room where there were several men who took my declaration. Then a tall man with a mustache comes in and starts beating me, saying that he had to wake up because of my "stupid games." They asked me to snitch on my lover who was my accomplice on the self-kidnapping. They made me kneel and a tall fat man starts unzipping his pants saying that I do to him as I did to my lovers. Then Federico Mayorga, my husband's boss and owner of the safety agency, comes in with Joel, his bodyguard; he starts calling me a bitch while I was being beaten.[33]

The previous testimony is part of a plot of underhanded schemes and violence that shows how difficult it is for women who suffer domestic violence to achieve justice, especially when their husbands are part of the power networks that foster criminalizing victims, taking their children away, and sending them to prison.

The next testimony is from Lucía Sosa, a Nahuatl-speaking woman imprisoned at San Miguel Puebla, arrested for killing a property owner who had taken away her land, who defines the sexual violence she experienced at the hands of judicial police during detention in the following terms:

> Why do they have to put down women? When I shot him everything engulfed me: the rage against my ex-husband; the anger for this man who was trampling on me. Why do men have to humiliate women? Why do the rich humiliate the poor? I stayed put waiting for the police. I wasn't going to run; I knew I should pay for what I had done. When the police arrived, they beat me a lot. Then three policemen raped me and took me to the precinct to lock me up and now I'm here.[34]

Just as domestic violence has become a natural part of married life, police and military violence have become a part of how women relate to the Mexican state. The country's militarization, under the auspice of the War on Drugs, has altered life in indigenous and rural communities and fostered uncertainty for women. The army, police forces, and paramilitary groups are all staging their battles on women's bodies. This counterinsurgency strategy implies dealing with social movements as if they were "terrorist groups" and treating women involved in drug trafficking as dangerous members of organized crime.

The Mexican government's neocolonialism is criminalizing social move-ments in order to disband organizations and incarcerate their leaders. It is also criminalizing poverty with the purpose of showing its commitment to fighting drugs cartels. Sexual violence has become a racialized subjugation weapon that prolongs sexual violence experienced during childhood. The paradox, though, is that gender violence exists as a key part of the Mexican government's counter-insurgency campaigns, and as a part of the War on Drugs, even as the govern-ment signs legislative reforms that allegedly promote the "elimination of all forms of cruelty against women" (Hernández Castillo 2010a).

A case exhibiting the complicities that allow for state violence against women was the rape and murder of a seventy-three-year-old Nahuatl-speaking woman, Ernestina Ascencio Rosario, at the hands of four soldiers on Febru-ary 25, 2007, at Soledad Atzompa in Veracruz, part of the influence zone of the Sierra de Zongolica Indigenous Organizations Regional Coordination. This was not an isolated case: according to Amnesty International, from 1994 to the present, there have been at least sixty sexual assaults documented against indig-enous and peasant women at the hands of members of the armed forces, mostly in the states of Guerrero, Chiapas, and Oaxaca, precisely where grassroots or-ganizations have been surging the most.

Indigenous and peasant women have been the hardest hit by the militariza-tion of the country in the prevailing climate of insecurity and intimidation. It is striking that of the thirty women imprisoned at Atlacholoaya and San Miguel, seven were apprehended at military roadblocks under suspicion of drug traf-ficking, and threatened with violence, with no access to interpreters to explain their rights. In view of the multiple instances of sexual violence committed by members of the Mexican Army (which have been denounced by international organizations), it comes as no surprise that the detained women were willing to accept the charges despite not properly understanding the accusations made against them.

In this book, it is impossible to reproduce the multiple testimonies of eco-nomic exploitation, racism, and violence that have scarred the lives of these incarcerated women, and which, to an extent, continues to taint their prison ex-perience. Each of these life histories[35] reveals the way in which the justice system deepens the complex structures of inequality that characterize Mexican society and that render destitute indigenous women as the last link in a chain of oppres-sion. However, they also evidence women's capacity to reflect on their situation and, from the limited surroundings of imprisonment, they evidence how writing and intercultural dialogue that nurtures their writings have become tools to challenge the practices and representations that victimize them.

PRISON RESISTANCE: BUILDING SORORITY IN RECLUSION

After documenting and analyzing the violence of the penal state and its complicities with other forms of patriarchal violence, it seems almost impossible to speak of prison resistance or social agency on the part of incarcerated indigenous women. However, even in the space of the prison, where state power manifests itself in an almost totalizing manner, it is possible to find a thread of continuity between the experiences of resistance documented in the previous chapters and the destabilizing discourses that incarcerated women have developed based on their collective projects.

The spaces of collective reflection that started to be built after the "Life Histories" workshop have allowed the indigenous and mestizo women who participated in it to share their experiences and reflections on the multiple forms of violence that have marked their lives. The possibility of naming the tortures suffered when they arrived at the prison, such as the *costalazos* described by Águila del Mar in chapter 2, as well as human rights violations or forced marriage with their rapists as a violation of their rights as women, has allowed them to denaturalize violence. The doxa has become a discourse, and by naming what was formerly silenced, a step was taken toward transformation.

The female prisoners who participated in the "Life Histories" workshop have turned a creative writing project into a community of critical and thoughtful women called Sisters in the Shadows Editorial Collective of Women in Prison. The Collective no longer only writes books; its members have appropriated the publishing process, designing and binding the books with manual techniques (see Ruíz Rodríguez forthcoming). The seven books published so far and the radio series *Cantos desde el guamúchil*, produced by several members of the collective who are already free, have not only served to denounce the violence of the penitentiary system and to pressure authorities to revise legal records, but they have also contributed to destigmatizing the representations of incarcerated women made by Mexican society (see appendixes 4 and 5).[36]

In this experience, as in many others, the process of elaborating the texts and the visual and radio materials has been as important as the products themselves.

FIGURE 13. Members of the Sisters in the Shadows Editorial Collective of Women
in Prison (Colectiva Editorial de Mujeres en Prisión Hermanas en la Sombra)
in Atlacholoaya Correctional Facility in Morelos. Photograph from
R. Aída Hernández Archives.

Building ties of sorority has involved everyday efforts not devoid of contradictions, confronting the endemic distrust that characterizes life in prison (see Ruíz
Rodríguez forthcoming). At the same time, the spatial hierarchies established in
the prison's geography were disrupted by breaking the existing borders between
indigenous and mestizo women. Since the process of creating their first book,
Bajo la sombra del Guamúchil: Historias de vida de mujeres indígenas y campesi-
nas en prisión (*Under the Shade of the Guamúchil: Life Histories of Indigenous and*
Peasant Women in Prison), the space of the prison started to be reconfigured. The
workshop took place under the shade of the only tree that allows the prisoners
to approach nature, albeit in a limited manner, in the midst of the sea of concrete that is the prison. Indigenous and peasant women sat under this tree to
weave and embroider; they had turned it into their space, leaving the classrooms
and the spaces of the workshops for the women with more schooling, most of

them mestizas. The cultural workshops were "traditionally" for those who "knew more" and had more resources to appropriate the new knowledge that arrived from the outside. In our workshop, we took it upon ourselves to break with these hierarchies and approach those women who silently embroidered "under the shade of the guamúchil." One of the writers described the importance of this privileged space, noting that "the green of the guamúchil, the birds that nest in it, and the laughter of the children that reaches us from the playground makes them feel like they're not in prison" (Cadena 2010, 48).

There, we met the grandma, Morelitos, a Nahuatl woman from Atlixtac, Guerrero, aged more than seventy years, who arrived at the prison without speaking Spanish and without knowing what she was accused of. She had left her four grandchildren alone at her ranch when her migrant sons stopped sending her money and she decided to take a bus for the first time to Mexico City to seek help. She was detained at a military checkpoint and accused of transporting drugs (see appendix 3).

Also present was Máxima, a Nahuatl woman from Santa María Soyatla, Puebla, who left ten children alone outside the prison walls, one of them with disabilities, when her husband's participation in small-scale drug dealing landed her in jail. Like most imprisoned indigenous women, she never had the aid of a translator. We also found Altagracia and Leo, two Tlapaneca peasants united by family ties and stories of impunity. Alejandra, Miranda, Lulu, and Lupita, of indigenous and peasant ancestry, completed the group of women who decided to tell their stories.

At first, the idea was for the women who knew how to write to tell the stories of those who did not, thus putting their "pen" at the service of their indigenous colleagues. However, the dynamics started to take their own course. Alejandra Reynoso, who would later take on the pseudonym of "Perla Negra" (Black Pearl), told her own story. She had started to write in Atlacholoaya and she still felt insecure, but her chapter, titled "Perla Negra: Since I Was Born, Violence Has Been a Part of My Life" (Reynoso 2010, 9–11) not only portrays the horrendous way in which racism and patriarchal violence have marked her life but also reveals her poetic sensibility.

Miranda, a woman from Apaxtla de Castrejón, a Nahuatl community in the state of Guerrero, made a similar decision. She decided to use a pseudonym to publish her life history. In her chapter, Miranda never describes the reasons for her imprisonment, a decision that was respected by the members of the workshop; with her words, she manages to take us on a journey through a life marked with violence. The murder of her mother at the hands of her violent and alcoholic father and the subsequent murder of her own son while she was in prison allow us to imagine the world of violence that Miranda temporarily escaped when she arrived at Atlacholoaya (Miranda 2010, 75–85).

Similarly, Marisol (Águila del Mar—Ocean Eagle) decided to write her own life history. Already recognized as "the poet" of Atlacholoaya for her collaborations in the *Gaceta penitenciaria ¿Ahora qué sigue?* (Prison Gazette: Now What?), she was perhaps the most skillful creative writer in the group. Her story, narrated with an erotic prose that breaks away from victimizing narratives, revealed how domestic violence is made possible and reproduced by the state's complicity. Her poetry is also a tool for denunciation and self-reflection, and it has become a central thread of our documentary film project (*Bajo la sombra del Guamúchil*). In the "Life Histories" workshop, Marisol found an opportunity to develop her talents and explore narrative prose, denouncing with her life history the corruption and violence of the prison system (del Mar 2010, 115–35).

In addition to Alejandra Reynoso, Miranda, and Águila del Mar, the group of writers included Susuki Lee Camacho, Carlota Cadena, Guadalupe Salgado, and Rosa Salazar. Susuki Lee Camacho is a survivor of patriarchal violence, and defending her own life has cost her over ten years in prison. A narrator par excellence, Susuki discovered the power of her pen in this workshop, and she has devoted herself to using it prolifically in the last seven years. Her dialogues with Flor de Nochebuena and Morelitos exposed her to indigenous Mexico and made her aware of the racism that prevails in our entire society (Lee Camacho 2010a, 2010b). Of Korean-Mexican ancestry, Susuki grew up in a less marginalized environment than her Nahuatl friends. However, she experienced abandonment growing up in a boarding school. Her dialogues with Morelitos allowed Susuki to reflect on her own privileges but also on her wounds: "I listen to her and I return to my childhood and ask myself: was it worth it to grow up in a boarding school? I might not have been beaten like Morelitos, but I always thought it was better to have my parents nearby. Morelitos interrupts my thoughts . . ." (Lee Camacho 2010b, 40).

Suzuki's fame as a writer transcended the limits of the women's prison, and a paid assassin in the men's prison offered to hire her as his biographer. Susuki accepted the challenge and started to interview him and to record his life history. However, her sensibility and critical spirit kept her from taking on the heroic tone regarding male violence that permeated the interviewee's testimony.

The project was cut short, but Susuki's fame as a narrator and poet continues to grow outside the prison walls through magazines such as *Específica* and the collective's new publications.

Guadalupe Salgado suffers from bipolar disorder, and during one of her crises she took her daughter's life, who had severe cerebral palsy, because she felt that "this world is not made for little angels born with that frailty." The poverty they lived in, paired with her own illness, made her feel that she could not withstand "the burden life had given her." She decided not to tell her own story, but that of Lulu, an indigenous woman who suffered a head injury and who was under Guadalupe's care during the time of the workshop.

Carlota Cadena, a survivor of her own addictions, found, in Doña Mica, "Altagracia," and Leo Zavaleta, people with whom she could share her sense of humor and her love of life. Carlotita always showed up at the workshop with Jell-O, candy, something to share, and a curious anecdote that made all of us laugh. For a while, we forgot the imprisonment, and the workshop became a feast. I dare think that it was her proclivity to smile that endeared her to Carlota and Mica, and that continues to unite them in a lifelong friendship outside the prison walls. Without much in common, Carlota approached tiny Micaela, a premature elder at the age of fifty-something, and offered her friendship and her writing. Doña Mica, a native of a community of the mountain region of Guerrero where women are "given *pueblo*" ("made public") through gang rapes if they do not accept a man's proposition, or if they walk in the hills without male protection, found in Carlotita an attentive ear and a chronicler who narrates in detail the patriarchal violence experienced in indigenous communities and the racism of state justice (see Cadena 2010, 31–37).

Doña Mica was so pleased with Carlota's work, which she came to listen to every week in our workshop, that she brought her cousin Leo to share with Carlota her story. Both Mica and Leo are natives of small communities of the Me'phaa (Tlapaneco) municipality of Tlacoapa, in the mountain region of Guerrero, and they share in common a life history of orphanhood and gender violence. In contrast with Doña Mica, Leo is beginning to accept the challenge of writing and, with no specific method, she has started to express her ideas with simple words, slowly weaving her thoughts. After the interviews with Carlota, they started to write together. They were both delighted with the experiment; the "interviewee" became a co-author and, together, Carlota and Leo narrated their life histories in *Guamúchil*, written in the form of dialogues sprinkled with tears and laughter (see Cadena and Zavaleta 2010, 51–79). This project was only the beginning. Leo, who is now free, is working on her own book, titled *Los sueños de una cisne en el pantano* (Dreams of a Swan in a Swamp), as part of the publishing collective.

During our weekly workshops, Doña Rosita Salazar, a peasant woman from Xoxocotla, Morelos, who worked in the prison kitchen, always came to offer us food. Even though she was illiterate, she enjoyed listening to her colleagues and, on the days of the workshop, her sales were meager because she arrived early with a plate of quesadillas or hot sopes, and she remained there for three or four hours, silent at first but participative with time, always with some commentary or advice for the writers.

Mama Rosa, as she was known to the prisoners, went through a similar process as Leo: one day, she wrote her name out of the blue; the next week she penned an intelligent phrase; and before we knew it she was doing the exercises with the others. Her brief reflections were also included in the collective book, and they reveal her critical awareness of all sorts of violence against women (see "Una mujer con mucho miedo" in Salazar 2010, 29). Her shaky writing still struggles to express all the wealth of her thoughts, but each week she gave us a lesson that brought us close to the universe of the countryside, nature, and the simple people who dedicate their poems to plants:

> I dedicate this poem to plants,
> the plants that cure
> illnesses
> the guava leaves,
> peppermint
> I dedicate this poem to epazote
> to horehound,
> to basil,
> to black tea,
> to mint
> . . . I dedicate this poem to plants
> I am a person of the people,
> I believe in them
> as my grandparents did.
> Rosa Salazar (Colectiva Editorial Hermanas en la Sombra 2012, 88)

Rosita (Rosa Salazar) was jailed because she was unable to repay the 40,000 pesos (around US$2,000.00) she borrowed from a moneylender to help her son migrate to the north in search of a better life. Having signed papers she could not read, the profiteer's bad will landed her in Atlacholoaya, where she lived for four years and where she earned many adoptive daughters who still miss her.

These were the women who came to the "shade of the guamúchil" and broke the language and cultural barriers that kept them apart from their indigenous colleagues. Together, they created a space for exchange and collective reflection that has allowed them to share knowledges and confront the racist and sexist ideologies that have justified the violences in their lives and their incarceration in Atlacholoaya. Building a community of sorority that produces collective knowledge and publicizes it through different means is itself a form of resistance against the governance strategies of the penal state.

FINAL REFLECTIONS

Contrasting the experiences of indigenous women before community justice with the experiences of those in the state justice system, it becomes evident that both positive law and indigenous law reproduce and reinforce gender inequality. However, as we have seen throughout this chapter, the institutionalized racism that characterizes the state justice system adds a new axis of exclusion for those indigenous women who must face this system as either claimants or accused.

The globalization of cultural rights discourses that indigenous movements throughout the continent have appropriated runs parallel to the globalization of the prison industrial complex that function as an updated form of colonialism toward indigenous peoples.

The emancipatory spaces created by multicultural reforms, described in other chapters of this book, cannot be denied. Still it is impossible to analyze the relationships that indigenous peoples have with the Mexican state without taking into account the regulatory and punitive character of legal reforms carried out alongside the recognition of cultural diversity, such as the penal justice and public security constitutional reform as well as the amendments to the Law that Establishes Minimum Norms for Social Readjustment of Convicts.

Neoliberal structural reforms have deepened the marginalization of indigenous peoples, driving them to migrate north or resort to the production or transportation of illegal substances as a means to overcome the peasant agricultural crisis. At the same time, they have created an alternative form of economic control and exploitation by incorporating this labor surplus into the prison industrial complex as well as a legal and judicial apparatus that allows for the incarceration and exploitation of the most impoverished sectors of society.

Indigenous women have been hit the hardest by the consequences of these policies since they frequently have to take charge of the domestic economy when their men migrate. This has led some scholars to speak about the feminization of the Mexican peasantry. Women have also faced the most violent impacts of the militarization of indigenous regions and the War on Drugs.

The sexual and domestic violence that still pervades the lives of women in indigenous communities has now been enhanced by police and military violence of which many testimonies have been registered at the Puebla and Morelos women's penitentiaries. Racist violence has also tainted the experiences of indigenous women before state law in that contempt and discrimination toward their cultural and linguistic specificities characterize their detentions and prosecution. Indigenous women face laws and judicial procedures that they do not understand. This racism is reproduced in the prison sphere, where nonindigenous women and prison staff frequently exclude indigenous women. Even their own state-appointed attorneys rarely take their defense seriously, nor do they offer them the legal resources provided by the Indigenous Cultural Rights Law, such as the right to an interpreter and the use of expert anthropological testimony when this is called for.

The increase in female indigenous detainees for their participation in small-scale drug-trafficking charges evidences the inability of the system to offer a dignified livelihood to this social sector still burdened by illiteracy, unemployment, malnutrition, and high mortality rates nationwide (Bonfil 2003).

The imprisonment, uprooting, child abandonment, and unraveling of family structure imposed on women is clearly not keeping indigenous communities away from drug-trafficking networks. Nor does it demonstrate that multicultural reforms have made justice more accessible to the country's indigenous population. Only a social policy that offers economic alternatives to the Mexican peasantry based on distribution of wealth and a real recognition of cultural and political rights of indigenous peoples can counter the advancement of drug cartels in indigenous lands and keep indigenous men and women away from organized crime.

In spite of the violence of the penal state described in this chapter, a small group of indigenous and mestizo women incarcerated in the women's prison of

Atlacholoaya have taken on the challenge of building community at the very place where institutional violence promotes distrust and isolation. Confronting racism and patriarchal violence, they have undertaken the task of rewriting their life histories and reconfiguring their victimized female identities through collective reflection. Although the Sisters in the Shadows Editorial Collective of Women in Prison is a small group that is hardly representative of the reality of incarcerated women overall, its work has reached many prisons in the country through its books, and its example is being followed by other artistic and cultural collectives in prison spaces (see Belaustegigoitia forthcoming).

FINAL THOUGHTS

THE ORGANIZATIONAL EXPERIENCES AND STRATEGIES of struggle of indigenous women analyzed in the five chapters of this book take place in the context of contradictory processes of criminalization of the indigenous population and multiculturalization of Latin American states. We are before new forms of governmentality that tend to promote "individual empowerment" and "market citizenship" while simultaneously using legality to criminalize social protest and dissidence. Through public policies, the work of nongovernmental organizations, and feminist projects themselves, a discourse of women's rights has been promoted that widens the gap between the individual and the collective. In this context, organized indigenous women in Mexico, Guatemala, and Colombia are destabilizing these discourses of power by demanding the recognition of the collective rights of their peoples as a necessary condition for the full exercise of their rights as women.

Critical views on the institutionalization of feminisms (See Schild 2015; Radcliff 2008, 2009) and multicultural agendas (Hale 2005; Yashar 2005; Iturralde 2000) are indispensable to nuance the optimism with which constitutional reforms on women's and indigenous peoples' rights are sometimes analyzed. However, to limit ourselves to a systemic analysis that does not recognize "the fissures in the discourses of powers" is to silence once again the voices and experiences of those who, with their everyday struggles, are creating new meanings around rights, culture, and justice.

While it is true that the "juridization of politics" has displaced more radical discourses and practices regarding revolution and social justice, it has also enabled the emergence of broader understandings of cultural and gender rights. Organized indigenous women's struggles have demonstrated that the struggle for land and territory is a fundamental part of the struggle for culture, and that the struggle against violence toward women must include the struggle against neocolonialism, racism, and territorial dispossession.

Throughout this book, I have attempted to demonstrate that the hegemony of the state is always an unfinished process. The political agendas of neoliberal multiculturalism and of penal states have not been entirely successful. The policies to decentralize and strengthen civil society, which characterize neoliberal states, have had contradictory results in those regions where previous organizational efforts already existed: indeed, they have enabled the appropriation of new collective spaces for the development of critical reflection and political organization.

The impact of multicultural reforms in spaces of justice has been as diverse as the regional histories, and while, in some cases, these reforms have become new strategies for neoliberal governance, in others, they have contributed to emancipatory autonomist projects in which indigenous women have actively participated, as we saw in chapter 3.

The internal heterogeneity of indigenous women's movements, as a product of their different political genealogies described in chapter 2, has influenced their acceptance or rejection of feminist discourses and their impacts (or not) in spaces of communal justice. Based on discourses regarding women's rights, human rights, cosmovision, or women's dignity, the negotiation of the meanings of "culture" and "tradition" confront both essentialist or purist views of what it means to be "indigenous," and racist and neocolonial views on progress and modernity.

Throughout the twenty-five years during which I have worked in alliance and collaboration with indigenous women, I have witnessed the emergence of different processes of vernacularization of rights discourses: from an initial rejection of the feminist agenda (stigmatized as neoliberal and separatist) to a vindication of indigenous and communal feminisms based on their own epistemologies. My own views regarding the possibilities of indigenous justice have changed from a complete disqualification of the patriarchal nature of indigenous law to the recognition of its historic nature and its emancipatory potential. As I have documented in chapter 3, in various regions of Mexico, Guatemala,

FIGURE 14. Zapatista member of the local autonomic government
in Chiapas. Photograph by Andrés Solorzano.

and Colombia, indigenous women have started to impact spaces of communal justice, vindicating "good customs" and rejecting the "bad customs" that violate and exclude them.

The "awareness-raising" methodologies underlying the collaborative research project "Indigenous Women Between Positivist Law and Community Justice in the Highlands of Chiapas" (1998–2000), described in chapter 1, continued to reproduce a feminist ethnocentrism that assumed an ability to "emancipate others." The "dialogues of knowledges" with organized indigenous women have led me to recognize this epistemic colonialism and to seek, in their theorizations, other ways of understanding gender justice. Their writings have been fundamental for the emergence of new theorizations regarding the decolonization of feminism.

Through different textual strategies, not always arising from academic spaces, indigenous women are theorizing their realities and confronting the discourses of power that attempt to reproduce neoliberal governance. With the memoirs of their political encounters, their literary texts, or the writing of their life histories, indigenous women in this book speak to us of other ways of imagining emancipation and social justice.

Concepts such as *cuatriedad*, developed in the documents of the First Summit of Indigenous Women, and examined in chapter 2, have been used to refer to the importance of totality, balance, and integrality in contrast with the fragmentation promoted by the neoliberal system. This term refers to a concept of the person whereby it is impossible to separate the individual from the collective, where nature is not a resource at the service of human beings but a part of the cuatriedad, of the totality of which we are only a small part. Breaking with the dichotomist analyses that characterize Western thought, indigenous women use the metaphor of the four cardinal points to refer to the importance of holistic thought.

Regarding communal justice, indigenous women from Oaxaca have appropriated concepts such as "communality" developed by the Ayuujk anthropologist and leader Floriberto Díaz to vindicate the importance of the "collective" from the perspective of more integral views of the community, which include men and women, as we saw in chapter 3 in the context of the communitarian laws in the municipality of Tlahuitoltepec. We also found theoretical elaborations and new concepts arising from dialogues with feminist organizations, such as "integral intercultural defense with a gender perspective," coined by Nahua women from Cuetzalán, Puebla, to name a legal strategy against domestic violence whereby indigenous defenders act indistinctly in the Public Prosecutor's Office and in the Indigenous Court.

In the case of Colombia, the concept of "integrality" has been fundamental in the theorizations arising from the certification course "Indigenous Families, Gender Participation, and Equity," where the women revisit Nasa mythology to speak of the balance between the male and the female in order to denounce women's current exclusion from certain communal spaces.

These new theorizations are also found in Inés Fernández Ortega's legal struggle in the Inter-American Court of Human Rights. Her notions of rape as part of a historic grievance against her people, and her demand of collective reparations, destabilized the liberal views of the body and sexual violence underlying international law. This litigation set a precedent in the Inter-American Court in terms of understanding sexual violence not only as a violation of sexual and reproductive rights but also as a violation of the collective rights of indigenous men and women and their right to self-determination and autonomy. Inés Fernandez's preoccupation with including all the women in her organization as beneficiaries of the Inter-American Court's sentence set a precedent in international litigation. As observed in chapter 4, the Inter-American Court acknowledged for the first time that a violation against an individual impacts the entire community, thus considering a person's cultural context as a key dimension in comprehending how gender violence is experienced and how to imagine justice.

In the case of the literary texts and the life histories written by indigenous women, members of the Sisters in the Shadows Editorial Collective of Women in Prison demonstrate a denunciation of racism in the justice system and the complicities of patriarchal violence. In addition, there are various theorizations regarding how freedom can be reconceptualized when the various prisons that control and limit female bodies are observed from a privileged place.

By describing and recognizing these different ways of theorizing justice, rights, and women's emancipation, I do not intend to disqualify or reject feminist discourses on women's rights or gender justice; instead, my intention is to point out that there are other emancipatory practices and languages oftentimes silenced by the "monoculture of feminist knowledge." One challenge faced by those of us who have taken on the difficult task of decolonizing our feminisms is to recognize our own ethnocentrism and reject the logics of power that produce the "non-existence" of indigenous and peasant women while simultaneously breaking away from "Orientalizing" strategies (Said 1978). These strategies represent indigenous women as our alterity, as the keepers of a "primordial knowledge" that will serve as the basis for our emancipation. Imposing on them, through our representations, the "responsibility of saving us" with their "alternative knowledges" is yet another form of colonialism and does not contribute to the critical intercultural dialogues that we need.

In the search for other ways of imagining the world and thinking of other possible futures, the temptation to idealize indigenous cultures has been present. In reaction to racism and ethnocentrism, indigenous intellectuals or scholars in solidarity have tended to present an ahistorical view of indigenous peoples, negating the internal contradictions and the power relations that exist in the communities, as well as the impact of colonialism on their contemporary cultural practices. These representations can become new forms of "discursive colonialism" that prevent us from seeing the dynamics of domination and resistance that develop among indigenous peoples. This book has been an effort to confront these ahistorical views and to demonstrate the cultural creativity of indigenous women in the realms of justice and law.

APPENDIX 1

CASE OF *INÉS FERNÁNDEZ ORTEGA V. MÉXICO*[1]

Official Expertise Anthropological Report

ROSALVA AÍDA HERNÁNDEZ CASTILLO AND HÉCTOR ORTÍZ ELIZONDO

(Presented orally in the Inter-American Court of Human Rights by Rosalva Aída Hernández Castillo, in Lima, Peru, on April 15, 2010)

INTRODUCTION

1.1 OBJECTIVES

- To analyze what kind of an impact the rape of Ms. Inés Fernández Ortega had on the indigenous community, especially among women.
- To analyze how this sexual assault and the impunity on the case have affected the social fabric of this community.
- To seek and propose appropriate measures of reparation.

This case was notified to the Mexican state based on the fiftieth article of the American Convention on Human Rights,[2] through the Inter-American Commission on Human Rights.

1.2 METHODOLOGY

This Official Expertise Report has been produced based on:

- The study of the anthropological and historical background of the Me'phaa population. Field visits to the communities of Me'phaa in Barranca de Guadalupe, Barranca Tecuani, and the municipal capital Ayutla de los Libres, in the Mexican state of Guerrero.
- In-depth interviews with Ms. Inés Fernández Ortega, her nuclear family, and her extended family.
- Group interviews with members of the Indigenous Organization of the Me'phaa People (Organización del Pueblo Indígena Me'phaa—OPIM).

During the interviews the experts focused on reconstructing the circumstances of the aggression that Inés Fernández Ortega endured and how these experiences affected her life, the members of her family, and the community. We also explored how the process of the pursuit of justice impacted the social fabric of the Me'phaa community and the organization to which the victim belongs (OPIM), considering the different effects these events have on men and women.

We inquired specifically into how the cultural concepts of personhood, violence, and lack of justice were an influence on how the rape, and the latter context of impunity, were handled.

Thematic areas included:

- The link between personal and communal experiences of violence.
- The soul and spiritual illnesses linked to the experience of rape, and how these affect the family and the community.
- How the presence of the army impacts the community's social fabric.
- The need for reparation, truth, and justice in the rebuilding of the social fabric and stability.
- How gender and cultural factors could have contributed to the lack of justice.

1.3 BACKGROUND AND SOCIOCULTURAL CONTEXT

Inés Fernández Ortega is identified by others and herself as a Me'phaa, one of the sixty-two indigenous communities officially recognized by the National Commission for the Development of Indigenous Peoples (Comisión Nacional para el Desarrollo de Pueblos Indígenas—CDI). The Me'phaa community, also known as "Tlapanecas," are located in the state of Guerrero, specifically in the following municipalities: Acatepec, Atlixtac, Malinaltepec, Tlacoapa, San Luis Acatlán, Zapotitlán Tablas, Atlamajalcingo del Monte, Metlatonoc, Tlapa, Quetzaltenango, Azoyú, and Acapulco, in addition to the municipality of Ayutla de los Libres, where the events took place. In 2007, official data reported the existence of 98,573 Me'phaa-speaking people, of which 92,206 lived in 276 different locations[3] in the state of Guerrero.

The majority of these communities are located in a rugged land that runs from the coast to a range of mountains within an area of approximately 3,000 square kilometers. Many of these communities are formed by scattered settlements with difficult access, as is the case of Barranca Tecuani, which is home to Inés Fernández Ortega and, therefore, where these events took place.

Guerrero's indigenous communities are characterized by high levels of marginalization, making it the Mexican state with the highest levels of illiteracy within indigenous communities (according to the information given by the CDI, National Commission for the Development of Indigenous Peoples, in 2005, 39.7 percent of the 534,624 indigenous people who lived in Guerrero could not read). The municipality of Ayutla de los Libres, which is where the Barranca Tecuani community is situated, has a population of 55,974, of which 21,930 are indigenous people (39.2 percent). This municipality has been classified as one with a very high level of marginalization by the National Population Council (Consejo Nacional de Población—CONAPO), where 9,120 inhabitants cannot read (sociodemographic indicators of total population and indigenous population, for each municipality; CDI 2005). The level of marginalization heightens in the case of indigenous women, who have higher indicators of monolingualism and illiteracy, and whose health conditions are among the worst in the country, occupying the first place in the country for maternal mortality.

The majority of the Me'phaa communities in Ayutla de los Libres are dispersed in ravines and do not have clean drinking water or drainage canals. The construction of latrines has not been adequately promoted in the area which is why people defecate out in the open, bringing with that a number of health implications. This is communal land used mainly for subsistence crop production, although, in some communities they grow coffee and hibiscus for sale purposes.

Barranca Tecuani is inhabited by approximately 120 families, making a total of 530 people, all Me'phaa-speaking people with a very rudimentary knowledge of Spanish. This is a community dispersed in a gully, with a primary school, a church, and a government commission in its center. As in most Me'phaa communities, the land tenure is communal and the highest agrarian authority is the Commission of Communal Lands (Comisariado de Bienes Comunales). There is a politico-religious authority that runs alongside this authority, which is composed of the *Mayordomos* of the three main religious festivals: The Virgin of Guadalupe, on December 12; San José, on March 19; and Santa Cruz on May 3.[4]

They were in charge of the spiritual healing rituals that took place after the rape and torture of Inés, and they attend to all the soul and spiritual illnesses that arise in the community.

The participation in the Mayordomía system is fundamental for a community's sense of belonging and, notwithstanding the internal differences that came with Inés's rape (due to the disagreements that emerged regarding how to handle the threat that the armed forces represented), every sector of the community participates. Inés's husband, Fortunato Prisciliano, was elected Mayordomo of the "Annual Virgin of Guadalupe Celebration" in 2010. According to Prisciliano: "It is a great deal of money, sometimes if you are elected you can spend up to $3,000 pesos (US$165.00) and one has to kill animals for the festivity, but it is important to participate, because if you don't, you are not worthy in the community" (Interview with Fortunato Priciliano, Barranca Tecuani, March 13, 2008). This social activity has been instrumental for both of them to reintegrate into the community after a period of social distancing since they started legal procedures.

As part of the Mayordomía system, they created a joint fund where 25 percent of the income from the celebrations is put aside in a savings account, to be used when a member of a community is in need. There is also an unpaid mutual aid known as *naguma xtaja* in which all the members of the community participate to help each other when needed.

Based on the interviews that took place, it is apparent that the communal ownership of the land, and the participation of the people in the Mayordomías and in community work, are essential in the reaffirmation of the Me'phaa people's identity and sense of belonging to the Barranca de Tecuani community. However, for Inés Fernández and Fortunato Prisciliano, these ties of belonging and solidarity had gone beyond the community's borders to their participation in OPIM (a civil organization that should be seen as an indigenous representative institution and which is a result of the indigenous communities' changes and adaptation to the forces of modernity).[5] This organization has approximately three hundred people and is present in six communities of the Ayutla municipality (Barranca de Guadalupe, Barranca Tecuani, El Camalote, El Salto, El Progreso, and Te Cruz) and in a community of Acatepec (Barranca Bejuco), and it has been fundamental in helping Inés Fernández with her allegation procedure.

In a search for alternatives to the high levels of marginalization and poverty that prevail in the region, the Independent Organization of the Mixteco and Tlapaneco People (Organización Independiente de Pueblos Mixtecos y Tlapanecos—OIPMT) was formed in 1998 and legally constituted in 2000. OIPMT developed as an organization where a number of different communities from two different indigenous groups established in the same region of Guerrero's mountains came together. Two years later, this organization was divided into two: the Organization for the Mixteco People's Future (Organización para el Futuro del Pueblo Mixteco—OFPM) and the Indigenous Organization of the Me'phaa People (Organización del Pueblo Indígena Me'phaa—OPIM).

This organizational process of the Me'phaa people was simultaneous with an escalation of the armed forces' presence in the area due to the development of counterinsurgent campaigns in the region and campaigns against drug trafficking. The army's presence brought with it a number of complaints regarding the violation of human rights by the armed forces. This situation is what induced OPIM to include the search for justice in regards to the violation of human rights that the population endures in their agenda.

These acts of repression have been experienced and interpreted in light of historical experiences that relate the presence of the army with violence and impunity since the 1970s, when the so-called *guerra sucia* (dirty war) took place in Guerrero against supporters of the guerrilla movements.[6] This was the case with the massacre of El Charco on June 7, 1998, where, according to the survivors, the army killed eleven people, injured five, and detained twenty-two (five of whom were under the age of 18).[7]

The rape and torture of Inés Fernández Ortega is interpreted, by herself and by other members of the community, not as an independent case of violence but as a continuum of violence that has characterized the relation between the indigenous groups and the Mexican Army.

The harassment of members of OPIM since they started supporting Inés Fernández Ortega and Valentina Rosenda Cantú (also a victim of rape committed by military forces on February 16, 2002),[8] is interpreted by its members as part of a relatively recent history of military violence. The murder of Lorenzo

Fernández Ortega (Inés's brother and member of OPIM) in February 2008, the anonymous death threats to Obtilia Eugenio Manuel (the president of OPIM), and the warrants and arrests in April 2008 of five of OPIM's main leaders (one of whom remains in prison—Raúl Hernández), have fueled the fear and the sense of vulnerability of OPIM members and Barranca de Tecuani inhabitants, erasing memories of a recent past of violence and impunity, causing in Inés mixed feelings when it comes to making the decision to file complaints and pursue justice.[9]

EVENTS AND CONSEQUENCES

2.1 EVENTS THAT TOOK PLACE

The available information indicates that, on March 22, 2002, at approximately 3 p.m., eleven soldiers from the 41st Battalion of the Mexican Armed Forces arrived at Inés Fernández Ortega's and Fortunato Prisciliano Sierra's home, located in the Barranca de Tecuani community, which is part of the municipality of Ayutla de los Libres in the state of Guerrero, Mexico. Three of the soldiers entered the room that was being used as a kitchen without Inés's consent. At that moment, Inés was accompanied by only her four children, all under the age of 18. The soldiers asked questions that she couldn't answer, after which one of them raped her. After the rape took place, the soldiers left, but not before stealing the meat that Prisciliano had been drying in his yard for his family. Two days after the incident, the victim presented a formal allegation to the attorney general's office[10] (Ministerio Público of Ayutla de los Libres), who determined that it was not the correct authority to investigate either the unauthorized and illegal entrance to Inés's property or the rape or theft due to the fact that the accused parties were part of the Mexican Army. In May 2002, the local authorities forwarded the case to the military authorities.

2.2 PERSONAL AND COMMUNAL IMPACT

In the Me'phaa community's cultural context, the idea of a person is not conceived as isolated from the community; the construction of subjectivity is always linked to the collective. In Mexican indigenous communities, as is the case in the Me'phaa community, the individual and the group are closely linked, which means that the violence experienced by an individual is perceived as an affront to the community, bringing with it communal instability. As a consequence, the damage caused by experiencing rape can reach up to a gnoseological level. This is because, in the Me'phaa culture, events that cause pain (such as an accident or violence) can lead to an illness called *susto* (fright): a condition with physical effects on the person who suffers from it, with the possibility of transcending to those surrounding the person. This is why it is necessary to understand how Inés's rape affected not only her but also her family and community.

Both Inés Fernández Ortega and her mother-in-law, María Sierra Librada, made reference to the illness produced by the "fright" (called *gamitú* in Me'phaa) when they testified, which they both suffered from after the rape took place. According to their beliefs, the soul leaves the body (*nanda tiga akiin*) due to fear caused by the violence, which produces intense headaches, goose bumps, body tremors, loss of appetite, and insomnia. The cause is also linked to the violence that Inés's "nahual" (*kuiñú*) suffered, her nahual being her spiritual animal protector. According to Mrs. Sierra Librada, this nahual is still hurt somewhere in the mountain and hasn't been able to go back to his home for nine years, since the rape happened.

Even though candles were lit in the sacred place of Barranca de Tecuani Mountain in the days following the rape and the proper rituals for the healing of the soul were executed, the lack of justice prevents Inés, her mother-in-law, and other women from the community to completely heal from the "susto." In regards to what María Sierra said, "As long as there is no justice our spirits cannot be in peace, there is a lot of fear and we cannot sleep soundly, because we know that if the *guachos* (word used to refer to the military forces) are not punished for what they did, they will be able to do it again. The lack of justice produces *va jui* and *garmitú* (different Me'phaa words for fright) (Interview with María Sierra Librada, in Barranca de Tecuani, March 13, 2010).

The community's imbalance caused by the "susto" still affects Inés and many other women in the community because justice is an element that allows order to be restored. However, from the community's perspective, there has not been closure due to the fact that the guilty parties have not been punished. This is how the imbalance produced by the lack of justice becomes the cause of other acts of aggression suffered by other members of OPIM, among them the murder of Inés's brother, Lorenzo Fernández.

In every narrative about the rape, there has been a continuum between the sexual aggression and the aggressions following the accusation and search for justice. A single event, like the rape of Inés, has its consequences in other events because it has not been possible to have closure without a proper punishment. In this regard, we can acknowledge once again that it is not possible to separate Inés's personal experience from the collective experiences of repression and fear in the community and among the members of OPIM.

The responses from the members of Barranca de Tecuani community and members of OPIM have been very different from those of the bordering communities. First of all, the inhabitants of Barranca de Tecuani came together to expel the soldiers from the communal lands where they were camping. The limits of the communal lands that encompass ravines and cultivation areas mark the borders of the community's collective area, which means that the canvassing of the military forces and their camping in that communal space with no prior authorization from the owners of the land is perceived as an affront to their collective rights.

However, this social cohesion demonstrated initially in the collective actions to expel the military forces has been fragmenting with time due to the disagreements of how to deal with the threat that the military represents. According to Inés Fernández's testimony, "Before the rape, the community was very united, but it was the government and the fear that divided us. Alfonso Morales, who works for the military, told the women that they shouldn't accuse the guachos (soldiers) because they would get into trouble. They are afraid that what happened to me will happen to them, this is why they don't want to support me" (Interview with Inés Fernández Ortega, March 13, 2010). This fear is stimulated by the ongoing presence of military forces in the area. According to Inés Fernández Ortega's testimonies, in the beginning of February 2009, military units once again parked in front of their community, and many soldiers entered their lands, stealing part of the harvest and damaging the rest. In these circumstances, Inés Fernández and her husband, Fortunato Prisciliano, expressed the same perception about having part of the community abandon them in their fight to seek justice. Inés is especially upset by the lack of support and the stigma that she has suffered from the women of Barranca de Tecuani who single her out as "the soldiers' woman" (la mujer de los guachos).

However, Inés and Fortunato still see themselves as part of the community and are recognized as such due to the fact that they still participate in charges that their communal citizenship rights grant them. Fortunato was elected Mayordomo in the "Virgin of Guadalupe Celebration" on December 12, 2010, and Inés has just been elected as a delegate in the community's social program called *Oportunidades*[11] (Opportunities). Cultural institutions like the Mayordomías and religious festivities are traditional mechanisms that help rebuild the indigenous collective space and are rarely affected by political ups and downs.

Nevertheless, the ongoing military presence in the indigenous territory, and the impunity that has brought with it insufficient law enforcement in conflicts such as Inés Fernández's, affect other mechanisms in the community's social fabric. For instance, the community has experienced social fragmentation that put the social reproduction and the viability of an ethnic collectivity that depends on a healthy, harmonic, and safe development at risk. This is especially true for women who are mainly in charge of transmitting the cultural values and the socio-cultural reproduction of the Me'phaa community. This social fragmentation can be seen in Barranca de Tecuani's community through the fear experienced by part of the community when Inés Fernández presented her case to the attorney general and, later, to the Inter-American Court of Human Rights, because this could have made the soldiers "mad" and put the members of the community in a more vulnerable position.

Parallel to this, the lack of justice in the case, and the impunity of Inés's attackers, have proved the point of those who argue that it is better to keep quiet than to report rapes to human rights authorities. Inés's mother-in-law, María Sierra Librada, explains the community's indifference and even its rejection when it comes to seeking justice for her daughter-in-law as yet another consequence of the garmitú: the population is paralyzed with fear, and cannot think.

In this context, the community's togetherness, and the solidarity of those who agree with Inés's claim for justice, have been reconstructed in the collective space of OPIM, where she has found the support that her fellow women of Barranca de Tecuani have refused to give her. "The OPIM is now my family and my community to me, they have suffered with me because of the lack of justice, they are like my father and my mother" (Interview with Inés Fernández Ortega on March 13, 2010). This is why, for Inés, the possible measures or reparations are not only for her but for the girls and women of her community and her organization, as we will see further on.

2.3 THE IMPACT ON THE WOMEN OF THE REGION

In the Me'phaa culture, as in most of the Andean and Mesoamerican cultures, women are the ones in charge of the children's education and transmitting the values and the world vision of their community, which is why they play an important role in the social and cultural reproduction. This is why violence against indigenous women is experienced not only as a problem in the community but as a communal experience that puts the community's culture and social reproduction at risk. Inés Fernandez's rape, the impunity that has prevailed during the last eight years, and the ongoing military presence in the area have created a vulnerable atmosphere for the Me'phaa women and thus puts the cultural reproduction of this community at risk.

As the rape and the conflicts that have come after the allegation to the authorities have impacted Barranca Tecuani's social fabric, their effects have been particularly harmful to the young girls and women of the region. Many of them say that they have the "susto" and have limited their outings from the community due to the fear of suffering Inés's luck.

The organized spaces that Inés and other members of OPIM had been promoting (where women of the community had started to reflect about their rights as women and as indigenous people, and where they could propose productive projects that would help them rise from their situation of extreme poverty) were suspended. According to Andrea Eugenio's testimony (one of the Me'phaa trainers from OPIM who held some workshops in Barranca Tecuani), "Women are now afraid of getting together and organizing anything, because they think that what happened to Inés was because she was involved and was involving other women" (Interview with Andrea Eugenio in Ayutla de los Libres, March 13, 2010). This disassembling of collective work, in a region that is characterized by its isolation, and where there are no projects for women, has brought with it a deeper marginalization and lack of productive alternatives for all women.

Parallel to this, the fear of sexual violence because of the constant military presence has deepened because of the impunity following Inés's rape and has had an influence on many women when it comes to letting their daughters play freely in the fields as they used to do. In many occasions, these women don't even let their daughters go to school when they know that military forces are canvassing the region.

The region's geography, where houses are dispersed in ravines, makes the children's and teenagers' social lives take place mostly out in open spaces, such as cornfields, ravines, or in the vicinities bordering the school, all of which have become insecure since the rape occurred. Due to the geographical isolation of Barranca Tecuani and other communities of the region, to get to the largest town in the municipality, people have to walk three hours to a crossroads where a bus passes (as the only means of transportation). In the current situation of fear of military presence, and with the ongoing threat of sexual violence, mothers have opted to keep their daughters at home and out of school, or send them to live with middle-class mestizo (mixed race) families in the main city of the municipality, Ayutla de los Libres, where the nearest middle school is located. The living conditions of these young and teenage girls are described very vividly by Noemí Prisciliano Fernández, Inés's eldest daughter:

> There are about thirty other girls from Barranca Tecuani studying over there in Ayutla, who work for the mestiza bosses without pay. Sometimes we get woken up at 6 a.m. and work until 4 p.m., which is when we leave for school. When we come home at night after school, we sometimes have to make dinner, wash or iron laundry. I came to live in Ayutla when I was twelve so I could go to school, and I've lived in 5 different households, because I'm not treated well and I'd rather change houses. Now I live in the house of OPIM, but my sister does live with a teacher and she works all day and doesn't get paid a cent, she is just given a bed to sleep on and food. (Interview with Noemí Prisciliano, March 14, 2010)

Not only do teenage girls live in fear, but they have also lost the freedom that they had before the rape and the acts of repression brought on by the allegation. Having a safe and dignified place to live while they are studying becomes a pressing need in the unsafe context of the community.

2.4 THE LACK OF JUDICIAL ACCESSIBILITY FOR INDIGENOUS WOMEN

Various studies surrounding indigenous women's access to justice in this state have shown that the discriminatory gender ideologies and the lack of cultural sensibility on the part of the authorities have differentiated the relations between this sector of the population and the rights granted to the rest of the country.[12] This study maintains that we can see the triple discrimination that indigenous women suffer (due to their ethnic identity, their gender, and their low economic resources) through the re-victimization that comes when they are trying to seek justice. The fact that the authorities don't know the indigenous language, and the monolingualism and illiteracy on part of the indigenous women, makes it harder for them to have access to justice.

The experience that Inés Fernández Ortega had with the attorney general of Ayutla de los Libres, and with the military authorities, confirms this triple discrimination tendency. As in most of Mexico's indigenous regions, Ayutla de los Libres's attorney general is a non-indigenous government official, who is unfamiliar with the indigenous languages spoken in the region (Me'phaa, Tu'un sávi, or Mixteco). This office does not employ the support of a translator or an interpreter, which is why Inés requested Ms. Obtilia Eugenio's (leader of OPIM) help to present an allegation. In Inés Fernandez's interviews, she talks about the bad treatment and lack of interest on the part of the judicial authorities when she presented her allegation. These were the authorities who determined that they were incompetent to take on the case due to the fact that the accused parties were part of the Mexican Army, and they decided to turn it over to the military attorney general (*ministerio público militar*).

The studies stated above, regarding indigenous women and their trouble accessing justice, maintain that Inés's experience is almost the rule when it comes to indigenous women's and men's judicial processes in the state's judicial system, although the Mexican Constitution in its second article establishes the right to a translator and defense attorney who are familiar with the indigenous cultures and anthropological expertise reports.[13] Attorney generals do not have personnel who fit the profile or who "know the plaintiff's culture."

This violation of their linguistic and cultural rights is not only a product of the lack of trained personnel to enable a more accessible justice system for indigenous people, but it goes hand in hand with the degrading treatment on the part of the public officials, in many ways contributing to the racial hierarchy that distinguishes Mexican society. In the case of indigenous women, this structural racism reproduced by the state is deepened with gender discrimination, and, in many cases, it re-victimizes women when it comes to sexual violence because of the lack of sensibility that takes form as a symbolic violence. This is the case of the medical expert who first tried to certify Inés Fernandez's rape, answering her request to be examined by a woman by saying, "Who cares if a man examines you, was it women who raped you?" (Interview with Inés Fernández on March 13, 2010).

If the discriminatory treatment that Inés Fernández received when she presented her allegation led her to distrust the state's judicial institutions, her experience with the military authorities only deepened her distrust and put her in a vulnerable state with the military's presence in her house, where military authorities showed up with no prior notice and, once again, without a translator.

Inés Fernandez's experiences with state justice, and the impunity that prevails regarding her rape, have influenced women in the region to not consider the state's justice department as an option for the resolution of conflicts. This is why the creation of an attorney general specializing in sexual crimes did not resonate amid the means of reparation that Inés and other members of OPIM demanded.[14]

CONCLUSIONS

After analyzing the harm that Inés's rape produced in the social fabric of Barranca de Tecuani's indigenous community, the experts appointed by the offended party's representatives, Rosalva Aída Hernández Castillo and Héctor Ortíz Elizondo, have come to the conclusion that:

- The social cohesion of Barranca de Tecuani's indigenous community was, in fact, affected by the events that Inés Fernández Ortega endured on March 22, 2002.
- The situation that Inés Fernández Ortega went through generated a state of fear in the Me'phaa communities of the mountain region, with far-reaching repercussions that impact women most of all.
- The context of impunity that prevails since these events took place to this date means, both to the members of the community and the members of OPIM, an ongoing harm that has to be repaired in order to recuperate the social situation that prevailed before the events.
- The lack of justice has been a product of triple discrimination: ethnic, gender, and class discrimination that Inés has lived throughout her whole allegation process and that should be repaired by creating new spaces for justice with officials who are more sensitive to the difference of cultures and gender.

REPARATION MEASURES

The demand for justice concerning Inés Fernández Ortega, her family members, and other members of OPIM is presented in symbolic, moral, social, and economic terms, and it is expressed in concrete reparation actions.

Because of the way that the harm was perceived as unspecific and suffered by a collectivity and not by one person in particular, these reparation measures are understood by the victim of the events that took place on March 22, 2002, as acts that have to be compensatory to the community without preventing her from requiring reparations for her family and herself as well. Among the reparation measures available to compensate for the harm caused in this case, we would like to point out the ones that have to do directly with this expertise report.

SATISFACTION MEASURES

PUNISHMENT FOR PERPETRATORS

The geographical isolation that characterizes the mountains of Guerrero where the Me'phaa people reside has an influence on that the state, and this isolation often results in punishing the people and preventing the guarantee of their rights. This is the same situation that has allowed them to preserve their own justice system as a means to resolve conflicts. In other words, implementing the national law and rights is something to which the indigenous peoples rarely aspire.

In that sense, the fact that a Me'phaa woman exposed herself nationally to make an allegation about such an intimate crime as rape, and to require punishment, is a test to the Mexican justice system to the point where achieving the application of national law in a local case would reestablish the relationship between the inhabitants. This is what justifies, by applying the rule of law, the prosecution of the perpetrators of the crime committed against Inés Fernández Ortega.

COMPENSATION

As mentioned in part 2.2 above, it is important to highlight the impact of the case on women: once teenage girls finish primary school, they have to leave their community to keep studying secondary school in the state's head municipality which, in most cases, means living as a semi-slave servant in mixed-race houses in Ayutla de los Libres. This is a result of the difficulties experienced by affected parties and other members of the community when it comes to paying for food and living expenses for their children to keep studying in the state's head municipality.

Because of this, and as a way to address the victim's economic situation, a just measure of satisfaction in this case would be to grant scholarships to Inés Fernández's and Fortunato Prisciliano's children, which would guarantee their continued enrollment in school and prevent the minors from dropping out.

As Inés Fernández's eldest daughter put it: "Financial compensation for my mother and us, her children who have suffered from poverty . . . because we were denied many things, that we could probably have today."

PAYMENT OF EXPENSES AND COSTS

Inés Fernández's and Fortunato Prisciliano's economic situation was already precarious before these events took place but has worsened since they have had to make several trips to the state's head municipality and other expenses linked to the legal prosecution of the case, including providing food for people who have attended their home to learn more about their case, as is the case of the experts writing this report. Parts of these expenses have been provided by OPIM, whose members also provide their own expenses when accompanying the victims. Therefore, it is justifiable to request that the state pay the reasonable and necessary expenses that have originated and will originate from the ongoing case, considering that most of the expenses were paid "in-kind"; in other words, the payments come from their rural indigenous community's economic subsistence crops and, therefore, are not verifiable.

APOLOGY, REDRESS, AND RECOGNITION OF LIABILITY

Applying publicity measures to the case's resulting sentence such as broadcasting it and publishing it in local and national newspapers is not as important to the Me'phaa people compared to other reparation mechanisms. Although it is also true that the Me'phaa peoples' dignity has been tainted in the eyes of the region's mixed-race population due to the wide dissemination of these and many other acts of repression and violence. In this sense, the relation between the Me'phaa population and both the mixed-race people and the state will remain affected until a public apology takes place on the part of the state in the presence of OPIM's members. In fact, an essential element in conciliation mechanisms that prevail in the indigenous justice system is the admission of guilt, without which it is not possible to reach forgiveness and restore order.

As a consequence of the above, and as a means to fight prejudice and promote tolerance,[15] it appears justified that the state sends an official government authority with a high enough ranking to represent it to the region in order to apologize to the victim and her family in a public way and with enough anticipation to guarantee a wide-ranging attendance to make the state's motives public.

PROTECTION AND PREVENTION MEASURES

COMMUNITY SCHOOL

For the given reasons, to justify scholarships, we must understand that the rest of the Me'phaa population in the mountain region is in a similar situation to Inés Fernández and Fortunato Prisciliano when it comes to taking care of their children. This situation means permanently putting teenagers at risk of suffering sexual violence due to the fact that most of them have to "pay" for their studies with this servant-like system.

On the other hand, the implementation of an informal education system in these communities must take into account the degree of scattered settlements. This means that a fixed education and training system, as it would be to establish a local school in each community may be impractical, as opposed to other more mobile options, which trainers and promoters of OPIM have started to apply in different communities of the region.

In this sense, as experts, we propose, as a prevention and protection measure related to the access of services by the victims who live in isolated areas,[16] the previously proposed community school for the education and advocacy of women's rights be replaced with a boarding school to be installed and run in the head municipality of Ayutla de los Libres. This boarding school will be able to function as a place to house the Me'phaa families' children who are studying secondary school or high school, while at the same time providing an informal education on different subjects, with the women of the OPIM in charge.[17]

AN OFFICE TO ATTEND VICTIMS OF VIOLENCE

Establishing an office to attend victims of violence in the head municipality of Ayutla de los Libres is a demand that doesn't satisfy Inés Fernández Ortega's needs. This comes from the fact that her lack of trust toward the state overcomes any possibilities of linking this reparation directly to the facts that produced the allegation.

Nevertheless, we have to consider that the double victimization experienced by the victim was a product of the lack of training and sensitivity on the part of the working personnel of the attorney general's office, which is why it would be ideal to have female personnel attending sexual violence cases, and to be able to count on interpreters and translators to help the indigenous women. There are active programs in the country such as Family Violence Prevention and Attention Units (Unidades de Atención u Prevención de la Violencia Familiar—UAPVIF) from the federal secretary of public security, and the Program for Attention to Intra-family and/or Sexual Violence Victims that functions in Chilpancingo, Guerrero. The correct function of these programs also depends on the integrity and accountability to which they are subject; this makes it feasible to establish cooperation between these institutions and a civil society, in this case with an indigenous institution such as OPIM.

Because of the above, as experts, we propose that this demand be kept but on the condition that these institutions sign an agreement to cooperate with civil associations at their request.

GUARANTEE OF NON-REPETITION

Finally, as it is one of the most heartfelt demands expressed by Inés Fernández Ortega, her family, and other members of the Me'phaa people, we request the withdrawal of the military forces as a necessary measure to assure non-repetition.

The very presence of the military forces without applying international legislation regarding armed conflict puts the people in a state of defenselessness, which leads to both the inhabitants of the area and the armed forces' lack of knowledge about whether the population should be recognized as civilians or non-belligerent forces. The unexpected presence and lack of official documentation of military forces without there being an armed conflict implies the suspension of the local authority's power, who ask, "What can we do if they are the military?" when a resident is victimized by one of them, as is the case of Inés Fernández.

The public interest causes that allegedly justify the military's presence are diminished by the fact that there is no explicit announcement on the part of indigenous people who are allegedly interested in military presence in their lands.[18] In other words, the army's presence in the area responds only to the state's interest and not to the "public's interest," while there is no announcement from civil societies requesting military presence.

From this general state of legal defenselessness comes a mutual distrust that promotes conflict, and therefore the violation of human rights, which diminishes people's peace and security rights.[19]

Because of this, and as a way to reestablish social peace in the region and prove that the Me'phaa people are not the enemy of the army, we consider it necessary that the state of Mexico recognize the indigenous communities' right to make decisions on fundamental issues about their culture, according to the Mexican Constitution's 2nd Article regarding their autonomy and recognition of their local authority for legal and administrative matters.

APPENDIX 2

LEGAL FILES OF INDIGENOUS WOMEN PRISONERS IN MORELOS AND PUEBLA

NAME	AGE	LANGUAGE	ORIGIN	SCHOLARSHIP	OCCUPATION
H.M.	70	Nahuatl	Huiztlacotla, Guerrero	None/unlettered	Peasant widow/ communal lands holder
M.E.B	38	Tzotzil	Huixtla, Chiapas	None	Peasant
M.C.R	38	Nahuatl	Atlixtac, Guerrero	Elementary school, fifth grade	Peasant
H.M.A.	22	Nahuatl	Atlixtac, Guerrero	Elementary school, fifth grade	
B.V.H.		Nahuatl	Atlixtac, Guerrero	Elementary school, sixth grade	Employee
M.A.V.H.	31	Nahuatl	Huiztlacotla, Guerrero	Elementary school, second grade	
R.S.P	29	Nahuatl	Copala, Guerrero	Elementary school	Hogar
M.J.R.P	55	Nahuatl	Tehuestitla, Guerrero	None	Peasant
M.P.E	47	Nahuatl	Itzucar de Matamoros, Puebla	None	Peasant
C.T.R.	49	Nahuatl	Huecahuaxco, Morelos	Elementary school, first grade	Peasant

DATE AND PLACE OF DETENTION	FELONY	SENTENCES	TRANSLATOR	CRIMINAL RECORD	VISITS
2002, military checkpoint	Crimes against health	11 years	No	No	No
2000, at home	Child abduction	17 years	No	No	No
2002, at a military checkpoint where she was threatened with rape	Crimes against health	15 years	No	No	Yes
Military checkpoint	Crimes against health	15 years	No	No	No
2003, Taxqueña	Crimes against health	11 years	No	No	No
2003, at a military checkpoint	Crimes against health	11 years	No	No	Yes
2000, at a military checkpoint	Crimes against health	10 years	No	No	No
2002, arrested with two other men who came by her little store	Crimes against health	15 years	No	No	Yes
2003, arrest at house for giving marijuana to a relative	Crimes against health	15 years	No	No	No
1996, military checkpoint	Crimes against health	15 years	No	Same Felony	Yes

NAME	AGE	LANGUAGE	ORIGIN	SCHOLARSHIP	OCCUPATION
J.F.P.	37	Nahuatl	Huachinango, Guerrero	None/unlettered	Embroidery/ housewife
C.S.	27	Totonaco	San Felipe Tepatlán, Puebla	None/unlettered	Peasant
L.S.O.	38	Nahuatl	Zacatlán de las Manzanas, Puebla	None/unlettered	Housewife
R.R.M.	33	Nahuatl	San Sebastián Tzinacatepec, Puebla	technical career unfinished	
R.B.Z.	41	Nahuatl	Tehuacan, Puebla	None/unlettered	Employee
J.P.R.	46	Nahuatl	Huaquechula, Puebla	Elementary school, first grade	Embroidery/ housewife
E.C.C.	58	Nahuatl	San Francisco Altepexi, Puebla	Elementary school, first grade	Housewife
M.R.E.	45	Spanish	Palmasola, Veracruz	Elementary school, six grade	Selling handicrafts
F.S.R.	45	Nahuatl	San Nicolas Tolentina, Puebla	None	Peasant
S.O.C.	58	Nahuatl	Acatepec, Puebla	None/unlettered	Housewife

DATE AND PLACE OF DETENTION	FELONY	SENTENCES	TRANSLATOR	CRIMINAL RECORD	VISITS
2006, military checkpoint	Crimes against health	5 years	No	No	No
2006	Homicide	Indicted	No	No	No
2001	Homicide	26 years	No	No	Yes
2000	Kidnapping	50 years	No	No	No
2001	Crimes against health	11 years, 5 months	No	Same felony	No
2009	Attempted kidnapping	24 years	No	No	No
2009	Crimes against health	Indicted	No	No	Yes
2000	Crimes against health	10 years	No	No	Yes
2005	Infant theft	Indicted	No	Same felony	No
2005	Pandering	5 years, 9 months	No	No	No

continued

(continued)

NAME	AGE	LANGUAGE	ORIGIN	SCHOLARSHIP	OCCUPATION
L.A.T.	46	Nahuatl	Izucar de Mata-moros, Puebla	None/unlettered	Owner of a beauty salon
A.O.O.	40	Nahuatl	Llano de en Medio, Veracruz	None/unlettered	Peddler
V.L.A.	58	Nahuatl	Izucar de Mata-moros, Puebla	High school	Housewife
M.S.X.	74	Nahuatl	Papalotla, Puebla	None/unlettered	Merchant
P.L.L.	34	Spanish	San Miguel Hacienda, Puebla	None/unlettered	Housewife
P.E.G.	53	Nahuatl	San Cristóbal Tepatlazco, Puebla	Elementary school, second grade	Housewife
M.M.S.	28	Nahuatl	Cuautla, Morelos	Elementary school, third grade	Employee
P.F.C.	38	Totonaco	Tlaxcala, Puebla	None/unlettered	Owner of a grocery store
P.C.J.	51	Espl	Puebla, Puebla	High school	Restaurant worker
M.J.P.	47	Totonaco	Tlacuilotepec, Puebla	Elementary school, sixth grade	Merchant

Source of information: Judicial records. Data collected by Meztli Yoalli Rodriguez and R. Aída Hernández Castillo.

DATE AND PLACE OF DETENTION	FELONY	SENTENCES	TRANSLATOR	CRIMINAL RECORD	VISITS
2003	Pandering	8 years, 8 months	No	No	Yes
2002	Infant plagiarism	17 years	No	No	Yes
1995	Homicide	45 years	No	No	No
2008	Crimes against health	6 years, 8 months	No	Same felony	Yes
1997	Homicide	20 years	No	No	No
1995	Kidnapping	18 years	No	No	Yes
1999	Kidnapping	50 years	No	No	Yes
2004	Crimes against health	10 years	No	No	Yes
2003	Crimes against health	10 years	No	No	Yes
2000	Kidnapping	50 years	No	No	Yes

APPENDIX 3

FROM THE "LIFE HISTORIES" WORKSHOP IN ATLACHOLOAYA, MORELOS[1]

Morelitos: His Word Against Mine

WRITTEN BY SUSUKI LEE CAMACHO

When I see your slow walk and frail-looking figure, I think about all you must have gone through in life. It is this experience that has made you into someone full of wisdom. Perhaps it is because of my desire to travel back to the past, my desire to know you better, or simply a desire to acquire some of that wisdom you have managed to use so well throughout the years, that I invite you to write your story. Truly, I do not know the precise reason, but here I am trying to make it possible through this medium, so that you, Morelitos, become known. Revealing, just maybe, a part of your introspection.

I find myself inside the prison cell of Morelitos, as every other one it is a small place, approximately three-by-two meters, including the bathroom and bed. The so-called bed is only a concrete block with a cushion on top that serves as a mattress. There is also a tiny table where you have your meals, over the table there is a shelf where Morelitos places the few belongings she owns.

She invites me to sit down and have a cup of water, and that is how she begins to tell me that she was born in Huizacotla, municipality of Atlixtac, in the state of Guerrero. Her parents also came from the same place. They were born and died there. The rancho consisted of only a handful of homes made with mud and palm leaves and, of course, without any furniture. Morelitos, you describe your

Published in Hernández Castillo, Rosalva Aída. *Bajo la sombra del Guamúchil: Historias de vida de mujeres indígenas y campesinas en reclusión.* Iwgia, Oremedia, CIESAS, México, 2010b.

life to me by saying: *We slept on a mat; we ate on top of it. We cooked outside on the fire and during the rainy season inside. The rancho was far away from any large settlements; we were surrounded by hills. When we needed to stock up on supplies, we would walk to the nearest town. We did not have a doctor or a sewer system, let alone power or drinkable water. To get our hands on some water we would have to carry it with donkeys or other animals, and if you had none, then you would have to walk. It would be approximately thirty minutes from the house to the waterhole. Our job consisted in planting corn, squash, and beans. That is how we fed ourselves. We also herded livestock and raised chickens. The people of my town speak mostly Náhuatl. Among my fondest memories is my life at the rancho. It was a peaceful life; almost everybody knew each other and people were very friendly. Although there are also things that I did not like and still exist, for instance: the fact that there is no light, drinkable water, doctor, school, street lighting and other things needed to live well. During that time there were six of us in the family. My dad, mom, two brothers, a sister and me. I was the youngest. My mom and I were very close, you could say so because instead of rejecting my gender she would always say: "I am glad you were born a woman, that way I will have someone to talk to about certain things without being ashamed." On the other hand, my dad was more of a hitter and he would find any reason to scream at us. He was usually in a bad mood.* She adds: *My parents were always fighting each other, sometimes it was his hand, other times it was his belt which struck against my mom's back. Sometimes because there was not enough salt in the salsa, others because the food wasn't ready in the moment that he asked for it.*

I interrupt her story to comment on the fact that in my house scenes like these also took place. I think that it was a very common thing among older marriages because with my parents it was exactly the same thing. The only difference is that my parents fought over money, while we stood like spectators.

Upon hearing this, Morelitos says, *Yes, but you did not get beaten, and that makes a big difference.* She then continues her story: *As a child I remember that I liked very much to play in the fields, my cousins and I would run after each other in the open meadows. The times we were sent out to take care of the goats, we would be playing; we would spend most of the day picking flowers, swimming in the river or simply laying down underneath a tree to talk about the boys that lived near. I believe those were my best years. However, I also have sad memories of my childhood, like not having any clothes to wear. My poor mother would save the sacks of sugar that she could find, so she could make us some rags with which to cover our body. I never used shoes, and sometimes rocks would hurt my feet; other times thorns would pierce through, so I would have to sit down and pull out the thorns in order to be able to keep walking. I remember very well that I asked my mother how I was born, she said: "Here, there is no way of finding out a kid's weight, we can only tell if a kid is chubby or if he is skinny. You were very small and skinny, we even thought you would not be able to make it, but thank god, you are here, despite the fact that the midwife was not close by. When the pain started in the middle of the night, without any company but my machete, I walked for an hour. I was brought back to the house, carried by animals." A birth was no reason to rejoice, work would only increase and food would dwindle. Such an event, far from making us happy, would only annoy us, and more so if the baby was born a female. They would say: "Ugh, another girl! They only cause problems, and don't help at all." However, if it was born a boy, congratulations would be in order for the father, comments like: "Finally, a boy! He can help us work the field and our name will endure. I wish only boys were born."*

However, Morelitos says to me: *My mom was different. She would tell me: "It is good that you were born a woman; that way the housekeeping will be less demanding." She would sometimes hit me because we were not supposed to answer back to my parents when they scolded us, regardless of whether we were right or wrong; also for looking at them in the eye when they were correcting us. This would always happen with my father. He almost always treated me like someone outside of the family. He never treated me nicely or talked to me in any other way. He would always say: "Why did I have women?" My father was the one who would hit me the most and there never was anyone to defend me. Never! Not even my mother would dare contradict any man, so let alone the head of the family. With my sisters, I would get along fine, we would talk about a thousand things and we would always play together. It was not the case with my brothers, they kept their distance, for they thought: "Men do not play with women, boys should only play with other boys, otherwise they would become queer." I can't recall if they would fight or not, I did not pay much attention to them. I remember this one time my sister stepped on a chick by accident and killed it. To cover up the evidence we dug up a small hole and buried it, we even put some flowers and a cross. When my dad arrived, the beating was such that I still remember it until this day, he said: "Since nobody did it, I am going to hit both of you." I did not want to tell on my sister, so when he asked me I answered: "I do not know Dad!"*

Back then, I would only speak Náhuatl, since it was my first tongue. Later, in order to survive, I had to teach myself to speak Spanish. Amongst my brothers and myself there was a huge difference in the treatment our parents gave us, for instance my brothers would get more food because my mother would think that they were the ones who worked the most; according to my parents, women were only good to raise children. When my brothers returned to the house after a day's work they would go to bed, while the women we would have to keep doing the household chores. The same thing happened when the boys went to the field and the women would rarely go. Normally we would help by carrying the water, cleaning everyone's clothes in the river and grinding nixtamal in the metate to make tortillas. In my town, there were no mills, schools, or clinics, hence the reason why we never went to school. We would hear our parents say, "Better to have a half-full stomach, than a head filled with letters." Therefore, I did not have any good or bad moments as a student, since I never set foot in a school.

Life on the ranch did not allow us to have big plans, you did not think of anything besides surviving. The girls, from a very young age, learned handicrafts; the boys usually went to the field and girls were taught to sell their crafts. Other times, we carried flowers or produce to sell or to exchange for beans, among other goods. Children learned to respect the elders and if an older person yelled at us or hit us, we could not say a word; we would complain to our parents and leave it up to them. The treatment towards boys and girls was different: the boys learned that they were the ones that were in charge in the house and the girls learned that you should not contradict a man and that having a boy is a blessing, because otherwise you are no good.

Our religion stated that the head of the household is the man. When the whole family went to church, we would all go to the same one. There was only one and that was the Catholic Church. When I went to Sunday school the nun would tell us: "Is not good to change your husband, a decent woman only marries once and forever, regardless of the behavior of the husband. To be a good woman we must carry our cross."

Back then, the courtship process was all about intercepting the girls. If someone liked a girl, he would spy on her when she left her house and stood in her way; this would happen three or four times until the girl would accept to be his girlfriend. Relationships would only be verbal. Never could you hold your partners hand! Moreover, you would not think about a kiss in the mouth! The relationship was only for talking, and it happened in secret or with the parent's consent. These relationships did not always lead to marriages; sometimes, when there was no rapport, the relationship ended. I remember my first fiancé. When he asked me to be his girlfriend, it felt nice, right away, he asked for a present as a signal of our pact, I gave him one of my earrings and he gave me his handkerchief. Maybe we would still be married today but the traditions of my town would not allow it. The one who would later become my husband was who separated us, all with the excuse that I could not marry an "outsider." The day that a dance was taking place in our town, he found out who was my boyfriend and persecuted him in the company of others, saying that no outsider could have a girlfriend from the community, because the girls where strictly reserved to the men from the town. Up until today I still remember my first relationship fondly, says Morelitos.

She continues her story, and with a bit of sadness she tells me that during her teen years she never learned about her period. She describes this first traumatic experience by telling me: *The first time that I got my period I was very frightened, I also felt deeply ashamed since we were at another ranch which my family got invited to, so I did not know what to do or why was I bleeding. Since my clothes got stained, my mother discreetly gave me a rag. We then went to a spot where nobody could see us and she told me how to use it, but without explaining why it had happened. Shortly after getting my first period I got married. It was then that I became acquainted with sexual relationships. My boyfriend first forced me into having sex; we were out by the field when he caught me. I was yelling while I ran, I thought that maybe he would feel sorry for me and would leave me alone, but the more I begged, the crazier he got. Finally, he accomplished his goal. For me it was not a pleasant experience, quite the opposite, I felt disgusted. Instead of loving him, I detested him. I even thought that this was something normal that happened in relationships. Because of that, they married me. I obeyed, but I did not understand why I had to stay with a man that had hurt me, since I only wanted to stay a kid and not a grown up with responsibilities and children. My mother never talked to me about what could happen or how to act. At the time, my parents only talked about their poverty and problems in the family. In the ranch if a woman had sexual intercourse before being married or if she decided not to get married, she would grow old without ever marrying. Back then a woman that was not a virgin was not accepted, if it became known that you have had sexual relationships and not gotten married you would be excluded from the social groups that were made up by other women and, when having a celebration, men would not take you out to dance. Generally, a woman that was not a virgin and was still single would go out exclusively with married men. What I learned in my hometown is that a married woman cannot go out with other men, she should be respectful and save herself only for her husband; otherwise she is not worthy of socializing with other married women. In my community there were no recreational activities. We made the most out of our day by working in the field, be it gathering material to make hats, cutting flowers; there were not many duties. When the village festival took place, young people had barely any involvement. One of the few activities that young people had to do at the festival was to pray along with the older folk, to give out food and to clean up after it was all over. In my village, the differences between men and women were very pronounced. Since a very young age we were educated in a very different way, and the set of rules we had to follow was drastically different. Women were not allowed to be alone with the boyfriend or to have a say in domestic matters, or decide how many children we wanted to have. That was not the case when it came to the boys. They, for instance, would do whatever they wanted, without answering to their parents, much less their mother. They would come home at whatever time they pleased. They were not censured at all; their actions were not questioned. On the other hand, decent girls were not supposed to laugh with anyone. Since we used shawls, if a boy was interested in you, we would cover our face with it and we would bow without giving any answer until he got tired and left. Working positions were not for young people, you needed to be an adult, preferably married and of mature age. Never young people, much less women, because we were only good at raising kids and cleaning the house. If any female demanded her right to participate or to have some position, she would be thrown out of the assembly amongst insults, laughter, and ridicule. I got married at thirteen years of age. I met my husband in the ranch and we grew up together. My memories at his side were very sad, he demanded from me a lot; he would hit me for anything, saying that it was my fault. For every daughter that was born, I was blamed. He would tell me that I could not even give birth correctly. He would never cooperate with the household spending, but when it came to giving out beatings he was most enthusiastic. I would tell him: "Here is my back. Take it out on me but do not touch the kids, you leave them alone." I always thought of leaving him, but he would threaten me saying, "If you leave me I will kill you or I will make you crippled, because you are my woman, just deal with it. Besides, who will want you, you are no longer worth anything and you are full of kids." My poor mother, when she wanted to defend me he would attack her; so she would sometimes prefer to pray so he would not hit me so much.*

I still remember the day that I arrived in this place: I was sixty-three years old. It seems like it was yesterday. A few days before my arrest, I was working to clean up a piece of land in order to plant it later. In that afternoon, I boarded the bus that would take me to Mexico City. How far I was from thinking that it was the last time that I would see my hut. While I was traveling I was thinking all the time of going back to my village and planting in order to survive. That was going through my head when approximately at 11 p.m. or 12 p.m. at night, I can't recall exactly, the driver woke us up and told us to leave the bus. When I did it was really frightening because before me were countless soldiers. They surrounded us right away. In the corner of the bus were some bags and since I was seated right next to them, they told me: "¿This is yours right?" I told them that it was not the case, I was only carrying a bag of seeds, plums, and a bit of beans that I was planning to give to my relative. That is how I responded. Nevertheless, they said: "Do not play games with us, grandma; you are traveling right next to the package." Regardless of the many explanations I gave, it was their word against mine. Later they took me to a holding area, my things and the alleged package never appeared, but they kept saying that it was mine. Three days later I was transferred to the prison, where someone read to me an alleged statement I had made, but I had not said a thing, I could hardly understand a word of Spanish. No matter how much I tried to explain that I had not said any of those things that were written in the statement, they did not believe me and I was sentenced to eleven years and nine or eight months. I would say my arrival to the prison was good, I thought I would get beaten; but other than waking up at six o'clock in the morning to do my forced labor, everything was good. For the most part all the mates were kind to me. I remember the day I fell sick. I felt I was dying. My mates wrote me letters of encouragement; I even got a visit from Elena de Hoyos. When I saw her standing I could not recognize her, until she spoke to me in the sweetest tone of voice. Right away, I felt immediate trust. Upon my return, my mates received me with hugs and smiles. My moments of happiness are when a gathering happens, or when they support me by saying: "You are almost out Morelitos." Then my face lights up with happiness, because I think of my little hut, my son and of the field. There are sad moments in this place. For instance, for me Christmas was a symbol of family unity, in my ranch, although we were poor, we were always together on this day. Here the partners only gather with conflicting and noisy people. Older women like me and some others that do not like to spend time with them, are often labeled as bitter and are the target of mocking and insults. Generally, the inmates that receive visits in the male area are those who hire other interns to do the cleaning for them, among other things. Usually the poorest women, the ones that hail from rural areas, are always humiliated, even more so, if you are indigenous, there is a lot of racism. In this place, there are some groups of people with higher economic possibilities, which are the same women who are protected by the authorities of the prison. Another group are the lesbians, for the most part conflictive, where there is no space for women like myself. We are the group made up of indigenous and humble people, some women from the city spend some time with us and teach us to do some handicrafts, but they too suffer the consequences of being with us. That is how we spend our time, between embroidering, knitting and attendance lists, since we do not have the proper resources to buy material that we require for the different courses.

I have concluded the history of Morelitos. Writing your story has been for me an open door, which allowed me to travel to your past; even I would dare say that you have left in me the legacy of your essence for life, and maybe I could describe my experience with you with a thousand details; however, in this occasion with simplicity allow me to thank you for sharing with me the greatness of your years.

A few months after the publication of this book and the documentary that complements it we managed to have Morelitos's judicial file reviewed, and she was freed due to the miscarriage of justice in her case. Six months after being set free, Morelitos died due to a gastric ulceration that developed during her years in prison.

APPENDIX 4

FROM *BITÁCORA DEL DESTIERRO: NARRATIVA DE MUJERES EN PRISIÓN*[1]

HORRORS TO THE FLAG/AMATISTA LEE

"It's time for honors ladies!" A call that we all fear. Only mentioning its name, we start aching all around, the head, the stomach, the feet. Oh! And how many errands to run, wash clothes, clean the cell, oh well, enough said, we even become experts in constitutional articles. Article 8, any convicted person loses his duties and rights, like voting or saluting the flag.

The purpose is being absent, after all we are no patriots, if we have died for society. Why would we revive ourselves to honor the country?

MOTHER, ACCEPT ME/LEO ZAVALETA

Mother, I'm your daughter, the unwanted, your shame, the one who caused you disgrace and condemned you to a life of heartbreak, the one that cries begging for mercy on your behalf. If one day I came to hate you because of the beatings that I received at the slightest provocation, and the difference between my sisters and me, forgive me. I never knew that you loved me just the way you were taught, without a hug, without an "I love you."

I've grown, now I have kids and grandkids, however my wish remains to hear you say the words: "daughter, I'm your mother, the one who caused you so much pain." There is an empty heart and I want to fill it up. Day in and day out I ask God that you love me mother. I am thirsty for you; I want to die in peace.

APPENDIX 5

FROM *DIVINAS AUSENTES. ANTOLOGÍA POÉTICA DE MUJERES EN RECLUSIÓN*

La Malquerida/The Unloved[1]

AGUILA DEL MAR/MARISOL HERNANDEZ DEL AGUILA

The look of love has grown pale in the eyes
Of the one I loved best.
The look of anger gleams in the eyes
Of the monster who shapes us
And pronounces us guilty:
Society.
And yet, I want to weave my own dreams
And to craft my own destiny:
Be the wife of one who does love me,
Be the lover of one who longs for me.
A child disowned—a rebel child—
I like collecting love stories.
I am romantic, I never give up,
I'm always, always passionate.
Those sea eagles, scattered here and there
Each one minding her nest—
I am their sister.
We are Amazons tempered by fire.
Their sister eagle is here, held back, captive.
But my soul is ready to take flight.
My being has borne fruit.

My soul gave birth.
I am the mother of the night,
The mother of the day.
A sun child, a moon child,
A princess in a story of old,
A fairy in a fairy tale.
A holy trinity.
We are one:
One spirit and one flesh.
Who is the weaver, the dreamer,
The sea eagle ready to take flight?
I am
Aguila del Mar.

NOTES

INTRODUCTION

1. In a previous publication I have a detailed analysis of the etymology of the concept of *indigenous* and the manner in which it has become a field of power in the struggles for meaning (see Hernández Castillo 2010c). In this work, I state that, according to authors who have reconstructed the history of the concept, the word *indigenous* appears in some colonial documents from the fourteenth century and is defined as "people bred upon that very soyle [*sic*]," to distinguish the inhabitants of the Americas from those brought over as slaves by the Spanish and Portuguese (see de la Cadena and Starn 2007). Nevertheless, before the 1950s the concept of indigenous was used primarily in botanical works to refer to the native origin of plants. The term appeared for the first time in an international document in 1957 in Convention 107 of the International Labor Organization (ILO), in reference to the "Protection and Integration of Indigenous and Other Tribal and Semi-Tribal Populations in Independent Countries" (see Niezen 2003).

2. The *resguardo* is a system of communal landholdings. Under this system, indigenous peoples were allowed to use the land but could not sell it. Similar in some respects to the Native American reservation system of the United States, the resguardos have lasted (with some changes) even to the present and have been an enduring link between the government and the remaining highland groups.

3. *Cosmovision* (*cosmovisión*) is the term used by indigenous intellectuals in Mayan and Andean regions to refer to their "worldview" or their own epistemology. In the framework of the International Rights of Nature Tribunal held in Lima, Peru, in December 2014, the participating organizations defined indigenous cosmovision in the following terms: "According to their cosmovision, indigenous peoples experience nature in a holistic way imbued with a sacred quality. Nature is revered as the primary source of life; it nourishes, supports, and teaches humanity; nature is the center of the universe. All life is regulated by a single and totalizing 'set of rules of conduct'" (see http://therightsofnature .org/framework-for-tribunal/). Some authors relate the meaning of cosmovision to the original German term *weltanschauung* as an image or general view of existence, reality, or the "world" that a person, society, or culture develops in a given time period.

4. I use the concept of *governmentality* developed by Michel Foucault to refer to the forms of social control in disciplinary institutions (schools, hospitals, psychiatric institutions, etc.) and to refer to forms of knowledge (Foucault 1991). Power can manifest itself positively by producing knowledge and certain discourses that get internalized by individuals and guide the behavior of populations. This leads to more efficient forms of social control, as knowledge enables individuals to govern themselves.

5. In Latin America the term *indigenismo* is used to describe the ways that nation-states have formulated their vision of indigenous social inclusion and the state policies that they have developed toward indigenous peoples.

6. The Puebla Panama Plan is a multibillion dollar development plan formally initiated in 2001, intended to promote the regional integration and development of the nine southern states of Mexico, all of Central America, Colombia, and the Dominican Republic.

7. Unless otherwise noted, all translations from texts written originally in Spanish are my own.

8. Although Kimberlé Crenshaw's work is the most frequently cited when referring to the concept of intersectionality, Chicana feminists had proposed this idea almost a decade earlier in their critiques of white feminism. *Chicana Voices: Intersections of Class, Race, and Gender*, an anthology of Chicana scholarship, articulated the theory and its basic elements, stating that, "for Chicanas, as for other women of color, the discussion that we offer is one that combines analyses of class, race, and gender. We cannot separate any of the three from our experience. It is the combination that makes our experience

unique" (Córdova et al. 1984, 3). I thank my colleague and friend Francisca James-Hernández for sharing this information with me.

9. An analysis of the racism that continues to permeate an important sector of Latin American urban feminism, and that has contributed to many indigenous women's rejection of the concept of feminism, can be found in Blackwell (2012).

10. I use the term hegemonic feminism to refer to the feminism that has emerged from urban centers and has been theorized from the academy, wherein the struggle against abortion and reproductive rights has been central.

11. Interview with Alma López by Ixkic Duarte (2002).

12. I use the concept "to Orientalize" in reference to the process described by Edward Said in *Orientalism* (1978) as a general patronizing Western attitude toward Middle Eastern, Asian, and North African societies. According to Said's analysis, the West essentializes these societies as static and undeveloped, thereby fabricating a view of "Oriental culture" that can be studied, depicted, and reproduced. Implicit in this fabrication, writes Said, is the idea that Western society is developed, rational, flexible, and superior (Said 1978).

13. This section is part of a longer chapter published in an edited volume in which I developed the link between the colonization of indigenous women's bodies and the colonization of indigenous territories (see Hernández Castillo 2014).

14. I was member and co-founder of the Grupo de Mujeres de San Cristóbal de las Casas, a women's organization that ran a shelter: the Women and Children's Support Centre (CAMM).

15. Both projects were supported by a grant by the National Council for Science and Technology (Consejo Nacional de Ciencia y Tecnología—CONACYT).

16. As part of the collective project on which this chapter is based, we conducted interviews with members of indigenous organizations from the three countries and created an anthology of life histories of indigenous leaders from Mexico, Guatemala, and Colombia (see Hernández Castillo 2006b).

CHAPTER 1

1. Juridization is the growing recourse to legal intervention: growing litigiousness.

2. The Declaration of Barbados can be found at http://servindi.org/pdf/Dec _Barbados_1.pdf.

3. The concept of "action research" was developed by German-U.S. psychologist Kurt Lewin in 1944 in order to define a research methodology based on

democratic, participatory processes with local populations. Attention was given, once again, to these formulations at the end of the 1960s in Latin American social sciences from various perspectives committed to social justice. Contributions made by Brazilian pedagogue Paulo Freire were vital in this process. For an analysis of action research and collaborative research processes, see Mora Bayo (2008).

4. For an analysis of action research by feminist academics, see Lykes and Coquillon (2007).

5. To consult the publications made by imprisoned women in the context of this project, see http://rosalvaaida.wix.com/rahc#!hermanasenlasombra/cin54.

6. For an English translation of the Women's Revolutionary Law and other Zapatista documents related to gender demands, see Speed, Hernández Castillo, and Stephen (2006).

7. *Zapatismo* is the noun used to refer to the Zapatista Army of National Liberation (Ejército Zapatista de Liberación Nacional—EZLN).

8. My journalistic work on these issues can be downloaded from my blog http://rosalvaaida.wix.com/rahc#!artculos-periodisticos-/chbr, and the radio series *Cantos desde el Guamúchil* can be heard at https://soundcloud.com/radio -encuentros/sets/cantos-desde-el-guamuchil.

9. The Unión por la Nueva Educación para México is an independent organization founded in 1994 with education promoters in the zone of Zapatista influence who took the place of the official teachers from the secretary of public education (Secretaría de Educación Pública—SEP). The teachers from SEP were thrown out of the communities for failing to appear and to comply with community commitments. The Asamblea Nacional Indígena por la Autonomía Plural is a national, independent organization that was originally founded in Chiapas in the 1980s. The latter was the first Mexican indigenous organization that made autonomy a central axis of their struggle. A description of the Zapatista autonomous regions in Chiapas and how they operate can be found in Cerda García (2011) and Mora Bayo (2008).

10. For an analysis of the impact of militarization and para-militarization on the daily lives of indigenous women in Chiapas, see Hernández Castillo (2002b).

11. A "red alert" is a military term used by the EZLN to declare a state of emergency at times of military tension or mobilization of federal army troops.

12. *Memorias de talleres legislativos*, Taller No. 8 Evaluación, San Cristóbal de las Casas, Chiapas, January 2001 (manuscript).

13. In Mexico City these modifications to the Criminal Proceedings Code, recognizing the rights to an interpreter and to cultural affidavits, were made in January 1991, representing pioneering legislation for cultural reforms in the area of justice.

14. In Latin America the term *Indigenism* (*Indigenismo*) is used to describe the ways that nation-states have formulated their vision of Indigenous social inclusion and the state policies toward indigenous peoples that they have developed.

15. An excellent analysis of the various epistemological and political dilemmas posed by cultural expert witness reports and the various positions regarding their usefulness, their objectivity, and the essentialisms they can reproduce can be found in the collective book edited by Armando Guevara Gil, Aaron Verona, and Roxana Vergara (2015), which includes works by several anthropologists with significant experience in developing cultural expert reports in Mexico, Argentina, Peru, and Colombia. For an ethnography of the agreements and disagreements between the legal and the anthropological fields based on an analysis of cultural expert witness reports presented in title claims in Australia that can be found, see Burke (2011).

16. Interview with Inés Fernández Ortega, translated by Andrea Eugenio, Barranca Tecuani, March 13, 2009.

17. The children are allowed to live with their mothers in the prison until they are six years old, at which time they are given to their non-incarcerated relatives or they are kept under state custody.

18. The *Colectivo Editorial* has published with support from IWGIA and CIESAS, a book/video titled *Bajo la sombra del Guamuchil: Historias de vida de mujeres indígenas y campesinas presas* (2010); with support from the Instituto de Cultura de Morelos, the handmade books titled *Fragmentos de mujer* (2011) and *Mareas cautivas: Navegando las letras de las mujeres en prisión* (Colectiva Editorial Hermanas en la Sombra 2012); and with a scholarship from the Instituto Nacional de Bellas Artes, a three-book collection titled *Revelaciones intramuros*. For an English version of one of the life stories, see appendix 2. For the creative writing work, see appendixes 3 and 4.

19. *Costalazos* is a form of torture in which a person's body is wrapped in gunny sacks before being beaten (to avoid leaving marks).

20. Exercise by Guadalupe Salgado in the "Life Histories" workshop at the Atlacholoaya Women's CERESO, May 17, 2009.

21. Exercise by Susuki Lee, in the "Life Histories" workshop at the Atlacholoaya Women's CERESO, May 17, 2009.

22. In this regard, Ben Olguín (2009) contrasts the experience of Jean Trounstine (2001) with the work of James B. Waldram (1997). Trounstine ran a literary workshop project known as "Shakespeare Behind Bars," in which the writer taught English theater from the sixteenth century to female prisoners, most of them women of color, while disregarding the prisoners' own writing (Trounstine 2001). Waldram, by contrast, used Paulo Freire's pedagogy in his workshops to recover the spirituality and traditional knowledge of Canada's imprisoned Native population (Waldram 1997). Sara Makowski, for her part, asserts that the literary workshop held in the Mexico City women's prison known as the Reclusorio Preventivo Femenil Oriente, where she conducted her research, was a space of counter-power: "In the Literature Workshop things that cannot be even mentioned in any other corner of the women's prison are spoken about and discussed. There, anxieties are shared, and the group increases its awareness of ways to transform complaints and pain into critical judgment" (Makowski 1994, 180).

23. During the last four years, three literary gatherings have been organized, with workshop participants reading their work to the prison population at the Morelos CERESO. Writers and musicians from outside the prison have been invited to hear their work. We have also organized a number of presentations of the book titled *Bajo la sombra del Guamúchil*, with participation by the authors who have been released from the prison.

CHAPTER 2

1. A *huipil* is a handmade traditional blouse with embroidery.

2. Zapotec is one of the sixty-three indigenous languages spoken in Mexico, mainly in the state of Oaxaca.

3. PROGRESA (Programa de Educación, Salud, y Alimenación) and Solidaridad were part of a larger poverty alleviation strategy developed in 1997 by the Salinas de Gortari administration. The programs offered conditional cash transfers to the rural poor in exchange for sending their children to school and in exchange for regular attendance at state health and education workshops. For a critical perspective on the counterinsurgency use of those programs, see Mora Bayo (2008).

4. Lucio Cabañas was a Mexican schoolteacher who became a guerrilla fighter and led a guerrilla group known as the Army of the Poor and Peasants' Brigade Against Injustice (or Party of the Poor as it was known in the Mexican state of Guerrero) from 1967 to 1972. For a film version of his life, see *La guerrilla y la esperanza: Lucio Cabañas* by the Mexican film producer Gerardo Tort.

5. For a history of the Communist Party and the guerrilla movement in Guerrero, see Bartra (1996). For a history of the Communist Party in Mexico, see Carr (1997).

6. Benita Galeana was a mestizo woman of rural origin born on September 10, 1907, in San Jerónimo de Juárez in the state of Guerrero. In 1927, Benita joined the Communist Party and became a social and political activist. During the administration of Plutarco Elías Calles (1924–1928), she suffered political repression. When Joseph Stalin took power in the Soviet Union, she became a radical Stalinist. Always a militant of the Communist Party, she supported the policies of nationalization of oil and railroads by Lázaro Cárdenas. She was the wife of Manuel Rodríguez, also a militant of the Communist Party. For more information about her life, see her autobiography *Benita: Memoir of a Mexican Activist*, translated by Amy Diane Prince (1994).

7. For a comparative analysis of women's participation in guerrilla movements in Nicaragua, El Salvador, Chiapas, and Cuba, see Kampwirth (2002). For the experience in Guatemala, see Colom (1998) and Soriano (2005). For Colombia, see Meertens (2000) and Otero Bahamón (2006).

8. For an analysis of the use of sexual violence during the "dirty war" in Mexico, see Rayas Velasco (2008, 2009); for the Guatemalan context, see Méndez Gutiérrez and Carrera Guerra (2015) and Equipo de Estudios Comunitarios y Acción Psicosocial (2009); for Colombia, see Sisma Mujer (2015).

9. During the late 1960s and 1970s, we see the emergence of guerrilla movements throughout the continent: the Rebel Armed Forces (Fuerzas Armadas Rebeldes) in Guatemala in 1960; the Tupamaros in Uruguay in 1962; Red Flag in Venezuela 1964; the National Liberation Army (Ejército de Liberación Nacional—ELN), the Revolutionary Armed Forces of Colombia (Fuerzas Armadas Revolucionarias de Colombia—FARC), and the Popular Liberation Army (Ejército Popular de Liberación—EPL) in Colombia.

10. The murder of the presidential candidate and radical liberal, Jorge Eliécer Gaitán in 1948, started the movement known as Bogotazo, a popular uprising in the capital and in different regions of the country. The conservative party

responded with indiscriminate repression. This uprising started the spread of violence throughout the country. This era is known as *La Violencia* ("The Violence") that left around 200,000 people dead.

11. For a history of the political-military organizations in Colombia, see Offstein (2003); Casas (1990); and Sánchez and Meertens (2000).

12. For a brief history of this organization and an interview with one of its leaders, see Emanuelsson (n.d.).

13. For the role of indigenous women in the armed conflict in Colombia, see Berrío Palomo (2005, 2008).

14. In one of Camilo Torres's articles, published in *Frente Unido*, he said: "I had to leave my religious vestments, my soutaine, to become a truth priest; the duty of every Catholic is to be a revolutionary, the duty of each revolutionary is to make the revolution; the Catholic that is not revolutionary is living in a mortal sin" (Torres 1965, 8).

15. For a deeper analysis of the philosophical principles of Indian theology, see CENAMI (1991, 1994).

16. Interview with M. C. M, May 1998, San Cristóbal de las Casas, Chiapas.

17. The Maya-Cakchiquel feminist intellectual Emma Chirix has developed a deep critique of the colonizing Project of the Bethlemite Sisters in Guatemala through a historical ethnography of the Socorro Indigenous Institute (see Chirix 2013).

18. The "scorched earth campaigns" were a counterinsurgency strategy launched by the Guatemalan government of Efrain Ríos Montt (1982–1983) that involved destroying anything that might be useful to the guerrilla while advancing through or withdrawing from an area. It is a military strategy where all of the assets that are used or can be used by the enemy are targeted, such as food sources, transportation, communications, industrial resources, and even the people in the area. More than four hundred Mayan communities were destroyed by these campaigns.

19. Ibid.

20. Interview with the Dominican nun, R. A. C. May 1998, San Cristóbal de las Casas, Chiapas.

21. Interview with M. C. M, June 1998, San Cristóbal de las Casas, Chiapas.

22. Women for Dialogue (Mujeres para el Diálogo) was formed in 1979 with the objective of influencing the decision process in the Third Episcopal Latin American Conference that took place in Puebla, Mexico. Presently the group has developed strategies to influence public opinion and to work with grassroots

organizations around issues of gender inequality. Its central offices are in Mexico City, but they work in the rest of the country through educational workshops (see Mujeres para el Diálogo 1992).

23. The project was titled "New and Old Spaces of Power: Collective Organization and Daily Life Resistance" (CONACYT) and included ten case studies from Mexico, Guatemala, and Colombia, with the participation of ten researchers: Márgara Millán, Silvia Soriano, Morna Macleod, Lina Rosa Berrío, Beatriz Canabal, Patricia Artia, Susana Mejía, Ixkic Duarte, Violeta Zylberberg, and myself.

24. As a part of this project, eight indigenous women wrote their life stories in dialogue with a member of the research team and published the book *Historias a dos voces: Testimonios de luchas y resistencias de mujeres indígenas* (Hernández Castillo 2006b).

25. For a history of the colonization of the Lacandon rainforest in Mexico, see Garza et al. (1995) and de Vos (2003). For a history of the colonization of the rainforest region in Guatemala, see Camacho Nasar et al. (2003) and Garst (1993).

26. For a definition of *resguardo*, see note 2 in the introduction. The *cabildo* is a government body of Spanish colonial origin that governs a municipality and has become an important space for the construction of community consensus. Cabildos are sometimes appointed, sometimes elected, but are considered to be representative of all land-owning heads of households and, among many indigenous peoples, this excludes women.

27. The Colombian government of Lleras Restrepo (1966–1970) formed the Association of Peasant Users (Asociación Nacional de Usuarios Campesinos National—ANUC), but rapidly the Colombian peasants broke up with the institutional links and created a non-official ANUC that promoted the occupation of lands de facto through the entire country. The response to these land occupations was the repression of thousands of peasants, and both members and non-members of ANUC were put into jail and tortured. After these traumatic experiences, many peasants left the ANUC, considering that their demands for territorial rights were broader than the agrarian demands of ANUC.

28. In part, as response to the indigenous movement demands, the new Colombian Constitution of 1991 gives legal recognition to the indigenous at the same time that it recognizes the cultural and linguistic diversity of the country, giving to indigenous communities the right to preserve their languages and allowing

certain degrees of political autonomy, as well as respecting their political and legal systems.

29. There is pioneering work on the history of urban popular feminism and its articulation with civil feminism, such as that of Massolo (1992) and Espinosa Damián and Sánchez (1992); for the history of rural and indigenous feminisms, see Espinosa Damián (2009).

30. CIDHAL is one of the oldest feminist organization in Latin America with political work in the popular sectors. It was formed in 1969 in the Mexican state of Morelos as a documentation and distribution center of feminist materials. Later on, it reoriented its work with the popular sectors (especially urban sectors) and with the Base Ecclesial Communities (CEBs). For a history of CIDHAL, see Espinosa Damián and Paz Paredes (1988).

31. For a history of this organization, see Freyermuth and Fernández (1995).

32. Comaletzin was constituted as a civil association in 1987 and stated its main lines of action: "the organization, education, investigation with gender as an axis of analysis" (Comaletzin 1999, 1). This organization plays a very important role in the formation of the National Network of Rural Assessors and Promotors, formed by organizations working on gender and development in diverse rural regions of Mexico.

33. CIAM was founded in 1989 by Gloria Sierra, Begoña de Agustin (lawyer), Pilar Jaime (feminist), and Mercedes Olvera (anthropologist), and registered in Nicaragua, Mexico, and Guatemala. The initial objective was to work with women affected by armed conflict (refuged, displaced, and returned) in Central America and Mexico and, through participative investigation, they develop gender and identity awareness and exercise their rights and defend them before ACNUR and their own organizations of refugees and displaced, and the countries of refuge. They worked with organized women in popular movements; refugees in Mexico, Nicaragua, Costa Rica, Honduras, Belize, and Panama; and with displaced persons in El Salvador, Nicaragua, and Guatemala. (I am grateful to Mercedes Olivera for this information.)

34. The Team of Women in Solidarity Action was founded in February 1985 and centered its work on themes like health and popular education with the popular sectors in the Mexico City and with indigenous women in diverse parts of the country.

35. There is a long road traveled with respect to international agreements on women's rights: Declaration of the United Nations (1945); Universal Declaration of Human Rights (1948); Agreement on Suppression of Illegal Traffic of Persons and Exploitation of Prostitution (1949); Agreement on Equal Pay

for Equal Work (1951); Convention of the Political Rights of Women (1952); Agreement on the Nationality of Married Women (1957); Agreement on Discrimination in Relation to Employment and Occupation (1958); Agreement Against Discrimination in Education (1960); Agreement on Necessity of Consentment and Minimum Age for Matrimony (1962); International Pact of Civil and Political Rights (1966); International Covenant of Economic, Social, and Cultural Rights (1966); Declaration on the Elimination of Discrimination Against Women (1967); Declaration on the Protection of Women and Children in Cases of Conflict and Armed Conflict (1974); Agreement on the Equality of Opportunities and the Treatment of Workers (1981); Agreement Against Torture, Punishment, or Cruel, Inhumane, or Degrading Treatment (1985); and Declaration on the Violence Against Women (1993). In the Latin American context, there is the Agreement to Avoid, Sanction, and Eradicate Violence Against Women, known as the "Agreement of Belem do Pará" (approved in 1994).

36. For a critical analysis of the use of "development discourses" in indigenous communities from a gender perspective, see Radcliff (2009).

CHAPTER 3

1. The so-called Laws of the Indies (Leyes de Indias) established the legislation about public law, jurisdictions, and functions of indigenous local authorities.

2. In other publications, I have analyzed the importance of this generation of critical Latin American anthropologists, the use of activist-research and collaborative methods, and the important contribution of Latin American social sciences to the decolonization of knowledge (see Hernández Castillo 2007). It was through these methodologies that political alliances were constructed between the continental indigenous movement and the academy. In the context of these dialogues, a critique of the colonial uses of anthropology has developed and was expressed in the Barbados Indigenous Conference I and II (see www.google.com.mx/#q=declaracion+de+barbados+1971)

3. Several authors have analyzed the multicultural legal reforms promoted by the Latin American states: see Assies, van der Haar, and Hoekema (2000); Sieder (2002); Van Cott (2000).

4. These numbers are not exact because there are different criteria to define who is and who is not indigenous. For an analysis of the demographic data about indigenous peoples in the continent, see González (1994).

5. These projects are "Indigenous Women, Collective Rights, and Gender Demands" (CONACYT 2002–2006), which I directed and which included the cases of Mexico, Guatemala, and Colombia; "Globalization, Justice, and Rights from a Gender Perspective" (CONACYT 2007–2010), a collective project that María Teresa Sierra and I coordinated, which included the cases of Mexico and Guatemala; and "Women and Law in Latin America: Justice, Security, and Legal Pluralism" (2010–2013), coordinated by Rachel Sieder, with the support of the NORGLOBAL Program of the Norwegian Research Council and which included case studies in Mexico, Guatemala, Colombia, Bolivia, and Ecuador.

6. In those years, I was a member of the feminist organization Grupo de Mujeres de San Cristóbal las Casas.

7. The document was translated to English and published in Speed, Hernández Castillo, and Stephen (2006). The documentary film *Sentimos fuerte nuestro corazón* is in the library of the NGO Colectiva Feminista Mercedes Olivera in San Cristóbal de las Casas.

8. For an analysis of Zapatista autonomy, see Baronnet, Mora, and Stahler-Sholk (2011).

9. Testimony of Judith (Mora Bayo 2014, 159).

10. Testimony of Alicia (Mora Bayo 2014, 162).

11. Floriberto Díaz was invited as an advisor in the Peace Dialogues between the Mexican state and the Zapatista commanders, a few months before his death. His complete theoretical work was published after his death by the National University, UNAM: *Floriberto Díaz: Comunalidad energía viva del pensamiento Mixe* (*Floriberto Díaz: Communality, Lived Energy of the Mixe Thought*) (Díaz 2007).

12. Article 25 of the Constitution establishes that the law will protect the practices and cultural traditions of indigenous communities that have been used until now to elect their local authorities.

13. In a case study, as a part of our collective project, Juan Carlos Martínez has analyzed how governmental human rights officials have limited indigenous autonomy in Tlahuitoltepec, confronting legal decisions taken in their local spaces of justice (Martínez 2013, 127).

14. Interview with Rufina Villa, founder of the cooperative Maseualsiuamej Mosenyolchicauanij, Cuetzalán, Puebla, May 13, 2003.

15. Two international entities that have been fundamental in promoting reforms to the justice system have been the United Nations Verification Mission in

Guatemala (MINUGUA) and the United Nations Development Program (UNDP).

16. For an analysis of the various cases of disputes between collective rights and individual rights, see Sánchez Botero (2001).

17. These associations are Asociación de Cabildos Indígenas del Norte, Asociación de Cabildos del Territorio Ancestral Sa'th Tama Kiwe, Asociación de Autoridades Tradicionales Indígenas de la Zona Occidente, Asociación Nasa Sxha, Asociación de Cabildos Genaro Sánchez, Asociación de Cabildos Juan Tama, Consejo de Autoridades Tradicionales Indígenas del Oriente Caucano, Cabildo Mayor Yanacona, Organización Zona Baja Eperara Siaperara, and Reasentamientos.

18. Yolanda Durán, Curripaco, Guainía, Colombia. Interview conducted in September 2007 (Berrío Palomo 2008, 201).

CHAPTER 4

1. See the list of international litigations promoted by the feminist organization Latin American and Caribbean Committee for the Defense of Woman's Rights (Comité de América Latina y el Caribe para la Defensa de los Derechos de la Mujer—CLADEM): http://www.cladem.org/programas/litigio /litigios-internacionales.

2. Interview with Santiago Aguirre, legal representative of Inés Fernández Ortega, Tlapa, Guerrero, February 11, 2013.

3. Expert witness report on the case of Valentina Rosendo Cantú, elaborated by Héctor Ortíz Elizondo, April 2009.

4. Interview with Inés Fernández Ortega, March 13, 2009.

5. On June 7, 1998, eleven people were killed by soldiers of the Mexican Army in the community of El Charco, in the municipality of Ayutla de los Libres. The peasants killed in the massacre were among a group of seventy Mixteco indigenous persons who met in the elementary school in El Charco to discuss the situation of marginalization and poverty in their communities. The army accused them of being guerrilla fighters.

6. The American Convention of Human Rights has been ratified by twenty-five countries in the continent: Argentina, Barbados, Bolivia, Brazil, Colombia, Costa Rica, Chile, Dominica, Ecuador, El Salvador, Grenada, Guatemala, Haiti, Honduras, Jamaica, Mexico, Nicaragua, Panama, Paraguay, Peru, Dominican

Republic, Suriname, Trinidad and Tobago, Uruguay, and Venezuela. This regional treaty is an obligation for all the countries that signed, and it represents the end of a process that started toward the end of World War II, when nations of the American continent gathered in Mexico to work on the composition of a treaty that would later be adopted as a convention. The declaration, called the "American Declaration of Rights and Duties of Man," was approved by all member nations of OEA in 1948.

7. The sentence of the Inter-American Human Rights Court reports that for the Mexican state, the representatives were Juan Manuel Gómez Robledo, Multilateral Affairs and Human Rights Sub-Secretary for the Secretary of Foreign Affairs; Alejandro Negrin Muñoz, General Director of Human Rights and Democracy for the Secretary of Foreign Affairs; Rogelio Rodríguez Correa, Sub-Director of International Affairs for the Secretary of National Defense; Yéssica de Lamadrid Téllez, General Director of International Cooperation for the National Attorney General's Office; Carlos Garduño Salinas, Associate General Director of the Human Rights Promotion and Defense Unit for the Secretary of Government; Jorge Cicero Fernández, Chief of Chancellery of Mexico and Peru; Rosa María Gómez Saavedra, Secretary of the Women Institute of the State of Guerrero; María de la Luz Reyes Ríos, General Director of the Defense Service for the Government of the State of Guerrero; José Ignacio Martín del Campo Covarrubias, Director of the International Litigation Area Regarding Human Rights for the Secretary of Foreign Affairs; Luis Manuel Jardón Piña, Chief of the Department of Litigation for the Chancellery; Katya Vera, Chief of Department of the International Litigation Area Concerning Human Rights for the Secretary of Foreign Affairs; and finally, Guadalupe Salas y Villagomez, General Associate Director of Politics for Violent Crimes Against Women and Human Trafficking.

8. Participation of the legal representative of the Mexican state in the public hearing for the Inter-American Court of Human Rights, in its XLI Extraordinary Session Period, in Lima, Peru, April 15, 2010.

9. These were the three topics that the Inter-American Court requested from us in the expert report.

10. See sentence of the Inter-American Human Rights Court in case *Fernández Ortega & Others v. México*, August 30, 2010, and the sentence on the case of *Rosendo Cantú & Others v. México*, August 31, 2010.

11. For the entire sentence of the Court, see http://www.corteidh.or.cr/docs/casos /articulos/seriec_215_esp.pdf.

12. See *Masacre Plan de Sánchez v. Guatemala* (sentenced November 19, 2004) and *Comunidad Moiwana v. Surinam* (sentenced June 15, 2005).

13. Speech of the Secretary of Interior Alejandro Poiré Romero in the "Act of Acknowledgment of Responsibilities of the Mexican State," for the case of *Valentina Rosendo Cantú v. México*, December 15, 2011, Mexico City.

14. According to reports of Amnesty International, from 1994 to the present, there have been sixty sexual aggressions against indigenous and peasant women on the part of members of military forces, especially in the states of Guerrero, Chiapas, and Oaxaca.

15. Interview with Inés Fernández Ortega, translated by Andrea Eugenio, March 13, 2009.

16. Ibid.

17. Memories of the Workshop on Communitarian Compensations, organized with Inés and the members of OPIM in Ayutla de los Libres, February 2009.

18. Interview with Abel Barrera, Tlapa, Guerrero, February 11, 2013.

19. On September 26, 2014, forty-three male students from the Raúl Isidro Burgos Rural Teachers' College of Ayotzinapa went missing in Iguala, Guerrero, Mexico. According to official reports, they commandeered several buses and traveled to Iguala that day to hold a protest at a conference led by the mayor's wife. During the journey, local police intercepted them and a confrontation ensued. Details of what happened during and after the clash remain unclear, but the official investigation concluded that, once the students were in custody, they were handed over to the local Guerreros Unidos (United Warriors) crime syndicate and were, presumably, killed. Mexican authorities claimed that the Mayor of Iguala, José Luis Abarca Velázquez and his wife, María de los Ángeles Pineda Villa, masterminded the abduction. Both Abarca and Pineda Villa fled after the incident but were arrested about a month later in Mexico City. Iguala's police chief, Felipe Flores Velásquez, remains a fugitive. The events caused social unrest in parts of Guerrero and attacks on government buildings, and they led to the resignation of the governor of Guerrero, Ángel Aguirre Rivero, in the face of statewide protests. For an analysis of the Ayotzinapa case and the role of the narco-state in the disappearance of the forty-three students, see Hernández Castillo and Mora Bayo (2015).

20. Rosendo Radilla was a distinguished social leader of the municipality of Atoyac de Álvarez in Guerrero. He worked for the health and education of his people and had a charge as the major of the municipality. On August 25, 1974, he was detained illegally in a military checkpoint and was last seen in the

ex military headquarters of Atoyac de Álvarez, Guerrero. Thirty-four years later, his whereabouts continue to be unknown. His daughter, Tita Radilla, took the case to the Inter-American Court of Human Rights, obtaining a sentence against the Mexican state.

21. This constitutional reform has not yet been implemented, for it has encountered resistance from military power.

22. See "Entran 400 militares a pueblos de Ayutla: Causan temor," in *La jornada de Guerrero*, http://www.lajornadaguerrero.com.mx/2013/02/07/index.php?section =politica&article=003n1pol.

23. Ibid.

CHAPTER 5

1. A Spanish version of this chapter was published in Sierra, Hernández Castillo, and Sieder (2013).

2. Meztli Yoalli Rodríguez, a technical intern with the CIESAS program of fellowships for undergraduate students, was in charge of in-depth interviews in San Miguel and the review of the penal files. Life stories of Atlacholoaya inmates were done by the inmates themselves during the "Life Histories" workshop. See their collective book *Bajo la sombra del Guamuchil: Historias de vida de mujeres en prisión* (Hernández Castillo 2010b). The author headed the workshop and systematized the legal files data (see appendix 2).

3. The Law of Indigenous Rights and Culture recognizes the right to self-determination for indigenous peoples and communities. Nevertheless, the same law also shackles its enforcement, making it difficult, if not impossible, to implement. For example, establishing the ways to exercise self-determination was handed down to state constitutions and laws. Collective management of natural resources is limited to preferential treatment, and customary laws were not recognized. Actually, the new legal framework does not grant legal personhood to indigenous peoples themselves but only to their communities (the whole is recognized but only the individuals have rights). Furthermore, communities are built as government welfare recipients as a result of categorizing them as public interest subjects instead of as public law persons, as was originally stated (López Bárcenas 2000; Hernández Castillo, Sierra, and Paz 2004).

4. Amendments were made to articles 16, 17, 18, 19, 20, 21, and 22; other reformed articles were fraction XXI and XXIII of Article 73, fraction VII of article 115,

and fraction XIII of paragraph B of article 123, all of the Political Constitution of the Mexican United States.

5. For the entire document of the legal reforms in the Penal Code, see http://www.diputados.gob.mx/sedia/biblio/archivo/SAD-07–08.pdf.

6. Finally, the leaders of Atenco were freed after a national movement demanding their liberation. Although in March 2016, the congress of the state of Mexico, where Atenco is located, approved a new law (dubbed the Atenco Law), which will provide security forces the legal power to use lethal force and other degrees of violence in social protests.

7. When this manuscript was in revision (May 2016), the Mexican president Enrique Peña Nieto sent to the Mexican Senate a bill to legalize the medical and therapeutic uses of marijuana. This initiative marks a change in the national drug policy that in the last decades has been characterized by criminalization. But this reform, if approved, will benefit the consumers and will not be relevant for the poor indigenous prisoners involved in the drug trade, considering that the legalized amount would be 28 grams (about 1 ounce).

8. For an interview with the director of Amnesty International in Mexico about the case of Nestora Salgado, see http://mexico.cnn.com/videos/2015/05/29/amnistia-acompana-caso-de-nestora-salgado. For an analysis of judicial racism in that case, see Hernández Castillo 2015.

9. See "Overview of Critical Resistance on the Prison Industrial Complex" (Braz et al. 2000).

10. *La Razón*, September 23, 2009.

11. See a summary of these reforms in "Reformas a la ley que establece las normas mínimas sobre readaptación social de sentenciados:" http://www.diputados.gob.mx/LeyesBiblio/pdf/201_130614.pdf.

12. www.edomex.gob.mx/portal/page/portal/readaptacionsocial/industria.

13. Interview by Sergio Castañeda in *El Universal*, Mexico City, April 16, 2009.

14. "Dar trabajo a presos en México: Sueldos mínimos y sin impuestos en el periódico," Special report by Eduardo Alonso, in *El Universal*, January 2, 2007.

15. Information registered by Meztli Rodríguez in the CERESO of San Miguel Puebla.

16. When I was revising this manuscript, the CDI revealed some general data from its 2013 penitentiary census, but it did not allow me to access it even though I requested it in writing. However, according to the general data leaked to the press, 8,558 people in prison defined themselves as indigenous, 8,240 of whom were men, and 318 were women.

17. CNDH, *Informe especial de la Comisión Nacional de los Derechos Humanos sobre las mujeres internas en los centros de reclusión de la República Mexicana*, CNDH, México D.F., 2015.

18. In Morelos, the census reported the existence of 93,737 persons distributed in 721 communities in which Nahuatl language is used in the municipalities of Amacuzac, Axochiapan, Cuautla, Cuernavaca, Ocuituco, Puente de Ixtla, Temixco, Temoac, Tepoztlán, Tetela del Volcán, Tlalnepantla, Tlayacapan, Totolapan, and Yecapixtla. In the case of Puebla, the INEGI census of 2005 reported that 957,650 persons identified themselves as indigenous, that is to say 18.9 percent of the state's population. The languages most frequently spoken were Nahuatl with 397,207 speakers, Totonaco with 97,064, Popoloca with 14,688, and Mazateco with 13,033.

19. "Life History of Morelitos," written by Suzuki Lee in June 2009, within the "Life Histories" workshop, coordinated by Rosalva Aída Hernández Castillo. For the entire "Life History of Morelitos," see appendix 3.

20. "Que Alguien Me Explique: Voices of Atlacholoaya; Sharing the Story of Flor de Nochebuena." (Colectiva Editorial Hermanas en la Sombra 2009b).

21. "Cargando Nuestra Cruz: La Historia de Morelitos," written by Amatista Lee in March 2009, within the "Life Histories" workshop, coordinated by Rosalva Aída Hernández Castillo, in *Ahora que sigue?* 2, no. 13 (March 2009).

22. Interview done by Meztli Yoallo Rodríguez in CERESO San Miguel, Puebla.

23. "La Historia de Altagracia: Entre la pobreza y el narcomenudeo," written by Carlota Cadena in March 2009 within the "Life Histories" workshop, coordinated by Rosalva Aída Hernández Castillo, in *Ahora que sigue?* 2, no. 15 (May 2009).

24. "Life History of Flor de," Nochebuena written by Amatista Lee in June 2009.

25. "Life History of Perla Negra," written by Alejandra Alarcón on May 15, 2009, within the "Life Histories" workshop, coordinated by Rosalva Aída Hernández Castillo.

26. "Life History of Concepción Pérez Santiago," written by Meztli Rodríguez in the CERESO San Miguel Puebla, April 2009.

27. "Life History of 'Mujer de las Cañadas,'" written by Mercedes Pisoni in March 2009, within the "Life Histories" workshop, coordinated by Rosalva Aída Hernández Castillo.

28. "Life History of Victoria," written by Carlota Cadena on September 1, 2009, within the "Life Histories" workshop, coordinated by Rosalva Aída Hernández Castillo.

29. "Life History of 'Mujer de las Cañadas.'"

30. "Life History of Victoria."

31. "Life History of 'Mujer de las Cañadas.'"

32. Exercise by Guadalupe Salgado, in the "Life Histories" workshop at the Atlacholoaya CERESO, May 17, 2009.

33. "Life History of Águila del Mar," written by Marisol Hernández on March 7, 2009, within the "Life Histories" workshop, coordinated by Rosalva Aída Hernández Castillo.

34. "Life History of Lucía Sosa," written by Meztli Rodríguez in the CERESO San Miguel Puebla, April 2009.

35. See the film *Bajo la sombra del Guamúchil: Historias de vida de mujeres presas*, https://vimeo.com/17755550, and the book under the same title (Hernández Castillo 2010b) in http://media.wix.com/ugd/be8021_9cf2dc65fefc4e44b2de8df92 68175d5.pdf.

36. The Collective's publications can be downloaded for free here: http://rosalva aida.wix.com/rahc#!hermanasenlasombra/c1n54. The radio programs can be listened to here: https://soundcloud.com/radio-encuentros/sets/cantos-desde -el-guamuchil.

APPENDIX 1

1. Translated by Adriana Pou Hernández and Tiffany Tinoco Smith.

2. See Inter-American Court of Human Rights, "American Convention on Human Rights."

3. This is not the totality of the Me'phaa population due to the fact that the national census took into account members of the population who were five years and older (INEGI 2007).

4. The Mayordomía system has a colonial origin and is a collection of secular and religious positions held by men or households in rural indigenous communities throughout Mesoamerica. These revolving offices, or *cargos*, become the unpaid responsibility of men who are active in civic life. They typically hold a given post for a term of one year and alternate between civic and religious obligations from year to year. Office holders execute most of the tasks of local governments and churches. Individuals who hold a cargo are generally obligated to incur the costs of feasting during the fiestas that honor particular saints.

5. Article 33, 2nd paragraph of the United Nations Declaration on the Rights of Indigenous Peoples.

6. The first time these violations of human rights were given formal recognition was in 2001, when the National Human Rights Commission examined 532 cases of torture and missing people during the *guerra sucia* and emitted a recommendation that stated that there was enough proof to establish that at least 275 people had been arrested, tortured, and went missing, at the hands of the armed forces (CNDH 2001).

7. See Peace Brigades, International-Mexico Project, "Violence Against Human Rights Activists in the South of Mexico. Silenced," Newsletter for the Mexico Project, Ayutla de los Libres, May 2009.

8. Allegation 12.571, Inter-American Commission of Human Rights.

9. Since these events took place, the Inter-American Commission of Human Rights granted precautionary measures to Obtilia Eugenio Manuel, Cuauhtémoc Ramírez Rodríguez, and Andrea Eugenio Manuel, leaders of the OPIM, also granting them to Obtilia's and Cuauhtémoc's children. On September 4, 2007, the Inter-American Commission on Human Rights granted precautionary measures to Inés Fernández Ortega, Fortunato Prisciliano Sierra, and their children. On June 27, 2008, the measures given to Obtilia and her family were expanded to forty-one other members of OPIM after the murder of Lorenzo Fernández Ortega. On April 9, 2009, after Raúl Lucas and Manuel Ponce went missing and were later found killed, the Inter-American Court of Human Rights, as requested by the Inter-American Commission on Human Rights, granted provisional measures favoring 108 human rights activists in Guerrero.

10. In most common law jurisdictions, the attorney general is the main legal advisor to the government and, in some jurisdictions, he or she may also have executive responsibility for law enforcement, public prosecutions, or even ministerial responsibility for legal affairs generally.

11. Assistant police forces for communities with scarce resources that channel support through women.

12. See Sierra (2004a) and Hernández Castillo (2004b).

13. Also see articles 15, 18, 124, 128 paragraph IV, 154, and 159 of the Federal Penal Code of Legal Procedures, where it states that it is mandatory for the interpreters and translators to have knowledge of language, customs, and culture of the indigenous people. Also see articles 12, 84, and 110 of Guerrero's Penal Code of Legal Procedures.

14. Workshop regarding means of reparation in Barranca Guadalupe, March 3, 2010.

15. Article 15 of the United Nation's Declaration on the Rights of Indigenous People.

16. Human Rights Commission E/CN.4/Sub.2/1993/8, page 34.

17. Article 21 of the United Nation's Declaration on the Rights of Indigenous People.

18. Article 30 of the United Nation's Declaration on the Rights of Indigenous People.

19. Article 7 of the United Nation's Declaration on the Rights of Indigenous People.

APPENDIX 3

1. Translated by Efrén Hernández Hernández.

APPENDIX 4

1. Translated by Joanna Morris and Mary Macaulay.

APPENDIX 5

1. Translated by Adriana Alexander.

REFERENCES

Aguirre Franco, Felipe. "Dificultades de la teología india." Unpublished manuscript, SEPAI-CELAM, 1997.

Ajxup, Virginia. "Género, etnicidad, cosmovisión y mujer." In *Identidad, rostros sin máscara*, edited by Morna Macleod and María Luisa Cabrera, 57–71. Guatemala: Oxfam-Australia, 2000.

Alonso, Ana. "Rationalizing Patriarchy: Gender, Domestic Violence, and Law in Mexico." *Identities: Global Studies in Culture and Power* 2, no. 1–2 (1996): 29–47.

Álvarez, Carmen. "Cosmovisión maya y feminismo ¿Caminos que se unen?" Paper presented at the Congress of Mayan Studies, Guatemala City, August 20–24, 2005.

Álvarez, Sonia E. *Engendering Democracy in Brazil: Women's Movements in Transition Politics.* Princeton, NJ: Princeton University Press, 1990.

———. "Latin American Feminisms 'Go Global': Trends of the 1990s and Challenges for the New Millennium." In *Cultures of Politics/Politics of Cultures: Revisioning Latin American Social Movements*, edited by Sonia E. Álvarez, Evelina Dagnino, and Arturo Escobar, 293–324. Boulder, CO: Westview Press, 1998.

Álvarez, Sonia E., Evelina Dagnino, and Arturo Escobar, eds. *Culture of Politics/Politics of Cultures: Revisioning Latin American Social Movements.* Boulder, CO: Westview Press, 1998.

Anaya, James, and Claudio Grossman. "The Case of *Awas Tingni v. Nicaragua*: A New Step in the International Law of Indigenous Peoples." *Arizona Journal of International and Comparative Law* 19, no. 1 (2002): 2–15.

Aronowitz, Stanley. "The Situation of the Left in the United States." *Socialist Review* 23, no. 3 (1994): 49–80.

Arriola, Aura Marina. *Ese obstinado sobrevivir: Autoetnografía de una mujer guatemalteca.* Guatemala: Ediciones del Pensativo, 2000.

Artía Rodríguez, Patricia. "Desatar las voces, construir las utopías: La Coordinadora Nacional de Mujeres Indígenas en Oaxaca." MA thesis, CIESAS, Mexico City, 2001.

Assies, Willem, Gemma van der Haar, and André J. Hoekema, eds. *The Challenge of Diversity: Indigenous Peoples and Reform of the State in Latin America.* Amsterdam: Thela Thesis, 2000.

Avilés, Jaime. "Burgoa: los acuerdos de San Andrés, inexistentes," *La Jornada,* March 4, 1997, 10.

Azaola, Elena. *El delito de ser mujer.* Mexico City: CIESAS/Plaza y Valdez, 1996.

Azaola, Elena, and Cristina Yacamán. *Las mujeres olvidadas: Un estudio sobre la situación actual de las cárceles de mujeres en la República Mexicana.* Mexico City: Colmex-CNDH, 1996.

Azaola, Elena, and Marcelo Bergman. "El sistema penitenciario Mexicano." In *La reforma de la justicia en México,* edited by Alvarado Arturo, 745–81. Mexico City: Colmex, 2008.

Baitenmann, Helga, Victoria Chenaut, and Ann Varley, eds. *Decoding Gender: Law and Practice in Contemporary Mexico.* New Brunswick, NJ: Rutgers University Press, 2008.

Baronnet, Bruno, Mariana Mora, and Richard Stahler-Sholk. *Luchas "muy otras": Zapatismo y autonomía en las comunidades indígenas de Chiapas.* México City: UAM/CIESAS, 2011.

Barrera, Leticia. *La Corte Suprema en escena: Una etnografía del mundo judicial.* Buenos Aires: Grupo Editorial Siglo XXI, 2012.

Bartra, Armando. *Guerrero bronco: Campesinos, ciudadanos y guerrilleros en la Costa Grande.* México City: Ediciones Sinfiltro, 1996.

Bartra, Eli. *Feminismo en México: Ayer y hoy.* México City: Universidad Autónoma Metropolitana, 2002.

Belaustegigoitia, Marisa. "Una historia inconclusa desahacer la cárcel: Prácticas artístico/pedagógicas y maniobras jurídicas con una óptica de género" In *Resistencias penitenciarias. Investigación activista con mujeres en reclusión,* edited by Rosalva Aída Hernández Castillo. México: CIESAS, forthcoming.

Berrío Palomo, Lina Rosa. "Liderazgos femeninos indígenas en Colombia y México: Una mirada a sus procesos." MA thesis, UNAM, Mexico City, 2005.

———. "Sembrando sueños, creando utopías: Liderazgos femeninos indígenas en Mexico y Colombia." In *Etnografías e historias de resistencia: Mujeres indígenas, procesos organizativos y nuevas identidades políticas*, edited by Rosalva Aída Hernández Castillo, 120–55. Mexico City: CIESAS/PUEG-UNAM, 2008.

Bidegain, Ana María. "Bases históricas de la teología de liberación y atipicidad de la Iglesia Colombiana." *Texto y Contexto* 5 (1985): 15–28.

Blackwell, Maylei. "Weaving in the Spaces: Transnational Indigenous Women's Organizing and the Politics of Scale." In *Dissident Women: Gender and Cultural Politics in Chiapas*, edited by Shannon Speed, R. Aída Hernández Castillo, and Lynn M. Stephen, 115–57. Austin: University of Texas Press, 2009.

———. "The Practice of Autonomy in the Age of Neoliberalism: Strategies from Indigenous Women's Organising in Mexico." *Journal of Latin American Studies* 44 (2012): 703–32.

Bonfil Batalla, Guillermo. *Utopía y revolución: El pensamientos político contemporáneo de los indios en América Latina*. Mexico: Editorial Nueva Imagen, 1981.

Bonfil, Paloma. *Diagnóstico de la discriminación hacia las mujeres indígenas*. México: Comisión Nacional para el Desarrollo de los Pueblos Indígenas, 2003.

Boserup, Esther. *La mujer y el desarrollo económico*. Madrid: Minerva, 1983 [1970].

Bourdieu, Pierre. *Outline of a Theory of Practice*. Translated by Richard Nice. Cambridge: Cambridge University Press, 1977. Originally published as *Esquisse d'une théorie de la pratique, précédé de trois études d'ethnologie kabyle*. Paris: Seuil, 1972.

Brand, Karl Werner. "Aspectos cíclicos de los nuevos movimientos sociales." In *Los nuevos movimientos sociales*, edited by Russell Dalton and Mandred Kuechler, 45–71. Valencia: Edicions Afons el Magnanim, 1990.

Braz, Rose, Bo (Rita D.) Brown, Craig Gilmore, Ruthie Gilmore, Donna Hunter, Christian Parenti, Dylan Rodriguez, Cassandra Shaylor, Nancy Stoller, and Julia Sudbury, eds. "Overview: Critical Resistance to the Prison-Industrial Complex." *Social Justice* 27, no. 3 (2000): 1–17.

Brown, Wendy, and Janet Halley, eds. *Left Legalism/Left Critique*. Durham, NC: Duke University Press, 2002.

Bruchac, Joseph. "Breaking Out with the Pen." In *A Gift of Tongues: Critical Challenges to Contemporary American Poetry*, edited by Marie Harris and Kathleen Agüero, 286–94. Athens: University of Georgia Press, 1987.

Brysk, Alison. *From Tribal Village to Global Village: Indian Rights and International Relations in Latin America*. Stanford, CA: Stanford University Press, 2000.

Buenrostro, Manuel. "Reformas legales, espacios y modalidades de la justicia indígena de los mayas en Quintana Roo." In *Justicias indígenas y estado. Violencias contemporáneas*, edited by Teresa Sierra, Rosalva Aída Hernández, and Rachel Sieder, 89–121. Mexico: FLACSO-CIESAS, 2013.

Burke, Paul. *Law's Anthropology: From Ethnography to Expert Testimony in Native Titles*. Canberra: ANU Press, 2011.

Cabnal, Lorena. "Acercamiento a la construcción de la propuesta de pensamiento epistémico de las mujeres indígenas feministas comunitarias de Abya Yala." In *Feminismos diversos: Feminismos comunitarios*, 7–33. Segovia: ACSUR-Las Segovias, 2010.

Cadena, Carlota. "Altagracia: Apenas si teníamos para sobrevivir." In *Bajo la sombra del Guamúchil: Historias de vida de mujeres indígenas y campesinas en reclusión*, edited by Rosalva Aída Hernández Castillo, 31–37. México: CIESAS/IWGIA/Ore-Media, 2010.

Cadena, Carlota, and Leo Zavaleta. "Leo: ¿Quién te dijo que las mujeres tienen derecho a enamorarse." In *Bajo la sombra del Guamúchil: Historias de vida de mujeres indígenas y campesinas en reclusión*, edited by Rosalva Aída Hernández Castillo, 51–79. México: CIESAS/IWGIA/Ore-Media, 2010.

Calla, Pamela, and Susan Paulson. *Justicia comunitaria y género en las zonas rurales de Bolivia. Ocho estudios de caso*. La Paz: Oasis-Red de Participación y Justicia de Bolivia-Jiquisiña-Comai Pachamama, 2008.

Carr, Barry. *La izquierda mexicana en el siglo XX*. Mexico City: Ediciones Era, 1997.

Carrasco, Morita. "Diálogos de una antropóloga con el derecho a partir de su experiencia como perito en dos juicios penales." In *El peritaje antropológico: Entre la reflexión y la práctica*, edited by Guevara Gil Armando, Aaron Verona, and Roxana Vergara, 57–71. Lima: Centro de Investigación, Capacitación y Asesoría Jurídica del Decaptamento Académico de derecho (CICAJ), 2015.

Casas, Ulises. *Origen y desarrollo del movimiento revolucionario colombiano*. Bogotá: La Casa de la Libertad, 1990.

Castellanos Guerrero, Alicia, Jorge Gómez Izquierdo, Guy Rozat, and Fernanda Núñez. *Los caminos del racismo en México*. Mexico City: Plaza y Valdez, 2008.

Castro-Gómez, Santiago. "Latinoamericanismo, modernidad, globalización. Prolegómenos a una crítica poscolonial de la razón." In *Teorías sin disciplina. Latinoamericanismo, poscolonialidad y globalización en debate*, edited by Santiago Castro-Gómez and Eduardo Mendieta, 169–203. México: Miguel Angel Porrúa-University of San Francisco, 1998.

Castro-Gómez, Santiago, and Eduardo Mendieta, eds. *Teorías sin disciplina: Latinoamericanismo, poscolonialidad y globalización en debate*. México: Miguel Angel Porrúa, University of San Francisco, 1998.

———. "Ciencias sociales, violencia epistémica y el problema de la "invención del otro." In *La colonialidad del saber: eurocentrismo y ciencias sociales. Perspectivas latinoamericanas*, edited by Edgardo Lander. Buenos Aires: CLACSO-UNESCO, 2000.

Cavazos Ortiz, Irma. *Mujer, etiqueta y cárcel.* Mexico City: UAM-Instituto Nacional de Ciencias Penales, 2005.

CENAMI. *Teología india memorias del primer encuentro taller Latinoamericano*, Tomo I. Mexico City: CENAMI/Abya-Yala, 1991.

———. *Teología india memorias del segundo encuentro taller Latinoamericano*, Tomo II. Mexico City: CENAMI/Abya-Yala, 1994.

Cerda García, Alejandro. *Imaginando zapatismo: Multiculturalidad y autonomía indígena en Chiapas desde un municipio autónomo.* México City: Universidad Autónoma Metropolitana/Miguel Ángel Porrúa, 2011.

Chenaut, Victoria. *Género y procesos interlegales.* México: Colmich-CIESAS, 2014.

Chirix, Emma. *Alas y raíces, afectividad de las mujeres mayas. Rik'in ruxik' y ruxe'il, ronojel kajowab'al ri mayab' taq ixoqi'.* Guatemala: Grupo de Mujeres Mayas Kaqla, Nawal Wuj, 2003.

———. *Cuerpos, poderes y políticas: Mujeres mayas en un internado católico.* Guatemala: Ediciones Maya' Na'oj, 2013.

———. "Que Alguien Me Explique: Voices of Atlacholoaya; Sharing the Story of Flor de Nochebuena," *¿Ahora que sigue?* (March 2009).

———. *Mareas Cautivas.* Cuernavaca: Astrolabio Editorial, 2012.

Collier, Jane. *El Derecho Zinacanteco: Procesos de disputar en un pueblo indígena de Chiapas.* Tuxtla Gutiérrez, Chiapas: CIESAS-UNICACH, 1995 [1973].

———. "Mapping Interlegality in Chiapas, Mexico." *PoLAR: Political and Legal Anthropology Review* 21, no. 1 (1998): 150–71.

Collier, Jane F., Bill Maurer, and Liliana Suárez-Navaz. "Sanctioned Identities: Legal Construction of Modern Personhood." *Identities: Global Studies in Culture and Power* 2, no. 1–2 (1995): 1–27.

Colom, Yolanda. *Mujeres en la alborada: Guerrilla y participación femenina en Guatemala 1973–1978.* Guatemala: Artemio & Edinter, 1998.

Comaletzin. *Curriculum institucional.* Cuetzalan, Puebla: Unpublished manuscript, 1999.

Comaroff John and Jean Comaroff. *Of Revelation and Revolution: Christianity, Colonialism and Consciousness in South Africa.* Chicago: University of Chicago Press, 1991.

Commander Esther. "Discurso de la Comandanta Esther ante el Congreso de la Unión." *La Jornada*, April 3, 2001, 9.

Comisión Nacional de Derechos Humanos (CNDH). Recomendación 026–2001 México: CNDH, November 27, 2001.

Comisión Nacional para el Desarrollo de los Pueblos Indígenas. *Censos de la población indígena privada de su libertad*. México: CDI, 2006.

Conger Lind, Amy. "Power, Gender, and Development: Organizations and the Politics of Need in Ecuador." In *The Making of Social Movements in Latin America: Identity, Strategy and Democracy*, edited by Arturo Escobar and Sonia E. Álvarez, 10–25. Boulder, CO: Westview Press, 1992.

Consejo Regional Indígena del Cauca (CRIC). *¿Qué pasaría si la escuela? 30 años de construcción de una educación propia*. Bogotá: Editorial El Fuego Azul, 2004.

Coordinadora Nacional de Mujeres Indígenas en México. *Presentación de la Coordinadora Nacional de Mujeres Indígenas*. Panfleto de presentación, México, 1997.

Córdova, Teresa. "Chicana Voices: Intersections of Class, Race, and Gender." National Association for Chicano Studies, University of Texas at Austin, Center for Mexican American Studies, NACS Conference. Austin: University of Texas, 1984.

Crenshaw, Kimberlé. "Demarginalizing the Intersection of Race and Sex: A Black Feminist Critique of Antidiscrimination Doctrine, Feminist Theory and Antiracist Politics." *The University of Chicago Legal Forum* 1, no. 8 (1989): 139–67.

———. "Mapping the Margins: Intersectionality, Identity Politics, and Violence Against Women of Color." *Stanford Law Review* 43, no. 6 (1991): 1241–99.

Cuevas Sosa, Andrés, Rosario Mendieta Dimas, and Elvia Salazar Cruz. *La mujer delincuente bajo la ley del hombre*. Mexico City: Pax, 1992.

Cumbre de Mujeres Indígenas de América. *Memoria de la primera cumbre de mujeres indígenas de las Américas*. Mexico City: Fundación Rigoberta Menchú Tum, 2003.

Cumes, Aura Estela. *"Las mujeres son 'mas indias': Género, multiculturalismo y Mayanización. ¿Esquivando o retando opresiones?"* Unpublished manuscript, Guatemala, 2007a.

———. "Mayanización y el sueño de la emancipación indígena en Guatemala." In *Mayanización y vida cotidiana: La ideología multicultural en la sociedad guatemalteca, Vol. 1*, edited by Santiago Bastos and Aura Estela Cumes, 81–98. Guatemala: FLACSO-CIRMA, 2007b.

———. "Multiculturalismo y unidad nacional en Guatemala: Dinámicas de Mayanización en un contexto turbulento e ideologizado." Paper presented in the

International Colloquium "Ciudades multiculturales de América: Migraciones, relaciones interétnicas y etnicidad." Monterrey, Nuevo León, Mexico, October 29–31, 2007c.

———. "Mujeres indígenas, poder y justicia: de guardianas a autoridades en la construcción de culturas y cosmovisiones." In *Mujeres indígenas y justicia ancestral*, edited by Miriam Lang and Anna Kucia, 33–50. Quito, Ecuador: UNIFEM Región Andina/FLACSO Guatemala, 2009.

Curruchichi, María Luisa. "La Cosmovisión Maya y la perspectiva de género." In *Identidad, rostros sin máscara*, edited by Morna Macleod and María Luisa Cabrera, 45–55. Guatemala: Oxfam-Australia, 2000.

D'Aubeterre Buznego, María Eugenia. *El pago de la novia. Matrimonio, vida conyugal y prácticas matrimoniales en Acuexcomac, Puebla.* Zamora: COLMICH-BUAP, 2003.

Davis, Angela Y. *Women, Race and Class.* New York: Random House, 1981.

de la Cadena, Marisol. *Indigenous Mestizos: The Politics of Race and Culture in Cuzco, Peru, 1919–1991.* Durham, NC: Duke University Press, 2000.

———. 2005. "Are *Mestizos* Hybrids? The Conceptual Politics of Andean Identities." *Journal of Latin American Studies* 37, no. 2 (2005): 259–84.

de la Cadena, Marisol, and Orin Starn. *Indigenous Experience Today.* Oxford-New York: Berg, 2007.

Delgado, Richard, and Jean Stefancic. *Critical Race Theory: An Introduction.* New York: New York University Press, 2001.

del Mar, Aguila. "Sol: ¡Lo has perdido todo que Dios te bendiga!" In *Bajo la sombra del Guamúchil: Historias de vida de mujeres indígenas y campesinas en reclusión,* edited by Rosalva Aída Hernández Castillo, 115–35. México: CIESAS/IWGIA/Ore-Media, 2010.

de Sousa Santos, Boaventura. *Por una concepción multicultural de los derechos humanos.* México: UNAM-Centro de Investigaciones Interdisciplinarias en Ciencias y Humanidades, 1998a.

———. *La globalización del derecho: Los nuevos caminos de la regulación y la emancipación.* Bogotá: ILSA/Universidad Nacional de Colombia, 1998b.

———. *Toward a New Legal Common Sense.* 2nd ed. London: Butterworths Lexis-Nexis, 2002.

———. *Una epistemología del Sur. La reinvención del conocimiento y la emancipación social.* México: CLACSO y Siglo XXI, 2009.

de Sousa Santos, Boaventura, and Mauricio García Villegas. *El caleidoscopio de las justicias en Colombia, Análisis Socio-Jurídico,* Tomo I, Bogotá: Instituto Colombiano de Antropología e Historia-Universidad de Coimbra-Universidad de los Andes-Universidad Nacional de Colombia-Siglo del Hombre Editores, 2001.

———. "Law, Politics, and the Subaltern in Counter-hegemonic Globalization." In *Law and Globalization from Below: Towards a Cosmopolitan Legality*, edited by Boaventura de Sousa Santos and Cesar A. Rodríguez-Garavito, 1–27. Cambridge, UK: Cambridge University Press, 2005.

———. *Una epistemología del sur: La reinvención del conocimiento y la emancipación social*. México: CLACSO y Siglo XXI, 2009.

de Vos, Jan. *Una tierra para sembrar sueños. Historia reciente de la Selva Lacandona (1950–2000)*. México: FCE, 2003.

Díaz-Cotto, Juanita. *Gender, Ethnicity and the State: Latina and Latino Prison Politics*. Albany: State of New York University Press, 1996.

Díaz, Floriberto. *Comunalidad energía viva del pensamiento Mixe*. Mexico City: UNAM, 2007.

di Leonardo, Micaela. "White Lies, Black Myths." In *The Gender/Sexuality Reader: Culture, History, Political Economy*, edited by Roger N. Lancaster and Micaela di Leonardo, 53–71. New York: Routledge, 1997.

Duarte, Ixkic. "Conversación con Alma López, autoridad guatemalteca: La doble mirada del género y la etnicidad." *Estudios latinoamericanos, Nueva Época*, no. 18 (July–December 2002): 15–27.

———. *Desde el sur organizado: Mujeres Nahuas del Sur de Veracruz construyendo política*. México: UAM/Xochimilco, 2011.

Emanuelsson, Dick." La lucha cívica y la lucha armada de los indígenas El caso del Movimiento Armado Quintín Lamé." Accessed May 10, 2015, http://www.profesionalespcm.org.

Engle, Karen. *The Elusive Promise of Indigenous Development: Rights, Culture, Strategy*. Durham, NC: Duke University Press, 2010.

Engle Merry, Sally. "Gender Violence and Legally Engendered Selves." *Identities: Global Studies in Culture and Power* 2, no. 1–2 (September 1995): 49–73.

———. *Colonizing Hawai'i: The Cultural Power of Law*. Princeton, NJ: Princeton University Press, 2000.

———. *Human Rights and Gender Violence: Translating International Law into Local Justice*. Chicago: University of Chicago Press, 2006.

———. "Derechos humanos, género y nuevos movimientos sociales: Debates contemporáneos en antropología jurídica." In *Justicia y diversidad en América Latina. Pueblos indígenas ante la globalización*, edited by Victoria Chenaut, Magda Gómez, Héctor Ortíz, and María Teresa Sierra, 261–91. México City: CIESAS/FLACSO, 2011.

Engle Merry, Sally, and Susan Bibler Coutin. "Technologies of Truth in the Anthropology of Conflict." *American Ethnologist* 41, no. 1 (2014): 1–16.

Equipo de Estudios Comunitarios y Acción Psicosocial and Unión Nacional de Mujeres Guatemaltecas. *Tejidos que lleva el alma: Memoria de las mujeres mayas sobrevivientes deviolación sexual durante el conflicto armado.* Guatemala: ECAP, 2009.

Escalante Betancourt, Yuri. "Ética y verdad. La antropología frente al positivismo jurídico." In *Peritaje antropológico en México: Reflexiones teórico metodológicas y experiencias,* edited by María Antonieta Gallart and Laura Valladares, 33–43 México: Boletín Colegio de Etnólogos y Antropólogos Sociales, 2012.

———. *El racismo judicial en México: Análisis de sentencias y representación de la diversidad.* México: Juan Pablos, 2015.

Espinosa Damián, Gisela. *Cuatro vertientes del feminismo en México: Cruces y disyuntivas entre el cuerpo y la política.* Mexico City: Colección Teoría y Análisis, publicaciones Universidad Autónoma Metropolitana, Xochimilco, 2009.

Espinosa Damián, Gisela, and Alma Sánchez. *También somos protagonistas de la historia de México.* Cuadernos Para La Mujer, Serie Pensamientos y Lucha No. 7. Morelia, Michoacán: Equipo de Mujeres en Acción Solidaria/Centro Michoacano de Investigación y Formación Vasco de Quiroga, 1992.

Espinosa Damián, Gisela, and Lorena Paz Paredes. "Pioneras del Feminismo en los Sectores Populares: La Experiencia de CIDHAL 1977–1985." Unpublished manuscript, 1988.

Esquit, Edgar, and Ivan García. *El derecho consuetudirnario, la reforma judicial y la implementación de los acuerdos de paz.* Guatemala: FLACSO, 1998.

Ever, Christine, and Christine Kovic. *Women of Chiapas: Making History in Times of Struggle and Hope.* New York: Routledge, 2003.

Facio, Alda. "El derecho como producto del patriarcado." In *Sobre patriarcas, jerarcas, patrones y otros varones,* edited by Alda Facio and Rosalía Camacho, 60–78, San José, Costa Rica: ILANUD, 1992.

Fernández Christlieb, Paulina. *Justicia autónoma Zapatista: Zona selva Tseltal.* México: Ed. Estampa, 2015.

Fineman, Martha, and Nancy Thomadsen, eds. *At the Boundaries of Law: Feminism and Legal Theory.* New York: Routledge, 1991.

Fonow, Mary Margaret, and Judith Cook. *Beyond Methodology: Feminist Scholarship as Lived Research.* Bloomington: Indiana University Press, 1991.

Foro Internacional de Mujeres Indígenas (FIMI). *Mairin Iwanka Raya, Mujeres indígenas confrontan la violencia. Informe complementario al estudio sobre violencia contra mujeres indígenas del Secretariado General de las Naciones Unidas.* Managua: UNIFEM-HIVOS-Madre-Global Fund for Women, 2006.

Foucault, Michel. *Discipline and Punish: The Birth of Prison.* New York: Pantheon Books, 1977.

———. "Governmentality." In *The Foucault Effect: Studies in Governmentality,* translated by Rosi Braidotti and revised by Colin Gordon; edited by Graham Burchell, Colin Gordon, and Peter Miller, 87–104. Chicago: University of Chicago Press, 1991.

French, Jan Hoffman. "Mestizaje and Law Making in Indigenous Identity Formation in Northeastern Brazil: 'After the Conflict Came the History.'" *American Anthropologist* 106, no. 4 (2004): 663–74.

Freyermuth, Graciela, and Mariana Fernández. "Migration, Organization and Identity: The Case of a Women's Group from San Cristóbal las Casas." *Signs* 20, no. 4 (1995): 15–37.

Gabriel Xiquín, Calixta. "Liderazgo de las mujeres Mayas en las leyendas y mitologías según su cosmovisión." Unpublished manuscript, 2004.

Gall, Olivia. "Identidad, exclusión y racismo: reflexiones teóricas y sobre México." *Revista Mexicana de Sociología* 66, no. 2 (April-June 2003): 221–59.

Gall, Olivia, and Rosalva Aída Hernández Castillo. "La historia silenciada: Las Mujeres indígenas en las rebeliones coloniales y poscoloniales." In *Voces disidentes: Debates contemporáneos en los estudios de género,* edited by Sara Elena Pérez Gil and Patricia Ravelo, 120–58. Mexico City: CIESAS-Porrúa, 2004.

García Ramírez, Sergio. "La reforma del proceso penal: riesgos y desafío." Paper presented at the forum, *Reforma de la Justicia Penal y de la Justicia para Adolescentes,* UNAM: Instituto de Investigaciones Jurídicas, Academia Mexicana de Ciencias Penales, March 15, 2007. In *Biblioteca Jurídica Virtual,* Instituto de Investigaciones Jurídicas—UNAM, http://biblio.juridicas.unam.mx/libros/6/2680/15.pdf.

Garrido, Vicente, and Jorge Sobral. *La investigación criminal: La psicología aplicada al descubrimiento, captura y condena de los criminales.* Madrid: Nabla, 2008.

Garst, Rachel. *Ixcan: Colonización, desarrollo y condiciones de retorno.* Guatemala: COINDE, 1993.

Garza Caligaris, Anna María. "El movimiento de mujeres en Chiapas: Haciendo historia." *Anuario de Estudios Indígenas,* VIII. Instituto de Estudios Indígenas, UNACH. Tuxtla Gutiérrez, Chiapas: 109–35, 2000.

———. *Género, interlegalidad y conflicto en San Pedro Chenalhó.* México: PROIMMSE, UNAM/IEI, UNACH, 2002.

Garza Caligaris, Ana María, Fernanda Paz, Juana María Ruiz, and Angelina Calvo. *Nuevo Huixtan, Nuevo Matzam, Nuevo San Juan Chamula: Voces de la Historia.* México: CRIM-UNAM, 1995.

Garza Caligaris, Ana María, and Sonia Toledo. "Mujeres, agrarismo y militancia: Chiapas en la década de los ochenta." In *Tejiendo historias: Tierra, género y poder en Chiapas*, edited by Maya Lorena Pérez Ruíz, 15–19. Mexico City: CONACULTA-INAH, 2004.

Gebara, Ivonne. *Levántate y anda: Algunos aspectos del caminar de la mujer en América Latina*. México City: Editorial Dabar, 1990.

Giacomello, Corina, and Isabel Blas Guillen. *Propuestas de reforma en casos de mujeres encarceladas por delitos de drogs en México*. México: Equis-Justicia para las Mujeres e INACIPE, 2016.

Gilmore, Ruth Wilson. *Golden Gulag: Prisons, Surplus, Crisis, and Opposition in Globalizing California (American Crossroads)*. Berkeley: University of California Press, 2007.

———. "Forgotten Places and the Seed of Grassroots Planning." In *Engaging Contradictions: Theory, Politics and Methods of Activist Scholarship*, edited by Charles Hale, 31–62. Berkeley: University of California Press, 2008.

Gil Tébar, Pilar. *Caminando con un sólo corazón: Las mujeres indígenas de Chiapas*. Estudios sobre la Mujer. Mexico City: Editorial Atenea, 1991.

Gitlin, Todd. "The Left, Lost in the Politics of Identity," *Harper's Magazine*, September 1993, 16–20.

Gitlitz, John S. "El *otro* sigue siendo el *otro*: el concepto de cultura y los peritajes antropológicos." In *El peritaje antropológico. Entre la reflexión y la práctica*, edited by Guevara Gil Armando, Aaron Verona, and Roxana Vergara, 71–89. Lima: Centro de Investigación, Capacitación y Asesoría Jurídica del Decaptamento Académico de Derecho (CICAJ), 2015.

Gluckman, Max. *The Judicial Process Among the Barotse of Northern Rhodesia*. Manchester: University of Manchester Press, 1955.

Gómez, Magda. "Derechos indígenas: Los pueblos indígenas en la Constitución Mexicana." (Article 4, paragraph 1). México: INI, 1992.

González, Mary Lisbeth. "How Many Indigenous People?" In *Indigenous People and Poverty in Latin America: An Empirical Analysis*, edited by Harry Anthony Patrinos, 21–39. Washington, DC: World Bank, 1994.

Gross, David, and Stuart Plattner. "Anthropology as Social Work: Collaborative Models of Anthropological Research." *Anthropology Newsletter, American Anthropological Association* 43 (2002): 4.

Grupo de Mujeres Mayas Kaqla. *Algunos colores del arco iris, realidad de las mujeres Mayas*. Guatemala City: Editorial Kaqla, 2000.

———. *La palabra y el sentir de las mujeres Mayas de Kaqla*. Guatemala City: Editorial Kaqla, 2004.

Grupo de Mujeres de San Cristóbal. Memoir of the workshop "Los derechos de las mujeres en nuestras costumbres y tradiciones," San Cristóbal de las Casas, May 19–20: Mimeo. Partially reproduced in "El grito de la luna. Mujeres: derecho y tradición." *Revista Ojarasca* (August–September 1994): 20–27.

Gunn Allen, Paula. *The Sacred Hoop: Recovering the Feminine in American Indian Traditions.* Boston: Beacon Press, 2002 [1986].

Gutiérrez Chong, Natividad. "Autonomía con mirada de mujer." In *México: Experiencias de autonomía indígena*, edited by Araceli Burguete Cal y Mayor, 54–86. Copenhagen: International Group on Indigenous Affairs (IWGIA), 1999.

———. *Mujeres y nacionalismos en América Latina: De la independencia a la nación del nuevo milenio.* México: Universidad Nacional Autónoma de México, 2004.

Hale, Charles. "Does Multiculturalism Menace? Governance, Cultural Rights and the Politics of Identity in Guatemala." *Journal of Latin American Studies* 34 (2002): 485–524.

———. "Neoliberal Multiculturalism: The Remaking of Cultural Rights and Racial Dominance in Central America." *Political and Legal Anthropology Review* 28, no. 1 (2005): 10–28.

———. *Engaging Contradictions: Theory, Politics and Methods of Activist Scholarship.* Berkeley: University of California Press, 2008.

Hall, Bud L. "Investigación participativa, conocimiento popular y poder: Una reflexión personal." In *La investigación participativa en América Latina*, compiled by Gilberto Vejarano, 15–34. Pátzcuaro, Michoacán, México: Antología CREFAL, 1983.

Haraway, Donna. "Situated Knowledge: The Science Question in Feminism and the Privilege of Partial Perspective." In *Simians, Cyborgs and Women: The Reinvention of Nature*, 183–203. New York: Routledge, 1991.

Hartsock, Nancy. "The Feminist Standpoint." In *Discovering Reality*, edited by Sandra Harding and Merril Hintikka, 283–310. Boston; London: D. Riedel Publishing Company, 1983.

———. "Comment on Hekman's Truth and Method: Feminist Standpoint Theory Revisited: Truth or Justice?" *Signs* 22, no. 2 (1997): 367–74.

Harvey, David. *The New Imperialism.* Oxford: Oxford University Press, 2003.

Harvey, Neil. "Globalization and Resistance in Post-Cold War Mexico." *Third World Quarterly* 22, no. 6 (2001): 1045–61.

Herivel, Tara, and Paul Wright, eds. *Prison Nation: The Warehousing of America's Poor.* New York; London: Routledge, 2003.

Hernández Castillo, Rosalva Aída. "Reinventing Tradition: The Women's Law." *Akwe: Kon A Journal of Indigenous Issues* 11, no. 2 (1994a): 15–23.

————. "Entre la violencia doméstica y la opresión cultural: La ley y la costumbre a los ojos de las mujeres." *Americas & Latinas: A Journal of Women and Gender*, Center for Latin American Studies (1994b): 20–37.

————. *The Other Word: Women and Violence in Chiapas*. Dinamarca: IWGIA, 2001a.

————. "Entre el etnocentrismo feminista y el esencialismo étnico. Las mujeres indígenas y sus demandas de género." *Debate Feminista* 12, no. 24 (2001c) 206–29.

————. "National Law and Indigenous Customary Law: The Struggle for Justice of the Indigenous Women from Chiapas." In *Gender, Justice Development and Rights*, edited by Maxine Molyneux and Shahra Razavi, 384–413. Oxford: Oxford University Press, 2002a.

————. "¿Guerra fratricida o estrategia etnocida? Las mujeres frente a la violencia política en Chiapas." In *Estudios sobre la violencia: Teoría y práctica*, edited by Witold Jacorzynski, 97–122. Mexico City: CIESAS-Porrúa, 2002b.

————. "Indígenas y teología india: Límites y aportaciones a las luchas de las mujeres indígenas." In *Religión y género: Enciclopedia Iberoamericana de religiones*, edited by Sylvia Marcos, 319–37. Madrid: Editorial Trotta, 2004a.

————. "El derecho positivo y la costumbre jurídica: Las mujeres indígenas de Chiapas y sus luchas por el acceso a la justicia." In *Violencia contra las mujeres en contextos urbanos y rurales*, edited by Marta Torres Falcón. Mexico City: El Colegio de México, 2004b.

————. "Gender and Differentiated Citizenship in Mexico: Indigenous Women and Men Re-invent Culture and Redefine the Nation." In *Citizenship, Political Culture and State Transformation in Latin America*, edited by Willem Assies, Marco A. Calderon, and Tom Salman, 323–41. Amsterdam: Dutch University Press-COLMICH, 2005.

————. "Between Feminist Ethnocentricity and Ethnic Essentialism: The Zapatistas' Demands and the National Indigenous Women's Movement." In *Dissident Women: Gender and Cultural Politics in Chiapas*, edited by Shannon Speed, Rosalva Aída Hernández Castillo, and Lynn M. Stephen, 57–74. Austin: University of Texas Press, 2006a.

————. *Historias a dos voces: Testimonios de luchas y resistencias de mujeres indígenas*. Morelia, Michoacán: Instituto Michoacano de la Mujer, 2006b.

————. "Socially Committed Anthropology from a Dialogical Feminist Perspective." Paper presented in the *Panel for Critically Engaged Collaborative Research: Remaking Anthropological Practice* at the Annual Meeting of the American Anthropological Association (AAA), San Jose, CA, 2007.

————. *Etnografías e historias de resistencia: Mujeres indígenas, procesos organizativos y nuevas identidades políticas.* Mexico City: CIESAS-PUEG, 2008.

————. "Violencia de estado y violencia de género: Las paradojas de los derechos humanos de las mujeres en México" In *Trace* 57 (June 2010a): 86–98.

————. *Bajo la sombra del Guamúchil: historias de vida de mujeres indígenas y campesinas en reclusión.* Mexico City: IWGIA, 2010b.

————. "Indigeneity as a Field of Power: Multiculturalism and Indigenous Identities in Political Struggles." In *The SAGE Handbook of Identities*, eds. Margaret Wetherell and Chandra Tlapade Mohanty, 379–403. London: SAGE Publications LTD, 2010c.

————. "¿Del estado multicultural al estado penal? Mujeres indígenas presas y criminalización de la pobreza en México." In *Justicias indígenas y estado: Violencias contemporáneas*, edited by María Teresa Sierra, Rosalva Aída Hernández Castillo, and Rachel Sieder, 299–335. México: FLACSO-CIESAS, 2013.

————. "Cuerpos femeninos, violencia y acumulación por desposesión." In *Des-Posesión: Género, territorio y luchas por la autonomía*, edited by Marisa Belaustiguigoitia and María Josefina Saldaña-Portillo, 79–101. México: PUEG-UNAM/ Instituto de Liderazgo Simone de Beauvoir and Debate Feminista, 2014.

————. "El racismo judicial y las policías comunitarias en Guerrero," *La Jornada*, August 3, 2015, 15.

Hernández Castillo, Rosalva Aída, and Adriana Terven. "Methodological Routes: Towards a Critical and Collaborative Legal Anthropology" In *Demanding Justice and Security: Indigenous Women and Legal Pluralities in Latin America*, edited by Rachel Sieder. New Brunswick, NJ: Rutgers University Press, forthcoming.

Hernández Castillo, Rosalva Aída, and Anna Garza Caligaris. "En torno a la ley y la costumbre: Problemas de antropología legal y género en los Altos de Chiapas." In *Tradiciones y costumbres jurídicas en las comunidades indígenas de México*, edited by Gisela González Guerra and Rosa Isabel Estrada Martínez, 217–27. Mexico City: CNDH, 1995.

Hernández Castillo, Rosalva Aída, and Gisela Espinosa Damián. "New Political Actors in Rural Mexico: The Challenges and Achievements of Peasant and Indigenous Women." In *Cultural Politics and Resistance in the 21st Century*, edited by Kara Dellacioppa and Clare Weber, 21–49. London; New York: Palgrave and MacMillan, 2011.

Hernández Castillo, Rosalva Aída, and Mariana Mora Bayo. "Ayotzinapa: ¿Fue el Estado? Reflexiones desde la antropología política en Guerrero." In *LASA Forum* 46, no. 1 (2015): 28–33.

Hernández Castillo, Rosalva Aída, Teresa Sierra, and Sarela Paz, eds. *El estado y los indígenas en tiempos del PAN: Neoindigenismo, legalidad e identidad.* Mexico City: CIESAS-Porrúa, 2004.

Hernández Castillo, Rosalva Aída, and Violeta Zylberberg. "Alzando la vista: Impactos locales y nacionales del zapatismo en la vida de las mujeres indígenas." In *Tejiendo historías: Tierra, género y poder en Chiapas,* edited by Maya Lorena Pérez, 335–55. México: Instituto Nacional de Antropología e Historia, 2004.

Hill Collins, Patricia. *Black Feminist Thought: Knowledge, Consciousness, and the Politics of Empowerment.* Boston: Unwin Hyman, 1990.

Hill Collins, Patricia, and Margaret Andersen, eds. *Race, Class and Gender: An Anthology,* 6th ed. Belmont, CA: Thomson/Wadsworth, 2007 [1992].

Hirschkind, Charles, and Saba Mahmood. "Feminism, the Taliban, and Politics of Counter-Insurgency." *Anthropological Quarterly* 75, no. 2 (2002): 339–54.

Hirsh, Susan. *Law, Hegemony and Resistance.* New York; London: Routledge, 1994.

Hooker, Juliet. "Indigenous Inclusion/Black Exclusion: Race, Ethnicity and Multicultural Citizenship in Latin America." *Journal of Latin American Studies* 37, no. 2 (2005): 285–310.

Hobsbawm, Eric. "Identity Politics and the Left." *New Left Review* 1, no. 217 (May–June 1996): 38–47.

Iglesia Guatemalteca en el Exilio. *Iglesia Guatemalteca en el exilio: Martirio y lucha en Guatemala.* Guatemala: Edición Especial IGE, 1982.

Illicachi Guzñay, Juan. *Diálogos del Catolicismo y Protestantismo indígena en Chimborazo.* Quito: Editorial Universitaria Abya-Yala, 2013.

Instituto Nacional de Estadística y Geografía. *Perspectiva estadística de Guerrero.* México: INEGI, 2007.

Inter-American Court of Human Rights. *Sentencia de la Corte Interamericana de Derechos Humanos Caso Fernández Ortega y Otros vs. México.* August 30, 2010.

———. *Sentencia de la Corte Interamericana de Derechos Humanos Caso Rosendo Cantú y Otros vs. México.* August 31, 2010.

Iturralde, Diego. "El movimiento indígena como actor político: Lucha indígena y reforma neoliberal." *Revista: Iconos. Revista de ciencias sociales* 9 (2000): 22–30.

James, Joy. *The New Abolitionist. (Neo)Slave Narratives and Contemporary Prison Writings.* New York: State University of New York Press, 2005.

Jameson, Frederic. *Documentos de cultura: Documentos de Barbarie.* Madrid: Ed. Paidos, 1989.

———. *Postmodernism or the Cultural Logic of Late Capitalism.* Durham, NC: Duke University Press, 1990.

Jocón González, María Estela. "Fortalecimiento de la participación política de las mujeres mayas" (series Oxlajuj Baqtun). Chimaltenango: Maya Uk'u'x B'e, 2005.

Kabeer, Naila. *Realidades trastocadas: Las Jerarquías de género en el pensamiento de desarrollo.* México: Paidos-PUEG-UNAM, 1998.

Kampwirth, Karen. *Women and Guerrilla Movements.* University Park, PA: Penn State University Press, 2002.

———. *Feminism and the Legacy of Revolution: Nicaragua, El Salvador, Chiapas.* Athens: Ohio University Press, 2004.

Klein, Hilary. *Compañeras: Zapatista Women's Stories.* New York: Seven Stories Press, 2015.

Lagarde, Marcela. *Violencia feminicida en 10 entidades de la República Mexicana.* Comisión Especial para Conocer y Dar Seguimiento a las Investigaciones Relacionadas con los Feminicidios en la República Mexicana y a la Procuración de Justicia Vinculada de la Cámara de Diputados, LIX Legislatura. México, May 2006.

Lamas, Marta. "El movimiento feminista en la década de los ochenta" In *Crisis y sujetos sociales en México,* edited by Enrique de la Garza, 30–58. Mexico City: UNAM/Miguel Angel Porrúa, 1992.

Lamas, Marta, Alicia Martínez, María Luisa Tarrés, and Esperanza Tuñón. "Building Bridges: The Growth of Popular Feminism in Mexico." In *The Challenge of Local Feminisms,* edited by Amrita Basu, 324–50. Boulder, CO: Westview Press, 1995.

Lash, Scott, and John Urry. *Economics of Sign and Space.* London: Sage, 1994.

Latour, Bruno. *La Fabrique du droit: Une ethnographie du Conseil d'Etat.* París: La Découverte, 2002.

Lau Jaiven, Ana. "El nuevo movimiento feminista Mexicano a fines del milenio." In *Feminismo en México: Ayer y hoy,* edited by Eli Bartra, 120–52. Mexico City: Universidad Autónoma Metropolitana, 2002.

Lee Camacho, Susuki. "Flor de Nochebuena: Nacieron mujeres, ahora se aguantan!" In *Bajo la sombra del Guamúchil: Historias de vida de mujeres indígenas y campesinas en reclusión,* edited by Rosalva Aída Hernández Castillo, 19–31. México: CIESAS/IWGIA/Ore-Media, 2010a.

———. "Morelitos: Su palabra contra la mía." In *Bajo la sombra del Guamúchil: Historias de vida de mujeres indígenas y campesinas en reclusión,* edited by Rosalva Aída Hernández Castillo, 31–51. México: CIESAS/IWGIA/Ore-Media, 2010b.

Levitt, Peggy, and Sally Engle Merry. "Vernacularization on the Ground: Local Uses of Global Women's Rights in Peru, China, India and the United States." *Global Networks* 9, no. 4 (2009): 441–61.

Leyva Solano, Xochitl, ed. *Conocimientos y prácticas políticas: Reflexiones desde nuestras prácticas y conocimientos situados*. México: CIESAS-Universidad de San Marcos, 2013.

López Bárcenas, Francisco. "La diversidad negada: Los derechos indígenas en la propuesta gubernamental de reforma constitucional." In *Autonomía y derechos de los pueblos indígenas*, edited by Gabriel García Colorado and Irma Eréndira Sandoval, 40–67. México: Chamber of Deputies–Instituto de Investigaciones Legislativas, 2000.

López, Alma. "Aciertos y desaciertos de la participación política de las mujeres mayas Kichés: Un reto histórico de nosotras." In *La doble mirada: Luchas y experiencias de las mujeres indígenas de América Latina*, edited by Marta Sánchez, 23–31. México City: UNIFEM/ILSB, 2005.

Lozano Suárez, Leonor. "Participate, Make Visible, Propose: The Wager of Indigenous Women in the Organizational Process of the Regional Indigenous Council of the Cauca (CRIC)" In *Demanding Justice and Security: Indigenous Women and Legal Pluralities in Latin America*, edited by Rachel Sieder. New Brunswick, NJ: Rutgers University Press, forthcoming.

Lykes, Brinton, and Erzulie Coquillon. "Participatory and Action Research and Feminisms: Towards Transformative Praxis." In *Handbook of Feminist Research: Theory and Praxis*, edited by Sharlene Nagy Hesse-Biber, 297–326. Thousand Oaks, CA: Sage Publications.

Macleod, Morna. "Un canto por la justicia, un canto por la vida digna encuentro entre Ana María Rodríguez y Morna Macleod." In *Historias a dos voces: Testimonios de luchas y resistencias de mujeres indígenas*, edited by Rosalva Aída Hernández Castillo, 21–50. Morelia: Serie Teoría Feminista/Instituto Michoacano de la Mujer, 2006.

———. "Luchas político-culturales y autorepresentación Maya en Guatemala." PhD dissertation, UNAM, Mexico City, 2008.

———. *Nietas del fuego, creadoras del alba: Luchas político-culturales de mujeres mayas*. Guatemala: FLACSO Guatemala—Hivos, 2011.

Macleod, Morna, and Crisanta Pérez Bámaca. *Tu'n Tklet Qnan Tx'otx', Q'ixkojalel, b'ix Tb'anil Qanq'ib'il, En defensa de la Madre Tierra, sentir lo quesiente el otro, y el buen vivir. La lucha de Doña Crisanta contra Goldcorp*. México: Ce-Acatl, 2013.

Makowski, Sara. *Las flores del mal: Identidad y resistencia en cárceles de mujeres*. Master's thesis on social sciences, FLACSO, México.

Maldonado, Korinta, and Adriana Terven. *Los juzgados indígenas de Cuetzalán y de Huehuetla: Vigencia y reproducción de los sistemas normativos de los pueblos de la Sierra Norte de Puebla*. México: CDI, 2008.

Malinowski, Bronislaw. *Crimen y costumbre en la sociedad salvaje.* Barcelona: Ed. Ariel, 1982 [1926].

Martínez, Felicitas, and Paula Silva Florentino. "La experiencia de las mujeres en la policía comunitaria de Guerrero." In *Género, complementariedades y exclusiones en Mesoamérica y los Andes,* edited by Rosalva Aída Hernández Castillo and Andrew Canessa, 331–46. Lima: International Work Group for Indigenous Affairs (IWGIA)/Abya Yala Press/The British Academy of Science, 2012.

Martínez, Juan Carlos. "Oaxaca: un paso atras: Reforma neoliberal y regresión en el reconocimiento de derechos autonómicos de los pueblos indígenas; el caso de Tlahuitoltepec." In *Justicias indígenas y estado: Violencias contemporáneas,* edited by Teresa Sierra, Rosalva Aída Hernández Castillo, and Rachel Sieder, 123–53. México: FLACSO-CIESAS, 2013.

Massolo, Alejandra. *Por amor y coraje: Mujeres en movimientos urbanos de la ciudad de México.* Mexico: El Colegio de México, 1992.

Meckesheimer, Anika. "Sobre las tres agendas de una investigación con, y no solamente sobre la coordinadora diocesana de mujeres en San Cristóbal de las Casas, Chiapas." PhD dissertation, Metropolitan University of México (UAM-Xochimilco), Mexico City, 2015.

Meertens, Donny. *Ensayos sobre tierra, violencia y género.* Bogotá: Centro de Estudios Sociales-Universidad Nacional, 2000.

Mejía, Susana. "Los derechos de las mujeres nahuas de Cuetzalan: La construcción de un feminismo indígena, desde la necesidad." In *Etnografías e historias de resistencia: Mujeres indígenas, procesos organizativos y nuevas identidades políticas,* edited by Rosalva Aída Hernández Castillo, 453–502. México: CIESAS-PUEG-UNAM, 2008.

———. "Resistencia y acción colectiva de las mujeres nahuas de Cuetzalan: ¿Construcción de un feminismo indígena?" PhD dissertation, UAM-Xochimilco, Mexico City, 2010.

Mejía, Susana, Celestina Cruz Martín, and Carlos Rodríguez. "Género y justicia en comunidades nahuas de Cuetzalan: La experiencia de la Casa de la Mujer Indígena." Paper presented in the 5th Congress of the Latin American Legal Anthropology Network (RELAJU), Oaxtepec, México, November 2006.

Melville, Thomas. "The Catholic Church in Guatemala, 1944–82." *Cultural Survival Quarterly* (Spring 1983): 25–30.

Méndez, Georgina. "Mujeres Mayas-*Kichwas* en la apuesta por la descolonización de los pensamientos y corazones." In *Senti-pensar el género: Perspectivas desde los pueblos indígenas,* edited by Georgina Méndez, Juan López Itzin, Sylvia Marcos, and Carmen Osorio, 27–63. México: Editorial Casa del Mago/Red INPIIM AC/ Red de Feminismos Descoloniales, 2013.

Méndez, Georgina, Juan López Itzin, Sylvia Marcos, and Carmen Osorio, eds. *Senti-pensar el género: Perspectivas desde los pueblos indígenas.* México: Editorial Casa del Mago/Red INPIIM AC/Red de Feminismos Descoloniales, 2013.

Méndez Gutiérrez, Luz, and Amanda Carrera Guerra. *Mujeres Indígenas: Clamor por la Justicia. Violencia Sexual, Conflicto Armado y Despojo Violento de Tierras.* Guatemala: F&G Editores, 2015.

Mex. Const., Article IV.

Mex. Penal Code Amend. XVI, Sec. 1

Mex. Penal Code Amend. XIX, Sec. 1

Millán, Margara. "Nuevos espacios, nuevas actoras: Neozapatismo y su significado para las mujeres indígenas." In *Etnografías e historias de resistencia: Mujeres indígenas, procesos organizativos y nuevas identidades políticas,* edited by Rosalva Aída Hernández Castillo, 217–49. Mexico City: CIESAS-PUEG/UNAM, 2008.

———. *Des-ordenando el género ¿Des-centrando la nación? El zapatismo de las mujeres indígenas y sus consecuencias.* México: UMAM-BUAP, 2014.

Millán, Márgara, ed. *Más allá del Feminismo: Caminos para Andar.* México: Pez en el Agua/Red de Feminismos Descoloniales, 2014.

Miranda. "Miranda: todavía no acabo de entender." In *Bajo la sombra del Guamúchil: Historias de vida de mujeres indígenas y campesinas en reclusión,* edited by Rosalva Aída Hernández, 79–85. México: CIESAS/IWGIA/Ore-Media, 2010.

Mohanty, Chandra. "Under Western Eyes: Feminist Scholarship and Colonial Discourses." In *Third World Women and the Politics of Feminism,* edited by Chandra Mohanty, Ann Russo, and Lourdes Torres, 51–81. Bloomington: Indiana University Press, 1991 [1986].

———. "'Under Western Eyes' Revisited: Feminist Solidarity Through Anticapitalist Struggles." *Signs: Journal of Women in Culture and Society* 28, no. 2 (2002): 499–535.

Moore, Henrietta L. *Antropología y Feminismo.* Valencia: Editorial Cátedra, 1996.

Mora Bayo, Mariana. "Decolonizing Politics: Zapatista Indigenous Autonomy in an Era of Neoliberal Governance and Low Intensity Warfare," PhD dissertation, University of Texas at Austin, 2008.

———. "La politización de la justicia zapatista frente a la guerra de baja intensidad." In *Justicias indígenas y estado: Violencias contemporáneas,* edited by María Teresa Sierra, Rosalva Aída Hernández Castillo, and Rachel Sieder, 195–224. México: FLACSO/CIESAS, 2013.

————. "Repensando la política y la descolonización en minúscula: Reflexiones sobre la praxis feminista desde el zapatismo." In *Más allá del feminismo: Caminos para andar*, edited by Margara Millán, 155–82. México: Pez en el Agua/Red de Feminismos Descoloniales, 2014.

Mujeres para el Diálogo. "La dimesión feminista de la fe a los 500 años de evangelización." *Memoria de coloquio*. Unpublished manuscript, México City, 1992.

Nader, Laura. *The Disputing Process: Law in Ten Societies*. New York: Columbia University Press, 1978.

————. *Harmony Ideology: Justice and Control in a Zapotec Mountain Village*. Stanford, CA: Stanford University Press, 1990.

Ng'weno, Bettina. "Can Ethnicity Replace Race? Afro-Colombians, Indigeneity and the Colombian Multicultural State." *Journal of Latin American and Caribbean Anthropology* 12, no. 2 (2007): 414–40.

Naples, Nancy. *Feminisms and Method: Ethnography, Discourse Analysis and Activist Research*. New York: Routledge Press, 2003.

Niezen, Ronald. *The Origins of Indigenism: Human Rights and the Politics of Identity*. Berkeley: University of California Press, 2003.

Núñez, Concepción. "Deshilando condenas, bordando libertades: Diez historias de vida. Mujeres Indígenas Presas por Delitos Contra la Salud en Oaxaca." PhD dissertation, Oaxaca: Universidad Autónoma Benito Juárez (UABJ), 2007.

————. "Una historia inconclusa." In *Resistencias penitenciarias: Investigación activista con mujeres en reclusión*, edited by Rosalva Aída Hernández Castillo. México: CIESAS, forthcoming.

Offstein, Norman. "An Historical Review and Analysis of Colombian Guerrilla Movements: FARC, ELN and EPL." *Desarrollo y Sociedad* no. 52 (September 2003): 99–142.

Olguín, Ben. *La Pinta: Chicana/o Prisoner Literature, Culture and Politics*. Austin: University of Texas Press, 2009.

Ortíz Elizondo, Héctor. Informe Pericial para el caso de *Valentina Rosendo Cantú v. México*. Unpublished manuscript, 2009.

Painemal, Millaray. "La experiencia de las organizaciones de mujeres mapuche: Resistencias y desafíos ante una doble discriminación." In *La doble mirada: Luchas y experiencias de las mujeres indígenas de América Latina*, edited by Marta Sánchez, 77–87. México City: UNIFEM/ILSB, 2005.

Palacios Zuolaga, Patricia. "The Path to Gender Justice in the Inter-American Court of Human Rights." *Texas Journal of Women and the Law* no. 227 (2008): 1–97.

Pancho Aquite, Avelina, and Lina Rosa Berrío Palomo. "Ser mujer líder: Testimonios desde tierras Colombianas." In *Historias a dos voces: Testimonios de luchas y resistencias de mujeres indígenas*, edited by Rosalva Aída Hernández Castillo, 93–116. Morelia, Michoacán: Instituto Michoacano de la Mujer, 2006.

Paris Pombo, María Dolores. "Racismo y nacionalismo: La construcción de identidades excluyentes." *Política y Cultura*, no. 12 (Summer 1999).

Pelaez, Victoria. "La industria penitenciaria de los EEUU ¿Negocio o nueva forma de esclavitud?" *Global Research*, June 20, 2008, 10–17.

Prince, Amy Diane. *Benita: Memoir of a Mexican Activist*. Pittsburgh, PA: Latin American Literary Review Press, 1994.

Quijano, Anibal. "Coloniality of Power, Eurocentrism, and Latin America." *Nepantla: Views from the South* 1, no. 3 (2000): 533–80.

Radcliffe-Brown, Alfred Reginald. *Structure and Function in Primitive Society*. Glencoe, IL: The Free Press, 1952.

Radcliff, Sarah. "Las Mujeres indígenas ecuatorianas bajo la gobernabilidad multicultural y de género." In *Raza, etnicidad y sexualidades: Ciudadanía y multiculturalismo en América Latina*, edited by Peter Wade, Fernando Urrea, and Mara Viveros, 105–36. Bogotá: Universidad Nacional de Colombia-CES, 2008.

———. *Indigenous Development in the Andes: Culture, Power, and Transnationalism*. Durham, NC: Duke University Press, 2009.

Radcliff, Sarah, and Andrea Pequeño. "Ethnicity, Development and Gender: Tsáchila Indigenous Women in Ecuador." *Development and Change* 41, no. 6 (2010): 983–1016.

Rajagopal, Balakrishnan. *International Law from Below: Development, Social Movements, and Third World Resistance*. Cambridge, UK: Cambridge University Press, 2003.

Ramírez, María Clemencia. *Between the Guerrillas and the State: The Cocalero Movement, Citizenship, and Identity in the Colombia Amazon*. Durham, NC: Duke University Press, 2011.

Rappaport, Joanne. "Redrawing the Nation: Indigenous Intellectuals and Ethnic Pluralism in Colombia." In *After Spanish Rule: Postcolonial Predicaments of the Americas*, edited by Mark Thurner and Andres Guerrero, 310–46. Durham, NC: Duke University Press, 2003.

———. *Intercultural Utopias: Public Intellectuals, Cultural Experimentation, and Ethnic Pluralism in Colombia*. Durham, NC: Duke University Press, 2005.

Rayas Velasco, Lucía. "Subyugar a la nación: Cuando el cuerpo femenino es territorio de tortura a manos del estado." Paper presented at the Gender and State

Violence: Violence Against Activist and Revolutionaries Conference, México City, May 20, 2008.

———. *Armadas: Un análisis de género desde el cuerpo de las mujeres combatientes.* México: El Colegio de México, 2009.

Reinharz, Shulamit. *Feminist Methods in Social Research.* New York; Oxford, UK: Oxford University Press, 1992.

Reynoso, Alejandra. "Perla Negra: Desde que nací la violencia ha sido parte de mi vida." In *Bajo la sombra del Guamúchil: Historias de vida de mujeres indígenas y campesinas en reclusión,* edited by Rosalva Aída Hernández Castillo, 95–115. México: CIESAS/IWGIA/Ore-Media, 2010.

Richards, Patricia. "The Politics of Gender, Human Rights and Being Indigenous in Chile." *Gender & Society* 19, no. 2, (April 2005): 199–220.

Ríos, Margarita. *Diagnóstico del area femenil del CERESO Morelos.* Cuernavaca: Secretaría de Readaptación Social, 2009.

Rivera Zea, Tarcila. "Mujeres indígenas Americanas luchando por sus derechos." In *La doble mirada: Luchas y experiencias de las mujeres indígenas de América Latina,* ed. Marta Sánchez, 33–50. Mexico City: UNIFEM/ILSB, 2005.

Robichaux, David. *El matrimonio en Mesoamérica ayer y hoy.* México: Universidad Iberoamericana, 2003.

Rojas, José María. "Ocupación y recuperación de los territorios indígenas en Colombia." Unpublished manuscript, 2006.

Romay, Amalia. "Experiencia de las mujeres nahuas en la DPO." In *Género, complementariedades y exclusiones en Mesoamérica y los Andes,* edited by Rosalva Aída Hernández Castillo and Andrew Canessa, 416–28. Lima: International Work Group for Indigenous Affairs (IWGIA)/Abya Yala Press/The British Academy of Science, 2012.

Roseberry, William. "Hegemony and the Language of Contention." In *Everyday Forms of State Formation: Revolution and the Negotiation of Rule in Modern Mexico,* edited by James Scott, Gilbert M. Joseph, and Daniel Nugent. Durham, NC: Duke University Press, 1994.

Rovira, Giomar. *Mujeres de Maíz.* México City: Editorial Era, 1997.

Rowbotham, Sheila. *Women in Movement: Feminism and Social Action.* New York/London: Routledge, 1992.

Ruíz Rodríguez, Marina. "Flores en el desierto: Ensayo sobre las relaciones entre mujeres de adentro y de afuera del CERESO Morelos." In *Resistencias penitenciarias: Investigación activista con mujeres en reclusión,* edited by Rosalva Aída Hernández Castillo. México: CIESAS, forthcoming.

Rus, Jan, Rosalva Aída Hernández Castillo, and Shannan Mattiace. *Mayan Lives, Mayan Utopias: The Indigenous Peoples of Chiapas and the Zapatista Rebellion, Latin American Perspectives in the Classroom*. Boulder, CO: Rowman & Littlefield Publishers, 2003.

Said, Edward. *Orientalism*. New York: Pantheon Press, 1978.

Salazar, Rosa. "Una mujer con mucho miedo." In *Bajo la sombra del Guamúchil: Historias de vida de mujeres indígenas y campesinas en reclusión*, edited by Rosalva Aída Hernández Castillo, 29. México: CIESAS/IWGIA/Ore-Media,2010.

———. "Los retos de los liderazgos femeninos en el movimiento indígena de México: La experiencia de la ANIPA." In *Género, complementariedades y exclusiones en Mesoamérica y los Andes*, edited by Rosalva Aída Hernández Castillo and Andrew Canesa, 359–88. Lima: International Work Group for Indigenous Affairs (IWGIA)/Abya Yala Press/The British Academy of Science, 2012.

Sánchez Botero, Esther. *Justicia y pueblos indígenas de Colombia: La tutela como medio para la construcción del entendimiento intercultural*. Bogotá, Colombia: Universidad Nacional de Colombia, UNIJUS, 1998.

———. "Aproximación desde la antropología jurídica a la justicia de los pueblos indígenas." In *El caleidoscopio de las justicias en Colombia*, edited by Boaventura de Sousa Santos and Mauricio García Villegas. Bogotá: Colciencias-Instituto Colombiano de Antropología e Historia-CES, 2001.

Sánchez, Gonzalo, and Donny Meertens. *Bandoleros, gamonales y campesinos: El caso de la violencia en Colombia*. Bogotá: El Áncora Editores, 2000.

Sánchez Néstor, Martha. *La doble mirada: Luchas y experiencias de las mujeres indígenas de América Latina*. México City: UNIFEM/ILSB, 2005.

Santana, María Eugenia. "Mujeres organizadas de la Diócesis de San Cristóbal de las Casas: De la lucha por la dignidad a la lucha por el empoderamiento." MA thesis, El Colegio de la Frontera Sur, San Cristóbal de las Casas, Chiapas, 2001.

Schild, Verónica. "'Gender Equity' Without Social Justice: Women's Rights in the Neoliberal Age." Accessed May 10, 2015, https://nacla.org/article/gender-equity-without-social-justice-womens-rights-neoliberal-age.

———. "Emancipation as Moral Regulation: Latin American Feminisms and Neoliberalism." *Hypatia Special Issue: Emancipation* 30, no. 3 (2015): 547–63.

Segato, Rita Laura. "El Color de la Cárcel en América Latina: Apuntes sobre la colonialidad de la justicia en un continente en deconstrucción." *Nueva Sociedad* no. 208 (March–April 2007): 142–60.

———. "La escritura en el cuerpo de las mujeres asesinadas en Cd. Juárez." *Debate Feminista* 19, no. 37 (April 2008): 78–102.

Shih, Shu-mei, Sylvia Marcos, Obioma Nnaemeka, and Marguerite Waller. "Conversation on Feminist Imperialism and the Politics of Difference." In *Dialogue and Difference: Feminisms Challenge Globalization*, edited by Marguerite Waller and Sylvia Marcos, 143–58, New York: Comparative Feminist Studies/Palgrave, 2005.

Sieder, Rachel, ed. *Multiculturalism in Latin America: Indigenous Rights, Diversity and Democracy*. London: Palgrave, 2002.

———. "Subaltern Cosmopolitan Legalities and Ethnographic Engagement in the Grey Zone," *Universitas Humanística* no. 75 (January/June 2013): 221–24.

———. *Demanding Justice and Security: Indigenous Women and Legal Pluralities in Latin America*. New Brunswick, NJ: Rutgers University Press, forthcoming.

Sieder, Rachel, and Jessica Witchell. "Impulsando las demandas indígenas a través de la ley: Reflexiones sobre el proceso de paz en Guatemala." In *Los derechos humanos en tierras mayas: Política, representaciones y moralidad*, edited by Pedro Pitarch Ramón and Julián López García, 55–82. España: Sociedad Española de Estudios Mayas, 2001.

Sieder, Rachel, and John-Andrew MacNeish. *Gender Justice and Legal Pluralities: Latin American and African Perspectives*. Milton Park, Abingdon, Oxon; New York, NY: Routledge, 2013.

Sieder, Rachel, and Morna Macleod. "Género, derecho y cosmovisión maya en Guatemala." *Desacatos* 31 (September-December 2009): 51–72.

Sierra, María Teresa. *Discurso, cultura y poder: El ejercicio de la autoridad en pueblos ñhahñús del Valle del Mezquital*. México: CIESAS-Gobierno del Estado de Hidalgo, 1992.

———. *Haciendo justicia: Interlegalidad, derecho y género en regiones indígenas*. México: CIESAS-Porrúa, 2004a.

———. "Diálogos y prácticas interculturales: Derechos humanos, derechos de las mujeres y políticas de identidad." *Desacatos*, no. 15–16 (2004b): 126–48.

———. "Las mujeres indígenas ante la justicia Comunitaria: Perspectivas desde la interculturalidad y los derechos." *Desacatos* 31 (September–December 2009): 73–88.

———. "Indigenous Women Fight for Justice: Gender Rights and Legal Pluralism in Mexico." In *Gender Justice and Legal Pluralities: Latin American and African Perspectives*, edited by Rachel Sieder and John-Andrew McNeish, 56–82. Milton Park, Abingdon, Oxon; New York, NY: Routledge, 2013.

———. "Pueblos indígenas y usos contra-hegemónicos de la ley en la disputa por la justicia: La policía comunitaria de Guerrero." *The Journal of Latin American and Caribbean Anthropology* 20, no. 1 (2014): 133–55.

Sierra, María Teresa, and Rosalva Aída Hernández Castillo. "Repensar los derechos colectivos desde el género: Aportes de las mujeres indígenas al debate de la autonomía." In *La doble mirada: Luchas y experiencias de las mujeres indígenas de América Latina*, edited by Martha Sánchez, 105–20. Mexico City: UNIFEM/ ILSB, 2005.

Sierra, Teresa, Rosalva Aída Hernández Castillo, and Rachel Sieder. *Justicias indígenas y estado: Violencias contemporáneas*. México: FLACSO-CIESAS, 2013.

Siller, Clodomiro. "El punto de partida de la teología india." In *Teología india. Memorias del primer encuentro taller Latinoamericano*, 15–32. Mexico City: CENAMI/Abya-Yala, 1991.

Sisma Mujer y Colectivo de Abogados José Alvear Restrepo (CAJAR). "Violencia sexual, otra forma de guerra en Colombia." Paper presented in the International Criminal Court, The Hague, Netherlands, March 10, 2015.

Smart, Carol. *Feminism and the Power of Law*. New York: Routledge, 1989.

Smith, Andrea. *Conquest: Sexual Violence and American Indian Genocide*. Boston: South End Press, 2005a.

———. "Native American Feminism, Sovereignty and Social Change." *Feminist Studies* 31, no. 1 (2005b): 116–32.

Smith, Sharon. "Mistaken Identity; Or, Can Identity Politics Liberate the Oppressed?" In *International Socialist* 62 (Spring 1994): 4–13.

Soriano, Silvia. "Mujeres y guerra en guatemala y Chiapas." PhD dissertation, UNAM, Mexico City, 2005.

———. "María Teresa y el valor de encontrarse con ella misma: Diálogo de María Teresa con Silvia Soriano." In *Historias a dos voces: Testimonios de luchas y resistencias de mujeres indígenas*, edited by Rosalva Aída Hernández Castillo, 117–36. Morelia: Serie Teoría Feminista/Instituto Michoacano de la Mujer, 2006.

Speed, Shannon, Rosalva Aída Hernández Castillo, and Lynn M. Stephen. *Dissident Women: Gender and Cultural Politics in Chiapas*. Austin: University of Texas Press, 2006.

Speed, Shannon. "At the Crossroads of Human Rights and Anthropology: Toward a Critically Engaged Activist Research." *American Anthropologist* 108, no. 1 (March 2006): 66–76.

———. "Exercising Rights and Reconfiguring Resistance in the Zapatista." In *The Practice of Human Rights: Tracking Law Between the Global and the Local*, edited by Mark Goodale and Sally Engle Merry, 163–92. Cambridge, UK: Cambridge University Press, 2007.

———. *Rights in Rebellion: Indigenous Struggle and Human Rights in Chiapas*. Stanford, CA: Stanford University Press, 2008.

Stephen, Lynn. "Ser testigo presencial-Acompañando, presenciando, actuando" (LASA-OXFAM America 2015 Martin Diskin Memorial Lecture). *LASA Forum* 46, no. 3 (Summer 2015): 4–14.

Stoltz-Chinchilla, Norma. *Nuestras utopías, mujeres guatemaltecas del siglo XX.* Guatemala: Agrupación Mujeres Tierra Viva, 1997.

Sub-Commander Marcos. "Carta del Sub-Comandante Marcos sobre la vida cotidiana en el EZLN." *La Jornada*, January 30, 1994, 9.

Sudbury, Julia. *Global Lockdown: Race, Gender and the Prison Industrial Complex.* New York/London: Routledge, 2005.

Tamez, Elsa. *Teólogos de la liberación hablan sobre la mujer.* San José, Costa Rica: DEI, 1988.

———. "Justicia indígena en tiempos multiculturales: Hacía la conformación de un proyecto colectivo propio: la experiencia organizativa de Cuetzalan." PhD dissertation, CIESAS, México, 2009.

Terven, Adriana, and Claudia Chávez. "Las prácticas de justicia indígena bajo el reconocimiento del estado: El caso poblano desde la experiencia organizativa de Cuetzalan." In *Justicias indígenas y estado: Violencias contemporáneas*, edited by María Teresa Sierra, Rosalva Aída Hernández Castillo, and Rachel Sieder, 51–88. México: CIESAS/FLACSO, 2013.

Terven, Adriana, and Manuel Buenrostro. "Administración de justicia estatal y del pueblo náhuatl y maya (Puebla y Quintana Roo)." *Portal* 5, no. 7 (2010): 30–52.

Ticona Colque, Valentín (Viceministro de Justicia Comunitaria de Bolivia). "Políticas públicas del Gobierno boliviano acerca de la justicia comunitaria." In *Mujeres indígenas y justicia ancestral*, edited by Miriam Lang and Anna Kucia, 51–56. Ecuador, Quito: Fondo de Desarrollo de las Naciones Unidas para la Mujer (UNIFEM)—Región Andina, 2009.

Tilley, Virginia. "New Help or New Hegemony? The Transnational Indigenous Peoples' Movement and 'Being Indian' in El Salvador." *Journal of Latin American Studies* 34, no. 3 (2002): 525–54.

Torres, Camilo. "Reflexiones de Camilo Torres." *Frente Unido* no. 8, October 14, 1965, 7–10.

Touraine, Alain. *Actores sociales y sistemas políticos en América Latina.* Chile: PREALC-OIT, 1987.

Trigger, David. "Anthropology in Native Title Cases: Mere pleading, Expert Opinions or Hearsay?" In *Crossing Boundaries: Cultural, Legal, Historical and Practice Issues in Native Title*, edited by Sandy Toussaint, 24–33. Melbourne, AU: Melbourne University Press, 2004.

Trounstine, Jean. *Shakespeare Behind Bars: The Power of Drama in a Women's Prison.* New York: San Martin, 2001.

Valladares, Laura. "La importancia del peritaje cultural: avances, retos y acciones del Colegio de Etnólogos y Antropólogos Sociales AC (CEAS) para la certificación de perito." In *Peritaje antropológico en México: Reflexiones teórico metodológicas y experiencias,* edited by María Antonieta Gallart and Laura Valladares, 11–21. México: Boletín Colegio de Etnólogos y Antropólogos Sociales, 2012.

Van Cott, Donna. *The Friendly Liquidation of the Past: The Politics of Diversity in Latin America.* Pittsburgh, PA: University of Pittsburgh Press, 2000.

———. *From Movements to Parties in Latin America: The Evolution of Ethnic Politics.* Cambridge, UK: Cambridge University Press, 2005.

———. *Las mujeres de Tlahuitoltepec Mixe, frente a la impartición de justicia y el uso del derecho internacional 2000–2008,* México: INMUJERES, 2011.

Vargas Vázquez, Liliana Vianey. "Informe del proyecto: Las mujeres de Tlahuitoltepec mixe, frente a la impartición de la justicia local y el uso del derecho internacional," 2000–2007, September 2008.

———. *Las mujeres de Tlahuitoltepec mixe, frente a la impartición de justicia y el uso del derecho internacional, 2000–2008.* México: INMUJERES, 2011.

Velásquez Nimatuj, Irma Alicia. *La pequeña burguesía indígena comercial de Guatemala: Desigualdades de clase, raza y género.* Guatemala: SERJUS y CEDPA, 2003.

Velázquez Domínguez, María Graciela. "La prisión como territorio simbólico: Un rito de paso trunco en el área femenil del CERESO Morelos." Honors thesis, Escuela Nacional de Antropología e Historia, México, DF, 2004.

Verona, Aarón. "¿Pluma o espada? La desnaturalización del peritaje antropológico: Análisis de seis peritajes." In *El Peritaje Antropológico: Entre la Reflexión y la Práctica,* edited by Guevara Gil Armando, Aaron Verona, and Roxana Vergara, 205–19. Lima: Centro de Investigación, Capacitación y Asesoría Jurídica del Decaptamento Académico de derecho (CICAJ), 2015.

Villa, Rufina. "Las mujeres nahuas y su experiencia del juzgado indígena de Cuetzalán, Puebla." In *Género, complementariedades y exclusiones en Mesoamérica y los Andes,* edited by Rosalva Aída Hernández Castillo and Andrew Canessa, 346–52. Lima: International Work Group for Indigenous Affairs (IWGIA)/Abya Yala Press/The British Academy of Science, 2012.

Wacquant, Loïc. *Punishing the Poor: The Neoliberal Government of Social Insecurity.* Durham, NC: Duke University Press, 2009.

———. *Las cárceles de la miseria.* Buenos Aires: Editorial Manantial, 2000.

Wade, Peter. "Etnicidad, multiculturalismo y políticas sociales en Latinoamérica: Poblaciones Afrolatinas (e indígenas)." *Tabula Rasa*, no. 4 (January–February 2006): 59–81. Universidad Colegio Mayor de Cundinamarca Bogotá, Colombia.

Waldram, James. *Way of the Pipe: Aboriginal Spirituality and Symbolic Healing in a Canadian Prison*. Toronto: Broadview, 1997.

Wieringa, Saskia. "Women's Interests and Empowerment: Gender Planning Reconsidered." *Development and Change* 25 (1992): 829–48.

Willis, Paul E. *Learning to Labor: How Working Class Kids Get Working Class Jobs*. New York: Teacher College Press, 1981.

Wolf, Diane. *Feminist Dilemmas in Fieldwork*. Boulder, CO: Westview Press, 1996.

Wolkmer, Antonio Carlos. *Pluralismo jurídico—Fundamentos de una nueva cultura en el Derecho*. 3rd ed. San Pablo: Alfa-Omega, 2001.

Yashar, Deborah. *Contesting Citizenship in Latin America: The Rise of Indigenous Movements and the Postliberal Challenge*. New York: Cambridge University Press, 2005.

Yuval Davis, Nira. *Gender and Nation*. London: Sage Press, 1997.

Zamora, Barbara. "Criminalización de la protesta social y modificación de la legislación penal." Accessed May 10, 2015, www.ciaj.com.ar.

Zapeta, José Ángel. "Valores, principios y situación de la justicia maya en Guatemala." In *Mujeres indígenas y justicia ancestral*, edited by Miriam Lang and Anna Kucia, 197–200. Ecuador, Quito: Fondo de Desarrollo de las Naciones Unidas para la Mujer (UNIFEM)—Región Andina, 2009.

Zepeda Lecuona, Guillermo. "La reforma constitucional en materia penal de junio 2008: Claroscuros de una oportunidad histórica para transformar el sistema penal mexicano." *Análisis Plural* 3 (2008): 30–58.

Zylberberg Panebianco, Violeta. "'We Can No Longer Be Like Hens with Our Heads Bowed, We Must Raise Our Heads and Look Ahead': A Consideration of the Daily Life of Zapatista Women." In *Dissident Women: Gender and Cultural Politics in Chiapas*, edited by Shannon Speed, Rosalva Aída Hernández Castillo, and Lynn M. Stephen, 222–37. Austin: University of Texas Press, 2006.

———. "¿Queriendo se puede cambiar todo? Un acercamiento al proceso de discusión y cambio que se vive al interior de una comunidad zapatista." In *Etnografías e historias de resistencia: Mujeres indígenas, procesos organizativos y nuevas identidades políticas*, edited by Rosalva Aída Hernández Castillo, 145–63. México: CIESAS-PUEG/UNAM, 2008.

INDEX

ANUC (Asociación Nacional de Usurarios Campesino), 101, 281n27
Armed Revolutionary Forces of Colombia. See FARC
Asamblea Nacional Indígena Plural por la Autonomía. See ANIPA
Asociación Nacional de Usurarios Campesino. See ANUC
Assembly of Mixe Authorities (Asamblea de Autoridades Mixes), 142–43
Atlacholoaya. See under CERESO
autonomy: autonomic demands, 11, 19, 105; autonomous regions, 7, 47, 82, 137–38, 276n9; autonomic rights, 192, 251, 100; indigenous, 4–5, 7, 102, 124–26, 136–37, 140, 153, 158, 162, 177, 192, 276n9, 284n13; political, 123–24, 126, 134, 154, 282n29; territorial, 4, 102, 138; Zapatista, 138–43, 284n8
Azaola, Elena, 58, 196, 203–5, 296

Barranca Tequani (community in Guerrero), 53–54, 182, 184 fig. 11, 187, 236–39, 244–45, 277n16
Barrera Hernández, Abel, x, 174, 180, 287n18. See also Center of Human Rights of the Mountains of Guerrero Tlachinollan
Base Ecclesial Communities. See CEB
Berrio Palomo, Lina Rosa, xi, 84, 88, 97, 102, 159, 161, 280n13, 281n23, 285n18, 296–97, 314
Boserup, Esther, 116–17, 297

Cabañas, Lucio, 73, 76–77, 279n4
cabildos (Colombia), 101, 157, 281n26; Zonal Associations of Councils, 158, 285n17
Calderón, Felipe, 190, 193, 202
CAMM (Women and Children's Support Centre), 46–48, 275n14
"Campo Algodonero" case, 56–57
Caracoles (Zapatista administrative units), 139–40. See also Commission of Honor and Justice
catholicism, 76, 85–86; catechists, 91; and Catholic Church, 37, 85–96, 101–3, 131, 141, 264; organizations, 91; principles, 124. See also Indian theology; liberation theology; pastoral

CDI (Comisión Nacional para el Desarrollo de los Pueblos Indígenas), 193, 196, 202–3, 237, 215n16, 300
CEB (Comunidades Eclesiales de Base), 88, 282n30
CEJIL (Centro por la Justicia y el Derecho Internacional), 52, 173–77
CELAM (Second Conference of the Latin American Episcopate), 86–87
Center for Justice and International Law. See CEJIL
Center of Activist Research for Women. See CIAM
Center of Human Rights of the Mountains of Guerrero Tlachinollan, x, 29, 52, 166–68, 170–85
CERESO (Centro de Readaptación Social): Atlacholoaya (Morelos), x, 31, 57–60, 63, 191, 199–200, 201, 203–5, 208–11, 213, 219–28, 257, 259, 261–68, 277nn20–21, 278n21, 278n23, 288n2, 290n20, 291n32, 316, 321; San Miguel (Puebla), 31, 191, 199–200, 201, 203–4, 208–10, 219, 289n15, 290n22, 290n26, 291n34
CFPP. See Federal Penal Proceedings Code
Chirix, Emma, xi, 96, 135, 280n17, 299
CIAM (Centro de Investigación-Acción para la Mujer), 38, 79, 110, 282n33
CIDHAL (Comunicación, Intercambio y Desarrollo Humano en América Latina AC), 109, 282n30
CIESAS (Center of Research and Advanced Studies in Social Anthropology), x, 29, 39, 41
CIOAC (Central Independiente de Obreros Agrícolas y Campesino), 101, 104
civil feminism. See feminism
CLADEM (Comité de América Latina y el Caribe para la Defensa de los Derechos de la Mujer), 166, 285n1
CNDH (Comisión Nacional de Derechos Humanos), 203, 290n17, 292n6, 300
Coalition of Feminist Women, 107
CODIMUJ (Coordinadora Diocesana de Mujeres), 93, 142
COLEM (Colectivo de Espacios para Mujeres), 38–39, 46, 110

law (*cont.*)
Tribal Law, 31; Women's Revolutionary
Law, 43, 68, 80, 129, 137, 140, 144, 276n6.
See also customary law
Law of Culture and Indigenous Rights
(Ley de Derechos y Cultura Indígena),
137–38
legal monism. *See* interlegality
legal pluralism. *See* interlegality
liberal feminism. *See* feminism
liberation theology, 3, 37, 69, 85–95, 102,
108–9. *See also* Indian theology; pastoral
life histories: indigenous activist, 96, 275n16;
indigenous women, 231, 233; of indigenous women in prision, 29, 58, 60–66,
209–28; and "Life Histories" workshop,
60–66, 209–28, 261, 277n20, 278n21,
288n2, 290n19, 290n21, 290n23, 290n25,
290nn2–8, 291nn32–33
litigation, international, 31, 163–67, 172–
89, 177n1, 286n7
Lozano Suárez, Leonor, 158–61, 311

Macleod, Morna, xi, 16, 25, 78–79, 99, 103,
151, 154, 281n23, 295, 301, 311, 318
Marcos, Silvia, x, 307, 312, 317
"María da Penha Law" (*María da Penha v.
Brazil*), 56, 165
Maseualsiuamej Mosenyolchicauanij, 96, 98,
104, 145–47, 284n14
Mayan cosmovision. *See* cosmovision
Mayan feminist. *See* feminism
Mayan Law (Derecho Maya). *See* law
Mejía, Susana, xi, 104, 145–46, 148, 281n23,
312
Mexican Constitution: agreements regarding human rights in, 72, 186; Article 2,
177, 195, 246, 251
militarization, 11, 24, 25, 42, 47, 52–55, 97, 164,
181–82, 185–87, 191, 218–19, 227, 276n10; vs.
demilitarization, 11, 27, 84, 172, 177, 185,
276n10; and institutional military violence, 55, 176, 178; and Mexican Army, 24,
26, 52, 164–65, 168–69, 176, 178, 187, 219,
239–40, 246, 285n5; and military violence,
22, 42, 55–56, 167–68, 173, 175, 176, 178,
181, 184, 218, 227, 239; and paramilitary

violence, 85; vs. paramilitarization, 24, 75,
82, 83, 121, 187. *See also* counterinsurgency
Millán, Márgara, x, 40, 74, 82, 141, 281n23,
308, 313
Mohanty, Chandra, xi, 70, 308, 313
Mora Bayo, Mariana, x, 75, 81, 139, 140, 141,
276n3, 276n9, 278n3, 284nn8–10, 287n19,
296, 308, 313
multiculturalism, 49, 126, 190, 192, 300, 306,
308, 315, 317, 321; and constitutionalism,
4, 125, 161; neoliberal, 4, 7, 126, 191–93,
230, 306; and public policies, 125, 150;
and reforms, 4, 6–8, 28, 31, 49–50, 125–28,
146, 192–93, 197, 226–27, 230; state, 29–31,
190–228, 314

National Association of Peasant Users. *See*
ANUC
National Commission for the Development
of Indigenous Peoples. *See* CDI
National Commission on Human Rights.
See CNDH
National Coordination of Indigenous
Women of Mexico. *See* CNMI
National Indigenous Organization of
Colombia. *See* ONIC
National Institute for Statistics and Cen-
suses. *See* INEGI
National Liberation Army. *See* ELN
National Liberation Zapatista Army. *See*
EZLN
National Plural Indigenous Assembly for
the Autonomy. *See* ANIPA
neoliberalism, 39, 111, 126, 297; and neoliberal
policies, 65; and neoliberal state, 22,
65, 110, 120, 125–26, 230; and neoliberal
structural reforms, 34, 126, 190, 198, 226
Network of Mixe Women (Red de Mujeres
Mixes), 144
Network of Rural Promoters and Advisors
(Red Nacional de Asesoras y Promoto-
ras Rurales), 146

Olivera, Mercedes, xi, 37, 79, 282n33, 284n7
OMIECH (Organización de Médicos
Indígenas del Estado de Chiapas), 109,
128–32

ABOUT THE AUTHOR

Born in Ensenada, Baja California, **Rosalva Aída Hernández Castillo** earned her doctorate in anthropology from Stanford University in 1996. She is professor and senior researcher at the Center for Research and Advanced Studies in Social Anthropology (CIESAS) in Mexico City. She worked as a journalist since she was eighteen years old in a Central American press agency. Since she was an undergraduate, she has combined her academic work with media projects in radio, video, and journalism. Her academic work has promoted indigenous and women's rights in Latin America. She has done fieldwork in indigenous communities in the Mexican states of Chiapas, Guerrero, and Morelos; with Guatemalan refugees; and with African immigrants in the south of Spain. She has published twenty-two books and her academic work has been translated to English, French, and Japanese. She is a recipient of the Martin Diskin Oxfam Award for her activist research and the Simón Bolívar Chair (2013–2014) for her academic work. She is currently Tinker Chair in the Institute of Latin American Studies at UT Austin (2016–2017).